D1245836

A
HISTORY
OF THE
AMERICAN
STOCK
EXCHANGE

ROBERT SOBEL

BeardBooks

Washington, DC

Library of Congress Cataloging-in-Publication Data

Sobel, Robert, 1931 Feb. 19-
    AMEX: a history of the American Stock Exchange 1921-1971 / by Robert Sobel.
        p. cm.
    Originally published:. New York, Weybright and Talley, 1972.
    Includes bibliographical references and index.
    ISBN 1-893122-48-4 (pbk. : alk. paper)
    1. American Stock Exchange. I. Title

HG4575.2 .S66 2000
332.64'273—dc21

                                                                    99-089700

For

Delia Cortese

Preface

A few years ago I was one of several Americans called upon to help escort a group of Yugoslav economists through New York's financial district. These men and women were on their first visits to the United States, and had prepared for their trip by reading all they could find on our exchanges and related institutions. Their knowledge of them was impressive, and the questions they asked perceptive and precise. Indeed, they knew more of the history and structure of the financial district than did many of their guides. They understood the functions of banks, the New York Stock Exchange, and even the over-the-counter markets. The role of the SEC held no mysteries for them and, having dealt with government agencies in their own country, they knew its significance and the reasons for its apparent slowness and lack of activity. But they could not understand why the American Stock Exchange existed. What role could such an institution play? Why had it developed? What was its true relationship to the Big Board and the over-the-counter market? And why was it called the *American* Stock Exchange—indicating national coverage—while the senior market was called the *New York* Stock Exchange—implying only local interest?

The guides were able to offer what amounted to textbook

answers to their questions. The visitors were not satisfied with them. I'm afraid they came away with the impression that we did not know much about this second-most-important securities exchange in America.

A few years later, when I began my research for the first volume of this history, *The Curbstone Brokers: The Origins of the American Stock Exchange* (Macmillan, 1970), I knew little more than I had when taking the visitors through the district. But, like them, I wanted to know more. After five years of study, I think I do, and only wish I could send copies of these books to the Yugoslavs.

I soon learned that the Amex administration itself did not know much of the history. A good deal of it resided in the memories of old-timers, and was encrusted with myth and exaggeration after almost fifty years of indoor trading. Indeed, I had been invited to write this history because the exchange's leaders wanted to know more of where they had been and how they had gotten to where they were. They imposed no restrictions on this work, and both the Amex and I agreed that it would be an unsubsidized history, with the exchange having no control over its content, analysis, and conclusions.

The Amex has held true to its promise. Many of its members are not pleased with various parts of this book, but they have never attempted to have sections changed, modified, or deleted. At a time when many businesses are being criticized for dishonesty and manipulation, the Amex example shines as an indication that such need not be the case. This position was the result not only of the integrity of Amex officials, but a sense of security and position the exchange has today, which it arrived at quite recently.

Had this book been undertaken a decade ago, it would have been more complete. Several key figures in Amex history have died in the past few years, and so gaps in the study had to be filled in through the use of secondary material. The Amex would scarcely have considered asking an independent historian to write its history prior to the 1960s. Until then, the exchange believed itself shaky, merely an appendage to the industry, and one that might not survive. This is no longer a question today.

I trust that if my Yugoslav friends could read this book, they would come away with an understanding of why this is so.

Many people at the Amex cooperated with me in my researches, and they are listed in the *Bibliographical Essay* at the end of the book. But I would like to give special thanks to Vice-President Robert Coplin, who has opened doors for me when they needed opening, spent hours explaining Amex policies, helped gather statistics, and was always there to fill in gaps. Most of the time he would say, "I don't know, but I'll get the answer for you in a day or so." Not once was the answer in my hands in more than his "day or so." Amex Librarian Marian Isidore and Assistant Librarian Sheila Richardson dug deeply into the archives to find half-forgotten records and pamphlets. Finally, were it not for the efforts of Executive Vice-President Winsor H. Watson, Jr., this entire project might never have been undertaken.

ROBERT SOBEL
New College of Hofstra
March 1972

Contents

Introduction

Shortly before noon on June 7, 1971, a large van pulled up to the curb on Broad Street in New York, between Exchange Place and Beaver Street. Several people alighted to check a portion of the curb, which was covered with a tarpaulin, and the small, festooned grandstand nearby. All seemed in order, and they left. There was to be a celebration that day. It was not unusual in the area; such events occurred at least once a week.

It was a bright, warm day. Several tourist groups entering and leaving the New York Stock Exchange were hardly noticed by the small knots of exchange clerks out for an early lunch and passing the time of day. A vendor's cart was set up near the corner of Wall and Broad, and this too was part of the scene—not an unusual sight in that place, at that time. Many Wall Streeters were in the practice of grabbing hot-dog lunches from one of these stands, followed by ice cream from another. Most were tended by old men or middle-aged women. But the cart at the corner of Wall and Broad that day was different. It was tended by a strikingly voluptuous young woman, clad in the scantiest of short shorts, topped by a flimsy yellow cotton T-shirt at least two sizes too small, selling chocolate-covered bananas, and doing a brisk business. She and her bananas were the main attraction on the street that day, not the curbstone and the stand down the block.

Slightly more than a year earlier an even more well-endowed young woman, on her way to work, had caused a traffic jam in front of the Subtreasury building. The district's business ground to a near halt as the male community turned out to ogle and whistle.

People in Wall Street learn to play fads and fancies, and in this regard the vendors there are no different from the bankers. That summer several hot dog and ice cream carts were tended by beautiful girls, many of them college students or out-of-work actresses and models. But chocolate-covered bananas were something new, especially when sold with suggestive motions.

The intersection of Wall and Broad is recognized as a symbol of finance capitalism throughout the world. That it also is a place charged with sexual symbolism is recognized immediately by those who spend more than a few hours in the area. Perhaps the crackling atmosphere of money and power leads people to search for diversion, or perhaps the money drive serves to sharpen the sex drive in otherwise mild-mannered junior executives and clerks. Whatever the case, the canvas-covered curbstone was no match for chocolate-covered bananas.

When they were not passing comments on the girl and her wares, the onlookers near the curbstone talked of the rather stagnant market and the chances for the "traditional summer rally." Some spoke casually of the strike of New York's bridge operators, who had walked off the job that morning, just before the rush of cars was due in the city. Cleverly, they had left the drawbridges open, and in some cases sabotaged the mechanisms so they could not be closed. What several radical groups had tried to do in Washington during the past three years the bridge operators had done to New York: they had succeeded in paralyzing the city. Yet the event caused little anxiety or discussion. Such strikes had become commonplace in the late 1960s. To many, they coincided with the coming to office of Mayor John V. Lindsay, and, as had become almost traditional, blame for the strike was assigned to the Mayor.

Someone noted that Lindsay was due on Broad Street within the hour—something to do with the curbstone and the stand. As the news spread, people began to walk away from the banana cart and toward the grandstand. The glamourous Mayor had his supporters north of Canal Street, but he was anathema below it. Wall Streeters of every economic circumstance would not miss a chance to boo and hiss their mayor.

What was the occasion? Few of the onlookers seemed to know, even when the festooned portable stand was examined and found to have something to do with the anniversary of the old Curb Market. Most of the people in the crowd had no idea of what the Curb Market was, why it was important enough to have an anniversary, or what would be done. One old-timer said that the New York Stock Exchange had once been situated at that location, just before it moved to its present site up the street. (This was not so.) Another said the Curb Market was the ancestor of the American Stock Exchange, which had a building there before moving to Trinity Place a half-century ago.

He was half right. The old Curb Market was on Broad Street in 1921, but the brokers traded outdoors, not in a building. Most of the brokers had rented offices in the Mills Building (long since demolished), where they stationed their clerks, who manned batteries of telephones. The clerks would receive buy and sell orders from Wall Street firms, peer out the window, and locate their employers. Each street broker tried to wear a bright hat or jacket, so as to stand out in the crowd. When the clerk and his broker made visual contact, the clerk waved his arms and wagged his hands, in a set of unusual gestures. Each had a meaning , signifying a specific stock, the number of shares to be bought or sold, or other pertinent information. The broker wagged back his signals, sometimes screaming additional information. On a busy day it would resemble a packed can of gaily colored crickets.* These brokers and their clerks and runners moved from the outdoor market on Broad Street to an indoor market on Trinity Place in mid-1921.

It was this move indoors, a half-century before, that was being celebrated.

Such matters didn't seem to interest the onlookers, how-

---

* An account of the old Curb Market and its activities can be found in the first volume of this study. See Robert Sobel, *The Curbstone Brokers: The Origins of the American Stock Exchange* (Macmillan, 1970).

ever. Wall Streeters' interests in traditions generally are confined to those that can be translated into buy and sell orders—such as the traditional summer rally—and not the ones dealing with the history of the district. But they remained in front of the grandstand. They all wanted to see Lindsay, who, they were told, was on his way.

The grandstand filled as the crowd waited. Most of those in and around the grandstand were young men and women, some wearing brightly colored hats, given out to symbolize the headgear of the curbstone brokers. American Stock Exchange President Ralph Saul stood nearby, along with President-elect Paul Kolton and several other Amex officers.

The guests of honor were a half dozen elderly men, brokers who had been present in 1921 when the market moved indoors. Some pointed out windows in a nearby building, as though to say that their clerks had sat there. A few wagged signals while cameras recorded them. By then most of the onlookers seemed to know what was going on and who brokers were, and they had an idea of what would be found under the canvas: a curbstone, to mark the fiftieth anniversary of the move from Broad Street.

Still no Mayor Lindsay. But the ceremonies began. Exchange Senior Vice President Winsor H. Watson, Jr., tried to assure the crowd the Mayor would be there soon, and read a few words about the meaning of the dedication. Later on he had to inform the crowd that Lindsay could not make it, due to "pressing business at City Hall." The Mayor was absent because he had to deal with the strike of bridge operators. Most jeered and hooted, others just shrugged their shoulders in resignation, and some began to move away.

Ralph Saul said a few words about the curbstone brokers. A tall, balding man, shy in public, he kept it short. To complicate matters, a sound truck appeared at this time, announcing a bullfight scheduled to take place at Madison Square Garden that evening. It seemed appropriate to have such an announcement of bulls and/or bears on Wall Street, but Saul did not make the obvious crack about it; it was not his style. Instead, an American Exchange official asked the driver to lower the volume until he passed the stand, and he obliged.

After Saul completed his comments, his place at the microphone was taken by a young City Hall aide. He made a weak apology and joke regarding the Mayor's absence, and then offered a few words about the old Curb Market. More than a quarter of the crowd was gone, with the rest on its way. They had come to see Lindsay, and not a stone in the ground.

The memorial curbstone was then unveiled, and the old-timers joined Saul, Kolton, and other Exchange officials gathering for pictures. The last of the crowd had gone. Most went back to their offices; some went to take a last look at the banana girl up the block.

Another memorial marker had been added to the many that dot the financial district. A handful of onlookers stopped to read the inscription. It read:

FOR MORE THAN A CENTURY THE OUTDOOR BROKERS, PREDE-
CESSORS OF THE AMERICAN STOCK EXCHANGE, CONDUCTED A
MARKET PLACE ON THE CURBSTONES OF THE FINANCIAL DIS-
TRICT, SERVING INVESTORS AND AIDING THE NATION'S IN-
DUSTRIAL GROWTH. THEY MOVED INDOORS ON JUNE 27, 1921,
FROM THIS SITE.

Although the curbstone brokers had moved indoors on June 27, expediency had dictated the celebration date of June 7: some of the people involved in the celebration would be away on vacation three weeks later. No one in the crowd seemed to have noticed the change of date.

It might be carping to note that *all* the curbstone brokers did not move indoors on June 27. A small contingent, led by one Thomas Cook, opposed the change and vowed to continue trading out of doors. Cook attracted few brokers to his banner, but they were there on June 27 and during the next few weeks, struggling to maintain an outdoor market. They couldn't make a go of it, and disappeared soon after, on a date that is unrecorded. So we really do not know the exact date outdoor trading ended in New York.

Why did the inscription begin with the words, "For more than a century"? How much more? When did outdoor trading begin? Why couldn't the American Exchange find a specific date to put on the memorial curbstone? At one time the Exchange said its origins went back to the California Gold Rush of 1849, which sparked an active market in mining stocks in New York, almost all of which were traded outdoors. Curbstone brokers dealt in stocks of railroads prior to the Gold Rush, and before that were active in canal, bank, and insurance stocks. Indeed, New York's first brokers were unorganized, and some of them traded in the open as well as in their offices. In 1792 a small group of these brokers united to form an organization that many consider the forerunner of the New York Stock Exchange (the "Big Board," which dominates the financial district). This would mean that the curbstone brokers antedated the Big Board, which would imply either a common parentage for the two groups, or a longer genealogy for the Curb than for the New York Stock Exchange.

The pecking order in the financial district is strict. The American Stock Exchange—the "Amex"—is a proud but clearly "second" market in the city. It would ill-behoove such an organization to claim common ancestry with the prestigious Big Board, especially on a marker only a few dozen yards from the New York Stock Exchange itself. Suggesting that it was an even more ancient market would have been out of the question. Hence, the phrase, "For more than a century."

In any case, the Amex brokers aren't too interested in such matters. So far as they are concerned, the important date for their origins isn't 1792 or earlier, but 1921. To them, that is the true date of the beginnings of their marketplace.

The young floor brokers and specialists at the Amex seem little different from their counterparts at the New York Stock Exchange, but there are differences nonetheless. Significantly, they refer to their place of business as the "American," and a few still call it the Curb, although at one time such a reference would have cost the speaker a fine of twenty-five cents. The senior market is not called "the New York" or "the Big Board," but simply, "the Stock Exchange."

More Amex brokers seem to have been graduated from New York, Boston, and Duquesne universities than from Harvard, Yale, or Princeton. But in appearance, sophistication, and knowledge, they are the equals if not the superiors of their Ivy League counterparts at the Big Board. There are more Irish, East European Jewish, and Italian names at the Amex than at the Stock Exhange, though three or four generations of Americanization have diluted whatever immigrant traces had existed in their fathers' time. Today's Amex broker proudly notes that he operates in a tougher market than the Big Board, one where skill and the ability to think quickly are more necessary than at the Big Board.

Specializing in a stock like American Telephone and Telegraph or General Motors is relatively simple. There are large markets for such securities, and few risks are taken in dealing with them. Being a specialist in a young, small retail company's stock is another matter entirely. The specialist must take risks, use his judgment in almost every trade, and in general be on his toes all day. Many of the Big Board's best specialists were trained at the Amex, and bright young apprentice specialists are as likely to be sent there by their firms as to the Stock Exchange. The Big Board is the main arena for Wall Street, but a professional can learn much more, and faster, at the Amex.

Such was not the case for the men who went indoors in June 1921, as most young specialists at the Amex know. Brokers in their thirties and forties have heard tales of what the business was like in those days from their fathers and uncles. Brokerage at the Amex is very much a father-and-son business. Along with their seats, connections, and opinions, fathers attempt to pass on their memories, values, and traditions. They have been far more successful in this than has been the case in almost any other area of American life. There is not much of a generation gap at the Amex. This helps explain the essential conservatism of its brokers, and at the same time their aggressiveness and vigor. They want to retain what they and their fathers have achieved, and at the same time they recognize that a sense of daring and willingness to take chances is part of their heritage.

Sons of old Curb brokers know that in 1921 their fathers were young, arrogant, and insecure. They were ready to take chances in order to make a fast shaky buck because they were not certain they would survive another year at their marketplace. Brokerage at the old Curb was a risky business, not only because each broker could be undercut by his fellows, but because of dangers of an attack by the Big Board or one of the many governmental groups then investigating Curb operations. In 1921 Big Board leaders looked to a past that was glorious and a future that promised enhanced power. (Remember, this was the dawn of the Republican-sponsored "New Era," and the golden age of laissez-faire economics.) Curbstone brokers, on the other hand, knew little and cared less about the past and weren't certain they had a future—1921 was also a depression year, and at such times hundreds of curbstone brokers would go bankrupt and leave the industry. Those men who went indoors tended to live in the present. The move itself was made not so much as to assure a long future, but because Wall Street and related pressures had forced it upon them. Probably a majority of the brokers did not believe the new exchange would last very long. It did offer the opportunity to continue to make money for the time being, and that was all they seemed to care about.

Because of this attitude, most of the brokers of that time would have been surprised to learn that their heirs were able to celebrate the fiftieth anniversary of the indoor market. They would not have been surprised that along the way there were times when it seemed to be on the point of dissolution. Those who survive—the elderly men at the grandstand in 1971—admit as much, and because of this feel a greater sense of obligation and debt to the Amex than most NYSE brokers feel toward their institution. "Were it not for the American Stock Exchange," one said, "I would have been a delivery boy, a clerk, or a post-office employee, living on a small pension. In fact, even *with* the Amex I almost wound up that way. I worked at all those jobs, even while being a specialist there."

This is no exaggeration; during the bad times of the early 1930s, some of the brokers took part-time jobs at such occupations, and made more money pushing a hack or sorting mail than they did as specialists on the floor of the Curb Exchange. During World War II, office employees would work at the Exchange until five o'clock and then go to their second job—as stevedores on the New York docks—and work there until late at night. Yet today some of these men and their sons are millionaires. They haven't forgotten their pasts.

This is the tradition of the Amex, and what was being celebrated on Broad Street in early June 1971. It is also the subject of this book.

Amex

The New Curb Market

The curbstone brokers conducted their last session outdoors on June 25, 1921. It was the usual half-day Saturday, with trading beginning at nine-thirty and ending at noon. Volume was dull, and prices stagnated. There wasn't much business for those brokers and clerks who were in attendance. As was customary, many of the Jewish brokers did not participate in Saturday trading for religious reasons, and their places were taken by their clerks or, in some cases, their partners. Partnerships of Gentile and Jew were not uncommon at the Curb, especially those between Irish Catholics and East European Jews. Both groups were discriminated against at the New York Stock Exchange, and it seemed only natural for them to unite at the Curb.

A handful of brokers, among them Curb Market President Edward R. McCormick and former President and Chairman of the New York Curb Market Realty Associates John L. McCormack, were not present at the session. Together with Curb counsel Franklin Leonard, Jr., and Curb Secretary Alfred B. Sturges, they were on the other side of Trinity Church, on Trinity Place, inspecting the new home of the New York Curb Market. Work on the $1.2-million building had begun the previous December, and had been completed except for finishing touches in early June. As McCormick and the others watched and supervised, their few desks and file cases were moved into third-floor offices. Then the Curb officials examined the trading floor, complete with posts resembling light poles. This resemblance was important; the architects, Starrett & Van Vleck, had been told to make the trading floor as close to the outdoor market as they could. Brokers stood near light poles so as to be easily picked out by their clerks, sitting high above in office windows at the Mills and Broad Exchange buildings. Now, on the floor of the indoor market, they could stand at replica poles. Their clerks would sit in a banked grandstand on one side of the floor. Each clerk would have his place and his telephones, and he could contact his broker through the customary hand signals. This too represented an attempt to duplicate outdoor conditions. The curbstone brokers had made their desires quite clear; except for the roof over their heads, they wanted their new home to be no different from the old.

If this were the case, why make the move at all? Curbstone brokers had traded securities in New York's streets for almost two centuries, in good weather and bad. Was a roof now so important?

The Curb Market was not moving indoors to escape the elements, but rather to leave those who demeaned it, and achieve a certain kind of respectability. Throughout the history of securities markets, outdoor brokers were looked upon as second-class citizens of the districts. Respectability was to be achieved with a move to indoor, permanent quarters. At least such had been the case in London, Paris, and Amsterdam. The curbstone brokers hoped the same would happen to them in New York.

The quest for respectability alone would not have caused the move, however. While it was true that a handful of brokers, most of them in positions of leadership, wanted status, the majority couldn't have cared less. They were on the Curb to make money. Only if very successful would they think of their position in the community of Wall Street. Few curbstone brokers were that successful, and so respectability was considered a luxury they could forego.

More important were pressures from the New York Stock Exchange. J. P. Morgan and other members of the Wall Street Establishment needed office space, and looked to the Mills and Broad Exchange buildings for it. If the Curb were to leave Broad, the offices could be theirs. The Establishment wanted the move, and made its desires known. A call to relocate, made by certain powerful Stock Exchange leaders, could not be ignored. Approximately 80 percent of all Curb transactions originated at Big Board commission houses. Without the patronage of the Stock Exchange, the Curb would have been doomed.

Some Stock Exchange officials, noting the increased trading volume at the Curb in this period, spoke of a merger of the two markets. Actually, they considered engulfing the Curb, leeching it of its business and throwing out whatever was left over. According to one plan, the Curb would be situated in a large room in the Stock Exchange building. There it would be under the eye of Big Board leaders, who would direct its development. Stock Exchange rules would apply, and Curb brokers would be under the control of Stock Exchange officials. But they were not to be permitted to join the senior market; they were to remain the stepchildren of Wall Street. To escape this fate, the move to Trinity Place seemed vital.

There were other reasons for the move. It had been discussed for over two generations, at times when there was no office shortage on Broad Street, no attempt to make the Curb part of the Stock Exchange, and when weather conditions were as bad as they were in 1921. As early as the 1870s, when E. S. Mendels attempted to organize the curbstone brokers into some kind of viable community, a move to permanent indoor quarters was discussed.

In the 1870s and during the next half-century, the Curb was an unorganized market. In 1908 Mendels had formed the Curb Market Agency, a weak office with little power or ability to oblige its members to conform to its rules. The Agency made certain the street was cleared of snow after winter storms, put up ropes to separate the brokers from the tourists during busy trading days, and printed a set of directories. There were rules governing trading methods, deliveries, stock listing, and other aspects of exchange business. But there were no ways to enforce such rules. Should a broker take many liberties with them, he would be shunned by his fellows, and in time be forced to leave the district. This would have happened had there been no Agency and no rules. A code of honor and accepted practices existed at the Curb long before 1908. All Mendels did was to set that code down in black and white. The Curb was governed by common law in this period, and not statute law.

Even then, however, there were two sets of attitudes at the Curb regarding the market's future. A majority of the brokers looked upon the Curb as a place of business, a market to be used in advancing their own fortunes. They would take whatever steps necessary to keep the market going, but no more. If they failed, they would leave the Curb and get a job someplace else. Should they hit it big, they would retire, go into a "respectable" business, or—glory of glories—try to obtain a seat at the New York Stock Exchange. Gentlemen conducted business at the Big Board; brokers traded stocks at the Curb. Few of these people thought of remaining at the Curb permanently; for them, it would be a case of either up or out.

Other brokers—a minority—wanted to regularize Curb procedures, make it a respectable market, enhance its reputation, and so rise with it. They saw progress in terms of the institution itself, not only the individual operating within the institution. Such men knew they could never rival the Big Board in prestige or power, but that was not their aim. The cardinal rule of the Curb was that whenever one of it stocks achieved listing on the Big Board, Curb brokers would immediately cease trading in it. The Curb was a place for "unseasoned" stocks. Once a security qualified for the Big Board, off it went. In the past, at least, the same was true of the men. This minority group had no wish to change the situation so far as the securities were concerned, but they did want to make it a place where decent and respectable brokers would want to remain. Given the institutional structure of the New York financial community at the time, that was all they could hope for.

It was these men—the minority—who led the Curb indoors in 1921. The majority went along because it had no choice. Some of the Curb's most powerful men, including its major specialists and Big Board correspondents, wanted the move. Had the majority refused to join them, they would have seen their business shrivel up and eventually disappear. It was move or die. The majority moved.

Edward McCormick, Franklin Leonard, and Alfred Sturges were leaders of this powerful minority. They and a few others like them had organized the move indoors. That is why they must have felt a particular pride as they inspected the new facilities the morning of June 25.

The curbstone brokers arrived on Broad Street shortly after eight o'clock on Monday morning, June 27. Their clerks were in the streets with them, and not at their accustomed places in the Mills and Broad Exchange buildings. They had been told where they should station themselves within the new Curb building. Each broker was told where his stocks would be traded—around which posts the individual specialists could congregate. There was a holiday mood in the crowd, and not much in the way of anxiety and anticipation. The novelty of the day was more interesting to these men than its implications. McCormick and his circle were aware of the importance of the move, but not so the average broker. Most had paid the $1,500 initial fee for membership in the indoor market, as well as the $500 initiation and transfer fee. For some it had taken their last dollar, while others had to borrow to meet the price. If such was the cost of staying in business, they would pay it. Others, who had doubts the plan would work, refused to purchase a seat until the last minute. By that time their prices had risen. McCormick had made available additional seats for a price of $6,500 apiece, and a handful of unlucky brokers had to pay that inflated price. These men shrugged off their loss; Wall Street is a place of speculation, and the price for guessing wrong was often more than $5,000.

At nine A.M.—a half-hour before the new market was scheduled to open—McCormick announced that the march to Trinity Place would begin. He probably stood not more than a few steps from where the memorial curbstone of 1971 now rests. The curbstone brokers fell in behind him, and the walk began, most of the brokers going west on Wall Street, but some taking the Exchange Place route. Then across Rector or Exchange Alley, or through Trinity churchyard, to the new building on Trinity Place.

McCormick arrived just before nine-thirty, and received the key to the building from John McCormack. He stood in front of the building, a handsome but not imposing structure that bore the name "NEW YORK CURB MARKET," and called for silence. Then he addressed the members. Like Ralph Saul a half-century later, McCormick was not a particularly good public speaker, and his remarks were short and to the point. "The die is cast," he said. "The old order is gone forever."

Those who considered McCormick's statement probably assumed he meant that the outdoor market's history was ended, and that the move represented the beginning of a new stage in Curb history. McCormick, who had worked hard for Curb reform, might have meant something quite different. The important change from the outdoor market was not the roof, as many thought, but the door. The roof would protect against the elements; the door would forbid entrance to disreputable brokers. McCormick meant to limit membership to those brokers who could be counted upon to behave themselves. Crooks, chiselers, and confidence men would be prohibited entry. Or, at least that was his hope.

After McCormick's short speech, Eugene Tappen, the Curb's Assistant Secretary (and a disappointed opera singer), stood and led the brokers in singing the "Star-Spangled Banner." Then the doors were opened and the brokers and clerks rushed in. Trading began at nine-thirty, as usual.

To the uninitiated, Curb activities seemed hopelessly confusing. There was this writhing mass of brokers—some five hundred of them—and twice five hundred clerks, runners, and allied personnel serving and servicing them. Each person seemed to know what he was doing, but the whole mass of people appeared directionless.

Such would not be an inaccurate observation. For as long

as there have been securities markets, there have been critics of them: people who say that such markets make no contribution to the economy. In response brokers have said they provide liquidity (by which they mean a place where ownership in securities can be transferred from one person to another). This is the major difference between the securities market and the situation in other goods that are bought and sold—say, real estate. There is a central securities market, but there is none in real estate. Nor could there ever be one. Every one of General Motors' quarter of a billion shares is like the others. When a person wants to buy a share of GM, he doesn't care which he gets. Similarly, a person who wants to sell a share knows that the price paid for any one share at the time will approximate the price he can expect to receive. Such is not the case with real estate. No two houses are identical after they have been lived in for a few years, and no two plots of land are the same. The house and its land are unique, and so the seller must go into the market to find a person who wants to buy his property. Similarly, a person in the market for a house may spend several months or even years seeking exactly what he wants. In 1921 a person could buy or sell a share of stock traded at the Curb in a matter of minutes, but it would have taken weeks or months to dispose of his house. That's liquidity: the reason the Curb—and every other securities market—offers in defense against those who challenge its existence.

If the Curb's individual issues each had identical qualities, each Curb broker was different from the others in function and specialty. But all brokers fell into one of four categories: specialist, two-dollar broker, representative, or individual trader.

The specialist was the key to the market in 1921. In one way or another, he had managed to gather almost all the business in a particular stock or group of stocks. Those brokers wanting to purchase that stock knew he would sell them shares, and tell them the current prices offered and asked for them. Let us assume the broker was a specialist in Nixon-Nevada Mines at the Curb (Nixon-Nevada was the volume leader the week before the move indoors). The specialist would have an "inventory" of the stock—say, a thousand or so shares. He would also "make a market" in Nixon-Nevada. Should he be asked, "How's Nixon-Nevada?" he might answer, "a quarter to a half." This would not be enough to answer the question, but the specialist assumed the person asking the question knew something about Curb verbal shorthand and the price of the stock at the last trade or thereabouts. What he was saying was, "I am prepared to buy Nixon-Nevada common from you at two dollars and twenty-five cents, and to sell it to you at two dollars and fifty cents." Then the questioner would reply, "I'll take two hundred," meaning he would buy 200 shares at $2.50. The specialist and the broker then would each take the other's number, worn on a small badge, and mark the sale. A copy would be given to a Curb employee known as a reporter, who would take the slip and deliver it to a telegraph clerk, whose job it was to punch it onto the ticker, from which it would be reproduced on tickers in brokerage offices.

How did a person become a specialist at the Curb? Through pushing, shoving, luck, double-dealing, muscle, cheating, cleverness, or a combination of these qualities. A young would-be specialist may see a broker putting out quotes in a stock. The quotes may be 20½ bid, 21 asked, meaning he will buy the stock at 20½ and sell it at 21. The young broker may think he could do better than that at a smaller margin; or, in the words of the Curb, "make a better market in the stock." He might then get an inventory of the stock and set up his operation near that of the man he wants to replace. When the specialist bids "one-half to one," his new competitor may shout, "five-eighths to seven-eighths." In so doing he is saying he will buy the stock at $20.62½, while his competitor offered $20.50. And he will sell at $20.87½, or twelve and a half cents less than his competitor's offer of $21.

If he could keep this up for a while, make good on his deliveries, and prove he would honor his word, he might soon become the sole specialist in the stock, and keep his dominance in it until successfully challenged. All it took was sufficient funds to purchase an inventory, a willingness to take risks (remember, when the specialist offered his quote he didn't know whether the questioner wanted to buy or sell), a reputation for keeping one's word on a deal, and the good fortune to swing the right way with the market. Some specialists at the Curb lacked some of these qualities. They would renege on deals when it suited them, and they thought they could get away with it. If they had a particularly bad day they might simply vanish from the area, leaving the buyers and sellers holding the bag. They might enter specialization without an inventory, hoping to strike it lucky the first day by buying more shares than were sold of a stock on its way up or selling more shares than they had purchased of a stock going down.

All of these were serious abuses on the old Curb, which McCormick hoped would change indoors. Brokers guilty of such activities could be barred from the floor; there was no way of forbidding a person entry to part of New York City's Broad Street real estate. The indoor Curb would be a club, he thought, dominated by specialists, each of whom owned a seat, and each of whom could vote for the Curb's officers. In time the specialists would evolve a code of ethics not unlike that at the Big Board. Then it would be a simple matter to keep the crooks and deadbeats from the market.

What if a large number of specialists—with seats—were themselves participants in swindles? What if they agreed to transgress rules? What would happen if the crime were not breaking the rule, but getting caught? Such was the case outdoors in the pre-1921 period. It would continue throughout the 1920s. And it has changed only recently, since 1961.

The specialist or would-be specialist thrived on his portfolio of stocks. The more issues he had and the higher their volume of trading, the more money he would make in commissions, all other things being equal. Thus, each specialist attempted to obtain as many potentially high-volume stocks as he could.

There were three ways of getting a new issue. When a company applied to the Curb for listing, it was asked to fill out papers and make certain statements. After this was done and the stock admitted to listing, the committee on arrangements assigned the stock to a specialist. In so doing the committee took into consideration such matters as whether the would-be specialist had sufficient capital to handle the new issue, and whether he was qualified to deal in it. A popular new issue, certain to be traded in heavily, was not given to a novice specialist or one with limited financial resources. Fairness was also considered; given a choice between two specialists, the committee often selected the one who needed a new issue over a man who was doing well without it. Sometimes chance played a role: the committee appeared on the floor to make its selection, and gave the stock to the first person who caught its eye or who asked for it. Certainly favoritism was practiced, and committee members were not above using their power to pay off associates or store up similar favors for the future. The committee on arrangements was one of the most powerful committees at the Curb, one of the few with any true control over the membership.

Sometimes the investment banker for the newly listed firm requested that the security be placed with a named specialist. The banker might have heard that the specialist was particularly talented, or the specialist might have been a friend of someone at the company. In some cases the specialist may have been instrumental in having the firm's securities listed, and the grant was made in return for the favor. Older and more aggressive specialists won many issues this way; young specialists who encouraged firms to list made sure they received promises of selection after listing was granted.

Both of these methods applied to listed stocks and bonds: securities of companies that had made application for listing and received it. But most Curb securities were not listed, having instead "unlisted trading rights." Specialists obtained these in a different way.

Let us assume a specialist learned of a new mine in Nevada that was doing fairly well. He might go to Nevada and visit the site, speak with the officers, and then ask them to consider applying for listing at the Curb—in which case he could hope to become its specialist. What if the officers refused to make application? This refusal would be ignored. The specialist might purchase shares in the company and then, acting as a stockholder, apply for unlisted trading rights at the Curb.

This right would almost always be granted. Indeed, a large majority of Curb issues were in this category, which meant that the necessary papers had not been filed or important information about the company was lacking. In all other respects, however, listed and unlisted securities were treated the same way by specialists and other brokers. The general feeling, however, was that the listed securities made up the cream of the list.*

The successful specialist of 1921 had to be able to take stocks from his fellow, sniff out new issues and bring them to market, and have enough money, brains, and guts to survive in a financial jungle where few rules existed and those rarely were enforced.

A representative had a far simpler task. He worked for one of the large commission houses dealing with the public. It was his job to carry out orders transmitted by customers' men in the offices. He was the person who asked the specialist, "How's Nixon-Nevada?"

Some representatives owned Curb seats, but most did not. Instead, they had purchased associate memberships at the Curb Market. These cost $250 and a transfer fee. Associate members were permitted to use all Curb facilities and trade with the regular members, in this way deriving savings on commissions. They were not allowed a vote for officers, and did not own stock in the Realty Associates—a Curb subsidiary, which owned the building and the grounds. They would be bound by the rules of the Market, but would not have a direct voice in its affairs. There were 320 associate members in all, most of whom were representatives of Wall Street brokerages. President McCormick said they would "make it possible for banking and brokerage firms throughout the country to become identified with the association with special privileges."

In actuality some of the representatives had more power

* There were exceptions: for example, the Standard Oil stocks were unlisted. At times officers of major firms would refuse to make information public. These firms might have qualified for trading at the Big Board had they applied for it. Instead, their issues traded with unlisted status at the Curb.

than all but the most prominent specialists. As has been indicated, approximately 80 percent of all trades originated at Stock Exchange firms. The trades were handled by the representatives. If two or more specialists were attempting to control a security, the victor would be determined by the person receiving the orders and executing them: the representative. Under certain circumstances representatives could make or break a specialist, and both men knew it. It was customary for them to work out deals in such circumstances.

For example, a representative might receive an order to purchase 400 shares of a stock "at the market." This meant he was bound to try to get the lowest price possible for his client. He might approach the specialist and find that the buy price was $20.50. The specialist would be informed that the representative was willing to purchase the security at $21.00—a half point, and in this case $200 more than the price would have been at $20.50. The specialist could keep half the difference in price, while putting away the other half in the representative's "envelope," which was kept in a special drawer. Many specialists and representatives engaged in such practices, so that by the end of the week a busy specialist could count on a few thousand dollars in addition to his other income, while his representative colleagues were also well-rewarded. Those representatives who would not engage in such practices simply had smaller take-home salaries. The temptation to go along was great, at a time in Wall Street history when such activities were the rule, not the exception. All but the most financially and morally secure made a practice of it.

Those specialists and representatives who entered these deals did not consider themselves dishonest. To them, dishonesty consisted of cheating or lying to a fellow-broker—not to a customer.

If discovered in a breach of the Curb rules regarding falsifying prices, a broker could be brought before the proper Curb committee and tried. If found guilty he could be fined, suspended, or even expelled from the marketplace. Few brokers received such treatment in the 1920s.

One such case involved Emil Mosbacher, a prominent

Curb broker and leading specialist. Mosbacher was not a popular broker, and not altogether trusted. Like other brokers of the period, he would on occasion violate Curb rules. In October 1920 he purchased stock at one price and reported it to his customer at another. As a result, he made a profit of more than $3,700. Mosbacher's action was noted and reported. The law committee heard the case, and took the unusual step of reporting it to the press. Stories of Mosbacher's action appeared in several newspapers—a most unusual situation for the time.

The charges against Mosbacher were pressed by Curb Secretary Sturges, Arthur Myles, and Eugene Tappen, all of whom were men of prominence at the Curb. Mosbacher was found guilty of the charges on December 8, 1920, and was expelled from the Curb Market. If this had happened at the Stock Exchange, the former member would have been disgraced, and might have chosen suicide as the only way out. This was not the Curb style. Members of the Stock Exchange were supposed to be men of honor, while those of the Curb were supposed to be good businessmen who didn't get caught at misdeeds. Even those who voted to expel Mosbacher seemed to know this, and so Mosbacher did not lose hope of eventual return. He might also have reflected that Sturges and Tappen voted to acquit him of charges, along with Law Committee member Lew Teichman.

Mosbacher did leave the Curb in December 1920. But in January 1922, he purchased a seat at the indoor Curb Market. By then the matter had been forgotten, and Mosbacher had no difficulty passing the Committee on Membership. In time, he too would serve on committees and be part of the Curb administration.

Such dealings as Mosbacher's and the way it was handled were not unusual in the 1920s. It is important to judge these actions and people in their own contexts, however. Both the New York Stock Exchange and the Curb Market of that time would be considered thieves' dens by today's standards. Mosbacher and the specialists and representatives who dealt in envelopes were not the worst of the brokerage crowd. Indeed, some of them were leaders of the district's reform movements.

To understand what the district considered dishonest, one

must examine the trades not originating at Stock Exchange houses—some 20 percent of the total. Some came from floor traders, more of whom later. Most originated at brokerages specializing in Curb securities, or at "bucket shops." For the most part, these two establishments were the same.

Most of the Curb Market's securities were of the unseasoned variety. These were securities of young companies or marginal firms, many of which would disappear through mergers, bankruptcy, or other means. A few would survive and grow, and would in time transfer to the Big Board. In addition, the Curb had a group of high-quality issues. Among these were the successor firms of Standard Oil of New Jersey, United States Tobacco, and United States Sugar. Such firms could easily have qualified for Big Board listing had they so desired. But the Stock Exchange required listed companies to issue regular reports and file financial information at the Exchange office. These companies, largely controlled by single families and uninterested in the marketability of their securities, refused to do so. Instead, powerful Curb specialists filed papers for them at the outdoor market, paid the $100 listing fee, and took control of their trading. Such stocks were the jewels of the Curb. Far more common were stocks in firms like New York Engine Company, which had 35,000 shares outstanding and traded at below $10, or Michigan-Pacific Lumber, a penny stock with 150,000 shares. Georgia Development Company would not trade for weeks at a time; it had only 20,000 shares listed at the Curb.

There were brokerages in New York and other cities where one could buy and sell stocks and bonds listed at the Curb. Their proprietors owned seats on the Curb, and had several representatives on the floor. In addition, they had a working arrangement with a New York Stock Exchange house, so that any orders they received for Stock Exchange securities could be handled by them.

Most of these brokerages catered to the wilder variety of speculator. Curb securities were thinly capitalized: an order to buy 500 shares of Georgia Development was an unusual occurrence. Because of this, and because the Curb specialists were not interested in maintaining orderly markets in the same way and to the same extent as their Stock Exchange counterparts, the Curb lent itself to manipulation. That 500-share order for Georgia Development could send it from 5 to 10 with ease, since the "buy" represented a great demand for such a stock and there was little supply. Suppose a person had "bet" the stock would rise? (That is to say, he did not purchase the stock, but placed a wager on it, in much the same way as one might place a bet on a horse.) Clearly, he would be a big winner.

There were places where people could bet on stocks, which were called "bucket shops." While there were several varieties of bucket shops, the most common was one in which the customer would look at the ticker and see a stock at a certain price. He would then "buy" shares from a teller, using 90-percent margin in his purchase. If he "purchased" 100 shares of a $10 stock, the total price would be $1,000, for which he would put up $100 and borrow the rest from the broker, using the stock as collateral. Such was the theory, at least. Since the broker had no intention of buying the stock, the collateral arrangement was academic. In effect, the speculator was betting the stock would rise. If it fell more than 10 percent, his equity in the wager was lost and he was wiped out. If it rose 10 percent, he doubled his money.

Not all bucket shops were Curb Market brokerages, but almost all Curb Market brokerages were bucket shops. They catered to the gambling instinct among clerks, manual workers, farmers, and even schoolboys. There a person could "buy" 10 shares of a dollar stock for $10 (or one dollar with 90-percent margin). The bucket shop–Curb brokerages filled a function in America similar to that of lotteries in South America—and in parts of the United States today. It served the "little guy" who had dreams of making a quick killing.

The Curb bucket shops did a high-volume business, and some became quite large. Indeed, at the time of the move indoors one of them, Jones & Baker, advertised itself as the largest brokerage bar none in the western hemisphere. It had offices in Chicago, Pittsburgh, Philadelphia, and Boston, as well as several in New York. Jackson Sells, the brains of the organization, recruited a research staff, instituted a training program for customers' men, and in fact was one of the most innovative men of the financial district. L. L. Winkelman, another king of the Curb brokerages, had offices in Chicago, Akron, Milwaukee, Uniontown, Marietta—indeed, throughout the Midwest. Winkelman was a merchandising and promotional genius, a fact that went unrecognized because he operated what was considered a shady business attached to a secondary market. In his time—from 1910 to 1923—Winkelman & Co. was to bucket shops what Woolworth was to low-priced merchandising.

Between them, Jones & Baker, Winkelman, and the bucket shops accounted for most of the 20 percent or so of Curb business not taken by stock exchange houses. Winkelman and Jones & Baker had representatives on the floor of the Curb Market, where they worked alongside representatives of the large Wall Street houses. Like them, the Curb representatives were eager to get weekly envelopes. But, unlike the Stock Exchange representatives, they were a source of embarrassment to the Curb leadership, who would just as soon see them leave. Mendels, McCormack, and McCormick had all conducted crusades to rid the Curb of bucket shops, to give it a better name and increased prestige. They would accept crookery from Big Board representatives, since the prestige of having them there was worth it. But throughout the last days outdoors and the first indoors, McCormick tried to remove the bucket shop operators from membership.

There was a second kind of representative and a third category of broker at the Curb. This was the "two-dollar broker." They were free-lancers who made their livings conducting transactions for brokerages and representatives. If a representative was flooded with orders, he might give some of them to a two-dollar broker to be executed. For this service the charge would be two dollars a transaction (hence the name). Or a small brokerage might find it didn't pay to have a permanent full-time representative at the Curb. So it would use the services of a two-dollar broker.

Some two-dollar brokers represented several houses, while others were the favorites of major representatives. Such people could do quite well financially. Many were expected to give kickbacks to those who employed them, which, although against the rules, was common practice at the Curb. Other two-dollar brokers, because of bad reputations for unwillingness to give kickbacks or inability to execute orders efficiently, were marginal men at the Curb, and most would soon drop out.

Finally, there were the traders. Such men owned seats on the Curb, and worked for their own accounts. They would wander the floor, seeking what seemed good buying and selling opportunities, and then they would swoop down and start to trade.

A person who knew something about the markets and had even the smallest connections could make a living through trading. These men paid no commissions, since they were their own brokers. Hence, they could buy stock at 2 and then sell it at 2⅛, making 12½¢ per share on the transaction. Enough such small trades, and the trader could do moderately well financially.

Most Curb traders were uninterested in such penny-ante business. This was the period of the manipulator, the pool operator, the Wall Street shark. They were famous, even romantic figures in their own right. Some brought together a dozen or so associates, each contributing a few thousand dollars—or hundreds of thousands of dollars—and would push stocks up and down as it suited them, making profits on every turn of the wheel. Such pools and combines were against certain regulations, both at the Stock Exchange and the Curb, but they did not violate state, city, or federal laws. The exchanges rarely took action against pool operators and other traders, and so they remained, the glamour figures of the 1920s.

One leading trader, Jesse Livermore, could often be found on the Curb floor, his appearance enough to stop trading, as specialists, representatives, and two-dollar brokers watched his every move, trying to anticipate where he would strike next. When he did, the news spread rapidly. A rumor that Livermore was bulling a stock would send it zooming, as lesser traders and others rushed to jump on the bandwagon. Livermore knew this, and at times would spread the rumor himself. Then, as others bought, he would sell, reaping his killing that way.

Those caught in such traps were disappointed, but the action itself was not considered unworthy of the man or unusual. It was merely one of the breaks of the game. Next time they would catch Livermore, and not he them.

These, then, were the four kinds of brokers who worked at the Curb Market. The specialists had most of the power within the organization, but they could not survive without the leading representatives of Wall Street firms, who exercised their power from without. The traders provided the glamour, but no trader had much influence in the operations of the market. The two–dollar brokers had no power as a group, although individual brokers, through connections or ability, managed to become prominent in Curb affairs. Yet no two–dollar broker ever rose to a position of leadership at the market.

In 1921 the administration was weak, inexperienced, and unable to force its will on the members, even if willing to try. The Curb didn't even have a constitution until 1912, and this was a rather weak document. Under its terms, the basic governing body was a Board of Representatives, with its chairman serving as Curb president, even though the title was not used until 1922. John McCormack, first chairman under the constitution, was a pleasant man who did little but make sure operations continued. Edward McCormick, the second chairman and the first president, spent much of his time in office arranging for the move indoors and making certain it succeeded.

Neither of these men was a full-time executive. Both were specialists who spent only a part of their time caring for Curb business. The same was true of the members of the Board of Representatives. According to the constitution,

> It shall fix the amount of initiation fee, listing fee and salaries; and through its Finance Committee the method of collection and payment of the same; regulate all business and make such other requirements for the purpose of insuring economy, safety and the protection of its members, as many appear to the Board to be necessary and proper.

A broad mandate—so broad as to be almost meaningless. The board was dominated by the major specialists, in any case, and existed as a forum to carry out their wills. The chairman was to preside over the board and be an *ex officio* member of all other committees. He was the board's creature or, to put it another way, an instrument of the specialists. And that body's power was derived not from the constitution, but from its members' positions at the Curb as major specialists.

The Curb had eight standing committees. The finance committee set initiation fees and handled Curb ledgers. All other fees were handled and set by the committee on commissions. The committee on listings was to set standards for admission of new securities to the Curb, but in fact took almost any stock brought in by a specialist. The committee on complaints and the arbitration committee regulated the brokers themselves. The law committee and the committee on constitution were charged with interpreting the laws and by-laws of the Curb. The membership committee screened new members.

During its first eight years indoors, Curb records indicate that only one member was expelled, and there is no record of a security being refused admission once it had the sponsorship of a specialist. In theory, either the committee on listing or the finance committee might have been given the power to determine the allocation of securities to specialists. Such was not the case. Again, throughout the 1920s there is no record of a security being taken from one specialist and given to another for any reason. Nor would a specialist bringing a stock to the Curb fail to receive it as his own.

In 1921 the Curb had no provision for the delivery of certificates, nor way of discovering whether such delivery had been made. At the end of the business day each specialist went over his slips to determine who owed him how many certificates, and to whom he owed certificates. Then he arranged for deliveries. According to the Curb manual:

> All deliveries in stocks except certain mining stocks must be made in 100-share certificates or in amounts equal thereto, except in case of odd lots, when the exact amount must be deliv-

ered in certificates or by transfer if the purchaser agreed to take the same in this manner.

The buyer must not later than two fifteen o'clock p.m. accept and pay for all or any portion of a lot of stock contracted for which may be tendered in lots of one hundred shares or multiples thereof; and he may buy in cash the undelivered portion, if having made the usual demand for the entire contract. This rule applies to bonds in lots of not less than $1,000. . . . All stocks and bonds must be delivered before 2:15 P.M. unless otherwise specified.

What this meant was that small armies of clerks would scurry around the Curb and to nearby brokerages, making deliveries as fast as they could, receiving five cents for each delivery. If the customer who purchased the stock demanded delivery of the certificate with his name on it, the customers' man would have to deliver the newly received certificate to the transfer agent, get it entered into the books and properly inscribed, and then send it on to the buyer.

There was no central clearing house in 1921. Clearly, one was needed. So was a tighter administration, better regulations, and higher standards—indeed, all the things the move indoors implied. Central clearing would come, for it was necessary for business and profits. But higher standards and regulation would have crippled the activities of many specialists and representatives. These would not come until forced on the brokers.

It would be helpful to think of the Curb Market in 1921 as a large department store. Although they never spoke of it as such, the brokers of that time indicated they considered it that way. In the store are several boutiques, a handful of departments, and a few concessions. Each acts on its own, but all know the store itself exists, and has to be maintained in order for them to continue their individual operations. So they pay a percentage of each transaction to an administration, expecting in return cleaning services, maintenance of facilities, and whatever other services the departments might require. The management of the building has no control over individual departments; it is the servant, and not the master, of the department heads. Each man hopes to maximize his profits, and most do not believe a fine store is needed for such returns.

A few department heads believe the store could be improved. If successful, they would turn their store into one of the finest in the land. They would not carry the quality merchandise offered by the store down the road (the Stock Exchange), but they would have no reason to apologize for what they did offer. Each piece of merchandise would be exactly as represented. Customers would be assured of fast, efficient, and honest service. Dishonest concessionaires would be expelled, and every attempt would be made to bring in better ones.

What could be the future of such a store? What would be the future of the Curb Market, which resembled the store? One faction wanted to maximize profits in the short run and the devil take the hindmost. Another wanted to forego profits if necessary in order to assure status, respectability, and perhaps even greater profits in the long run. The history of the Curb Market (and, later on, the American Stock Exchange) is one of constant struggle between these forces. As in the case of the department store, both worried about the state of mind of the customers. Would they come in the door? If the store were very disreputable, they would not. On the other hand, if the store were too well-run, if the merchandise were too high-toned, the store would be competing with the Big Board down the block, and this would be fatal, for the Wall Street Establishment would brook no such challenge.

For the moment, however, other problems seemed more important. The securities markets were in the doldrums in 1921, when the move indoors took place. This was followed by one of the most spectacular bull markets in American history. It offered opportunities for those who would make their fortunes at the Curb and others who wanted to make it a firmer market. These two factions would struggle against one another in the 1920s, and would continue the fight for decades beyond.

A Matter of Survival

More than a few curbstone brokers expected the indoor market to fail. They had been told that the move was necessary for two reasons. First of all, the outdoor market had become too large for Broad Street to contain, and harassment by the New York Stock Exchange and the local police was such that the new indoor market was a necessity. In addition, the brokers would be protected from the elements, and would be spared the bother of the cumbersome system of wagging signals from street to window clerk and then back again. The pessimists thought the solution to the overly large market could be a move to a new outdoor location, or even an advance down Broad Street. Deals had been worked out with the Stock Exchange and the police before, and they could be concluded again. The Curb system had worked well for generations, and there was no reason it could not continue to do the job. Finally, although the curbstone brokers grumbled about the weather, they didn't seem to mind it that much. In fact, they missed the elements that first winter indoors. Men who had never missed a day while trading on the street developed colds and the grippe for the first time in their lives; they were not used to heated rooms, and missed snow and rain in their faces.

These brokers thought that the expense of the move, the

cost of interest on loans, and the fact that the market was in the doldrums would combine to destroy the indoor market. As they saw it, the administration would be unable to meet payments on loans, and within a few months would declare bankruptcy. Then the curbstone brokers would return to Broad Street, never to leave. What would happen to the handsome new building? There were many guesses as to its fate, but the most popular in 1921 was that it would become an indoor sports palace, used for roller skating in the summer and ice skating in the winter.

Yet these brokers purchased seats at the Curb Market and went indoors. They were willing to spend $1,500 plus fees to remain in the good graces of the administration. Some said a half-century later that they looked upon the price as a small one to pay for the privilege of remaining a part of the Curb.

Other brokers offered a second reason to anticipate failure. McCormick had said that the move had been made to enable the administration to refuse admission to marginal and crooked brokers and to questionable and worthless securities. It was McCormick's intention to upgrade the Market in every way, beginning with its membership and the securities in which they dealt.

The pessimists thought that McCormick's failure would mean the Market would survive, but if the President succeeded, the Curb would surely vanish.

Throughout its history, they said, the Curb had been a place where brokers who could not hope for admission to the Stock Exchange dealt in securities unacceptable to the Big Board. That was the Curb's historic role, and now McCormick meant to change it. By raising standards he would be competing with the Stock Exchange for both men and securities, and down that road lay failure and bankruptcy. Should McCormick succeed, a new outdoor market would appear: one that consisted of men who could not obtain membership at the Curb Market, and securities that did not qualify for listing. Such a market would receive sponsorship from the Stock Exchange, which would frown on a second respectable market in the city and nation. Like the first group, the second expected failure within a short period of time. They too expected to be ice skating at the Curb building in the winter of 1922.

Securities markets, like other businesses, are at the mercy of forces they often cannot control. A business may survive bad management in good times; wise leadership in a very bad period may not save a firm or exchange from destruction. During its first three years indoors, the Curb leadership underwent both good and bad times, over which it had no control. Paradoxically the bad news was really disguised good news, while what seemed good fortune would in time create major problems for the Curb.

The worst news for business in general and the securities markets in particular in 1921 related to the expected post-war slump. In 1913, the last peacetime year prior to World War I, the United States was in the midst of what today would be called a recession. At that time, the United States was the world's leading debtor nation, while Britain was the center of world commerce. The London securities markets ruled supreme, and made primary markets even in certain American railroad securities. The first question a Wall Street broker wanted answered on arriving at his place of work was "How's London?" As the London markets went, so went those in New York.

The war changed all this. It brought prosperity to the United States, but this was expected to end with the armistice, at which time the United States would once again enter its recession, one even worse than that of 1913. It was anticipated that London would once again dominate world securities trading, even though the United States had emerged from the war the world's leading creditor nation. In 1920–21, then, many American businessmen awaited a recession, while Wall Streeters expected a crash on the order of 1907.* Such a crash would cause

* Americans have expected depressions after wars ever since the nation was founded. Such was the case after the Revolution. But the period of adjustment after every other important American war has been followed by prosperity. This had happened after the Civil War and the Spanish-American War, and there were brokers who remembered these conflicts in 1920–21. Such was also the case after World War II and the Korean War. Yet there are brokers today who expect a recession of great magnitude after the Vietnam war is over.

grave damage to accounts at the New York Stock Exchange. It might wreck the Curb Market.

There was a recession in 1921, as expected. Steel production, which had been geared for war, fell from 42 million tons to less than 20 million. There were almost 100,000 business failures that year, and 5 million unemployed workers. Railroads reported that freight loading was down 25 percent, and there was talk of nationalizing the lines. In sympathy, and in anticipation of worse news yet to come, prices on the New York Stock Exchange and the Curb went into their sharpest decline in history—even worse than that of the autumn of 1929.

There was recovery in 1921—just in time for the Curb's move. Gross national product rose from $74 billion in 1921 to $86.1 billion in 1923, while industrial production rose almost fifty percent in the same period, and real per capita income went from $682 to $769. It was the beginning of one of the biggest economic booms in world history.

Wall Street didn't believe it. The brokers and their customers still expected the depression to come at any moment. There was no index at the Curb in this period, but an indication of Curb prices may be gained from the Dow-Jones quarterly averages at the Big Board. In this same period volume remained stagnant at the Big Board, and even fell, from 261 million shares in 1922 to 237 million in 1923.

Dow-Jones Quarterly Averages, 1921–23

| | Quarter | | | |
Year	1	2	3	4
1921	75.2	74.3	68.3	75.6
1922	83.8	92.9	97.6	97.5
1923	101.0	96.2	90.2	91.0

Source: Ralph Nelson, *Merger Movements in American Industry, 1895–1956* (Princeton, 1959), p. 116

Prices fell at the Curb Market as well; as is natural, Curb (and later American Stock Exchange) price levels moved in sympathy with those at the senior market. But brokers do not earn their commissions on stock movements, but on volume. In this period, volume rose sharply at the Curb, going from 15.5 million shares in 1921 to 21.7 million in 1922 to almost 51 million shares in 1923.* The figures for bond trading were as spectacular, rising from $25.5 million worth of bonds (face value) to $90.8 million in 1923. While the economy recovered, the Big Board prices rose and then declined once more, in anticipation of a slump, but the new indoor Curb Market was doing quite well, and the curbstone brokers making what for them were fortunes.

The newspapers noted the phenomenon, and offered explanations. The *New York Times* believed the activity at the Curb was due to the added trust speculators had in the indoor institution, while the *Wall Street Journal* attributed it to a mania for securities in small firms which would do well once recovery began. The New York *World* thought the large volume a sign that manipulators had retained control at the Curb and were milking the public dry. The *World* called for an investigation of the bucket shops in the district, and for disclosures of their connections with the Curb administration.

It is difficult to say which of these explanations was true —if any was valid—or whether all contained grains of truth. There had been a large amount of savings deposited in banks during the war, and ordinary people had been urged to purchase government bonds—their first experience with securities. At least part of the speculation must have come from the spending that accompanied peace, and the desire for quick killings on the part of small speculators.

Whatever the reason, the increased interest in Curb securities enabled the indoor institution to sink firm foundations at Trinity Place. In June 1921 the Curb had a bank balance of $162,306, considered quite high in terms of the outdoor market. But the organization now had to pay off a mortgage, provide housekeeping and heating, and spend money for other services not provided when the Market was outdoors. A good deal of the Curb's income came from fees charged on each

* These figures and others relating to the Curb Market have been taken from the *Amex Data Book* (A.S.E., 1971), a substantial portion of which is reprinted in the back of this book.

transaction, in much the same way as the house at a gambling parlor takes a cut of every pot. The larger the pots, and the more of them, the larger the total take from fees.

Additional sums were derived from initiation fees. The more valuable Curb membership became, the more brokers sought seats, and the Curb treasury benefited with each turnover. Volume did rise, as did the turnover of memberships. Within a year or so of the inauguration of indoor trading, it was clear that whatever else might happen, the Curb Market would not fail due to financial pressures.

It was at that time the Curb faced a second, even more serious problem. In this case, the move indoors may well have saved the organization from utter destruction.

Ever since the turn of the century, the New York financial community had been under the influence of one investigating body or another. Municipal, state, and federal investigators, originating from the executive, legislative, and judicial branches of government, had gone to the financial district to look into its operations and make suggestions for reform and change. This was an aspect of the Progressive movement, and the slogan some progressives put forth was "Break Up the Money Trust."

"The Money Trust" referred to the nexus of big banks, brokerages, insurance companies, and trust companies, which dominated American finance. Their symbol was the New York Stock Exchange, however, and not the Curb. For the most part, the progressive reformers either ignored the Curb or defended it against the power of the Big Board.

Other reformers, at times allied with the first group, investigated the Curb as well. They called for "honesty on Wall Street," assuming that once the crooks were harried from the district, all would be well there. They might have considered the Stock Exchange too powerful an institution, but believed it was at least honest (in the way the term was used at the time). As to the rest of the New York financial community—including the Curb—it was believed capable of almost any financial manipulation.

The reformers were interested in ridding the Curb of

bucket shops, but for the moment they concentrated their attention on the Consolidated Stock Exchange, considered the focus of thievery in the financial district.

Like the Curb, the Consolidated consisted of non-Big Board brokers, but, unlike the Curb, it traded in Stock Exchange securities as well as almost anything else that interested speculators. The Stock Exchange considered the Curb a place for rabble, but at least that market knew its place, and would not attempt to take business from its betters. Not so the Consolidated. Ever since its founding in 1885, the Consolidated battled the Big Board for trades. There were days in the early twentieth century when the Consolidated did a larger volume of business than the senior market. Part of the reason for this was the Consolidated's willingness to innovate. Small investors could not purchase or sell odd lots (less than 100 shares of stock) at the Stock Exchange, but they were welcomed at the Consolidated, which was called the "Little Board." The Consolidated also traded in pipeline certificates (a form of petroleum futures), and almost any other commodity that found traders.

Despite many and repeated attempts on the part of Big Board administrations to destroy the Consolidated, the Little Board grew rapidly around 1908, in the aftermath of the panic of the previous year. Under the capable leadership of Miguel de Aguero, the Consolidated made plans to expand to Chicago and other Midwestern cities, and de Aguero spoke of the possibility of a chain of Consolidated branches, open twenty-four hours a day, where traders would always find buyers and sellers of securities. When New York passed a law forbidding the Big Board from interfering with the Consolidated, and the federal government indicated that a new investigation of the Big Board might be forthcoming, it seemed the Consolidated might in time challenge the Stock Exchange for dominance on Wall Street.

For all its willingness to innovate and serve small investors, the Consolidated had few honest brokers. In fact, the Consolidated served odd-lot customers because only habitués of bucket shops purchased securities in denominations below 100 shares (today's odd-lot investor would, if alive in 1900, have purchased a round lot on margin, and not considered odd lots at all). De Aguero wanted to establish his network of stock exchanges to increase business and attract clients from Stock Exchange houses. Even those at the Consolidated who supported him, however, had visions of all-night brokerages functioning like a pre–World War I version of Las Vegas.

A majority of the Consolidated's members were affiliated with bucket shops or officially ran these establishments. In fact, such brokers had no choice but to join the Little Board. They were barred from membership at the Stock Exchange, and frowned upon by the reform element at the Curb. Membership at the Curb could be had, but it did not enable the bucket shops to deal in Big Board stocks, which were not traded at the Curb. On the other hand, both Big Board and Curb securities were traded at the Consolidated, where membership could be obtained for a few hundred dollars, with no questions asked. And since so many customers of bucket shops gambled in odd lots, the methods of trading there suited the business well.

All of this was known prior to World War I, and resulted in several investigations of the Little Board. While these were taking place the Consolidated put up a façade of reformism. The election of de Aguero was one sign of this, and Consolidated campaigns to clean up the bucket shops made good reading in the press. By the end of the war, however, reform seemed dead; a conservative mood was evident in America. Now the Consolidated dropped its reformist stance, and signaled the change by electing William S. Silkworth its president in 1919.

Silkworth operated several bucket shops, and had a hand in many shady deals of the period. He also was a fine salesman, a man of considerable charm, and an excellent publicity director for his market. Silkworth aggressively sought business for the Consolidated, and succeeded. The brokers were delighted, as the price of their seats rose, bucket-shop business zoomed, and volume increased. Silkworth easily won re-election in 1920 and again in 1921. His presidential career reached its zenith in February, 1922, when all trading records at the Consolidated were broken—at a time when volume was low at the Big Board. While the Curb congratulated itself on the move indoors, the Little Board stole the show, and Silkworth, not McCormick, was the talk of Wall Street.

Then, without warning, the Consolidated was hit by a strange series of brokerage failures, and some of the exchange's major firms, among them R. H. MacMasters & Co., warned Silkworth they needed additional capital if they were to remain in business. The President asked the membership to subscribe to a fund to save such firms, and in short order raised some $102,000. Silkworth supposedly loaned the money to the endangered companies, many of which failed anyway. The MacMasters collapse, which came in late February, shocked the other houses and even led to a call for an investigation.

At the time the State Assembly was discussing a new anti-bucket shop proposal. Democratic gubernatorial candidate Alfred E. Smith was known to favor the measure, and pledged that if elected in November, he would investigate the financial district, beginning with the Consolidated, soon after taking office.

Silkworth responded in July. He conceded that some Consolidated brokers were corrupt, and claimed he was acting to rid the exchange of such men. Some of his enemies retaliated by charging he had misused the rescue fund, and asked for a full accounting. Silkworth called in reporters and denied the allegations. These were to be expected, he said, "as I have stepped on the toes of some of these people in the recent past." Yet the rumors persisted, along with talk that Silkworth was preparing to step down and would soon leave the country. Once more the reporters were summoned, and again they heard Silkworth deny the reports and assure them of the "basic soundness of the leading firms at our market."

Matters remained at that level for a week. Then, in mid-July, a new series of failures occurred at the Consolidated, and a leading brokerage, Edward M. Fuller & Co., joined the ranks of the bankrupt.

The Fuller collapse was unexpected. The firm had been considered well-financed and ably-led. It had been doing a record business at the time of its failure, and there had been talk of new offices and additional personnel. Fuller had been the first firm to contribute to the rescue fund, sending Silkworth a check for $10,000. Finally, George Silkworth, William's brother, was a partner at Fuller, and the firm was said to be on the inside of Consolidated's management.

There seemed only two possible explanations for the collapse. Either Fuller had made unwise investments, or was being robbed by insiders. If the latter were true, then George Silkworth must have been involved in some way. And should that be the case, then the Consolidated's President might also be implicated.

William Silkworth denied all allegations, and embarked on his reform program, hoping to turn attention from the failures. It didn't work. Then Smith was elected governor, a sign that an investigation of the district would soon begin. The Assembly passed the Martin Act, which gave the attorney general the power to issue cease-and-desist injunctions against suspected bucket shops. Attorney General Carl Sherman promised quick action and a complete investigation of the situation at Fuller. Albert Ottinger was placed in charge of the Anti-Fraud Bureau, and began work on the case in December, 1922.

Fear of what was to come resulted in a panic at the Consolidated, and the collapse of additional houses. M. C. Schneider went under, followed by Courtlandt, Ward & Co., and others joined them. Silkworth welcomed their failures, claiming they had resulted from his work in cleaning the exchange. He felt vindicated by his re-election in April, 1923, and in his acceptance speech promised cooperation with Sherman, Ottinger, "or anyone else" in ridding the Consolidated of corrupt houses and men. "We feel the public interest is paramount, and that any movement started in the interest of the public will prove to be in the interest of the Exchange."

The Ottinger investigation began in late May, and Silkworth testified on June 6. Assistant Attorney General William F. McKenna tried to implicate Silkworth in the Fuller bankruptcy, but failed to prove his charges. But he did uncover irregularities in Silkworth's own finances.

An examination of Silkworth's bank accounts showed that he had made large deposits in March, 1922—at the time he supposedly was using the rescue fund to help the besieged brokerages. Although he had never made more than $10,000 a year as a Consolidated president, Silkworth had deposited $133,000 in his bank accounts during the two years prior to the Fuller collapse. McKenna produced checks drawn on Fuller's account, made out to William Silkworth. He showed that Silkworth had shared in Fuller's profits throughout the 1920–22 period. The President strongly denied the charge, but admitted he was a "close friend" of W. Frank McGee, a Fuller executive.

Silkworth resigned from his post on June 21. Soon after he went on a "long vacation." The Silkworth scandal ruined the Consolidated, although the President's connections with the Fuller collapse were never proven. McGee refused to say why he paid Silkworth the money, even after he pleaded guilty to fraud charges later on. "We plead guilty rather than have innocent friends who extended many courtesies to us dragged deeper into the mire," he said. "We sacrifice ourselves to save our friends further embarrassment." *

As Attorney General Sherman prosecuted the Fuller case, he promised more of the same. At a press conference in June he said that twelve more brokerages were under investigation. Some were Consolidated houses, but others were leading Curb organizations. In some cases, he hinted, the houses under investigation belonged to both markets. This turned attention to the Curb, and in particular to the one major firm that belonged to the Consolidated as well (in contravention of published Curb rules): L. L. Winkelman & Co.

The Fuller investigation hurt all the Little Board houses,

* Silkworth may have escaped prosecution in 1923, but he did go to jail later on. After leaving Wall Street he became a confidence man, and was caught in 1926. Silkworth was convicted of mail fraud that year and served three months in jail. He was also convicted of fraud in connection with the failure of the Little Board house of Raynor, Nicholas & Truesdell, in a case that had nothing to do with the events of 1922–23. In 1933 Silkworth was charged with a third fraud, this one in the sale of a boat, but was not convicted. After that he disappeared from sight.

but Winkelman seemed capable of surviving. The firm's finances were good; it was the largest Consolidated member firm, and the second largest non–Stock Exchange house in America. In the parlance of the day, Winkelman was known as an "honest crook," one who cheated only the public, while Fuller was a dishonest one—a firm that bilked other brokers as well. Furthermore, Winkelman's attorney, Isaac H. Levy, was considered one of the shrewdest Wall Street lawyers of the time, and Attorney General Sherman was thought no match for him.

Winkelman might indeed have survived were it not for the failure of the largest Curb house, Jones & Baker, on May 31, 1923. The news came as a great shock; Jones & Baker had not even been under investigation, and was considered the strong rock of the Curb. When Jones & Baker offices closed throughout the Northeast and Midwest, shudders ran through the board rooms of every other Curb brokerage. Which would be next?

Winkelman gave the answer little more than a week later; it declared bankruptcy on June 8.

Suspecting that the Winkelman failure would reveal even greater scandals than those suspected in the Fuller case, Sherman invoked the Martin Act and moved to seize the firm's records. Levy refused to surrender them, and was threatened with contempt of court if he persisted in denying access to the records. Sherman obtained a writ from Federal Judge William Bondy and delivered it in person to Levy, who promptly announced that he would appeal the writ at the Circuit Court of Appeals. He noted that although Winkelman had announced bankruptcy, the firm had yet to be *adjudged* bankrupt by the courts. Sherman's writ had stated the firm was bankrupt; it was an error that invalidated the writ. This opened a legal battle that waged for months, though in the end Sherman received the books. Even before then, it was learned that Winkelman went under with liabilities of $10 million, making it one of the biggest collapses on Wall Street since the 1907 panic.

Meanwhile, other, smaller Curb houses failed in the wake of the Winkelman announcement. M. S. Wolfe & Co., with liabilities of $425,000, announced its closing on June 9. As in the Winkelman case, Sherman tried to obtain access to the books, but once again he was stopped by a clever lawyer, this time Arthur Garfield Hays, of the firm of Hays, St. John & Moore.

Hays was at the beginning of a brilliant career in 1923, one that would lead him to fame in civil rights cases later on. But in 1923 he was considered an expert in Wall Street law, one who knew where every loophole could be found. Hays claimed Wolfe & Co. would be able to meet its obligations if given a little time to do so. The firm had assets of $325,000, including $129,482 in cash. If Sherman insisted on invoking the Martin Act, he would cause Wolfe's 3,500 customers to lose whatever chance they had of obtaining a substantial part of their accounts. Hays claimed that every account was in order, and that Wolfe had never used customers' certificates illegally.

Hays, St. John & Moore was one of the firms representing Fuller & Co. Moore and several junior partners had tied that case in knots, and Sherman had respect for the firm. He went along with Hays in the Wolfe case, thus saving the firm's customers some money and at the same time easing the growing panic at the Curb.

While Sherman prepared for another attack on the Curb, the Board of Governors acted to institute a reform program. Curb President John W. Curtis, who had been in office less than a month when the investigations began, announced a clean-up campaign. In several public statements, he observed that the Curb had moved indoors in order to cleanse the bucketeers from the rolls—which was a half-truth at best. Most had already been uncovered and expelled, he said. (In fact, the Curb had done no such thing in its first two years indoors.) Now he and the board would act to rid the Curb of the rest of these disreputable and dishonest men. But Curtis, a weak and indecisive man, really did not know what to do. Were it not for the prodding of some board members, most notably Arthur Myles and Mortimer Landsberg, and the deft assistance of Curb counsel William A. Lockwood, he might have permitted the Curb Market to be lumped together with the Consolidated.

As it was, he acceded to a purge of bucket shops that began in the summer of 1923 and lasted almost half a year. Broker Benjamin Alexander was expelled in late June for violations of Article XVII, Section 6 of the Constitution, which covered "conduct or business of members, or any conduct or proceeding inconsistent with just and equitable principles of trade." A. B. Morley, of A. B. Morley & Co., was suspended for one year for violations of Article XVII, Sections 7 and 8. Section 7 provided that "a member of the Exchange shall submit to the Board of Governors or any standing committee, for examination, such portion of his books or papers as are material and relevant to any matter under investigation by said Board, or by any standing committee." Others followed, while several Curb bucket shops merely declared bankruptcy, sold their seats, and left the organization.

Was this true reform—or fair? The Curb records, complete in other details, contain no mention of this purge or accounts of hearings. Some of those firms singled out for expulsion were indeed bucket shops, but others were not. For example, Morley was no angel, but neither was he a prominent bucketeer. Angry at his suspension, he told reporters that he had been slandered.

> Facts regarding A. B. Morley & Co.'s suspension from the New York Curb Market have been garbled. The firm had decided not to carry Curb stocks on margin and recently issued a letter calling upon their customers who had accounts in Curb stocks to take them up, sell them or transfer them to another house, the principal reason being that owing to failures of several large firms who belonged to the New York Curb Market many Curb stocks were not regarded as acceptable for collateral for bank loans.
>
> In view of this decision the firm saw no reason for continuing as members of the Curb Market and therefore made arrangements for sale of its seat and tendered its resignation, continuing as members of the Consolidated Stock Exchange and as dealers in unlisted securities.
>
> The firm therefore failed to make an appearance before the Board of Governors of the Curb Market upon demand after

their resignation had been tendered, for which reason the Curb
Market suspended them for one year as a fine for a technical violation of rules. . . .

Morley indeed had indicated his intention to sell his seat
prior to the Curb's action against him. Was it a case of the
Board of Governors taking a parting slap at a person or firm in
order to give it a reform image in the press? Probably so, although such matters cannot be proven.

The climax of the Curb purge came in late December
1923, when the Governors suspended trading in the shares of
Southern Oil Corporation. The Curb stated that the firm was
not as represented to the public, and trading would cease in
order to protect both customers and brokers from being taken.
It was one of the first cases in which a securities market acted
to delist a stock for that reason—and one of the last during the
1920s. By so acting, the Curb indicated a willingness to reform
and a hope that it would not be placed in the same category as
the Consolidated.

The scandals of 1922–23 were quickly forgotten in the district, as the great bull market beginning in 1924 occupied the
attention of brokers and customers alike. But its affects remained, as Sherman and later Ottinger continued their crusade
against the bucket shops. Laurence Tweedy, who succeeded
Silkworth at the Consolidated, did all he could to cooperate
with the Attorney General. He insisted that all Consolidated
members sign waivers of immunity, and he expelled dozens of
bucketeers from membership. It was evident, however, that the
Consolidated could not be reformed without also being destroyed. For if Tweedy managed to expel all the bucket shops,
who would remain to trade at the market? Unlike Curtis, he
could not make gestures at reform and claim victory over evil.
Ottinger never relented, and by 1924 he had abandoned the
Curb to concentrate all his attention on the Consolidated.

Thomas B. Maloney, who succeeded Tweedy in 1924,
hoped to transform the Consolidated into a respectable market
by keeping its shell but ridding it of its substance. Maloney became more Catholic than the Pope; he not only cooperated

with Ottinger, he even insisted on more stringent reforms than the by then Attorney General had asked for. Maloney supported a proposed law that would have required all brokerages to deliver a sales or purchase slip to a customer within twenty-four hours of execution. The customer would be entitled to receive either his money or his security on demand at that time. If passed, this law would have made the manipulation of customers' accounts, quite common at the bucket shops, impossible. The law failed to pass, and the new Assistant District Attorney, Ferdinand Pecora, claimed the Consolidated had provided funds for those who had opposed it.

Unable to convince the government it wanted to reform, and perhaps unable to actually reform in any case, the Consolidated announced its closing in 1926. Actually, it dragged on for another two years before finally closing permanently. But its real demise came in 1923, with the disclosures of that year. After that, the ultimate failure was just a matter of time. Ironically, the Consolidated failed as a market for stocks and bonds at a time when the nation was in the midst of its greatest speculative binge in history—one tailor-made for a market like the Consolidated.

What of the Curb? It had been saved from possible bankruptcy and failure by two factors. The first was the bull market and boom in low-priced securities, which began soon after the indoor move enabled the brokers to prosper, and the Curb Market as an institution to prosper along with them. Had volume fallen those first two years, the Curb might indeed have collapsed.

The bull market brought increased speculation, and at the Curb that always meant good times for the more dishonest members of the organization. In all probability, the Curb was a more honest place to do business in 1922 than was the Consolidated. The Curb's working arrangement with the Big Board meant that it could not engage in certain practices the senior market frowned upon. The legacy of Mendels and others of the outdoor market—one stressing respectability, if not always honesty—was genuine at the Curb; there was no parallel movement in the Consolidated's history.

The move indoors had come at a most fortuitous time for the Curb. Time and again Curb spokesmen would refer to the new building as a sign of the Curb's intention to purify itself. Perhaps it gave the Curb brokers a psychological lift as well; they must have felt more secure and respectable indoors than they did while trading in the open on Broad Street. To be sure, the Consolidated also was an indoor market, and had been almost since its founding. But the doors at the Consolidated in 1922 were viewed as barriers to investigation by officials, while those at the Curb were publicized as a means to keep the bucketeers from the new building.

From what we know of both markets in 1922–25, it would seem that the Consolidated's leaders after Silkworth were interested in reform and honesty, but were unable to overcome the legacy of the past and the rot of the membership. The Curb was concerned with the image of respectability, but did less than the Little Board in the way of reform. The Curb had double protection in this period. The Little Board acted as a lightning rod for the reformers' ire, which would have been directed against the Curb had not the Consolidated been in existence. And the Stock Exchange's patronage was useful. Finding itself in this situation, the Curb's leaders did what was necessary to satisfy Sherman, Ottinger, and others of their group, but no more. Morley would be condemned, while Mike Meehan, the most famous of the Curb brokers and one of the sharpest shavers of rules during the 1920s, remained an honored and valued member of the Curb community.

THREE

The Inner Market

The Curb Market survived the difficult times of 1922–23, and that survival, by itself, was no mean accomplishment. Fearing a depression of one kind or another, the curbstone brokers of 1921 congratulated themselves on still being around in 1924.

By then the fate of the Consolidated seemed sealed: it would disappear in a few years, perhaps months. Those Curb brokers with ties to the Consolidated quickly severed them after the Silkworth revelations. Others collapsed in the wake of the Jones & Baker and Winkelman failures. The Curb was a more honest place to do business in 1924 than it had been at any previous time. This was due not to sudden conversions to respectability on the part of the membership. Rather, it was caused by fear of investigation and lack of opportunity. The investigations would end and the opportunities would come. And when they did, the Curb would teach even the New York Stock Exchange some lessons in how to cheat customers and fellow-brokers.

Until the opportunities presented themselves, the brokers could do little but wait and watch, and survive. Such is the testimony of some of the brokers who survived that period into the present. There is even a better barometer of sentiment, both pessimistic and optimistic, and that is the price of a seat on the Curb. As we have seen, the original subscription price in 1921 was $1,500. Then, just before the building opened, and at a time when it seemed the Curb Market would be a success, additional seats were sold for $6,500 apiece. The euphoria subsided by the end of the year, when a seat changed hands at $5,500. The price fluctuated between $3,600 and $10,000 for the next three years, not a wide range as such things went. It was a sign of insecurity mixed with hope at the Curb.

From the first and throughout the 1920s, the Curb's leaders strove to achieve four objectives: a *modus vivendi* with the Stock Exchange, increased business for Curb brokers, efficiency in operations, and a more honest organization.

Good relations with the Big Board were vital. After the move indoors it was generally agreed that the Curb would remain independent insofar as day-to-day operations were concerned, but in all important matters the leadership would take its cue from the Wall Street Establishment. For a while the New York State Attorney General's office was also important in this regard, but after 1924 the Stock Exchange was the only institution that concerned Curb administrations. Throughout the 1920s the Curb would clash with other securities markets outside of New York and with the over-the-counter market in the city. The Big Board maintained a hands-off attitude toward such matters, and on the few occasions when it did interfere in one way or another, it did so to support and protect the Curb. It made sense to do so. When the Curb battled with the Chicago Stock Exchange, for example, it was a case of a market that did not deal in Big Board securities opposing one that did. It behooved the Stock Exchange to defend its "little brother" in such a struggle, and it did.

The fight with the Chicago Stock Exchange was one that lasted throughout the decade, and lingered until 1933. The Chicago market's quarrel with the Curb was simple: the Curb was dealing in several securities listed on the Chicago Stock Exchange without the officials of the companies involved having asked for trading rights. A Curb specialist would note that a Chicago security had an active market, and had not applied for listing at the New York Stock Exchange. Under its constitution, the Stock Exchange could not trade in a security until and unless its management made proper application, filed certain papers, and was accepted for listing. This was not Curb procedure, as we have seen. The specialist would purchase his hundred shares or so of the stock and then, acting as a stockholder, make application for unlisted trading privileges, which were rarely denied.

Chicago was distressed, since its specialists would lose trades to the Curb. In some cases the companies themselves were angered, and asked that their securities be removed from the Curb. In the mid-1920s, the Chicago Stock Exchange had a measure of prestige, while listing or trading at the Curb indicated to conservative businessmen that the security might be second-rate.

The Big Board smiled at such moves, not because they helped the Curb, but because they hurt the Chicago market. In the early 1920s, the Chicago financial community mounted a challenge to Wall Street. This was the tail end of a period in which Chicago's leaders thought their city was destined to replace New York as the nation's center of power. Chicago was more centrally located than New York, was growing more rapidly than its eastern rival, and was more ambitious.

Harold L. Stuart, head of the investment house of Halsey, Stuart & Co., was a leader in this movement. Under ordinary circumstances, he would have had no difficulty in obtaining a niche on Wall Street, but Stuart preferred to remain in Chicago and build that city's financial center instead. His ally in this was Samuel Insull, also of Chicago, and the head of Commonwealth Edison Company, one of the nation's largest utilities. Insull had plans of spreading his interests throughout the Midwest, and making Commonwealth the hub of the biggest utilities complex in the world. Halsey, Stuart was his banker. Both Insull and Stuart were patrons of the arts, and dreamed of a new Chicago that would be a cultural and financial center more important than New York. Naturally, such ambitions distressed Wall Street's leaders, the House of Morgan in particular.

Many Chicago-based companies had their shares listed on

the New York Stock Exchange as well as the Chicago Stock Exchange. They had no choice but to do so, for at the time listing at the Big Board could be vital to a firm's ability to raise additional capital. The Insull-Stuart interests were not eager for listing; they were out to prove that a large firm could succeed with the backing of Chicago financiers and without that of the New York Establishment. So Commonwealth Edison was not traded at the Big Board.

There was nothing the Stock Exchange's administration could do about it. Unless and until Insull filed the proper papers, they could not admit the security to trading privileges.

The situation was different at the Curb. Seeing a major security that was not listed at the Stock Exchange, a Curb specialist purchased a hundred shares of Commonwealth Edison, applied as a stockholder for unlisted trading rights, received the same, and was then assigned Commonwealth Edison as its specialist.

Stuart was livid, as was Insull. Both men protested the action. The Chicago Stock Exchange attempted to force the Curb to delist the security, at one point issuing veiled threats against the Curb if the action were not taken. At the time, the Curb was expanding its ticker service throughout the country, and was making a special effort in the Midwest. Under certain circumstances, the Chicago Exchange suggested, Illinois might pass a law forbidding the selling and buying of securities on "disreputable" markets. Should the Curb Exchange be classified as such, all of its tickers could be removed from the state. During such a reform period, at the tail end of the Wall Street investigations, such an action would be both expected and proper. It was an important lever to be used against the Curb.

The Curb refused to bow to this pressure. By itself it might not have stood against the Chicago interests, but with the backing of the Big Board it could and did. In late July 1924, the Curb issued a statement to the effect that by granting Commonwealth Edison unlisted trading rights, it was performing a public service for the investors of the eastern states. At the same time, volume in Commonwealth Edison had not declined at the Chicago Exchange. Indeed, statistics indicated that volume actually had risen since the Curb began trading in the issue. For these reasons, the Chicago Exchange's demand was rejected.

Stuart was unhappy at this decision, but took no further action in the matter. Retaliation was not forthcoming.

Throughout the 1920s the Big Board and the Curb maintained a friendly relationship. The two markets had divided the nation's securities between them. The Big Board would take whatever it wanted from among those issues seeking listing, while the Curb could have those left over. They would unite in the face of governmental investigations or threats from other, non–New York markets. With the Consolidated all but dead, and the reformers on the decline in a conservative age, such an arrangement was possible and profitable to both parties. In this way, the Curb's leadership was able to achieve the first of its four objectives: good relations with the Stock Exchange and harmony within the financial district.

The second objective was to obtain additional business. This could be done in two ways, one of which the Curb could not control. If the nation's prospects appeared favorable, additional customers would be drawn to the securities markets, and trading per person might increase. Such had been the case even before the great bull market, and, as we have seen, it grew throughout the decade.

Trading Volume on the New York Curb Market, 1921–29

Year	Stocks (shares)	Bonds (principal amount)
1921	15,522,415	$ 25,510,000
1922	21,741,230	55,212,000
1923	50,968,680	90,793,000
1924	72,243,900	200,315,000
1925	88,406,350	500,533,000
1926	115,531,800	525,810,000
1927	125,116,566	575,810,000
1928	236,043,682	834,893,000
1929	476,140,375	513,551,000

Source: *Amex Databook*, pp. 30, 32

All such figures for this period must be used carefully, however. Reporting was not what it is today, and errors were frequent. In addition, manipulation could cause volume figures to balloon. For example, traders and even a specialist might chose to "churn" a security, a practice contrary to Curb ethics but one quite common nevertheless. If a broker or floor trader wanted the public to believe interest was developing in a particular security, he would buy and sell it simultaneously. In such a case, no money would change hands—indeed, none was needed to churn a stock—but the transaction would show on the tape. This was called "painting the tape," and was in vogue in the late 1920s. A speculator might accumulate a large position in a stock and want to encourage others to buy, so that he could increase its volume and price and then "dump" it on newcomers. He might take one or more of three actions, timing them carefully. First, he would "leak" a story about the stock to friendly newspapermen. Then he would enter buy orders for several hundred shares in order to cause the quotations to rise. Finally, the manipulator would start churning the issue. The next day unsuspecting people would read of good news out of XYZ headquarters, note that the price of the stock had risen, and that volume was high. The public would be sucked into the stock, while the speculator unloaded his holdings at a profit.

All of this led to higher-volume figures, and created profits for brokers in the form of commissions. As the Curb members tended to view it, that was the only real reason for the Curb Market to exist.

The second method of obtaining additional business was to increase the number of securities traded at the Curb, and to expand the Market's operations to other cities.

There is no way of knowing exactly how many issues were traded at the Curb in the 1920s. From time to time the Curb would announce that so many issues were listed, and an additional number had unlisted trading privileges. These figures, accurate so far as they went, didn't take into account unknown quantities. During the 1920s the Curb admitted so many issues to trading that it often did not know what was on the list and what was not. For example, it was not uncommon to admit as many as five to ten new issues to trading on a given day. In this period the Curb also traded stocks that had applied for Big Board listing but had not yet begun trading on the senior market, and these NYSE "when issued" securities complicated the count. Also, the Curb had a form of listing designated as "temporary," to provide an auction market for newly issued shares that qualified for Stock Exchange listing, but had not yet been filed at the Big Board. The Curb had no statistical department in those days, and so records here, too, are incomplete.

Another variety of stock was traded at the Curb that belonged to none of these categories. A Curb broker might trade in over-the-counter shares, which did not and could not qualify for Curb listing. He would pocket the commission, and try to keep the fact secret from the administration. In effect, these brokers were part-time over-the-counter market dealers, and at times conducted their non-Curb business on the floor of the exchange itself. Attempts on the part of the Curb administrations to end this practice were largely ineffective. Their policy seemed to be not to interfere with the profits made by members so long as no other broker was involved, or the broker was not rocking the boat. Indeed, the Curb not only ignored trading in unlisted and unauthorized securities, but in other forms of speculation and gambling having nothing at all to do with securities.

During the spring and summer of 1924, the board passed several resolutions forbidding the taking of bets on the coming presidential elections by members. Yet the word was out in New York that year: if you wanted to place a few dollars on either Coolidge or Davis, the Curb brokers would be happy to oblige. Curb brokers were also bookmakers for horse races and other athletic and sporting events, a throwback to the outdoor days, when bookmakers used Broad Street as a base for their operations. Much of the money bet in the famous "Black Sox scandal" of 1919 had been placed with Curb bookmakers, and the betting tradition continued throughout the 1920s. The same was true of ticket scalping. It was no accident that Horace Stoneham, owner of the New York Giants, was a broker as well, in addition to being the proprietor of what was reputed to be an excellent bucket shop, while Mike Meehan, one of the Curb's leading brokers, got his start in business as a ticket scalper.

There was a reform element at the Curb which attempted to limit if not end such practices. From his earliest days at the market, Edwin Posner belonged to that group. So did E. Burd Grubb and Fred C. Moffatt, and in time all three would become presidents of the organization. They lacked power in the 1920s, however, and could do nothing of importance except issue proclamations and introduce resolutions. Eugene Tappen, the Curb's secretary, spoke and wrote often of the need for reform, but his achievements were more in the way of preventing abuses from becoming institutionalized than in ending them.

In 1925, for example, several brokers attempted to amend the constitution to allow specialists to trade for their own accounts at reduced commission rates. This proposal would have increased Curb volume and turned the organization into more of a gambling den than it was already. It would also encourage brokers to speculate for their own accounts, at a time when the opposite kind of regulation was needed. The amendment had wide support among the wealthier and less conservative specialists, but was opposed by Posner and Tappen. The Secretary led the movement to reject the amendment, and succeeded.

Other reformers tried to limit the practice of trading in securities of those companies that did not want their stocks dealt with at the Curb. Had they succeeded, volume would have fallen, and several brokers who specialized in these securities would have been badly hurt. Only in this way, said the reformers, could the Curb achieve the kind of status it needed for permanence in the financial district. Unauthorized trading was becoming a scandal, they said, and giving the Curb a bad name. On that basis, it should be stopped. James S. Dustan, a member of the board, led the campaign in 1926–28, both at the Curb and in the press. Curb counsel William Lockwood supported the proposal. The next reform wave surely would strike the Curb, they felt, and the time to clean house was before, and not after, the reformers hit. Besides, business was good at the Curb, and the market should cut back on dealings at such times, when the brokers could afford to do so, and not in slack periods, when every trade was important.

Dustan and Lockwood were unheeded. Dustan's campaign was not taken seriously, and few brokers came to his support.

In 1926 Lockwood convinced many board members to support a plan to ask the president of each company with unlisted securities at the Curb whether or not he wanted the trading to continue. The plan did not include, however, a proposal as to what would be done if the answer was in the negative. In any case, nothing more was heard of the plan, and the practice of trading in unlisted securities continued.

Some corporation presidents tried to have their unlisted shares removed from trading. The directors of one firm, Apco Mossberg Corporation, pleaded with the Curb to end unlisted status. Theirs was a small company, and the shares were traded irregularly. The quotation was very low, giving the public the impression that the company was in bad shape, when it actually was not. The Curb continued to trade in Apco Mossberg, although the issue remained very inactive. The reason given was usually the same in all such cases: the fact that the security was traded at the Curb provided the stockholders with an important service. If the security were delisted, the stockholders in particular and the investing public in general would be deprived of such a market, and this would be against the best interests of both the public and the Curb.

The real reason for the refusals are not difficult to discern. The Curb leadership existed to increase rather than decrease securities trading, and would take no action to do the opposite unless obliged to act against its will. Some Big Board leaders had sufficient influence at Trinity Place to force reform had they so desired, but such was not the wish in the mid-1920s. So long as the Curb concentrated on marginal issues such as Apco Mossberg, it represented no threat to the senior market. Nor would New York state act in the matter. Although several measures designed to affect securities markets were introduced in the Albany legislature after 1923, none was aimed at the Curb.

The federal government showed even less interest. So unlisted trading continued, and served to increase Curb business.

After World War I the United States was the prime source of capital for the rest of the world, a position London had held prior to 1914. European and Latin American bankers, companies, and governments used American investment bankers to float stock and bond issues in the United States, and these were sold in turn to American investors. The bonds were in dollar denominations, and were traded in the United States only, and not in the country from which they originated. Most did not qualify for listing at the Big Board, but they were eagerly accepted at the Curb. The increase in bond trading at the Curb was due in large part to the rapid listing of these European and Latin American bonds. By 1928 the Curb was trading a larger volume of bonds than the Big Board. Several brokers, the most prominent of whom was Charles Leichner, dwarfed most Stock Exchange houses in this kind of security.

Foreign stocks, however, presented a problem. Since the primary market for such issues was made overseas, and since there were difficulties in transferring shares from the registry of one nation to another, they could not be traded in so easily. To solve this problem, the Curb Market and the Guaranty Trust Company joined forces to develop the American depository receipt.* In essence, it meant that Americans could purchase receipts that represented shares of stock deposited in a foreign bank. These receipts could be taken to the bank designated on their face and redeemed for the actual shares. In practice this was rarely done. Most people who purchase and sold "ADRs" did so for speculative purposes. Since this was the case, trading volume in foreign shares was high, which was translated into commissions for Curb brokers.

By the end of the decade, the Curb had more individual foreign issues on its list than had all other American securities markets combined. This situation exists to this day.

---

* Howard Sykes, a future Curb president, was instrumental in establishing the ADR system, which he did through his connections at the Trust Company.

Finally, there was the matter of expansion of the ticker network. Without newspaper reports, investors and speculators could not check the prices of securities, and modern brokerage could not exist. There was no way to convince newspapers that Curb prices were worth following, but the spreading network of tickers was a good litmus of how the Curb was faring in the hinterlands. The rapid growth of the Curb Market's ticker network in the late 1920s was indeed impressive.

Number of Curb Tickers in Operation, 1921–30

Year	Number of Tickers in Service
1921	266
1922	360
1923	398
1924	399
1925	474
1926	835
1927	931
1928	1,068
1929	1,805
1930	2,643

Source: American Stock Exchange

By 1928 Curb ticker service was available in almost every large city in the United States. Through Mike Meehan's brokerage, passengers aboard several ocean liners had Curb tickers at their disposal. They were there because a demand for them existed, and once installed, they helped create new demand. The growth of the ticker network was a clear sign that the Curb leadership had succeeded in its second objective: that of obtaining additional business and volume for the brokers. The price paid for such business would be great, as would be seen in the nightmare years of 1932–34.

The leadership's third objective was to make the Curb a more efficient place to do business than had previously been the case. At the same time, the membership made it clear it would not sacrifice profits for efficiency. In other words, the

Curb brokers would support those changes which made life easier for them, but not those that would really be masked reform measures.

The most important change in the first five years indoors was the initiation and development of the clearing house. As trading volume increased, brokers found it difficult to make deliveries of securities within the prescribed time limits. It made little sense, too, for a broker to try to deliver a thousand shares of stock to ten different buyers while awaiting delivery of a thousand shares of the same stock from other brokers who sold it to him. Here was a clear case where change was needed in the name of efficiency.

The problem did not exist at the Big Board, where a clearing house had been in operation for several years, performing well while also showing a profit. The clearing house there operated in much the same way as a bank. At the close of trading each broker would "deposit" his slips, each of which indicated the purchase or sale of a specified number of shares in a specified security, and the person or firm from whom the security had been purchased or to whom it had been sold. Then the clerks would match the slips, and the next day inform the broker of his "balance." In the case mentioned above, the broker who bought a thousand shares of stock and also sold a thousand would have a clear record. If a broker sold more shares of the stock than he purchased, he would be informed that he "owed" the difference, and could send the certificates to the clearing house by messenger.

Several members of the Curb asked the administration to explore the possibility of having a clearing house of their own. McCormick approached the Big Board leaders and asked for assistance, which was given. Samuel F. Streit, president of the New York Stock Exchange Clearing House, offered his cooperation, as did Duncan McGregor, who had established the clearing house on a model drawn from several German organizations. Edward Callahan and Richard Foster, two Curb clerks, were also involved in the operation. Under their direction, the Curb clearing house was put into operation on April 7, 1923.

Foster was named manager at a salary of $5,500 a year, while Callahan was assistant manager at $4,400.

The clearing house was a great success from the start, even though its operations were limited at first to selected securities. In 1923 only the most active securities were accepted by the clearing house. In effect, a security had to qualify twice at the Curb—the first time for listed or unlisted status, the second at the clearing house. During the very active markets of the late 1920s, the second qualification was almost as important as the first, but by then obtaining it presented little difficulty.

The clearing house was a financial as well as a technical success. For each clearing the broker paid a fee of five cents, and after salaries, rent, and supplies were paid for, a handsome surplus remained. The managers were rewarded for their efforts: in 1925 Foster's salary was raised to $6,000, and Callahan's to $5,000.

The clearing house was ruled by the Curb Committee on Clearing House, established in 1924. It was not considered a key committee, and did not attract those members interested in obtaining power at the Curb. But it proved to be a good first step for such men, and several major Curb figures began their administrative lives as members of the Committee, while former presidents would be named to the chairmanship as a sign of honor.

Fred C. Moffatt was one of the few administrators who showed any real interest in the clearing house, and by the late 1920s was acknowledged the Curb expert on the organization. His career was typical of that of many brokers of this period, and is worth sketching. Moffatt was born in New York in 1888, but his family soon moved to Scranton, Pennsylvania, where he grew up. He left school at the age of fifteen to take a job as messenger boy for the Postal Telegraph Company, and while there became interested in finance. The following year, 1904, he went to New York, where he worked as office boy for a Wall Street brokerage house, and then as a telegrapher for a second house. In order to make extra money Moffatt worked evenings in the telegraph rooms of several New York newspapers, including the *Sun, Herald,* and *Times.* Both types of work involved him in learning more about finance, and he decided to apply for a job at the Big Board.

World War I interrupted his plans, however. Moffatt enlisted as a private and served in France. He participated in the battle of the Argonne, where he was gassed and wounded. Although he recovered, the effects lingered. Moffatt always had stuttered badly, and the gassing made matters worse. Also, he was an inveterate smoker, and refused to quit. Because of these factors, Moffatt seemed destined to be a semi-invalid. He left the Army in May 1919, a decorated officer, and returned to the financial district.

Moffatt had been a telegrapher at J. W. Davis & Co. prior to enlisting. He returned to his old job, and continued the practice of part-time work in the evening as well. He managed to scrape together enough money to purchase a Curb seat in 1923, and for a while worked as a two-dollar broker. In 1925 he joined with William Spear to form the firm of Moffatt & Spear, a specialist unit.

Moffatt's firm was never a major one. Neither partner was particularly aggressive, though each was well-liked. Moffatt's health recovered, and he went to night school to overcome his stuttering handicap. He also became interested in Curb administration, and indicated a desire to serve on committees.

Moffatt was pleasant, honest, and rather bland. He posed no threat to other brokers, and was trusted by most. He was a war hero, when military service was a decided asset in business. In a period when all Curb administrators—including the president—were unsalaried, he was willing to take a job. Nor did he do so out of desire for personal profit (for some Curb positions were useful for business purposes). Moffatt was interested in the clearing house when few brokers cared to work for it, though all considered it vital to Curb prosperity.

In 1929 Moffatt was elected to the Board of Governors, and also took a place on the Committee on Clearing House. From that time on he was the key figure there. When in 1931 the Securities Clearing Corporation was formed from the clearing house, Moffatt became its chairman. Later on Moffatt would serve two separate terms as president and one as chairman of the Board of Governors. Moffatt was on one committee or another (and often several at once) from 1929 to 1949, when he retired from brokerage. His first important contribution— the administration of the clearing house—was also his most lasting, while the clearing house itself was a major attempt by the administration to make the Curb a more efficient place in the 1920s.

The very factors that made it possible for a man like Moffatt to become a major figure at the Curb were the causes of a second movement in the direction of internal reform. In 1925 some brokers asked for a scrapping of the old constitution and the writing of a new one. The constitution then in force was a remnant of the outdoor marketplace, and had been written when the curbstone community was diverse, unmanageable, and more than slightly disreputable. Conditions had changed by 1925. The events of 1922–23 had rid the Curb of many bucket shops, but the bull market beginning in 1924 had increased opportunities for gamblers and dishonest brokers, and these men operated on a larger scale than their counterparts at the old outdoor market. A stronger administration was needed to end such practices and expel the men who specialized in them. Earlier the Curb had been the handmaiden of the Big Board; the reform element thought the time was ripe to cut some of the ties with the senior market. They talked of raising standards for both brokers and securities, in this way competing with the Big Board for both.

By 1925 many Curb stocks were going over to the Stock Exchange, and there was nothing the Curb could do to prevent the exodus. As the bull market gathered steam, large brokerages would use the Curb as a minor league for brokers. New, unseasoned partners would be sent to the Curb for training. Then the best of them would be transferred to the Big Board. Such activity did not affect the specialists, but the level of floor brokerage at the Curb seemed to decline every year. Higher standards would change this situation. The reformers thought the Curb might also consider elimination of associate memberships: the Big Board houses would either purchase full memberships or leave the Curb. The reformers hoped these houses would opt for the second alternative. Then new brokerages, specializing in Curb securities, could be formed. Unlike Jones & Baker and Winkelman, these would be respectable places, and honest ones. It would mark a new era for the Curb, one in which separation from and competition with the Big Board would take place.

Finally, the reformers wanted to do away with salaried market employees. These were men who worked for members who, for one reason or another, did not appear on the floor. Some charter members of the Curb, now wealthy, had purchased seats at the Stock Exchange and spent their time there. Clerks performed their operations at the Curb. Like the associate members, such men would be told to take their places at the Curb or sell their seats. The reformers noted that if the seats were sold by specialists, their stocks could be distributed among those who were left, and so reward individuals who remained true to the Curb.

The reformers failed. The program was defeated by an alliance of Big Board houses and their satellites, conservative brokers, those fearful of retaliation, and realists who felt the Curb could not survive without business from Big Board houses. There were those who pointed to the fate of the Consolidated as an example of what would await the Curb should it challenge the Establishment. Most brokers were doing very well in 1925. Why rock the boat?

The reformers did manage to convince a majority that a new constitution was needed. Under Lockwood's direction, a committee was chosen and work begun. The new constitution was ratified and went into effect on September 7, 1926.

The 1926 constitution marked no drastic change from the previous document. All power remained in the hands of the board, and the president's job was to carry out its will. Some reformers hoped for a full-time salaried staff and a president who would be a full-time occupant of the office, not just a broker with time on his hands and friends on the board. They were voted down, and conditions remained as before.

Nor did the Curb make unconstitutional some of the speculative abuses of the 1920s. For example, the market at that time was in the hands of cliques, known as pools, that manipulated certain stocks for their own profits. As a stock moved upward, others would sell it short. This meant they would sell stock they didn't own, in the expectation of its decline, at which time they would purchase the stock on the open market and deliver it to the person who had lent it to them. A speculator might believe XYZ too high at 50, and sell it short at that price. Then, if the stock fell to 30, he might buy it and deliver, and in the process "make" 20 points.

But what would happen if the pool "cornered" the stock —controlled most of the issue? Then the short-seller would be unable to cover his position or, if he did so, his purchase would serve to send its price even higher. In the end he would be forced to buy from the manipulators, at which time the pool would be said to be "squeezing the shorts."

There was a move afoot at both the Big Board and the Curb to ban pools and corners, but it didn't get very far. The new Curb constitution provided for suspension of cornered stock and the posting of a settlement price by the Board of Governors. It was not much of a reform, but it was the best one could hope for in such times.

Article XVII set forth grounds for suspension and expulsion; this was a new feature. Among the grounds were fraud, fictitious transactions (painting the tape and churning), "demoralization of the market," dealing in securities outside of the market, and "acts detrimental to the welfare of the Exchange." None of these referred to dealings with customers—only to dealings with other brokers and houses.

No action was taken on the reform program of 1925. Throughout the rest of the decade and into the 1930s, the Curb would remain the satellite of the Big Board. Even such minor points as the elimination of associate memberships and the ending of salaried market employees were not considered. Walter Sykes, Jr., a wealthy broker and reform leader, became chairman of the committee on business conduct in 1927, and from that post asked for a reconsideration of the rules and an amendment of the constitution to end the practice of Stock Exchange houses being represented by salaried market employees, instead of partners, at the Curb. So long as the major Wall Street houses had such representation at the Curb, he said, the organization would have the aspect of a second-class market. As Sykes saw it, the big houses should be told to either put good men on the floor or leave the Curb. He realized the dangers such a move might bring: among them, the possibility of being taken up on his threat, or of retaliation from the Big Board. Sykes's move was met with a flood of protest to the board, and he withdrew from the fray.

This was the fate of even minor reform at the Curb in 1927. It is no wonder, then, that major reforms were not even considered.

The third and most visible attempt to make the Curb a more efficient establishment was the plan to expand the original building and in other ways provide additional space for the brokers and their staffs.

The original Curb building had no facilities for brokers' offices, another indication of the modest aspirations of the founders. McCormick had expected the brokers to find offices nearby, or retain their old ones on Broad Street. Funds available in 1921 would not allow offices even had the founders thought them wise.

Conditions had changed by 1927. Not only had the indoor market succeeded, but Curb brokers were wealthier than ever before in the market's history. The key indicator of this was

Prices of a Seat at the Curb Market, 1921–29

Year	First	High	Low	Last
1921	$ 6,000	$ 6,800	$ 3,750	$ 5,500
1922	5,500	10,000	4,200	7,000
1923	6,000	9,500	3,600	4,500
1924	4,000	9,000	4,000	9,000
1925	9,250	37,500	8,500	32,000
1926	34,000	35,000	17,500	32,000
1927	28,000	67,000	22,000	67,000
1928	56,000	170,000	56,000	170,000
1929	150,000	254,000	150,000	160,000

Source: Amex Databook, p. 12

the price of a Curb seat. The now-affluent brokers wanted offices within the Curb building, and were willing to pay high rents for them. Some of the men who had gone indoors were at the Big Board in 1927, installed in plush offices. Those who remained at the Curb wanted offices equally ornate, if not more so.

In April, 1928, the Board of Governors began consideration "in the matter of erection of a building in front of the Curb Exchange." * At the time the Curb building had a large lawn; the boast was that it was the biggest south of Canal Street. Now the board proposed to erect a building that would cover the lawn and then surmount the existing structure. The members had no idea at the time how high it should be, but all agreed it should be higher than the Stock Exchange building. And it wouldn't be as "old fashioned" as the senior market's home. Instead, it would be tall and graceful, in a style that would later be called "skyscraper modern."

Plans proceeded slowly as the governors collected funds for the project. On May 9, 1929, the board reported that it would construct the new building, which would cost "in excess of $1,100,000." Some thought the price would go as high as $1,375,000.

Meanwhile the board recommended the purchase of the Hamilton Building, an old structure nearby, which was the home of several Curb brokerage offices. The other occupants would be ousted, and offices made available for members of the Curb, as well as the clearing house. The board proposed to offer $1,000,000 for the Hamilton Building. Afterward, when the Curb addition was completed, the Hamilton Building could be used for other purposes or sold at a profit. In the lush days of May 1929, a million dollars didn't seem too high a price to pay for the convenience.

Nor did the board change its mind in the immediate aftermath of the stock market crash of October. The following month they presented a revised estimate for the addition,

* The New York Curb Market changed its name to the New York Curb Exchange in 1929, another sign of the new status of the organization.

which then stood at $1,772,000. It was another sign that the Curb had succeeded in its third objective—that of making the Market a more efficient place in which to do business. In this matter, as in those of obtaining increased volumes of business and maintaining good relations with the New York Stock Exchange, the Curb could claim success.

There was a fourth objective considered in the early 1920s, and here the Curb failed miserably. At the time of the move indoors McCormick had pledged the Curb to honesty, and steps had been taken in the first years to cleanse the Curb of its disreputable elements. This reform effort was short-lived, as we shall see. On November 23, 1928, Curb President William Muller, in a speech before the Delta Upsilon Club in New York, said that "regardless of what our listing requirements may be, regardless of what our rules of trading and our general policy may be, they are all meaningless unless they are interpreted by men of character." Muller would leave office in 1932. Before he did, the entire nation would learn how few "men of character" there were at the Curb in the 1920s.

The Shadow Administrations

The nation's securities exchanges were unincorporated concerns in the 1920s. In organization and theory, they were more like voluntary associations than corporations. According to the New York Stock Exchange, that market was a gathering of brokers who conducted business at a fixed location and operated under the terms of a constitution ratified by the members and rules promulgated by an elected board. It could be argued that internally the Exchange was a far more "democratic" entity than most corporations, which in theory were ruled by boards elected by stockholders, and not necessarily by the men who occupied important posts at the firm. It also meant that the Stock Exchange did not have to answer to any outside group or agency for its actions. As an unincorporated entity (its members often referred to it as a club), the Big Board did not come within the purview of the antitrust laws. Nor did the other exchanges, the Curb included.

When the Curb went indoors in 1921 the members purchased seats that gave them the right to trade. The seat also bestowed upon its owner the right to help select the Curb administration. The members were not really shareholders in the New York Curb Market. Instead, they received stock in the Realty Corporation, which owned the land, building, and other physical assets of the Curb Market. These shares could not be separated from the seat; they were an integral part of the package.

This may seem a fine and unimportant distinction, but it was not. It insured that the Curb Market would be an association of equals, with an administration directly answerable to a small constituency—its 550 members. No administration in this period and for years afterward could embark upon a program or policy contrary to the wishes of the members. Some Curb presidents would prod the members more than others, and a few pleaded with brokers to make certain needed changes. No president could afford to antagonize too many members at the same time, and none did.

It has been said that in a democracy the people get the kind of government they deserve. This assuredly was true at the Curb. Curb administrations were democratic in the sense that they reflected the nature and desires of the membership. In the 1920s the main body of brokers wanted to be left alone to do their work, and as a result Curb administrations in this period were weak. Curb brokers often slighted the rules, and the administrations were lax in their enforcement. On the other hand, the brokers spoke often of the need for an honest market, and so did the administrations, which often said reform was needed but did nothing about it.

As befitted voluntary organizations, the boards and presidents of all of the nation's securities markets were unsalaried. Leadership was drawn from the membership, which meant the leaders were *of* the members, and knew their problems and needs. It also meant that the leaders were nonprofessionals: men who often spent more time attending to their own affairs than to the business of the market. In some cases these men used their positions to enlarge their personal fortunes, as Silkworth did at the Consolidated. More often, market executives considered high office a matter of prestige, which brought benefits in a more indirect fashion; the example of Richard Whitney at the Big Board is a clear-cut instance. In so acting, the leaders at the Consolidated and the Big Board were also following tradition. At the corrupt Consolidated, it was natural for the president to be the biggest crook of the lot. The prestigious Big Board often sought for its president a man who had, or wanted, prestige.

The Curb tradition was somewhat different. Brokers there were either middle class or nouveau riche. They lacked the tradition of *noblesse oblige* one often found at the Stock Exchange, and some would have been as dishonest in their dealings as the Consolidated brokers were it not for pressures from the Big Board, hopes of achieving respectability, fear of exposure and censure by the few reformers at the Curb, and the bonanza from active trading in the 1920s that made shady deals unnecessary. Those who lacked fortunes wanted to make them; those who had a good deal of money wanted still more. Rarely did a Curb broker evidence willingness to serve on committees for no pay, in effect working for fellow-brokers who held such posts in low esteem. Membership on Curb committees could not ensure a beneficial distribution of new securities for specialists; as we have seen, allocation was not made that way. For that matter, far more money could be made in the 1920s by remaining on the trading floor rather than spending hours each week at committee meetings. Brokers who joined the administration in one office or another would hire clerks to take care of their floor operations, and the salaries came out of their own pockets.

For all these reasons, the Curb attracted a mixed bag of administrators in the 1920s. A majority appears to have been men of limited talents. Fred Moffatt was one of these. Some, like Edwin Posner, became outstanding administrators in time, and found that their willingness to take committee assignments was prized at the Curb. There were a few men of some substance at the Curb—such as E. Burd Grubb—who were able to rise rapidly by a combination of ability, charm, and prior status.

Since most brokers avoided committee work, the same names appeared over and over again during the 1920s. In 1927, for example, Grubb was on the arbitration committee, the committee on clearing house, the committee on membership, the committee on quotations, and the committee on arrangements, as well as the board. Joseph A. Cole was elected to the board in 1925; at the same time, he took a place on the committee on arrangements, the arbitration committee, the committee on membership, the subcommittee on securities, and the committee on constitution. From 1925 to 1933, Cole served on no fewer than four committees each year, and from 1934 to 1939 he was always on at least three. Posner purchased his Curb seat in 1921, when he was thirty years old. In 1925 he was elected to the board. During the next five years he served on almost every committee at the Curb. Mortimer Landsberg, Howard Sykes, Morton Stern, and David Page were others with wide committee experience during this period.

Contemporaries of these men say that none was a particularly good specialist. All were decent men, some were fine administrators, and all seem to have been drawn to administration through a desire to serve. None would have been a tycoon if he had remained only on the floor. Those who had that talent did not serve; they spent their time in brokerage.

During the Curb's first indoor decade Edward McCormick was the only president who combined intelligence, forcefulness, and sophistication. Before stepping down in 1923, he had hoped to make the Curb Market a respected and prosperous organization. As we have seen, these were often contradictory ambitions, but McCormick succeeded to a degree that had seemed beyond possiblity in the summer of 1921.

During the first year indoors the ticker service was extended throughout the Northeast, and McCormick thought the Midwest might be covered within the next decade. More than 450 new issues were admitted to trading, while less than half that number transferred to the Big Board. McCormick spearheaded a campaign to rid the exchange of shady operators and those who operated in semirespectability. Scarcely a month went by without one or more brokers being brought up on charges of malfeasance for one transaction or another. The committee on complaints, dominated by McCormick's group, usually issued warnings and severe reprimands to first offenders. One broker had to be called in twice.

The broker was James Gilligan, then a young specialist who had drifted into the periphery of what would later be called "the disreputable element." Gilligan was hard and shrewd, a specialist on the make. He had learned the ropes quickly, and used his abilities and knowledge to rise rapidly at the Curb. Gilligan was a tough customer; if a fellow-broker objected to some of his actions, he would be either ignored or cursed loudly. If this didn't succeed, Gilligan would attack him with his fists. Gilligan's combination of aggressiveness and conduct led to his first reprimand soon after the move indoors. In October 1921, Gilligan was charged with negligence in executing an order. The charge was not proven, and so he was exonerated. But Gilligan was reprimanded for using foul language at the time of the incident. He was warned to watch his step in the future, and obliged to take a pledge of good conduct.

A half-year later Gilligan was before the committee again, this time for having engaged in a fist fight on the Curb floor with another broker, E. E. Cerf. After a short hearing, both Cerf and Gilligan received fresh reprimands. In addition, both men were suspended for thirty days.

Gilligan was back at his post in late June, and continued to operate in the same fashion. Had such actions occurred at the Stock Exchange, he might have been expelled. The Curb was more tolerant of such individuals, even though McCormick hoped to strengthen standards. Gilligan would go on to become one of the most powerful men at the Curb, a broker not to be treated lightly. Almost forty years after this first suspension, further actions by Gilligan would almost destroy the organization.

Others engaged in similar practices. At one point two brokers were punished for engaging in a wrestling match in which one was injured. The other broker told the committee on complaints that he was extremely sorry about the entire matter, that he had never intended to hurt his adversary, and that he would be more circumspect in the future. Usually, that meant the opponents would meet in the street, and not on the floor.

An important move toward respectability took place in 1922, with the appointment of William Lockwood as Curb counsel. Lockwood was honest and intelligent, and from that time to the present he and his designated heirs and successors were strong influences for reform at the Curb.*

Lockwood was an aristocrat, a graduate of Williams College and Columbia Law School, and senior partner in the law firm of Morgan, Lockwood, and L'Heureux. Early in his practice he became interested in taxation, banking, and estate law. Lockwood was forty-eight years old in 1922, wealthy enough to pick his clients, and successful enough to confer prestige on those he represented. McCormick thought himself fortunate in obtaining his services. More important, Lockwood was impeccable in his dealings with the Stock Exchange and, later on, the government. With his Vandyke beard, clipped mustache, and British tailoring, he seemed the equal of any lawyer the Stock Exchange had. "Colonel" Lockwood (he had never been in the military, but he did not discourage those who addressed him as such) soon became an expert on exchange laws and regulations, and a formidable opponent for anyone investigating the Curb.

This presented a problem. Lockwood was every bit the reformer McCormick was, but his job was to defend the Curb against its opponents. At times this put him in a position of supporting programs and policies he thought unwise. For example, throughout the 1920s Lockwood thought it imprudent to continue the unlisted stock section. As we shall see, he was the man responsible for its retention in the 1930s. At other times Lockwood would salvage the Curb's existence at the price of foregoing reforms. Paradoxically, Lockwood the reformer made possible the kind of market the Gilligans and their ilk would one day exploit. Yet it may truly be said that Lockwood was the Curb's one indispensable man during its first three decades. His retainer, in 1922, was $2,400 a year.

The work of men like McCormick and Lockwood gave a façade to the Curb in 1921–22; the differing texture of a Gilli-

---

* Lockwood would be succeeded as Curb counsel by Francis Adams Truslow, his protégé, and later on Thomas McGovern would continue in their tradition. The only break in this service came from 1951 to 1961, when the "Lockwood faction" was out of power and Michael Mooney served in the post.

gan was also present, but it seemed to fade into the background. In July 1922, the American Economic Association polled its members to ask their opinion on the running of the securities markets. Of those who answered, 132 thought the Curb rules were "effective," 37 called them "fairly satisfactory," and only two said they were "inadequate." Without the Curb, the report concluded, there would be "a reversion to more primitive methods with scattered and localized dealings." It was still another indication of McCormick's success.

The Curb held its first elections since the move indoors in January 1922. In the past these had been formalities, with the regular re–election of those board members who wanted to continue in office and their replacement by like-minded people when they retired. But McCormick had angered a segment of the membership during the past year, with some opposing the move indoors and others resenting his reform policies. The Curb's counsel at that time, Franklin Leonard, was a member of the anti-McCormick faction, and some assumed he had ambitions to replace him.

Leonard was a sharp, tough lawyer, who had been instrumental in bringing the Curb indoors. He also had a reputation for speculation and for using his post to his own advantage. Leonard had several outside interests, including the Sutro Tunnel Co., of which he was a director and which his father headed. The Sutro Tunnel, which helped drain the Comstock Lode, was one of the longest of its type in the world, but had never been very profitable, and in the early twentieth century was on the verge of closing down. But Sutro was listed on the Big Board, and Leonard's connection with it gave him a certain amount of prestige in the eyes of Curb brokers, who also used Leonard's influence with western miners to obtain new listings. Leonard was also friendly with Eugene Tappen, and helped obtain the post of secretary of the Sutro for that Curb leader. Although it is not certain, it may have been that Tappen returned the favor by recommending Leonard for the Curb's legal department.

The split between McCormick and Leonard became evident in January 1922. The two men had said harsh things about one another, and had clashed at board meetings. Word of this had leaked to the membership. In addition to rumors of Leonard's speculation in securities, it was learned that the Curb's title to the land on which the exchange had been constructed was being challenged; apparently, Leonard had not done as thorough a title search as might have been expected. Leonard's friends and what might be called the anti-reform element joined to challenge the pro-McCormick board.

The administration group put forth its slate of eight men in late January. It included John Curtis and Arthur Myles, as well as E. M. "Briggs" Buchanan, Walter Sykes, and J. J. Stewart. The opposition ticket was headed by Vincent O'Neill, J. Robinson Duff, George Fanning, and George Leslie, Jr. A short but spirited campaign followed which concluded with the election of all the McCormick candidates with the exception of Stewart, who was defeated by Leslie.

The ill feelings were intensified during the election. As had been the case outdoors and would continue in the future, the Curb divided into factions at times when there were no outside pressures. Attacks from others usually resulted in a closing of ranks, and this occurred in June.

Ever since 1911, when he delivered a sensational speech entitled, "Is There a Money Trust?," Samuel Untermyer had been the symbol of muckraking in the financial district. As counsel for the "Money Trust" investigations of the following year, he had delved into every facet of Wall Street operations. Untermyer had served in a similar capacity for several other investigating groups, and in 1922 was chief counsel to the Lockwood Committee, which was looking into financial operations in the district.

Untermyer had always been considered a friend of the Curb, not so much because he thought it a reputable organization, but rather because of his dislike of the Stock Exchange, which he viewed as the source of much of the evil in the city. Whenever the Big Board made a move to put pressure on the Curb—whether to serve its own interests or to reform it— Untermyer would issue a blast about the arrogance and power of the Stock Exchange and the Money Trust. In 1922, however, Untermyer issued his first challenge to the Curb.

For many years the Curb had traded in "when, as, and if issued" stock. This would follow the announcement by an underwriter that a new security would soon be offered to the public, but prior to the filing of papers and the organization of a syndicate to market the issue.* With no knowledge other than a news item, a Curb specialist would begin to make a market in the security. Since the purchaser would not be able to receive his certificate until after the offering had been made, he was not required to pay a cent until then. The offering might take weeks to be completed, and during this period the specialist would accumulate perhaps hundreds of buy and sell orders, at varying prices. Settlement would take place after the certificates were ready. Since there was no clear way to determine the price of the security other than supply and demand, and since the specialist had a firm grip on both, the possibilities for manipulation were great. So was the gambling potential, for it allowed speculators to buy and sell without having to commit their funds. Finally, if for some reason the security was not issued, all orders were cancelled.

Untermyer thought this practice almost as pernicious as bucketing, and he made his feeling known in 1922. At that time Kuhn, Loeb & Co. was forming a new firm, North American Steel. The next day North American "when, as, and if issued" stock was traded at the Curb, and Untermyer decided to make this his battleground. He shot off a fiery letter to Curb Secretary Alfred Sturges:

> Unless the gambling operations now being conducted on your Exchange in the non-existent shares of the North American Steel Company "when issued" cease immediately by the with-

* This is very different from dealings today in "when-issued" stock. These securities have been authorized and filed, though not actually issued. It happens today after a stock split or merger, or at a time when a parent company decides to spin off a subsidiary. But now, as then, the buyer does not have to pay for his security until delivery can be made of the certificate.

drawal of the privilege of trading, the facts will be forthwith placed before the Grand Jury that is now in session for the purpose of dealing with cases arising out of the investigations of the Lockwood Committee, and an indictment will be asked of all concerned.

The fact that your Exchange admitted the phantom stock of this company to the privileges of trading "when issued" without having received a responsible application for listing or any facts on which a judgement could be based and without yourselves having or being able to furnish the slightest reliable information to the public of the size, color, or conversion value of the "chips" that were being used in the game in which you invited them and your own members to participate . . . [is reprehensible.]

Unfortunately not many rules have yet been prescribed for the game. . . . Until the game, as now being played, is stopped by constructive legislation that will convert your Exchange from a gambling hall into the great security market it should be, and will be when placed under proper governmental regulation, all the chips used must have their identification marks and redemption value plainly stamped on their face.

In the past Untermyer had criticized certain Curb activities, and when he did, the Curb complied with his wishes. The situation was different in 1922. The Curb had a new confidence now that it was a "respectable" market. The Stock Exchange would not bow to Untermyer, and why, they thought, should they? To fight would be a sign of having arrived. Furthermore, Kuhn, Loeb was pleased to have North American traded. The price was good, and would enable the underwriter to get a better market for the securities at a time when financing was still difficult. McCormick knew that to bow to Untermyer would further alienate his Curb opponents, who then could charge that he was cooperating with outsiders to take business away from the specialists. Finally, it was common knowledge that Untermyer was planning to leave for a European vacation in mid-June, and perhaps McCormick thought he wouldn't cancel it for the purpose of crossing swords with the Curb.

McCormick announced that trading would continue in

North American Steel. He saw no reason to change a practice at the Curb that was almost a century old and that had worked for the benefit of investors and brokers.

Untermyer never was a man to turn down a challenge. Calling in reporters, he told them that he had cancelled his vacation. He would go to the Grand Jury and ask for indictments against every Curb officer, as well as several brokers. Fifty supoenas were issued soon after, to McCormick, Sturges, and other key officials and brokers.

The next day McCormick announced trading would cease in North American Steel. In the future, he added, securities would not be traded on a "when, as, and if" basis. Within hours Untermyer withdrew his charges and took off for his vacation. McCormick had lost the battle, but in so doing had united the Curb community behind him and demonstrated a willingness to speak out for its interests, as well as the sense to know when he was licked. The dissidents were stilled. When, in June of 1923, a group of brokers announced their withdrawal from the Curb and their intention to form a new organization—the Curb Stock and Bond Market—few joined them. Among the staunchest defenders of the Curb Market were those men who had opposed the administration ticket in the 1922 elections.*

In early February 1923, McCormick announced his retirement; he would not seek another term. He told the members that he was stepping down on orders of his doctor, and that he would take a long rest. Then he would return to the Curb as a broker, and never again would serve as an administrator.**

McCormick's retirement came as no shock; he had served for nine years as chairman and president, and had often spoken of his desire to step down once the Curb building had been

---

* Talk of a new outdoor market had begun as soon as the announcement of the move indoors had been made. Its backers, Thomas Cook, A. R. Spacht, and Charles Finnigan, were marginal brokers who felt the Curb's "respectability" would mean a loss of business. This plan, like others before and since, received little support.

** McCormick's health recovered, and he did serve on several committees during the next decade.

completed. Nor was his choice of successor surprising. John W. Curtis, the Curb's vice-president, seemed the logical man for the post, and he was elected with McCormick's blessings and without opposition.

Curtis pledged himself to a continuation of the McCormick policies and programs. Like his predecessor, he would speak out often against the bucket shops; punishment of those who broke the rules continued. Curtis was particularly interested in persuading members to sell their memberships in out-of-town exchanges, and the board passed several resolutions in 1923 and 1924 condemning those who dealt in Curb securities on other markets. The new president hoped to convince many associate members that they would be better off if they purchased full memberships at the Curb. Curtis thought there was no room for "second-class" citizenship at the Curb—even though the second-class citizens were among the biggest and most prestigious investment banks in America. He urged the Curb to have higher commission-rate schedules for full members, and to oblige the associate members to pay a form of surcharge on all their transactions, but this plan had little support and died.

On several occasions Curtis spoke out in favor of what today would be called the "professionalization" of the Curb Market. The Curb was led by brokers, but day-to-day administration was in the hands of a paid staff. Curtis would enlarge the staff and cut back on the duties of the administrator-brokers. Salaries of paid employees were raised, and in his Christmas address of 1924 Curtis announced that he had hired an accountant to look over the Curb's books. Furthermore, accountants hired by the Curb would investigate listing applications and reports of all stocks enjoying listed status.

Curtis spoke often of the need for betterment, but little was done in that direction during his two years as president. That he lacked McCormick's prestige and shrewdness could be seen when the members simply ignored several of his pleas.

Curtis was not a wealthy man. He spent little time on administrative matters, and during his presidency the board gained far more power than it had under McCormick. The brokers grew arrogant as the great bull market of the 1920s gathered steam. They were in no mood to follow suggestions for betterment of the market at a time when all seemed well. Curtis stepped down in 1925, and was glad to do so. Now he, like many other brokers, could concentrate on the accumulation of a fortune.*

Curtis' vice-president was David U. Page, and during much of his administration Page was the *de facto* president. As Curtis tried to maximize his time on the trading floor, Page was obliged to spend additional time on administration. It was only natural, then, that Page be elected president in February 1925.

Like so many Curb brokers, Page came from a lower-middle-class family, and had started his career as a runner and clerk when he was sixteen years old. He was of medium size, slender, a very shy man, who was buffeted about by the others. But Page was honest and hard-working, and these attributes appealed to McCormick, who became his sponsor. In 1917, at the age of thirty-four, Page became a member of the board, and he served until 1923, when McCormick selected him for the vice-presidency. By then Page was considered a fine administrator, a good man at details, and a firm supporter of the McCormick policies. Like Curtis' administration, his was an extension of the McCormick period, without McCormick's vitality and an extension of the McCormick period, without McCormick's prestige.

Page was very much the puritan in Babylon, serving as he did from 1925 to 1928, the wild years of the bull market. No man could have run herd on the speculative brokers of this period—not McCormick nor any other figure the Curb might have produced at that time.

Page was able to upgrade one aspect of the Curb opera-

* Curtis did make his fortune in the 1920s, but, like so many others, he lost everything in the crash. His firm went bankrupt in 1931, and Curtis himself was suspended from Curb membership for "inability to meet obligations." Later on he found employment with a financial printer, serving as salesman and part-time executive, and then as president of a savings and loan association on Staten Island.

tions. Prior to his presidency so-called penny stocks dominated the list. These were low-priced issues of dubious value, the darlings of speculators. Now that times were better, the speculators moved into the higher-priced issues, and Page set out to remove the penny stocks from the list. Few opposed him and the board in this campaign; after all, why worry about the peanuts when the grapes are falling into your lap?

Page spent three years upgrading the list, and his efforts were successful. When he left office the Curb list contained over 1,700 issues (although not all traded regularly). Of this number, 1,150 paid dividends—and only 25 were selling at less than a dollar a share.

Neither Curtis or Page could be called strong executives. The Curb constitution did not permit the president to exercise much authority, and the members didn't want anyone puissant. McCormick had managed to transcend both the constitution and the membership because he needed power to answer problems and challenges. Curtis and Page faced far subtler difficulties, and the Curb of that period was not a very subtle place. So they faded into the background, as did administration in general.

Nor were these presidents powers on the board. Arthur Myles was far more important in the campaign against bucket shops than was either Curtis or Page. Myles, the Moore & Schley representative at the Curb, was a powerful broker from a prestigious Wall Street house. Myles had been a founder of the indoor market and a charter member of the Curb Market, and he spent most of his professional life at the Curb. But he was a representative and not a specialist; he had connections at the Stock Exchange as well as power among the Curb brokers. Myles was elected to the board in 1918, and served until 1931. Throughout this period he was one of the strong men at the Board, often presuming to speak as the Stock Exchange's representative to the Curb. Myles would serve or had served on almost all the major committees, and was one of the most respected men in the administration. Had he so desired, he might have become president himself in the 1920s. But Myles preferred to maintain his Moore & Schley–Stock Exchange position as well as that at the Curb, and so he contented himself with being a power behind lesser men like Curtis and Page.

Edwin Posner was Myles' ally and protégé. Unlike Myles, Posner was a specialist, with a commitment to the Curb and none to the Stock Exchange. Although a very junior member, Posner was a key man on the powerful arbitration committee from 1925 to 1928, and was on the important committee on listing from 1927 to 1933. From these positions he was able to learn quickly who held power and how they used it.

A short, stocky man, Posner had a tough appearance, a fabled temper, and a large reservoir of righteous indignation. He had come to the Curb after his father's firm had failed. With friends but little money, Posner rose rapidly, the result of an interest in administration and friendship with reform elements. He could not abide shady characters, and on occasion shouted down Curb veterans many years his senior, charging them publicly with breaches of conduct. Even then Posner was respected for his integrity and skill, while feared for his temper and hated by those who became his enemies. He made no secret of his desire for the presidency, but Posner had earned the hatred of powerful specialists. Not until these men were wiped out in the 1929 crash and its aftermath could he hope to gain such power.

If Myles was respected and Posner feared, Howard Sykes was disliked. Many brokers considered him pompous, a man who seemed to think Curb brokers disreputable. His older brother, Walter, was one of the leaders at Post & Flagg, an influential and rich brokerage firm of the time. Walter, an acknowledged leader, was a broker who served on many committees as a leader of the reformers. Although his crusades irritated many, he was believed sincere and able. The Sykeses were "old money" in the eyes of the Curb community, but Walter took pains not to show it. He had gone to the best schools and enjoyed good living, but he did not put on airs while at the Curb, and the brokers appreciated it.

Such was not the case with Howard Sykes. A graduate of Hotchkiss, he had gone on to Yale, where he played football. Howard was a great Yale fan, and would recount tales of his exploits to other brokers, much to their disgust and irritation. While many Curb brokers frequented the bike and horse races at Madison Square Garden and the nearby tracks, Howard looked forward all year to the Yale-Harvard game, and would speak of it for weeks before and after to his few Curb friends. He seemed to be sneering at the majority of brokers, those who had never finished high school, much less gone to college.

To make matters worse, Howard Sykes was a worldly man and an Anglophile operating in an arena of men who had never travelled much, many of whom were of Irish extraction. Before the war, Sykes had served as representative of Standard Oil of New York in Malaya and Java. He enlisted in the English army in the early days of the war, and served to its conclusion. Sykes transferred to the AEF in 1917, but he was always pro-English.

After the war Sykes became executive vice-president of the Shawmut Corporation of Boston (he sometimes said he liked Boston far more than New York), and in 1925 he came to New York to join his brother's firm. Sykes purchased a Curb seat that year, and two years later was elected to the board. At the time his enemies said he rose rapidly because of his brother's influence and sponsorship, and such would seem to have been the case. But Howard Sykes was also a man of ability, though his interests were narrow. He too wanted to upgrade the Curb, to attract a better kind of man and a more selective group of securities. While Posner would enlarge on the good that already existed at the Curb, Sykes gave the impression that he felt there were few elements of the Curb worth saving. He had the idea of seeking new British, continental, Canadian, and other foreign listings for the Curb, and in time transforming it into an international market. Let the Stock Exchange dominate trading in American securities, he often said. We will be the prime market for foreign stocks. Such an idea had appeal, but Howard Sykes' reasons for putting forth the suggestion were suspect. He seemed to want foreign stocks because he had contempt for Americans. Since most of the Curb brokers were intensely patriotic, they further resented Howard Sykes and all he seemed to stand for. Sykes might have been an excellent member of the Big Board, and one wonders why he didn't go there. He was out of his element at the Curb, and, although powerful, was never as respected as his brother and Edwin Posner.

There was some talk of Howard Sykes seeking the presidency in 1928, though it was evident he had little support. Instead, the board turned to the next man in the line of succession, William S. Muller.

Like his predecessors, Muller had been a member of the outdoor Curb and had supported McCormick in his move indoors. He was a more aggressive person than either Curtis or Page, and more ambitious as well. This was demonstrated by his election to the board in 1912, at which time he was only thirty-three years old. Muller did not remain on the board after his first term, concentrating his attention instead on affairs at his brokerage, Muller & Nash. When Nash left in 1914, Muller formed his own firm, and prospered during the war. As a result, he was a well-to-do if not wealthy man in the early 1920s. Unlike Curtis, he could afford time away from his own enterprise, and he was more forceful than Page.

Muller was not one to rock the boat. When he came to the presidency in February 1928, the great bull market was in its last and most dazzling phase. Optimism pervaded the financial district; all seemed right with the brokers' world; *laissez-faire* capitalism of the variety then preached by Republican leaders seemed fully justified. To be sure, there were still flaws in the financial picture and abuses in the district, but these appeared to be minor in the face of overwhelming success. Or so it seemed when Muller delivered his acceptance speech in February 1928. In it he congratulated the membership on the prosperity so evident in the district at that time. He said that most of the credit for this situation went to them, and little to the Curb Market, which was but an instrument of their desires. The Curb constitution, too, was theirs, and not the Market's as an abstract entity. If the Curb was to be kept clean, and the few remaining abuses removed, they, the brokers, would have to take the initiative and act.

In so speaking, Muller gave clear indication that his

would not be an activist administration. Muller would take no step to end abuses, and at no time show aggressive leadership, whether in the few good months left the bull market of the 1920s, or in the years that followed.

Volume rose sharply at the Curb soon after Muller took office. This seemed another sign of increased speculation. From time to time Muller conferred with Stock Exchange President E. H. H. Simmons and Vice-President Richard Whitney, but neither of these men indicated a belief that speculation was dangerous, prices too high, or the volume of trading unrealistic. On Saturday, June 16, 1929, volume at the Curb passed the 1.1-million mark, for the first time in history surpassing that of the Stock Exchange. Muller took no note of this, indicating instead that his campaign to oblige Curb brokers to quit other exchanges and cease trading in over-the-counter securities was proceeding smoothly.

Prices at both the Stock Exchange and the Curb fluctuated wildly in late September. Then they recovered in early October, and headed upward once more. Simmons and Whitney spoke daily to reporters, assuring them all was well. Muller remained silent, devoting his attention to Curb matters. He had learned that Joseph Reilly, who ran a cigar stand in the smoking room, was running a punch-board operation, by which members would pay for chances, hoping to win "costly articles, including automobiles and jewelry," while Reilly's lease stated "that the space leased shall be used as a Cigar Stand for the sale of cigars, cigarettes, pipes, tobacco, smoker's novelties, etc. . . ."

Muller went into some detail on the subject. He promised a further investigation and, if Reilly were indeed guilty, swift action.

The great crash began during the week of October 14–19, and the markets fell sharply in the days that followed. Muller remained quiet throughout this period. By month's end it had become clear that more than a "small minority" had been involved in speculation; it was, in fact, a large majority of Curb brokers. Scarcely a month would pass during the next decade without the appearance of a news story or magazine article or book about the speculative markets of the 1920s. Many of these studies were concerned with Curb brokers and their dealings. They demonstrated that while Curtis, Page, and Muller were talking about reforms and making token changes, the Curb trading floor was every bit as much a jungle as that at the Stock Exchange. The administrations of this period were but shadows; the substance was on the floor.

+ F I V E −

The Night Before and the Morning After

The Curb community prospered in the 1920s, as did almost every other part of the American financial structure. The large volume of business and the increased profits were welcomed, especially since they came at a time when many brokers had predicted a revival of the pre–World War I depression. This prosperity was not unusual insofar as profits were concerned. Many Curb brokers remembered the bonanza years at the turn of the century, prior to the 1907 panic. Some had been told of the huge profits of the Civil War era and after, which had come to an end with the panic of 1873. Now the Curb was in the midst of a new major bull market and speculative period. In the early 1920s most brokers expected it to come to a close as had the others, with a panic and crash. And there were periods of decline in the 1920s, when it seemed the upward movement had been halted, signaling the beginning of a new depression. But the market always recovered, and it went on to even greater heights.

By 1928 a pattern seemed to have been established, one of upward surge followed by minor decline and consolidation, and then another move to new heights. Earlier financial panics had been the handmaidens of economic collapse. Like their counterparts at the Stock Exchange, most Curb brokers believed the American economy of the 1920s to be quite different from that of the pre-war period, and not susceptible to depressions of long duration. Instead, there would be short, sharp, but correctable dips every few years. The Curb brokers were reasonably certain they could survive these, as they prepared for permanent prosperity in the New Era.

The Wall Street and Trinity Place financial communities like to talk of the lessons of history, but the Curb brokers seemed to have learned few from what they knew of the past. Many brokers had been ruined by the 1907 panic, and more went bankrupt as a result of the pre-war recession. For ten months after the declarations of war in 1914, all American securities markets were closed down, as their leaders were fearful of a terrific panic should trading be allowed. At that time, when brokers had no sources of income, dozens left the Curb, never to return.

In all those periods the careful husbanding of earnings of good years would have saved the brokers during the bad. One might expect such brokers to save part of their bonanza take to tide them over when the going got rough. The old curbstone brokers and their successors at the Curb Market learned no such lessons, or, if they did, they forgot them during the boom years. Surprisingly few brokers seemed worried about a crash in the late 1920s. Most spent their earnings freely, saving little against a time when reserves might be needed. During the night before they gave little thought to the morning after, even as they knew that in the past, experience had shown that the greater the boom, the more spectacular the bust.*

Bull markets on the Curb meant increased commissions and profits from manipulation and speculation. Commission rates were raised several times during the 1920s, while volume grew. Never before had the brokers known such returns from purchases and sales. Opportunities for manipulation and specu-

---

* The brokers of the 1960s were more prudent than their forebears. Although many suffered in the dips and dives of that decade's markets, the number of broker failures was much smaller. The firms that failed in 1969–70 did so more as a result of poor management and inadequate techniques than from insufficient capitalization.

lation were also great, though no more than they had been in previous bull markets. The scale was larger in the 1920s, and so were the returns.

As they had in the past, the Curb brokers enjoyed their lives during this bull market. There was a difference between the Curb brokers' life styles in the 1920s and those of other bull moves. The prosperous brokers of 1906 often were men of little education and limited horizons so far as their personal status was concerned. Their dreams were not ambitious by the Wall Street standards of the time. Most wanted to own their own homes in the suburbs—either Brooklyn or west Jersey— and have a small farm in "the country." When they splurged they did so by purchasing a small boat; a good time with the boys often consisted of attending a baseball game at the Polo Grounds. They drank beer, ate steaks, and puttered around the house on weekends. If one of their number took a European or Caribbean vacation, it became the talk of the curbstone community.

The prosperous Curb brokers of the 1920s had different ambitions. More of them were native-born than had been the men of 1906, and many were second-generation brokers. A high school diploma was no longer unusual at the Curb Market, although few brokers had any college experience. The world was different, too. America had emerged from the Great War the leading power in the world, and the Curb brokers knew it, were proud, and no longer quite so cowed by foreigners or fearful of contact with them. Most important, however, was the symbolism of the indoor market. Curb brokers no longer felt ashamed of their place of business. Though smaller than the Big Board and certainly not as prestigious, it was the nation's second-largest securities market at a time when stocks and bonds were prime topics of discussion. All of this had an effect on the Curb brokers. In 1906 they had dreamed of being as rich as Morgan; in the 1920s they also wanted to live like him.

If a prosperous Curb broker of the 1920s lived in New Jersey or Brooklyn, he was probably an old-timer or someone who could not manage something better. The goal of the 1920s was

Park Avenue or Fifth, or perhaps Riverdale. They could not hope to be admitted to Newport, the playground for the Big Board leaders, or aspire to the Hamptons or Montauk, both growing and prestigious areas, but they did buy land in Nassau and Westchester counties. Baseball still appealed to the brokers, but more for betting purposes than sport. Throughout the 1920s the board would warn against gambling on the floor, and the warnings went unheeded. Brokers would bet hundreds of dollars on important games, and thousands on the World Series. During the winter they switched interest to Madison Square Garden and the seven-day bicycle races, or to prize fights. Increasingly the brokers turned to "gentlemen's sports," such as contract bridge at their homes or clubs. The golf craze swept the Curb; scarcely a member lacked a set of clubs. The annual Curb golf tournament, held at one of the better clubs, was the event of the year. Many Curb brokers belonged to golf clubs in much the same way their predecessors had joined fraternal and ethnic organizations like the Elk, Moose, and Knights of Columbus. No longer did a European vacation seem unusual, and several Curb brokers vacationed in Cuba every year, mixing business with pleasure, as the increased number of Cuban issues traded at the Curb indicated. They became art collectors and aspired to culture. No longer did Curb brokers want their sons to leave school and join them on the floor. Now they insisted on college, and only the best would do. The sons of Curb brokers applied to Ivy League schools and socialized with the old aristocracy. As a result, the new men who came to the Curb Market in the late 1920s were often as well-educated as their Big Board counterparts, and they mingled freely with the Establishment from the other side of Trinity Place. The Curb seemed to have arrived.

Success brought an unexpected problem, however. As the securities markets expanded rapidly in the 1920s, a shortage of qualified personnel developed. Both the Stock Exchange and the Curb were affected, and brokers on each market made a determined effort to find trainees. Naturally, the Stock Exchange had an easier time of it. Wall Street had glamour in the 1920s, and to most the Big Board was synonymous with Wall Street. Trainees rushed to the district, eager to be at the center of action and make their fortunes.

One of these, aspiring poet and journalist Matthew Josephson, wrote of his own beginnings as a stock broker in this period. He was recommended by a newspaperman-friend to a member firm, and given a chance. "During a fortnight of orientation I familiarized myself with the machinery of the security markets, finding it complex but very neatly rationalized," he wrote. "Then I was put to work at the top instead of the bottom, after receiving some tutelage from an aged partner who planned to retire soon." Josephson did well at brokerage. "It was a beautiful game, I said to myself. I wondered why more people did not enter into it, rather than go on slaving in their dreary shops or just hoeing potatoes." But Josephson's customers lost money on tips and deserted him. The next rally brought a new group of customers, however, and prosperity to amateur brokers who specialized in handling accounts for amateur investors.*

There was a far better source for floor brokers and specialists, however, and that was the Curb Market. As we have seen earlier, Wall Street houses would use the Curb as a training ground for brokers, and the best of these would graduate to the Big Board soon after. The same was true of specialists. Some Curb brokers used their newly found wealth to purchase seats at the Stock Exchange, making a jump few ever had expected to accomplish in 1921. The effect was to invigorate the Stock Exchange with infusions of the best young blood in the district and to debilitate the Curb Market, which was now in the paradoxical situation of suffering from too much success.

It did serve to raise the Curb's reputation in the eyes of the Establishment. In the past, Big Board brokers had looked down on the Curb as a place for also-rans. Now that so many

* Many Wall Street brokers wrote of the level of personnel on the Street in this period, but Josephson's memoir is the best account of the reactions of a new man in the district, and what it seemed to be to an outsider. See Matthew Josephson, *Life Among the Surrealists* (Holt, Rinehart & Winston, 1962), especially pp. 275–310.

Curb brokers were making the shift, they could no longer make such statements, or at least not do so with as much assurance as before.*

The infusion of Curb brokers into the Big Board was both a reason for and a symbol of the relative harmony between the two markets during the middle and late 1920s. Now that the Consolidated had folded and outside investigations had become a thing of the past, there seemed no reason why the leaderships and members of the two markets could not work in harmony with one another. Many Curb securities left the junior market to seek listing at the Stock Exchange, but there seemed an endless supply of new firms for the Curb brokers to list in place of those that had moved on. With such bounty for all, there seemed little reason to bicker for scraps. The 1920s, in fact, was one of the more harmonious decades within the New York securities complex.

The 1920s was also one of the great speculative eras in American history, and the opportunities for manipulation were unsurpassed.** Here also the two markets would cooperate. Every week pools formed with the intent of bulling or bearing a stock; often they included leading Curb brokers as well as Big Board figures. Mike Meehan, who headed many pools in this period but specialized in Radio Corporation of America manipulations, was a member of both exchanges, and RCA itself began at the Curb and later transferred to the Big Board. Arthur Cutten, the most respected speculator of the decade, was involved in activities in both markets. Jesse Livermore, the "boy speculator" (who was actually a veteran of many pre-war conflicts), was one of the most glamourous figures in the district, and the most closely followed for several years. Most of Livermore's activities were in Big Board securities, but he also led several pools at the Curb. Livermore purchased a Curb

* A similar situation developed in the early and mid-1960s, and many of today's Big Board brokers have had training and experience at the American Stock Exchange.
** See John K. Galbraith, *The Great Crash* (Houghton Mifflin, 1955), Alexander Noyes, *The Market Place* (Scribners, 1938), and Robert Sobel, *The Great Bull Market* (Norton, 1968).

seat, which he held until 1926. He would from time to time make a personal appearance on the trading floor, and conduct his operations from there. On such occasions crowds would gather to watch Livermore in action, in much the same way as they would go see Babe Ruth at bat in Yankee Stadium or Bill Tilden playing tennis at Forest Hills.

This merging of Stock Exchange and Curb figures and markets began soon after the end of the war. The first major venture in this direction was the manipulation of Savold Tire in 1919. Savold was touted as "potentially the biggest factor in the tire business" by one journalist. The firm did not produce tires, but rather controlled the patents on a process to recap old tires at a far lower cost than the methods then employed. The syndicate that floated Savold included C. T. Morgan, Van Emburgh & Atterbury, and Tucker, Anthony & Co. of the Stock Exchange and B. J. Ferris & Co. and M. J. Meehan & Co. of the Curb. Louis Cartier, a prominent Curb broker who was a major factor in several automobile securities, became the specialist in Savold, and was charged with seeing to it that the price rose. And so it did. The underwriters purchased stock at 15 prior to the issuance, and the stock opened at 20, rising to 22 within a day. Volume was high, a sign of both interest and churning. Savold was the talk of the Curb.

Now other Savold issues were floated, each with rights to the patent in a different part of the country. Savold Tire of New Jersey, Savold Tire of Ohio, Savold Tire of New England, and Savold Tire of New York were equally successful, netting the underwriters and speculators small fortunes. Then the prices of the securities fell rapidly, probably due to the selling out by insiders. The pools were ended, and hundreds of speculators took losses. Cartier and B. J. Ferris then pocketed their profits and went on to bigger things. Indeed, it was through his skilful running of the pool that Cartier was given Chevrolet, and as its specialist he became independently wealthy.

How did the Savold group interest the public in the stocks? The churning helped, as did word-of-mouth advertising. Even more important, however, was the publicity given the issue in the newspapers. The Savold story appeared in many of the city's newspapers before and during the manipulation. Some of the interest was merited, to be sure. But other stories resulted from the approximately $100,000 in Savold stocks given to newspapermen in the form of bribes.*

Relations between newspapermen and both the Curb and Stock Exchange in this period were unusually good. Few journalists of the 1920s were of the muckraking tradition; most praised the securities markets as a symbol of the New Era. This was, in part, the result of a sincere belief that the new prosperity was real and lasting. But each New York newspaper had a financial page as well, and some of the reporters and columnists there received bribes from brokers to print favorable stories on individual stocks and bonds. The same was true for the few radio financial analysts of the period. W. F. Wamsley (*The New York Times*), Stanley W. Prenosil (Associated Press), Raleigh T. Curtis (New York *Daily News*), John F. Lowther (New York *Tribune*), and Arthur D. La Hines (*Wall Street Mirror*) were only a few of the leading journalists in the pay of one operator or another. There were many more. Some were contacted directly by brokers interested in planting stories. Others were in the pay of several "publicity counsels" who operated in the district in the 1920s, who acted as agents for the brokers or the newspapermen, and reaped fortunes through commissions or management fees.

Before the war Stock Exchange speculators had used journalists to spread stories and plant ideas. The curbstone brokers of the outdoor market had far more experience with such individuals. Speculators cannot operate without publicity, which is needed to draw in the unwary. If need be, that publicity would

---

* A good deal of information regarding the securities markets —speculator–journalist nexus appeared in investigations of the Wall Street area conducted in the early New Deal period. A more personal account may be found in A. Newton Plummer, *The Great American Swindle, Inc.* (Plummer, 1932). Plummer was a master swindler himself, and wrote this exposé in an attitude of mea culpa and to prove that he was only one of many men involved in such activities. The material in the book is damning, and Plummer named those involved and challenged them to sue if they felt slandered. No suit developed from this book.

be purchased. At the turn of the century few newspapers covered Curb developments, and only a handful reported on closing prices at the outdoor market. Curb brokers would bribe newspapermen to publicize those issues in which they were interested. Outright "gifts" were given, but more common were paid advertisements for brokerages. These were staid notices, stating that the brokerage dealt in Curb issues and was prepared to execute orders for the public. It was understood that the reporter who brought in such advertisements would receive commissions from the newspaper for them, and this would constitute payment for services rendered the advertiser. This close collaboration continued and grew in the post-war period. It also spread to the new securities services of the period. Together, the manipulators and journalists were able to create overnight sensations and reap large profits.

Opportunities for such dealings abounded in the 1920s, when new issues were eagerly received by a public eager to invest its money. Securities in the new fields of aviation and radio, and in the rapidly growing automobile industry, received the biggest plays. Market leadership rested with the blue chips in the early years of the bull market, but by 1924 the glamour issues were in greater demand. Since most of the new issues made their bows at the Curb, volume and speculation there grew rapidly in this period.

In 1924 Curb watchers could follow the antics of Ware, Inter-Ocean, Rova, Jones, and other radio companies. One of the group, Thompson Radio, seemed particularly attractive. Unlike some of the new firms, Thompson was already in production at the time its stock was floated. The company had a small factory in New Jersey, which it hoped to expand soon after going public. Still, it was clearly a speculation. Rivals like Radio Corporation of America, Westinghouse, General Electric, and Atwater Kent were much larger and better financed, and they advertised. There seemed little chance for Thompson or any of the dozen other small radio firms going public that year to survive. But the speculators were interested in their securities, and each enjoyed small booms before fizzling.

Plans to sell a public issue of Thompson were made in

early 1924. Then, in March, the New York Attorney General enjoined the underwriters for another new radio company, Federated Radio, from selling shares. Federated had violated several state regulations, and the underwriters had engaged in gross misrepresentation. Because of this, Federated never went public, and a pall was cast over all the new radio issues.

Undaunted, C. H. Hensel, E. W. Clucas & Co., and Morin S. Hare & Co. organized a syndicate to market 47,000 shares of Thompson Radio. In so doing, they would act for Robinson & Co., Thompson's banker. Under the agreement, Robinson would sell the shares to the three brokers at $10 a share, and do so before May 6. A week later the syndicate would offer the shares to the public at $12.50

All three underwriters had had previous experience with radio securities, and had little doubt the shares could be distributed. Clucas & Co. was particularly interested in the new issue, since it had been involved in the abortive offer of Federated shares and hoped to recoup both its losses and its reputation by success with Thompson.

The underwriters had a difficult time disposing of their shares. For almost a half year there was little activity or interest in Thompson Radio. Then, in early November, at a time when the stock was selling below 10, the underwriters employed Richard F. Hoyt, a partner in the Stock Exchange firm of Hayden, Stone & Co., to manage the issue. Soon after, A. Newton Plummer, then editor of the *National Financial News*, approached Hensel to solicit advertising. Hensel said he would advertise if, in Plummer's words, "I could get him some buying in Thompson." To this Plummer replied that he "might obtain a broker to help him if I could get a 'finder's commission,' and he agreed." Plummer then sent a friend, Cecil Rossi, to see Hensel and make arrangements for publicity. Together Rossi, Plummer, and Hoyt advertised and bulled Thompson Radio to new highs.

During the week of November 7, 1924, only 1,200 shares of Thompson were traded at the Curb Market, in a price range of between 7⅜ and 9⅜. Volume reached 35,200 shares in the week of November 22, and the price rose to 13½. Thompson's volume was 44,200 shares the week of January 3, 1925, and its price hit 24⅝. At that time interest in the firm was at its peak. It was then, too, that the pool began to liquidate its position. Thompson reached 25 on January 8, and then began to decline rapidly. The partners had made their profits, and were now content to allow the stock to reach its normal level. So it did. By April, Thompson was trading a hundred or so shares a day and was quoted at 6¼. Three months later Thompson Radio announced its need for additional financing, which was not forthcoming. In July 1926, Thompson went bankrupt.

The pool in Thompson was one of dozens at the Curb in this period. Almost every important upward move in the middle and late 1920s was the result of activities of one pool or another. The pools were not then illegal; they did not violate the letter of the law or of Curb regulations. Nor were they secret; pool managers were known not only on Wall Street but to the nation at large. Investors and speculators of the time were supposed to know such things could happen: a stock would rise or fall rapidly, for no apparent reason, as the result of pool operations. In the 1920s this added to the excitement of the game, and many investors took the chance of "riding a stock" in the hope of outguessing the pool managers or at least making a profit before the pool was dissolved.

Such was the case with the Thompson pool. The newspapers ran no major stories on Thompson as the stock rose, but Plummer was busy circulating rumors on the street. This was the way most Curb securities were bulled; the newspaper stories were reserved for Stock Exchange securities. Nor were the profits comparable to those obtainable at the Big Board. Hensel, Hoyt, and Rossi claimed the pool netted a profit of only $5,600. Such a pittance would not be worthy of note at the Stock Exchange. It would not have deserved notice in the press had it not been for Hensel's attempt to deny Plummer his commission. Plummer sued for his money in 1926, at which time Hensel testified quite openly about the pool's activities. The issue at question at the trial was not whether innocent customers had been duped, but whether Hensel owed Plummer money.

The important pools were organized in Big Board securities. The major organizers of pools—Harry Content, Mike Meehan, George Breen, William Danforth, Arthur Cutten, and Jesse Livermore—spent most of their time there, and usually ignored the Curb as not worth the trouble. Hoyt was not as important as these men, but even he did not consider Curb securities worth manipulating. One could obtain far more volume, interest, and profit at the Big Board. His return from the Thompson pool would appear to verify this.

The Curb produced not a single important speculator in the 1920s; all the sensational characters were at the Stock Exchange. When a Curb stock was finally seasoned enough to be taken for a ride, it would also be prepared for the move to the Stock Exchange. If a Curb broker wanted to participate in pools and had sufficient capital for the investment, he too would journey to Wall Street from Trinity Place.

This is not to say that the Curb lacked men prepared to take advantage of the public's lack of knowledge. At the Big Board the floor traders were plungers while the specialists were generally honest, according to the public standards of the day. The reverse was true at the Curb; there were not that many floor traders there during the 1920s, but the specialists were of a lower order of honesty than their Stock Market counterparts. One could expect an honest accounting and execution at the Stock Exchange; if the customer's order was executed at $40\frac{1}{2}$, it was reported as such. At the Curb a similar order might be reported at $40\frac{5}{8}$, with the specialist pocketing the extra eighth of a point. The Curb was not unaware of this practice, and attempted to end it, as the many rules violations brought before the floor committee indicate. It continued into the 1930s, and proved too widespread to control even then.

Another Curb problem lay in the execution of orders by floor representatives and two-dollar brokers. While most of them were reasonably efficient, they were not above attempting to make small amounts from trades given them to execute. The most common method of so doing was for the specialist and floor broker to enter into an agreement to raise the price for the order, and then split the difference between the true price and that charged between them. Or the floor broker might purchase shares for himself to raise the price artificially, then execute the order for his customer at the higher price by delivering the shares he had purchased a moment ago into the customer's account. A Stock Exchange broker of the time, David Salmon, wrote of a conversation he had with a friend, a two-dollar Curb broker, in the late 1920s.

> I remember another occasion, also, at a dinner to which my friend had invited me, when he told me in alcoholic confidence that, in spite of it having been a very quiet twelve hundred share day for him, he had nevertheless made $2,000.
>
> Now, my friend's share of the commission—he had to split his share with the firms that placed the orders with him—could have amounted to only $180. The difference between this amount and his day's winning—or $1,800—was made up by trading against his customers' orders.*

On another occasion the two-dollar broker offered a deal to Salmon: if he would give his firm's Curb business to him, the Stock Market broker would receive a "gift" of $500 a month. The broker turned the offer down, not because he knew the trades would be dishonest, but "because I couldn't afford to place myself in his power."

The Curb Market, then, was only a sideshow compared to what was happening at the Stock Exchange in the last phase of the great bull market of the 1920s. Speculation there mirrored what was happening on Wall Street.

When the crash came in October and November, Curb leaders issued optimistic statements. Both leaderships believed the sharp decline to be temporary, and made plans for a revival of business after the liquidations were completed. Curb brokers wore buttons reading "For Better Business Be Bullish" and "Prepare for Prosperity," with the head of an angry bull in the center of each. Brokers were urged to support President Hoover in his attempts to return the nation to an optimistic mood. As a sign of its faith in the future, the Curb leadership went ahead with its plans to purchase the Hamilton Building and

* David L. Salmon, as told to Dr. Edwin F. Bowers, *Confessions of a Former Customers' Man* (Vanguard, 1932), pp. 93–95.

construct an addition to the original Curb Market. The purchase was completed and the cornerstone for the Curb Market addition laid in 1931. Both projects left the treasury rather bare, but even then, in 1931, the leadership believed good times would soon return.

Meanwhile, the Market attempted to deal with problems created by the bear market. As prices fell in late 1929, those customers who had margin accounts were called upon to raise "more margin" or be sold out.* This created a great demand for "call money": the funds borrowed by margin customers against their securities. The higher the call rate, the more difficult it would be for customers to borrow, and if they could not borrow, stocks would collapse, causing greater demands for call money and still higher rates. The exchanges could do nothing to prevent this downward spiral, but they could create a market for call money so as to offer brokers the best rates possible. In April 1930, the Curb established such a "clearing house" on its floor. Funded by nine banks and trust companies, all of which were active in the call-money market, it brought together the banks and those who wanted funds in an auction market, and helped reconcile supply and demand.

In this way a market that had been quite active since the October 1929 crash became institutionalized a half year later. In so acting President Muller was taking cognizance of a pressing need among Curb brokers for assistance in serving the public. But the call-money post was not created as a public service. By then it was evident that the crash was not an aberration but the beginning of a long slide in values. As the liquidations continued, they threatened the positions of many specialists. These men needed a steady market in which to lighten their positions and salvage what they could. The call-money post was a step in that direction, and its heavy use from the first indicated the need was real. While there is no way of proving the

---

* If a customer purchased 100 shares of stock at $10 a share (for a total cost of $1,000), he might borrow up to 90 percent of the cost ($900 in this case) using the stock as collateral. Should the stock's price fall to below $9, the lender would ask the customer to raise additional collateral. If he could not, the position would be sold out at the market.

point, it is probable that it saved the business career of more than one broker.*

As part of the same program, the board "urged care be taken to salvage as much as possible of the firm's assets" in the cases of those corporations in the process of bankruptcy. This was stated in April and again in October. Many Curb-listed and unlisted companies, not so well capitalized as their Big Board counterparts, were in the grips of the decaying economy and filing bankruptcy statements, while there was little demand for new issues coming to the marketplace. Each bankruptcy added to the pessimism in the district and the nation at large, and the board wanted to do all it could to raise the level of confidence. Specialists were urged to do what they could to assist those firms whose shares they dealt in. What could these men do? During the lush years of the late 1920s a specialist might take an interest in such companies and their problems and opportunities, for this knowledge would aid him in his work and open possibilities for speculation. Such was not the case in late 1930, however, and the specialists rushed to save their own hides, ignoring the pleas.

The Curb leadership realized the difficult situation of the whole securities industry. Seeking a scapegoat for the depression, the newspapers fixed attention on Wall Street, which by late 1930 was the accepted symbol for the failure of capitalism to sustain the boom. In Albany there was talk of a revival of the investigations of the early 1920s.** Several congressional leaders spoke of the need for other investigations, to take place soon after the 1930 elections. It was urgent, then, for the dis-

---

* The importance of the call-money post was underlined by the way Muller put it into operation. In a rare show of power, and in violation of the constitution, Muller established the post without the prior consent or vote of the board.

** The talk of investigations might have worried Governor Franklin D. Roosevelt, who even then prepared for the presidential race in 1932. Roosevelt had been involved in several speculative schemes in the 1920s. He had been an officer and director of Consolidated Automatic Merchandising Corporation and president of United European Investors, Ltd., both extremely speculative ventures and the kinds of firms and underwritings certain to be investigated by state and federal probers.

trict to clean house as soon as possible. Commission deals and pooling would have to be stopped, or at least moderated. Marginal brokers must be swept off the floor. The financial district had to be made to appear less of a gambling den than it had been during the past half-decade.

Parts of the task were easy to accomplish. By late 1930 many of the marginal men and securities had already left the district, destroyed by the crash. In other respects, however, petty thievery actually increased. Unable to join large pools, and in desperate need of funds, floor brokers and specialists continued and even accelerated their work in bilking those relatively few customers who remained. The boards of both the New York and Curb exchanges must have known this was happening, but because of sympathy, conviction, or class feeling they did little to end such abuses. Their record in this regard had been poor in the affluent 1920s. How could they now interfere when some of them were desparately attempting to remain solvent?

The situation was acute at the Curb. If the board cracked down on its members, it might increase outside criticism by exposing corruption and wrongdoing, though at the same time such actions would indicate that a self-regulation process existed and that none was needed from the outside. Should the board look the other way, the practices would continue and perhaps even grow. But for the moment the public would not learn of them; before it did, the brokers could salvage their positions somewhat.

In effect, the leadership was obliged to chose between reform and a purge that might save the Curb on the one hand, and the continuation of a lax administration, which could save the brokers but might eventually destroy the Market.

It was a difficult decision, one the Curb leadership divided upon and ultimately avoided making formally. When it became apparent that the New York Stock Exchange would defy both Washington and Albany, the Curb followed suit. Meanwhile, there were no investigations by the board of Curb activities. Nor was there a concerted effort to single out wrongdoers and punish them. Indeed, there were fewer disciplinary actions against brokers in 1930 than there had been during the previous year, a sign that the committee on business conduct and the brokers themselves were unwilling to interfere with salvage activities of their fellows. The board limited itself to admonitions against wrongdoing, often couched in sentiments vaguely reminiscent of the Edwardian era.

There was no tradition of harsh discipline at the Curb, and the board consisted of men who themselves were faced with the problems of making livings in a rapidly shrinking market. In 1929 stock volume at the Curb Market had reached a record high of 476 million shares.* In each of the next four years the figure was halved, to 222 million shares in 1930, 110 million in 1931, and 57 million—or slightly above the 1923 level—in 1932. Little wonder, then, that specialists and floor brokers shaved eighths and quarters for a few extra dollars in earnings.

Many investors, now convinced common stocks were poor investments but still believing recovery possible, switched their accounts into bonds. As stock volume fell, bond volume rose, from $514 million (principal amount) in 1929 to $864 million in 1930 and $952 million in 1932. Many bond traders did well in the early years of the depression. Indeed, such trading was an important barometer of investor interest in securities in general. In 1935, bond volume reached an all-time peak of $1,171 million. Then it declined, hitting $442 million in 1937 and falling still further in the years that followed. Yet during this period of prosperity for bond brokers, several were brought before the administration for admonitions. It could not be claimed, then, that bad times alone led brokers to break rules; even those who prospered were guilty of offenses.

The tendency of the Muller administration was to tread water until it discovered which way the tide was going, and then go along with it. As far as the Curb was concerned, the tide was controlled by the Stock Exchange. At the time of the 1929 crash the Stock Exchange's president was E. H. H. Sim-

---

* Not until 1961, when volume reached 488,831,037 shares would the 1929 record be bettered.

mons, an able but colorless man. Then, in 1931, Richard Whitney took the helm. Whitney was a handsome, somewhat flamboyant individual, and an aristocrat to the core. He had attended Groton and Harvard, married the daughter of the president of the Union League Club, and was associated with J. P. Morgan & Co.

Whitney saw himself as the defender of Wall Street against those who would intrude upon its rights of self-government. When asked whether outside regulation was needed on Wall Street, Whitney's answer was quick and to the point. "You gentlemen are making a great mistake," he said. "The Exchange is a perfect institution."

Muller was content to go along with the Whitney line. During the remainder of his administration the Curb's leadership said little, permitting Whitney to speak for the entire financial community. Then, in February of 1932, the Curb gave Whitney a further sign of its endorsement. Muller stepped down as president and in his place Howard Sykes, another aristocrat, pledged cooperation with the Big Board. Groton and Harvard were fine symbols for the old order, but so were Hotchkiss and Yale. With men like Whitney and Sykes, the financial community attempted to regroup and defend itself against the reform elements gathering in Washington and Albany.

+S I X –

The Reluctant Reformers

Howard Sykes served as Curb president from February 1932 to February 1934. These were two difficult years in American financial history, and particularly perilous for the Curb. Throughout the period many Americans felt revolution was a real possibility in the United States. "I am not ashamed to record that in those days I felt and said I would be willing to part with half of what I had if I could be sure of keeping, under law and order, the other half," wrote speculator Joseph P. Kennedy. "Then it seemed that I should be able to hold nothing for the protection of my family."

Kennedy and other Wall Street figures recognized the dangers inherent in political and economic collapse, but they continued trading at the exchanges. Kennedy, Ben Smith, Floyd Odlum, and other bears led raids against stocks not very different from the bull pools of the late 1920s, reaping huge gains in the process. Both the New York and Curb exchanges saw major speculative efforts in the 1932–34 period, and the public knew of them. Now the leaders were villains, not heroes, and demands for reform were made in Albany and Washington.

Sykes and Stock Exchange President Richard Whitney firmly believed in self-regulation. Both men had recollections of earlier panics and depressions, which had ended without important government intervention, and they assumed the same would happen in the early 1930s. They also knew that such periods were usually followed by investigations of Wall Street and demands for regulatory legislation, and they opposed any attempt to put fetters on their activities. Leaders at both exchanges had memories of how J. P. Morgan saved the nation's financial integrity in 1907, during a panic that President Theodore Roosevelt had been powerless to halt. The Federal Reserve System, the major financial innovation resulting from the progressive period, was written in large part by businessmen and business-minded legislators, and during the 1920s administered by pro-business governors. If reform were to come, said Whitney and Sykes, let it come that way. Wall Street and Trinity Place could clean its own house, with no help from Albany and Washington. Investigations would cause more harm than good, for they might lead to an erosion of confidence in the nation's financial institutions. Too, at radical times such as the early 1930s, hot-headed reformers might convince others that the district should be eliminated or, even worse, "socialized." This would be a sign, thought Whitney, that a Soviet America had become a reality. To men like Whitney and Sykes, the financial district was the major symbol of democracy and free enterprise. Regulate it from the outside, or in any other way curb its freedom, and the Constitution itself might be next to go. The exchanges' presidents, then, viewed their roles as defending not only the district, but the nation itself.

Whitney and Sykes did little to reform their exchanges in 1932. Both men admitted that abuses existed and that speculation had been rampant in the late 1920s, but said that institutional changes would not have prevented the crash. Had the exchanges forbidden speculation in the late 1920s, the speculators would have found other places to operate—perhaps a revived Consolidated Stock Exchange. As it was, the New York and Curb exchanges had been run honestly, they claimed, and all a gambler could expect was an honest wheel. "You are trying to deal with human nature," opined Whitney later. "Speculation is always going to exist in this country just as long as we are Americans." To the nation's financial leaders, regulation of speculation would be as futile as regulation of alcohol. Prohibition had just failed, they said, and it would be foolish to institute a new prohibition to take its place. Was America to rid itself of speakeasies just to have a revival of bucket shops? Firm regulation, such as that demanded by reformers in the early 1930s, would cause the speculators to go underground, and set off a crime wave as bad as that the nation suffered through in the 1920s. This could be avoided through self-regulation. The district would be purged of marginal speculators. Existing exchange rules would be scrupulously enforced. That would suffice.

Along with most of the financial district's leaders, Sykes supported Hoover in the 1932 election, fearing what Roosevelt might bring to Washington. In early 1933, as parts of the Roosevelt program appeared in the press, Sykes spoke out on his ideas as to the cause of the depression and its cure. After noting that the depression would soon end, he warned against excessive spending programs. The nation needed a sound and stable currency, a balanced federal budget, and governmental economy, he said. If, as indicated, Roosevelt embarked on an inflationary financial program, the nation would suffer. As he was wont to do, Sykes referred to the British experience. When Britain went off the gold standard, he said, the supply of pounds sterling increased, causing a decrease in purchasing power. This in turn resulted in "disorder and unsettlement of investment confidence," and further chaos on the financial markets.

Then Sykes turned to the situation on Wall Street and Trinity Place. In March he charged that most of the blame was to be found in excessive speculation—unscrupulous individuals manipulating securities to their own advantage. The exchanges themselves had nothing to do with this, he said. Some of the speculators had been ruined in the crash, and laws might be considered to end the activities of those who remained. The Curb Exchange itself was free from blame.

> In all cases where securities dealt in upon an exchange are the subject of unscrupulous activities, the Exchange is vigilant to prevent the consummation of such nefarious schemes. To suspend dealings in any security when convinced that fraudulent

practices are being used is a powerful deterrent and always a remedy. With an exchange stock, the quotations serve as a selling argument, and it is of vital importance to the investing public, as well as to the welfare of the institution, that the unwarranted forcing up of prices as the basis of extended selling campaigns should be prevented.

Sykes further claimed that several corporations were attempting to manipulate the prices of their securities. "Occasionally a corporation itself, being in need of funds, would grant an option on a block of stock to be issued at various prices." Then the corporation's officers would plant rumors to attract public interest in the security. When its price rose, the officers would exercise their options and immediately sell the stock. "It may not be amiss for me to urge upon corporate officers the greatest caution in the giving of options," said Sykes. "The character of the optionee is of more importance than his financial responsibility."

Speculators, unprincipled corporation officers, and gulled investors were responsible for the ills of the financial district, continued Sykes. Public officials might well investigate them and pass legislation to curb their abuses. Why punish a storekeeper if his store becomes the hangout of criminals and fools? Such was Sykes's position throughout his administration.

Sykes spoke as New York State Attorney General John J. Bennett, Jr. prepared to investigate the Curb Exchange. Bennett's office had received complaints regarding listing practices at the Curb. Stocks admitted to unlisted trading had declined far more than the listed shares, and this led investors to demand an end to the practice. As Bennett put it,

> There is a widespread belief among the investing public that all securities traded on the Curb Exchange conform to the standards for listed securities established by that Exchange. The practice of admitting stocks and bonds to unlisted trading privileges presents an opportunity for serious abuses and my investigation will have for its object the elimination of this so-called unlisted trading.

Bennett noted that less than 1 percent of bond trading was in listed issues, and implied that the figure for stocks was not much higher. The Attorney General suggested that the Curb cease trading all unlisted securities or force the issuing firms to file appropriate papers. Given the situation in 1933, few firms would have applied; even if they had, they could not have met Curb requirements for listing. Thus, an enforcement of Bennett's suggestion would have destroyed the Curb Market.

Sykes vigorously opposed Bennett's plan. He defended unlisted trading, using the old argument that the exchange was performing a public service by providing a regulated open market for such shares and bonds. The exchange's methods of trading accurately reflected the forces of supply and demand, and enabled both the purchaser and seller to receive the best possible price. The alternative was to force unlisted securities to the over-the-counter market, he said, where prices were set by dealers. The would-be buyer or seller was at the mercy of such dealers, he claimed, and prices on the over-the-counter market had little relation to supply and demand factors. Sykes was seconded by former president Muller and Austin Neftel, former chairman of the listing committee. Neither man was responsive to suggestions that Curb prices were also rigged. Nor would Sykes produce records to substantiate his claims.

Bennett responded by announcing that in the future all hearings would be public, so the press could know how Curb leaders were dodging the issue. The Curb attitude stiffened; exchange counsel Lockwood informed him that no Curb officer would appear unless served with a subpoena. Nor would records be produced until and unless legal actions demanded it. At the same time Lockwood and Sykes acted to correct abuses: sixteen bonds and five foreign stocks—all unlisted—were removed from trading, and an announcement was released to the effect that more would follow. In this way, the Curb was prodded into reluctant reform.

Bennett's attack continued. On April 21 he charged the Curb with having continued the trading in Repetti, Inc., in 1929, even though it was public knowledge that the firm was insolvent. Another firm with unlisted shares, Standard Public Service, Inc., was also bankrupt, and yet the Curb permitted trading to continue, and several brokers manipulated the stock to their own advantage. One manipulator, Irving Walker, conceded he used "sucker lists" in his Standard Public Service manipulations. "You used high-pressure salesman's methods?" asked the committee counsel. "Well, if you call it that," was Walker's response. Then Irving Goldsmith, another broker, admitted to having alerted Walker to similar opportunities in Empire Trust Company stock, receiving in return a "finder's fee" of ten cents a share. This revelation was followed by an investigation of trading in a third unlisted security, Central Public Service. Its specialist, Frank Bethel, was told to bring his records to the committee, and a subpoena was served. Bethel appeared, but without the records. He claimed they were lost. His clerk corroborated the story, saying that he had been told by Bethel's former partner, "a Mr. Hyde," to "discard the records." Then the clerk and Bethel told the committee they had no idea where Hyde could be located.

Lockwood told the committee that such practices were not uncommon, since brokers could not be expected to keep the mountains of records they accumulated over the years. He insisted that no wrongdoing had taken place, and returned to the earlier claim that trading in unlisted securities was beneficial to the public.

Having made his point, Bennett turned to another charge. Not only did trading in unlisted securities lull the public into a belief they were of better-than-average quality, but such trading was contrary to the wishes of the companies whose securities were dealt in. Assistant Attorney General John McGohey read into the record the request of Maryland Casualty Company to have its stock removed. The letter was dated December 12, 1927. Austin Neftel admitted to having received the letter, and recommending that trading continue. Then McGohey asked, "In all there were forty-seven corporations who made requests to have their stock removed from trading because they did not know they were being traded on the exchange, were there not?" "I think so," was Neftel's reply.

With this Lockwood conceded defeat. He no longer attempted to defend the practice of unlisted trading as beneficial to all. When Bennett said the investigation had demonstrated "The existence of practices which, in my opinion, constitute serious abuses," Lockwood agreed. In a prepared statement, the Curb counsel said:

> The examination by the Attorney General has been of great value to the Curb Exchange in that it has shown the Exchange ways in which its so-called unlisted department might be strengthened in the interests of the investing public. The Exchange has already adopted principles whereby the future admission of dealings of such securities is predicated on the filing of additional information and the making of more searching analysis.
>
> The Exchange respectfully suggests to the Attorney General a temporary suspension of hearings in order that it may present to him certain requirements and rules which it believes will meet and eliminate all possible criticisms of the unlisted department. For that reason an adjournment until further notice is requested.

The inquiry was halted for three weeks in order to give Bennett an opportunity to examine the reforms. These were few in number, and relatively unimportant. In the future all companies whose shares or bonds were to be traded at the Curb would be notified of the fact and given an opportunity to protest. All protests would be considered by the Board, and if an equitable arrangement could not be arrived at, the shares or bonds would be removed from the list. Information similar to that required of listed securities would apply to the unlisted ones as well. Unlisted trading would continue.

Bennett accepted these changes as victory. In reality, he had little choice. The entire investigation had been conducted on a shoestring. Only four staff members had been assigned to it, and now they were needed for other work. In the depression year of 1933, New York State could not afford to continue an inquiry that might prove costly. So the scheduled examination of listed securities was never made. It would be the state's last major investigation of the securities market.

The Bennett investigation proved beneficial to the Curb, which was able to clean house before the federal investigations began the following year. Lockwood, Posner, and Miles had argued for reform during the past two years, but little had taken place. Frightened by the state probe, the Curb leaders began to set their affairs in order. The Stock Exchange, which was not investigated, took no such action. As a result, the Curb was better prepared for the congressional investigations of 1934.

The Curb also changed leadership, in part a result of the Bennett investigation. There had been no startling evidence of malfeasance uncovered; in no way had Howard Sykes been embarrassed by the probe. It was clear to all that the federal investigations, if and when they came, would be far tougher than those of the state. It also seemed evident that Curb practices throughout the 1920s would need defending, and a man of Sykes' personality and philosophy would not be the most effective person for the job. The Bennett investigation thrust Lockwood into the limelight, and he might have made a fine president. Lockwood was not a broker, however, and in any case had no interest in the position. He did stress the need for a new president whose activities had been beyond reproach, who could present a good face to the public, and who would defend vigorously the Exchange's right to survive.

By late 1933 the first of the New Deal measures to affect the securities industry had been signed into law. The Securities Act of 1933 required full disclosure of pertinent information by underwriters. This "truth in securities" law had been accepted with little dissent; Wall Street had come to think such an act wise and necessary if confidence were to be restored. The Banking Act of 1933 (more commonly known as the Glass-Steagall Act) was also passed. This measure established the Federal Deposit Insurance Corporation, and required commercial banks to divest themselves of their investment affiliates. This too had been expected, and caused few ripples on Wall Street. Late in 1933, however, it became known that President Roosevelt would ask for a measure to regulate the securities exchanges. This was an entirely different matter, one the leaderships of both exchanges reacted against vigorously. Stock Exchange President Whitney led the charge, and it was expected that he would be followed by the new president of the Curb Exchange.

Lockwood and Miles also opposed regulation, but, unlike Whitney, saw it as inevitable. They took the view that the Curb could live with regulation, but would die if the unlisted securities were removed from the market. They concentrated their attention on that issue, allowing the Big Board to say and do what it would in the area of regulation.

The new president, then, had to be a man acceptable to the Big Board, attractive to the public, a moderate insofar as politics was concerned, and willing to take a strong stand on the question of unlisted securities.

E. Burd Grubb was such a man. He was forty years old at the time, and a member of the Curb since 1923. Grubb had begun his Curb career as floor representative for McQuoid & Coady, but he soon joined Moffatt & Spear. He came to the board in 1931, and served on several committees, among them the committee on the clearing house, where he worked with his friend and mentor Fred Moffatt. Grubb was well-known at the Curb in 1934, and could always be counted upon to stand out in a crowd. He was handsome, gregarious, and well-spoken. His personal credentials would appear to have made him a natural ally of Sykes. Grubb was the son of a Civil War general, the nephew of T. O. M. Sopwith, the British aircraft designer and sportsman, and a sportsman in his own right. He served in World War I as a dispatch rider, and came out of the war a hero with a Croix de Guerre. In this period he won the middleweight boxing championship of the AEF, and afterward became one of the nation's finest amateur golfers. Grubb seemed an F. Scott Fitzgerald hero: the man Jay Gatsby would have wanted to be.

Grubb was popular at the Curb, respected as a man and friend. He was not considered a good broker; his interests didn't seem to be in that direction. He had native intelligence and a forceful way of speaking that masked his occasional lack of information or deep study. Grubb had little interest in politics, but believed reform was needed at the Curb. He disliked Sykes, and hoped the president would step down in 1934. Grubb intended to ask Moffatt to run for the post.

On learning of Sykes's intention to step down, Grubb visited Moffatt and asked him to run. Moffatt refused; he wisely realized that he lacked the personality needed at such a perilous moment, and besides, business was poor, and he couldn't afford to spare time from the brokerage to assume the presidency. Instead, he suggested that Grubb himself make the race. Grubb agreed, with the understanding he would accept a single term and then support Moffatt as his successor.

This solution pleased Lockwood, who had hoped a man like Grubb would accept the post. The new president would have to spend a good deal of his time in Washington dealing with federal officials. Sykes surely would have antagonized them; Moffatt would have appeared an indecisive man, someone who could be pushed around. Grubb, on the other hand, was forceful enough to make an impression, moderate enough to please Washington, and pliable enough to be influenced by Lockwood's strategies. The counsel wanted an attractive spokesman for the Curb Market, someone he could use as an echo chamber for his ideas, and yet a personality who would not be bullied by Whitney and others at the Big Board. In Grubb he found the man for the job.

Grubb took office in February 1934. Within three weeks he was in Washington to offer testimony on the proposed Fletcher-Rayburn bill, designed to regulate the stock exchanges. He hardly had sufficient time to master the intricacies of the subject, but such was not necessary. Lockwood was better equipped than he for the task, and prepared a good deal of the material Grubb used during the hearings. Grubb did understand the politics of the situation, and politics, not legalities, determined the official Curb position toward regulation.

The initial draft of the Fletcher-Rayburn bill placed restraints on the use of margin and declared illegal such activities as pools, matched orders, and other techniques employed "for the purpose of raising or depressing the price of . . . securities or for the purpose of creating . . . a false or misleading appearance of active trading." The Federal Trade Commission would regulate the markets and be entrusted with enforcement of the law. In itself this would have been a major change for the securities markets. In the past the federal government had investigated Wall Street, but never before had there been an attempt at continual and permanent regulation. Previous inquiries had been aimed at forcing the exchanges to cease certain practices and make reforms. At times congressmen spoke of the need for new legislation that the exchanges would have to follow or face criminal prosectuion. But the idea of an agency designed to take an active part in the running of the exchanges, to which the exchanges would answer, and which would have day-to-day powers, was novel. Ever since its beginnings the New York Stock Exchange had been committed to the principle of self-regulation. The Fletcher-Rayburn bill would end this by "putting a policeman at the corner of Wall and Broad." This, the Stock Market, speaking through Richard Whitney, vigorously opposed.

Only slightly less distasteful and radical was section 10 of the proposed bill. Under its terms brokers would be forbidden to trade for their own accounts or function as underwriters. This would eliminate all floor trading. It could easily be interpreted to mean that specialists could not buy and sell securities to "stabilize the market" in them. The bill read that specialists could not trade for their own account and could not buy or sell "except on fixed price orders." If accepted, this section would have ended the specialists' primary function—indeed, the measure would have ended any reason the specialists might have had to justify their existence. No longer could the specialist "make a market" in a stock; he would serve instead as a focal point for floor brokers, who themselves would make the markets between them on a negotiated basis. Section 10 might be interpreted as limiting exchange membership to commission brokers whose task it was to execute public orders. In terms of exchange structure, it would end the domination by specialists that had begun in the 1870s. Instead, the exchanges would be led by the floor traders and commission houses, which since that time had played a secondary role at the exchanges themselves, even though they had great power in the financial district. Needless to say, Richard Whitney, who spoke for the Stock Exchange—and therefore for the specialists—was adamant in his opposition to section 10.

The Curb Exchange occupied an uneasy position in this struggle between the New Deal and the Stock Exchange. Historically the Curb had always followed the Stock Exchange in its attitude toward outside regulation, the structure of the district, and view towards politics. This could be seen in the struggle with the Consolidated, but that was only one of many such examples. Curb leaders knew such a stance was a price that had to be paid for survival and prosperity. If Whitney opposed the New Deal, then, the Curb would have to follow his lead.

On the other hand, the Curb was also sensitive to governmental probers. It was not strong enough to stand firm against demands for change. This happened in the North American Steel case, when, as we have seen, Untermyer's threat by itself was sufficient to cause a change in policy. The recently ended Bennett Investigation was an even more striking example of this, when the Curb Exchange bowed before the will of the New York State Attorney General. The Stock Exchange could have withstood both challenges; the Curb could and would not do so.

The division of power at the Curb was different from that at the Stock Exchange, and this also complicated matters. In 1934 the Stock Exchange was controlled by the specialists. At that time the Curb specialists controlled their own market, but the floor brokers—representatives of the large commission houses—had a powerful veto over day-to-day operations, just as the Stock Exchange specialists could oblige the Curb to change its basic strategy. Without the floor brokers, the Curb would lose almost all its business; without acceptance by the Stock Exchange Establishment, the Curb could be crushed.

In March of 1934, a division developed in the district over the proper response to the Fletcher-Rayburn bill. Whitney was strongly opposed to it, and mounted a massive offensive against strict regulation. He would go so far as to accept "supervision" of new legislation by a "new board of seven members," which would include two Stock Exchange officials, the Secretary of the Treasury, and the Secretary of Commerce. As he understood it, the board would be dominated by the Stock Exchange

—in other words, it would be disguised self-regulation, or at least Stock Exchange enforcement of federal statutes. Furthermore, Whitney would have new legislation drawn loosely and interpreted in a manner that he called "flexible and mobile."

Whitney's opposition to the Fletcher-Rayburn bill was seconded by representatives of the regional exchanges, who claimed they could not survive if it were passed. Local underwritings would be impossible if the bill were strictly enforced, said W. W. Gradison of the Cincinnati Stock Exchange. Only the New York capital market could survive the regulations, and so the affect of the law would be to concentrate power on Wall Street instead of diffusing it through the nation, as the framers claimed they desired. Gradison and other representatives of the regional exchanges thus took stands behind Whitney and asked for the defeat of the measure.

There was an element on Wall Street that supported the proposed bill. The large commission houses, which dealt directly with the public and which could not revive unless confidence in the securities industry was restored, asked for passage of the bill. The specialists had little contact with the public, and did not realize how strong anti–Wall Street sentiment had become, they said. Until and unless the investing public believed the exchanges were honest and stocks worthy of purchase, volume would stagnate. Roosevelt had saved the banks through the instrumentality of deposit insurance. Now a depositor knew that his savings were insured by a federal agency. This was not possible at the exchanges, but if investors felt that federal presence at the securities markets guaranteed honesty in dealings and prices, a measure of confidence might be restored, and with it a higher volume of trading.

The commission houses were not overjoyed with the idea of regulation, but they saw no alternative to it. Speaking through the Association of Stock Market Firms, the commission houses testified in favor of the Fletcher-Rayburn bill. Such influential brokers as James V. Forrestal of Dillon, Read; Robert A. Lovett of Brown Brothers, Harriman; and E. A. Pierce of E. A. Pierce & Co. either spoke out at hearings of the Senate Banking Committee and the House Interstate Commerce Committee or through the newspapers, and endorsed the main lines of the measure.*

What was the Curb Exchange to do in such a situation? Whatever stand Lockwood and Grubb might take, they would antagonize one or the other of their two patrons. Lockwood knew the commission houses were not acting entirely in the public interest; if section 10 passed, they would benefit enormously at the expense of the specialists. Still, he had to make certain he left the stand with both their support and that of the Stock Exchange. Overriding even the regulatory issue was that of unlisted securities. There was a chance for the Curb to survive without the good will of either the specialists at the Stock Exchange or the commission houses, but if unlisted securities were banned from the Curb, it would collapse. Under the terms of the Fletcher-Rayburn bill, such might be the case. Though it went unmentioned in the press and was hardly discussed in Washington, Lockwood knew that if it was interpreted strictly, the bill would effectively destroy the Curb Exchange.

Grubb and Lockwood decided to divide the work between them. Grubb would testify on the issue of regulation, the one that interested most committee members and the country as a whole, while Lockwood would concentrate on the issue of unlisted securities.

On February 27, while Whitney testified before the Senate Banking Committee, Grubb appeared before the House Interstate Commerce Committee. He told the members that regulation was needed—but of a mild variety. Grubb thought the Whitney proposal for a regulatory body should be substituted for the Fletcher-Rayburn version:

> Study of the admitted problems by a highly intelligent body, expert in the various branches of the subject, in advance of the imposition of drastic rules, is of the utmost importance, and to

---

* This division on Wall Street would become important later on. In 1940, when Roosevelt restructured his administration to deal with the problems of war, he called several of the pro–Fletcher-Rayburn brokers to Washington and offered them positions in the government.

the end that evils or dangers are shown to exist and may be ob-
viated or minimized, the Exchange is in full sympathy.

In this way, Grubb tried to establish himself as a moderate, one willing to accept and even support regulation, and
then go further, to study the problem and perhaps give still
greater powers to the regulatory commission. His statement
and testimony won Whitney's approval without alienating the
Association of Stock Market Firms. Privately he told Whitney
that the plan had little hope of success; all the district could
hope for was a modification of some aspects of the draft law, especially section 10.

Grubb appeared before the Senate Banking Committee on
March 7. He told the committee that the proposed measure
"goes beyond the exchanges and their memberships in an effort
to extend a powerful Federal influence over the capital structure of the country."

> The Curb Exchange believes that it has adopted rules and reg-
> ulations to prevent manipulative practices which, when all
> things are considered, are at the bottom of great swings in the
> market. It does not believe that any rules will obviate rises and
> falls in the price of securities. Stabilization, in the last analysis,
> depends upon economic conditions and public psychology.

Nevertheless, he added, the Curb Exchange was prepared
to recommend the licensing of exchanges and the enactment of
prohibitions against certain manipulative practices "which fan
the flames of public buying."

Once again, Grubb managed to please both sides in the
conflict, and maintained friendships among the commission
brokers and the Stock Exchange specialists. He had done his
job well.

Lockwood was charged with the delicate and difficult task
of convincing the committee to permit continued trading in
unlisted securities at the Curb Exchange. In so doing he
adopted a reform position. Throughout its history, he said, the
Curb had continually attempted to raise standards for both securities and traders. He cited recent reforms made during the
Bennett inquiry as an example of this effort. Then he noted

that the Curb was a public exchange, one open to all who wished to buy and sell, and an institution that could be regulated by whatever agency Congress established. Its brokers were known and highly visible; they could be seen trading by any who wished to come. The Curb had a regulatory mechanism, which could he improved upon if necessary, but which was being reformed in any case while he talked.

What was the alternative to this market? What would happen if unlisted trading were banned from securities exchanges? First of all, it would destroy the Curb Exchange. Some 82 percent of all Curb transactions were in unlisted securities, and without them there would be no possibility for the market to survive. These securities would still be traded however—at the over-the-counter market. This market was conducted over the telephones, had no central location, and could be entered into by almost anyone. The difficulties of regulating the over-the-counter trading were enormous, probably insurmountable. Nor did the over-the-counter market maintain standards for securities, in contrast to the Curb's ever-higher ones. Prices were set by dealers, claimed Lockwood, and not by the forces of supply and demand, as at the Curb Exchange. In all, he concluded, there was no public interest to be served by having the unlisted stocks—valued at $17 billion at the time—traded over-the-counter.

In time Congress might decide to force the over-the-counter market into a central location, where it could more easily be observed and regulated. Such was the situation at the Curb in 1934. Why destroy a viable and working institution only to have to recreate it in a different guise but essentially the same form at some future date?

Lockwood's reasoning was convincing. When the final bill emerged from committee, the section on listed and unlisted securities was quite different from what it had been in the original version.

The Securities Exchange Act provided for the registration of all listed securities with the SEC. The Commission was to empower a study group to look into the matter of unlisted securities and report back with suggestions. These would be incorporated into the original act in the form of an amendment.

The study was made, and embodied in section 12(f) of the Act as amended. Its provisions were contained in three clauses. The first provided that any security admitted to unlisted trading privileges on an exchange prior to March 1, 1934, could be continued on that exchange. Clause 2 set down the conditions under which a security might be admitted to unlisted trading rights in the future. It stated that an exchange could apply for unlisted trading privileges in a stock registered under the Act as a fully listed stock on some other exchange, provided the exchange could establish that the stock had a widespread distribution and enjoyed an active market in the "vicinity of the exchange." Clause 2 would not be used by the Curb, since all it did was to open to it securities fully listed on regional exchanges. But it was of great importance to the regional exchanges, since it enabled them to bring in for unlisted trading privileges many Curb and Stock Exchange securities that were fully listed on the New York exchanges.

Clause 3 was of great importance to the Curb. It provided that any exchange could admit to unlisted trading privileges a security that had not been fully listed and registered with the SEC provided the exchange could also establish that there was an active market and widespread public distribution in the vicinity of the exchange. The law also stated that in order to qualify for unlisted trading under this clause, the issuing company had to be subject to substantially the same duties and obligations as a fully listed company.

It seemed to Lockwood that this clause held great promise for the Curb in the future, though it meant little in 1934. What might happen, for example, if the SEC obliged *all* companies to submit specified information, such as financial statements, proxies, and stock-ownership reports? In such a situation the Curb could raid the over-the-counter market freely, probably with SEC blessing, and enlarge its list enormously. In effect, clause 3 gave the Curb Exchange a vested interest in a strong, vigorous Securities and Exchange Commission, enforcing stiff regulations and adding to them. At the same time, an active and reform-minded SEC would also serve as a spur to all exchanges to rid themselves of disreputable men and securities. Without the SEC, the Curb might have become a semi-slum of American finance capitalism; in 1935 it seemed to a few Curb leaders that a strong SEC could enable the market to gain new respectability and at the same time enlarge the list of securities by picking and choosing what it wanted from the over-the-counter market.

These hopes never materialized, but they persisted throughout the 1930s. The SEC lost its vigor soon after, and the Curb reverted to old ways. For a while, however, the Curb Exchange became a far more enthusiastic supporter of the SEC than the Stock Exchange and even the regionals. Lockwood had gone to Washington in the hope of salvaging unlisted trading; he returned to New York with a promise of great benefits and the hope of new prosperity for the Curb, accomplished in such a way as to benefit both brokers and investors.

Whitney and Grubb also won a victory that, if not as impressive as Lockwood's, was far more widely heralded. Section 10 was eliminated from the final draft; the specialists would remain in control of the Stock Exchange, and Wall Street's Establishment would be given an opportunity to save itself. Congress rejected Whitney's proposed seven-man commission, and at the same time took operation of the Act from the FTC. Instead, the final draft provided for the establishment of a Securities and Exchange Commission which would be given power to enforce both the Securities Act of 1933 and the Securities Exchange Act of 1934, as well as any amendments or new acts that might pass in the future.

The revised measure passed the House by a vote of 280–84 and the Senate by a vote of 62–13. President Roosevelt signed it into law on June 6, 1934.

Whitney and Grubb hoped the SEC would be manned and headed by individuals sympathetic to the industry, though they understood that that was too much to expect. Still, there were Wall Streeters who had supported the Fletcher-Rayburn bill with reservations, but at the same time remained part of the Establishment. John M. Hancock of Lehman Brothers, Dean Witter, and James Auchincloss were prominent in this group. Assistant Secretary of Commerce John Dickinson was known to Wall Streeters, and at the same time was popular with New Dealers; he was thought a good choice for the post of chairman. Anti-business New Dealers hoped Ferdinand Pecora, James Landis, George Matthews, and University of Chicago president Robert Hutchins would be named, with Hutchins as chairman.

Three members of the five-member board pleased the reformers. Pecora, Landis, and Matthews represented this group. Robert Healy of the FTC, only slightly more moderate, was the fourth member. The fifth member and chairman was a surprise and delight to many in the financial district. Joseph P. Kennedy, a former Wall Street speculator who only a few months earlier had been engaged in the very kind of operations that the Securities Exchange Act declared illegal, was named by Roosevelt in what the *New York Times* called a "bombshell." The appointment was political: Roosevelt owed Kennedy a debt of gratitude for having supported him prior to his nomination for the presidency in 1932. He also realized Kennedy would be acceptable to financial leaders, and help balance the other four members of the board. Finally, as one writer indicated, Roosevelt was setting a former thief to work catching the other thieves. More likely, however, was the view that F.D.R. in this way tried to soothe feelings at Wall and Broad, and heal the breach created by the congressional hearings.

In mid-September the SEC members visited New York to establish contacts with the exchanges. At that time the report on unlisted securities was still in preparation, but Curb leaders already knew the securities would not be removed from their floor. Kennedy and the others visited the floor, chatted with brokers, and discussed common problems with Grubb, Lockwood, and other Curb leaders. The meeting was friendly. Regulation had come to Trinity Place, and it wasn't so bad as had been feared a year before.

+S E V E N –

The Dismal Years

The Great Depression would last until World War II. Not until American factories were called upon to provide arms and munitions for the Allies would true economic recovery take place. On several occasions in the 1930s it appeared the business cycle had taken an upward turn. These were false signals, and were followed by new declines and a further loss of confidence. The nation seemed to have lost its ability to find proper solutions for economic problems. President Roosevelt was able to maintain his popularity through much of the decade, and prevent the institution of radical programs that might have brought recovery—but at the price of destroying or at least drastically modifying the nation's political, economic, and social fabric.

The American business community was the scapegoat for these difficulties, and the New York financial district its prime symbol. Never before or since has the reputation of the American businessman been so low. As for Wall Street, it was able to withstand reform demands for drastic change and radical cries for its elimination. The district survived not so much as a result of its own wisdom and strength, but due to the inability of reform elements to combine on a single program and Roosevelt's reluctance to press for drastic and far-reaching changes.

115

The district's sufferings were not limited to those involving reputations. Business was extremely poor during the 1930s. As the economy stagnated, fewer firms came to the market to sell new securities, and those that did attempted to float ever-smaller issues. The market for these stocks and bonds was poor; investors either had lost confidence in securities or hadn't the funds to buy them. Bond and stock yields soared, with no takers. Although SEC Chairman Kennedy was able to end a so-called "capital strike," in which firms refused to float new issues in protest against F.D.R.'s programs, when they did they found little interest in new issues.

Most Stock Exchange brokers who survived the 1929 crash thought they would be able to "hold on" until conditions corrected themselves. The correction did not come, and each year more and more were obliged to leave the district. A large majority of these men were able to find positions elsewhere; the 1929 crash had alerted them to the dangers of failure, so that by 1930 Stock Exchange brokers were busily renewing contacts with friends and other industries, in preparation for a new career if the old one went sour. Although Stock Exchange firms went out of business, its members often had sufficient funds to live comfortably, for a while at least. And, given family connections and their status, they knew they would not be out on the street if and when an orderly closing of the old firm took place.

The situation was different at the Curb Market. The brokers there had money in 1928, but their status was still uncertain. More often than not, their contacts and friends were men like themselves: the kind of people who would be unable or unwilling to help them if the depression continued for very long. Few Curb brokers had private fortunes; most had all their assets tied up in their brokerage operations. Many specialists, on the edge of failure and wanting to leave the securities industry, found they could not do so, simply because they could find no better positions elsewhere. Brokers who in the late 1920s had earned excellent livings from their operations were now reduced to a slightly better than a subsistence level of income. There were times when Curb brokers, traveling from their homes to Trinity Place for Saturday morning activities, would spend more money for carfare and lunch than they earned in commissions. Tattered and frayed shirt and jackets were not the rule in the middle and late 1930s, but they were to be seen on the floor.

Many brokers sought part-time jobs to supplement their Curb earnings. Brokers would leave the district at four o'clock and go to Railway Express, where they put in eight hours on the night shift. Or they would use connections to get a job sorting mail at the post office. A few drove taxis, trucks, or vans. Some were able to get back-office jobs as clerks at Stock Exchange firms; they were the fortunate ones, and the best trained. At a time when millions of Americans were out of work (the unemployed in 1933 reached 12.8 million, almost a quarter of the labor force), no Curb broker went hungry. But peanut-butter sandwiches in a brown bag took the place of lunches at exclusive clubs, and one-bedroom walk-ups the place of fine houses in The Bronx or Brooklyn or duplexes in Manhattan.

This fall from wealth was hard on young brokers, the men who had come to the district after 1921. Older Curb brokers took the depression more in stride, for they had had experience with such periods prior to World War I. In the recent past, however, such dismal periods had ended after only a few years. The last prolonged depression period for the financial industry had occurred in the 1880s and early 1890s, and not many brokers remembered it or were prepared for a repetition of the experience.

Finally, the brokers assumed that business would pick up when a measure of growth and confidence returned to the economy. This was not to be. The economic depression would end around 1940, to be replaced by the wartime boom. The depression lingered longer in the financial district, the upswing coming in 1945, quickly followed by another decline. Not until the early 1950s would a sustained advance take place in the financial district. By that time, brokers at both the Stock Exchange and the Curb Exchange had developed a depression mentality that was hard to overcome or change. For twenty years, then, American finance would be depressed, and brokers would undergo a time of low returns, small commissions, and, for salaried employees, low wages.

The Curb's statistics tell part of the story. The price of a Curb seat reached a high of $254,000 just before the 1929 crash. Then began a steady decline that continued throughout much of the decade and did not "bottom out" until World War II. As we shall see, a Curb seat would exchange hands at $650 in 1942.

Price of a Seat at the Curb Market, 1929–39

Year	First	High	Low	Last
1929	$150,000	$254,000	$150,000	$160,000
1930	140,000	225,000	70,000	95,000
1931	100,000	137,500	38,000	38,000
1932	40,000	55,000	16,500	30,000
1933	30,000	50,000	25,000	25,000
1934	31,000	40,000	17,000	20,000
1935	21,000	33,000	12,000	30,000
1936	38,000	48,000	26,000	34,000
1937	34,000	35,000	17,500	17,500
1938	15,500	17,500	8,000	12,000
1939	12,000	12,000	7,000	8,500

Source: *Amex Databook*, p. 12

The market for seats also declined in this period, when there were more sellers than buyers. Sixty-eight changed hands in 1929; 25 were transferred in 1939, and only 14 the following year.

This decline was due in part to the loss of confidence in Wall Street, but more to the lower volume of trading in the 1930s. As has been noted, stock volume declined from 476 million shares in 1929 to 57 million in 1932. There was some recovery thereafter, but the trend was downward. Furthermore, the average price per listed and unlisted share declined throughout the period, reaching $12.26 in 1939. It would fall to $8.47 in 1941 before recovering during and after the war. Lower-priced stocks brought lower commissions, so although the decline in trading volume was not as sharp as that in the price of the Curb seat, commissions were hard hit.

Annual Stock Volume on the
Curb Exchange, 1932–39

Year	Volume
1932	57,108,543
1933	100,916,602
1934	60,050,695
1935	75,747,764
1936	134,845,196
1937	104,178,804
1938	49,640,238
1939	45,729,888

Source: *Amex Databook*, p. 30

The market value of all stocks listed on the Curb was in excess of $25 billion in 1929; in 1939 the figure was $7.6 billion. There were 1,745 listed and unlisted common and preferred issues in 1928, and 1,077 in 1939. In 1929 the common stock turnover ratio was over 50 percent; in 1939 it was 6.7 percent.

Million-share days were not noteworthy in the last months of the 1929 bull market. There were no million-share days in the 1930s, and many days when volume fell below 100,000 shares. The daily average for 1939 was 183,654; in 1942 it would reach a record low average of 89,566.

The statistical record corroborated the human story. Little wonder, then, that many brokers of that period were pessimistic about their personal futures and that of security and finance capitalism.

Grubb's major task after passage of the Securities Exchange Act was to make certain the Curb market conformed to those provisions that applied to it and assure the members the exchange would not go under. He was convinced the latter would not be possible without the former. Rarely had the Curb been able to stand on its own, without the support and patronage of other, larger, and more powerful institutions. Only when assured of government support prior to World War I had the Curb defied the Stock Exchange even mildly, and the move indoors in 1921 had been made in the same spirit. Once again the Curb found itself allied with the government, and tacitly at least opposed to Stock Exchange attitudes. Throughout the 1930s the Stock Exchange criticized the SEC and accepted its authority reluctantly. Not so the Curb. Grubb and Moffatt not only accepted the SEC, they did so with more enthusiasm than some Stock Exchange leaders thought seemly.

In this period of declining business and possible closing, the Curb Exchange as an institution and brokers as individuals had to face a choice, one not too dissimilar from that a suspected criminal would have. The Curb could "go clean," watch its step in all matters, and cooperate fully with the SEC. If it took this path, profits might be low, but at least they would be safe. On the other hand, Curb brokers faced with declining earnings might try to shave fractions, enter into small pools, and in other ways supplement their commissions. If discovered, however, they and their organization would be condemned, and perhaps closed down. The Curb leadership realized this, as did most brokers. They chose the former course. As a result, the Curb Exchange was cleaner and less corrupt in the mid-1930s than it had been at any previous time in its history. This is not to say that a few brokers did not violate the rules, or that all the manipulations of the 1920s had ended. Rather, they were fewer in number and smaller in scope, and brokers would refuse to enter into them in fear of what might happen if found out. Grubb made certain everyone understood this through vigorous prosecution of whatever wrongdoers were discovered.

Early in the summer of 1934 Grubb and Lockwood commuted between New York and Washington, making certain the Curb Exchange fulfilled all requirements of the new law. Francis Adams Truslow, the Curb's junior counsel, remained in Washington much of the time, working directly with Commission members and lawyers, and drawing up questionnaires and forms for Curb members and listed unlisted companies. Truslow would confer with a Commission lawyer, often Sherlock Davis, to discover what would be needed. Then he would retire to construct the regulation or write the questionnaire, after which he would submit it to the SEC for approval. This work was not completed until early October.

The result was a 765-page presentation, including exhibits and schedules, which was made available to the SEC and the Curb Exchange brokers. It was accepted by both without additions, and the Commission complimented the Curb Exchange on its efficiency and willingness to cooperate, while Davis indicated "amazement" that the task had been completed so rapidly.

Meanwhile, the Curb administration prepared applications for permission to temporarily continue unlisted trading for 1,432 individual securities, and filed large numbers of papers for each. At the same time, substantial work was done to fully register the 362 listed securities. Grubb estimated that in a four-month period some quarter of a million items were completed and filed to satisfy all the new regulations. The bulk of the work was done in the last three weeks in September, when Grubb, Lockwood, and the Curb administration and clerks worked fourteen-hour days and seven-day weeks.

Lockwood was also charged with drawing up the papers that would enable the Curb Exchange to become a national securities market under the terms of the new law. This task was completed in late August and sent off to Washington, where it was quickly approved.

Grubb notified the press of all these activities, and proved an excellent publicity man and "image maker" for the Curb Exchange. Although news of the Stock Exchange continued to dominate the financial pages, items about the Curb and its activities were now more common than they had been during the Sykes administration. These news items were uniformly favorable; they presented a picture of an organization intent on reform, eager to cooperate with the government, and open to public scrutiny. Grubb took pains to deny all rumors that the Curb might go out of business. On August 22, bleary-eyed and tired from working all night directing the processing of forms, Grubb told reporters that he had been asked by several of them whether the Curb might soon close down. "I emphatically answer no," he said. "We are definitely not going out of business. Nothing is farther from our thoughts or anticipations." He said the members also were confident of the Curb's future—an exaggeration, to be sure, but a necessary one given the circumstances. "If any one sought to sell a Curb Exchange seat today, he would receive a price somewhat above the last sale," which was $18,500, he added. All realized such a seat had sold for over a quarter of a million dollars in 1929, and as recently as March a seat was transferred at $40,000. Yet the fact that the price had appeared to have stabilized, and that it still was worth $18,500 or so, indicated at least some measure of confidence that a closing would not take place that year.

Grubb had taken the job with the understanding it would be for a single term, after which he would turn it over to Fred Moffatt. He was successful in all his activities and achieved his objectives, although this would not have been possible without the work of Lockwood and Truslow. When he stepped down in February 1935, Grubb did so with the gratitude of most brokers and the admiration of the SEC. At the same time, he had kept contacts with the Stock Exchange, and relations with the senior market, though bruised, were intact. Grubb would move on to the Stock Exchange, and become a governor of that institution soon after. But he was far too "advanced" to hope for the presidency there. Instead, he would continue to interest himself in Curb affairs and be an important influence at the Curb and spokesman for its interests at the Stock Exchange for the rest of the decade.

Rarely is a protégé succeeded by his mentor, but such was the case in 1935. Moffatt praised Grubb and Lockwood on taking over in February, and promised to continue the work they had begun. He was not completely successful in this, though through no fault of his own. Grubb had been able to take advantage of events to help save the Curb, but he always had been forced to swim with the tide. The tide shifted during the Moffatt administration. Like Grubb, he reacted to forces he could not control, and these were stormier after February 1935 than they had been prior to that time.

Moffatt's first major problem was the so-called Meehan Scandal, news of which broke in October.

As has been noted, Michael J. Meehan had been one of the most widely followed plungers of the 1920s. His pools in RCA and other glamour issues had been followed by hundreds of speculators, and a rumor that Mike Meehan was "interested" in an issue would suffice to send it up a score of points. Meehan was a broker as well as an operator and manipulator, and this gave him greater power than might otherwise have been the case. It also cast doubt as to the honesty of markets in the 1920s.

Meehan had survived the crash of 1929. Although the New Deal securities legislation of 1933 and 1934 had made illegal almost all of his manipulative practices, he still had his brokerage, which did a good business while others were folding. Meehan was not as wealthy as he had been prior to the crash, but neither was he in danger of bankruptcy. So while other speculators left the district, Meehan remained. Like others who had speculated in the 1920s, he indicated he would accept the laws and work within them.

Yet Meehan could not resist an opportunity to take a flyer from time to time. Nor was he reluctant to engage in pooling operations, always hopeful he could do so without publicity. The big chances and expectation of reward were no longer present in the district in the mid-1930s. But there were possibilities of small speculations and profits. And Meehan took them, perhaps not so much for profit as for a chance to test his skills one more time.

Meehan's vehicle was Bellanca Aircraft Corporation, a small manufacturer of airplanes, which had been formed in 1927, and which rode the crest of the Lindbergh aircraft mania of that period. Bellanca had some good patents, and its president, G. M. Bellanca, was a respected inventor and businessman. Like many other aircraft companies, Bellanca Corporation was touted as the "General Motors of the industry," while Bellanca himself was compared to Henry Ford. Bellanca Aircraft never was more than a minor factor in the industry, which

even in the late 1920s was still in its early stage of development, and by the early 1930s demand for airplanes and compo-
nents was very low. Bellanca had only $564,500 in sales in
1929, with a loss of $109,000. The following year sales rose to a
record $740,000, but so did the deficit: $324,000. Bellanca
started a program of cost-cutting, to little avail. In 1934 sales
were $538,000, and the loss, $139,000. From 1929 to 1934, Bellanca showed sales of $3,512,500 and a net loss of $1,122,000.
The company was close to bankruptcy, and the price of its
common stock reflected the fact: it traded around $3 a share at
the Curb.

Early in 1935 Bellanca made application to the Reconstruction Finance Corporation for a loan of $150,000. The loan
was refused on the grounds that Bellanca lacked sufficient collateral, and because the loan would not suffice to put the firm
on a sound operating basis. Then G. M. Bellanca turned to his
banker and tried to float a new stock issue to raise that amount
of money; he was told the market could not absorb additional
Bellanca stock. Finally, Bellanca spoke with a minor speculator
who had survived the 1920s, and agreed to a deal. The speculator would purchase 50,000 shares from Bellanca, who would
then use the money to help save the company. The understanding was that the speculator would then "manage" the stock and
make profits through this action. Meehan, acting through Mrs.
Meehan, was part of the syndicate, as was a former director of
the company.

On May 17, the syndicate agreed to purchase the shares at
an average price of $5 a share. On May 15, Bellanca had closed
at 2½; on the 16th it closed at 3⅝, and the price reached 4¼
on May 17. Clearly, news of the deal had been leaked to other
speculators, who scrambled to get on a new Meehan bandwagon. Hammons & Co., a small underwriter, was also brought
in, since Meehan planned a new stock issue sometime in
the future, and didn't want to use his own firm for the purpose.

Meehan began his operations at once. Until June 7 he supported Bellanca's price at 4, buying all stock offered below that
price. Then he began buying in earnest, raising the price so as

to draw outsiders to the issue. Through buying and selling, he managed a small profit but, more important, gave Bellanca the reputation of an "interesting speculation."

On June 17, Bellanca, Hammons, and Meehan met to put the second stage of the plan into operation. Hammons & Co. would purchase 100,000 shares of Bellanca from the company at $4 a share, this stock to be sold at the market, with dealers receiving a commission of 50 cents a share. In addition, the syndicate would receive warrants for 72,000 shares, exercisable within three years at $5 a share, and an option to purchase 25,000 shares at $4, exercisable within sixty days. Warrants for an additional 52,500 shares would go to Bellanca himself and other officers, who would step down and permit the syndicate to name a new management. Ballanca agreed not to sell any of his shares for the next 144 days—apparently the period in which Meehan and the others expected to force the stock's price to a new high, sell out, and pocket their profits.

Meehan did his job well, manipulating Bellanca at the Curb and selling an additional 16,000 shares over the counter. In so acting he relied upon tips, planted stories, rumors—in fact, on all of the devices so familiar in the 1920s, and illegal in the post-1934 period. Activity in Bellanca stock was noted in the newspapers and at the Curb. Yet the Exchange did not investigate the matter, and took no official action to prevent it. It failed the first test of self-regulation.

The SEC began an investigation of Bellanca activities in October 1935, and soon uncovered the link to Meehan. Registration of the new issue was halted, and the Commission issued a show-cause order asking the company to demonstrate why a stop order should not be issued suspending the effectiveness of its registration of other securities.

The Commission heard testimony in November, at which time the entire matter was aired. By then Bellanca common was trading at below 3, and headed down to even lower levels. The manipulation was ended with an SEC attack on the existence of such practices and the foolishness of the public. "The naïveté of all the purchasers is almost beyond belief," the report concluded. "They purchased on the mere say-so of respondent and without even the semblance of an intelligent inquiry into the stock."

> On the face of this record it is not difficult to assay the nature of respondent's activity in Bellanca stock during the period from June 19 to October 26. We see him active in bringing new buying power into the market, encouraging his friends to buy, inducing persons in the brokerage business to recommend the stock to their customers. We see his associates . . . trading heavily in the stock on narrow price fluctuations. We find a market, when weakness in the stock developed, supported and banked by heavy scale buy orders placed sometimes directly by respondent for M. J. Meehan and Company, at other times by respondent for the account of his alter ego, Mrs. Meehan. . . . The record leaves us in no doubt that respondent during this period was actively responsible for a series of transactions in Bellanca stock, the purpose of which was to maintain its price at or about the level that the stock had reached on June 18.

Meehan rejected this conclusion and through his lawyer, Monroe Goldwater, contested the charges. The case dragged on, but in the end Meehan was forced from the district.

The Meehan Scandal was important as an indication that speculation still existed on Wall Street and at the Curb Exchange. Beyond that, it indicated that the passage of the Securities Exchange law was insufficient to halt speculation; New Dealers felt stronger legislation was needed, and throughout the decade they would persist in their efforts. Although the Curb Exchange was not attacked directly during the hearing, it was involved by implication. Much of the good will Grubb had created was now dissipated. In February, at the time Moffatt took office, it seemed the SEC was content to allow the Curb administration oversee the securities legislation on its own floor. Such was no longer the case. For the rest of the decade and beyond, the SEC's presence would be felt at the Curb Exchange.

The meaning of the Meehan case was not lost at Trinity Place. Surveillance activities increased in 1936, and although the SEC would criticize other aspects of Curb management, its regulatory and disciplinary roles were superior to those of the Big Board, and models of their types.

At the same time, both the SEC and the Curb administration realized they had a common interest: regulation and the survival of the Curb Exchange. If the Curb failed, most of its securities would be traded at the over-the-counter market, which the SEC viewed as hardly reputable. Throughout the 1930s the work to bring additional securities under regulation and surveillance continued. This task could be accomplished far better and more easily at the Curb Exchange and the regionals than at the over-the-counter market.

One provision of the Securities Exchange Act provided for the full registration of all unlisted securities if they were to be continued at the exchanges after June 1, 1936. The Meehan case—the first major violation of the Securities Exchange Act —might seem to have indicated that the SEC would press harder than before to obtain full registration. On the other hand, the Curb Exchange was unable to accomplish the task, due to the inability of many unlisted securities to meet registration requirements.* This posed a dilemma. If the SEC enforced the law it would destroy the Curb, with the subsequent enlargement of the over-the-counter market. Or it could ask for a change in the law, with the continuation of unlisted trading, which might invite repetitions of the Meehan Scandal.

The SEC chose the latter approach. An amendment to the Securities Exchange Act, passed in 1936, gave the SEC increased powers in regulating unlisted securities. They could continue at the exchanges, but under careful regulation and with the SEC evaluating each case individually.

This amendment led to a relaxation of tensions at the Curb. In the aftermath of the Meehan case the SEC had recommended a thorough revamping of Curb procedures, including the framing of a new constitution and the election of a paid president. These recommendations were ignored; without the amendment, they might have been taken seriously and perhaps acted upon.

* It should be noted that Bellanca had full listing at the Curb.

Now the Curb had to face a new challenge, this one from the regionals. If section 12 of the Securities Exchange Act helped save the Curb, it also gave a new lease on life to the regional stock exchanges, of which there were fifteen in 1936. That year the SEC Chairman James Landis told the Senate Banking and Currency Committee that unlisted trading had to be continued, and indicated his support for the proposed amendment to continue the practice. "If tomorrow . . . unlisted trading should be abolished, the result would be that many small exchanges would be forced to close." All of these exchanges were in dire trouble, he testified, and most were losing money. They needed help to survive, not the enforcement of rules that would surely result in their closing. The 1936 amendment, used by the Curb as an excuse to ignore SEC recommendations for changes in procedure, thus was framed more to protect the regionals than to aid the Curb. Landis went even further than he had to in his support of the amendment. The regionals should be encouraged to seek new unlisted securities, he said, and he implied that this might be done at the expense of the Curb as well as the Big Board and the over-the-counter market. Lewis Castle, president of the Buffalo Stock Exchange, recognized the thrust of Landis' argument. "Should the Buffalo Stock Exchange fall by the wayside," he told Landis, "I know it will be through no fault of mine or yours."

Thaddeus Benson, president of the Chicago Stock Exchange, assumed leadership of the regionals in their drive for increased listings. Benson was interested in odd-lot trading in Stock Exchange issues and the absorption of over-the-counter issues in the Chicago area. But he also gazed longingly at the Curb list. In October 1936 he said the Curb Exchange was the "real competition." "The officials of the Curb are out after business, and are getting considerable that should be ours. I will say, too, their members are out aggressively seeking business, and at our expense."

Benson was correct; the Curb indeed made a major effort to secure new listings in this period. As had been the case in the 1920s, some Curb securities simply disappeared as a result of their companies' going out of business, while others were transferred to the Big Board. And as the Stock Exchange also wanted business, it would not drop companies that did not come up to its minimum requirements, but simply overlooked such cases. Also, the Big Board bent the rules in admitting several issues that otherwise would not have been accepted due to insufficient capitalization or earnings. This was to be expected, and so the Curb brokers had to intensify their search for new listings to compensate for the losses.

The search was difficult. Business was poor, especially for small industrial corporations. Such companies had little chance of survival, and not all that did survive could qualify for Curb listing. At the same time, the ban against admitting new issues to the unlisted section hurt the Curb. Each year the unlisted section declined as old firms went out of business and were not replaced by new ones. Grubb and Moffatt were able to attract new issues, which made up for some of the losses. Although the total stock list dwindled in size, the increase in new listings, especially after mid-1934, helped compensate for the decline in the unlisted area and kept the Curb Exchange in business.

Listed and Unlisted Issues at the Curb Exchange, 1930–40

Year	Stocks			Bonds		
	Listed	Unlisted	Total	Listed	Unlisted	Total
1930	534	1,758	2,292	23	565	588
1931	473	1,807	2,280	24	687	711
1932	397	1,753	2,150	21	852	873
1933	355	1,144	1,499	18	622	640
1934	346	818	1,164	16	600	616
1935	367	755	1,122	35	509	544
1936	405	688	1,093	51	410	461
1937	500	631	1,131	58	341	399
1938	510	606	1,116	71	316	387
1939	507	584	1,091	64	271	335

Source: *Amex Databook,* p. 33, and American Stock Exchange

Many members of the administration entered the search for new issues, and the specialists themselves were encouraged to seek them out in much the same way as they had in previous years. In each of his yearly reports from 1935 to 1939, Moffatt spoke of the need for new issues. "We may have but one answer to diminishing volume," he said in February 1938, "and that is more securities. We must provide for our membership. If volume falls off in the securities we have, we must bring in more securities to maintain the volume. That is our first and principal problem; attempts to solve it are unceasing."

Little wonder, then, that Benson and other leaders at the regional exchanges mounted their counterattack.

The loss of securities and the decline in volume damaged the specialists far more than the commission brokers, especially those who represented the large Wall Street houses. Declining volume hurt each, to be sure, but the commission houses lost nothing if a security transferred from the Curb to the Stock Exchange, since it could execute a customer's order in either market. In fact, it gained slightly, since commissions were higher at the Big Board. The Curb specialist could take no solace in this; in such a case he was minus one stock, and it could be the most important one he handled.

As a result, the power of the commission brokers grew while that of the specialists declined. The commission brokers always had a great deal of leverage at the Curb, representing as they did the Wall Street Establishment. This power and influence increased in the late 1930s, and it seemed some of them might mount a challenge and take over control of the Curb Exchange. Such a challenge, when it came, could be masked under the slogan of "reform." Those commission brokers wanting power could take that stance, charging the old-line leaders —almost all of whom were specialists—with a record of failure.

The Curb Exchange had reformed itself under the Grubb and Moffatt administrations, but its basic outline remained the same as it had been in the 1920s. Indeed, the Curb still operated under the much-amended but still intact 1921 constitution. Reformers could charge the old regime with failing to comply with part of the spirit of the Securities and Exchange Act, especially that calling for an open and public marketplace. Like the Stock Exchange, the Curb still operated as though it were a private club. Some reformers demanded an end to this practice and attitude, and went so far as to suggest incorporation of the Curb, with membership open to anyone who purchased shares.

The tinder was present, then, for conflict at the Curb Exchange. But, as had so often been the case in the past, the spark came from outside, in particular the market crash of 1937 and the new attack on the part of the SEC against the Stock Exchange late that year.

The origin of the 1937 crash may be found in the optimistic view of the economy shared by many New Dealers in the latter half of 1936. At that time it appeared the depression was ending. Roosevelt cut several major spending programs, in this way indicating pump-priming was no longer as necessary as it once had been. Such was not the case. Capital spending, which had been rising in late 1936 and well into 1937, began to slide in the summer. The stock market also declined, even more sharply than it had in 1930 or 1932. Seeking a scapegoat, Roosevelt set his sights on Wall Street. In August 1937, the SEC pressed criminal charges for the first time in its history. Later on Chairman William O. Douglas accused several Big Board brokers of manipulating the stock of Auburn Automobile Corporation, and he promised a more vigorous enforcement policy than previously had been the case.

As the stock market decline continued, Douglas intensified his attack on the exchanges. End abuses, he said, or the government will end them for you. The attack was directed at the Big Board; Douglas did not single out the Curb in this period, and even went so far as to imply that it was the victim of a Stock Exchange conspiracy to depress prices, and not a collaborator. When Douglas indicated that the Stock Exchange should consider a new constitution—one providing for outside regulation in one form or another—the Curb and the regionals showed interest in the idea for their own markets, while many Big Board leaders, former President Richard Whitney in particular, announced their opposition. To some it seemed a replay of 1933–34, with the non–Stock Exchange markets accepting regulation while the Big Board rejected it. And, as before, an important segment of the commission-house community sided with the government. These were the men who demanded a new constitution for the Curb Exchange as well as one for the Stock Exchange.

Stock Exchange President Charles Gay bowed to Douglas' pressures late in 1937, and agreed to appoint a committee on reorganization. It was headed by Carle Conway, president of the American Can Company, and included Kenneth Hogate of the *Wall Street Journal,* New Dealer Adolf A. Berle, Jr., and William McChesney Martin, who would later become the first salaried president of the New York Stock Exchange under its new constitution.

The Association of Stock Exchange Firms supported the Conway Committee with enthusiasm. E. A. Pierce was then a prime figure in the organization. His firm, E. A. Pierce & Co., was the largest commission house in the district at the time, and a powerful factor in the reform movement. It was known that Pierce felt a similar reform to be needed at the Curb Exchange, and he chided it for not having accepted the SEC's suggestions for change in 1935.

The Conway Committee issued its report in January 1938. In it the Committee recommended the drafting of a new constitution, the establishment of the post of paid president (to be filled by a non-member of the Stock Exchange), and the creation of a "professional administration." The seventeen standing committees would be reduced to seven, and the locus of power at the Stock Exchange would shift to a new thirty-man governing board. Significantly, it was to be composed of twenty commission brokers and only five specialists, as well as three non-members and two bond brokers.

Douglas supported the report, and tried to ease the blow by referring to it as "self-regulation." In a speech soon after, he said that by self-regulation he did not mean the government should adopt a hands-off attitude:

> I do mean, first, self-discipline in conformity to law—voluntary law obedience so complete that there is nothing left for government representatives to do; second, I mean obedience to ethical standards beyond those any law can establish. . . . This type of self-regulation has unquestioned advantages. From the view-

point of the business, they are obvious. Self-discipline is always more welcome than discipline imposed from above. . . .*

The Conway Report was accepted—with Whitney abstaining from the final vote—and became the basis for the new constitution. Still, many of Whitney's friends were selected as members of the first board, a sign that he might mount a campaign of sabotage soon after. Then it was learned that Whitney had been involved in the misappropriation of securities left in his care, and that he was in desperate financial condition as well. On March 8, Gay announced the failure of Whitney & Co. Although he did not say so, it also marked the failure of Wall Street opposition to regulation.

In 1938 Congress passed and the President signed the Malony Act, which completed the New Deal securities regulatory legislation. Under its terms the SEC was permitted to register national securities associations charged with the prevention of fraudulent practices in the over-the-counter markets. These associations were another manifestation of Douglas' call for self-regulation under SEC surveillance. Had the act been introduced prior to the Whitney collapse, some Wall Streeters might have protested. But there was no protest after Whitney's failure. The SEC won its battle with the district, but it still lacked the funds, personnel, and knowledge to use this power effectively.

In January, several days before the Conway Commission released its report, the Chicago Stock Exchange announced a complete reorganization, which included the creation of a paid presidency and outside board members. Other exchanges indicated they would soon follow suit.

Moffatt referred to the possibility of a Curb reorganization in his annual report on February 16.

---

* Douglas may have had other reasons to make such a speech. At the time he was discussed as a potential nominee to the Supreme Court. For the next year Douglas maintained a "low profile," refusing to suggest new legislation even though additional laws were necessary. In this way, he may have assured no Wall Street opposition to his nomination, which came in 1939.

Other problems, by reason of the interest taken in them by the press, have assumed an importance. Some, not previously commented on, are of interest to the Exchange. Probably the most discussed is whether or not we need or desire reorganization. Should we accept the general recommendation of the Conway Report and, starting from that, fit the report to the needs of the Curb Exchange? If such a plan is acceptable from the viewpoint of our public relations, and if we are in agreement that a plan be wise, I should be glad to appoint a Committee from the Board to undertake the survey.

The committee was selected, and the Curb Exchange began its consideration of a new constitution.

Acceptance of a new frame of government would be as difficult at the Curb as it had been at the Big Board. Just as old and new guards clashed at the Stock Exchange, so would they do battle at the Curb. To most, Moffatt represented the old guard, but this is not to say the Curb's ruling group was backward; indeed, it was considered at the time one of the most progressive administrations in the stock exchange complex. Nor were the "Young Turks" all reformers; some were self-seeking individuals who had been excluded from power due to reasons of corruption or a desire to make the Curb more dependent upon outside interests than it had been in the past. This difference between the struggle at the Curb and the Stock Exchange was not apparent in 1938, and would not become so until several years later. Because of this confusion, the financial community could not understand the motives and activities of the man who flashed across the Curb scene in 1938 and remained a source of contention for three years: Jerome Chester Cuppia.

Constitution and Crisis

The economy declined again in 1938. The gross national product, which had reached a recovery high of $90.8 billion the previous year, stood at $85.2 billion. Yet gloomy though the atmosphere in the country was, 1938 was the last year of decline during the great depression. The gross national product would rise to $91.1 billion in 1939 and exceed the $100 billion mark in 1940, the second time this had happened and the first since 1929. In 1941 the gross national product reached $125.8 billion, eclipsing all previous records. By then all the economic indices were in a sharp upward curve. In 1938 exports stood at $3.1 billion, for example, and the import surplus was over a billion dollars. In 1941 exports would be $5.2 billion, and the nation would record an export surplus of $778 million, the first since 1933 and the largest since 1928. By then it was clear the depression had ended.

Little of this could have been predicted in 1938. At the time many Americans, including a large majority of the Wall Street community, seemed convinced American capitalism would be unable to survive the crisis of that year. Ever since 1933 Roosevelt had seemed a political and economic savior; his great electoral victory in 1936 was the most dramatic sign of this, but there were many others. Now came the 1937–38 collapse, with F.D.R. unable to present a bold new program or even rhetoric that would capture the public imagination. His enemies claimed that the magician in the White House had pulled his last rabbit out of the hat; his supporters were uncertain as to what he would do next, if anything, to turn the economy upward once more.

Added to the economic problem was that of potential war in Europe. In 1938 Nazi Germany seemed strong, vigorous, and prepared for conflict with its Great War opponents. Hitler's Germany had survived the depression in far better shape than Britain, France, and the United States. And if Germany did not conquer Europe, world power might fall to the Soviet Union, which seemed scarcely less youthful and aggressive.

Potential investors took these factors into account in 1938, and remained far from Wall Street and Trinity Place. They were also influenced by the low industrial and farm profits of that year, which were the worst since 1934. Fear of war, the haunting suspicion that they were living in the twilight of western civilization, and the feeling that business was sick if not dying, made for a poor showing at the markets. In 1938 the Dow-Jones industrial average hit a high of 158.41. Then it began a long slide, reaching a bottom of 106.34 in 1941. Not until 1945—after World War II had ended—would the 1938 high be topped, and not until 1954 would the 1929 record be eclipsed.

As had usually been the case in the past, the Curb Exchange suffered more than the Stock Exchange during bad times. During the week of June 18, 1938, only 368,505 shares were traded at the Curb, an average of less than 62,000 shares a day. During the best week of the year—that of October 22— the average was only 327,000 shares a day, while the daily average for the year was 199,000 shares. And conditions would worsen: in 1941 the average would be 139,000 shares.

The Curb Exchange's leaders had doubts as to their ability to save the market in 1938. In February, Fred Moffatt noted that the Curb had shown a profit of some $75,000 in 1937, and that its cash and securities position amounted to $582,000. This showing had been made while other exchanges were losing money. Yet the cost-cutting program of the 1930s, which had made this profit possible, had reached a dead end. The custodial staff had reduced bulb wattage by half to save on electricity and on bulbs themselves; heat was kept low in the building; soap was rationed in the washrooms; the staff itself was down to a bare minimum. Further cutting was out of the question; the program had reached bedrock. Moffatt noted all this, and expressed doubts as to whether profits were possible in 1938 without a revival of volume:

> If you think it is easy for me to express myself, I may only say that I hide my emotions well. For today I have many doubts; not about the Exchange, for I have confidence in it, but doubts of myself, of my own ability to measure up to the things we need to have done. I can only say, gentlemen, that I will try, and in the trying I shall need your advice, your help, and your judgment more than ever before.

Moffatt was not enthusiastic about Curb reform, but was willing to accept it as the price to be paid for survival. He recommended acceptance of the Conway Report in the hope that a revamped Curb would increase investor confidence and lead to increased volume. Accordingly, he ordered a study of the report, aimed toward the framing of a new constitution. Arthur Myles was selected to head the committee charged with the task, which included Sykes and Muller. The committee was to draw up recommendations as soon as possible, and Moffatt promised to present them to the membership.

The reorganization plan was ready in early July, 1938. It represented a compromise between those members who wanted to keep power in the hands of brokers (mostly specialists) and others who would elect a professional management team, consisting of paid executives with no direct interest in brokerage (a position held by many major commission brokers). A third group, smaller than the first two, rejected the plan for a new constitution, claiming that amendment of the 1921 document was all that was needed.

Under the terms of the July draft, the number of Curb committees would be reduced, public members would be admitted to the board, and new election procedures would be adopted. For example, the president and vice-president would be elected by the board, as had been the case in the past, but the board itself would be restructured. It would consist of nine specialists, nine commissions brokers, six non-member governors from the Stock Exchange firms, and three non-members from over-the-counter firms. This differed from the Stock Exchange constitution in that it gave greater weight to the specialists and at the same time recognized the importance of outside forces at the Curb. Furthermore, Myles' insistence that the non-member governors be selected from the over-the-counter firms as well as Stock Exchange houses implied a closer relationship between these two markets than previously had been the case.

The major compromise was in the area of presidential responsibility. The president would be a member of the Curb Exchange, as before, and his powers would be restructured to resemble those of the Stock Exchange's chairman. He would be responsible for long-range planning and preside over board meetings. The president would name members to committees, and select chairmen of those committees, but day-to-day operations would be in the hands of an executive vice-president, who would be in charge of the technical staff and "the efficient working of the Exchange machinery." Although not spelled out in the original draft proposal, the executive vice-president would also be responsible for the appointment and dismissal of all staff officers, and through them all salaried employees.

The executive vice-president would not be a member of the Curb Exchange; if one at the time of selection, he would sell his seat. In return for his services, he would receive between $20,000 and $25,000 a year in salary. In a bow to the need for increased business, the Myles Committee provided for a new executive committee whose task it would be to spread news of the Curb Exchange and to get additional newspapers to carry Curb quotations. Finally, it recommended the engagement of a public relations firm to assist in such work.*

* Even before the constitution was ratified, the Curb engaged the public relations firm of Albert Frank-Guenther as a first step in its program "designed to acquaint the public with Curb activities and services as a national institution."

Several minor alterations were made in August. One of these was a change in titles. The president now was to be known as the chairman, while the executive vice-president received the title of president. The president was to receive powers in addition to those recommended by the Myles Committee. He could "examine . . . papers and records of any member, or the books, papers, and records of his firm." In other words, the paid president, who might not be a person who formerly had been a member of the Curb, could have direct power over individuals and firm members. In addition, he would be an ex-officio member of every committee, and have even broader powers over special committees. In effect, the president would have enhanced powers, while the chairman (the former president under the 1921 constitution) would relinquish these to the new officer.

In October a committee of Curb members traveled to Washington to present their plan to the SEC. The delegation was headed by Moffatt and Howard Sykes, and included Jerome Chester Cuppia and Henry Brunie. Former president William Muller was asked to join the delegation, but refused the invitation; he felt the new board would be too radical a group, and he led a dissident group of conservative brokers who demanded that all eighteen members of the board be Curb Exchange members, with no outside representation. On the other hand, Cuppia was one of several commission brokers who had wanted to increase the power of outside representatives; his membership in the delegation indicated not only that further concessions to the commission brokers were indicated, but that Moffatt was leaning heavily on them for support.

Douglas and other SEC members applauded the revised constitution. Douglas called it a "forthright and realistic approach," indicated his gratification at being consulted before it was placed before the membership for a vote, and urged its acceptance.

> The report of the governors . . . marks a great step forward along the lines on which the commission has been thinking and acting.
>
> These proposals, if adopted by the membership, will mean that another great stock exchange has voluntarily discarded its

private-club type of organization in favor of a public one. Adoption of these proposals will enable the New York Curb Exchange to develop a modern, independently managed public institution, organized along sound business lines and capable of effective regulation under government supervision.

We welcome the continuing evidence of the determination and capacity of national securities exchanges to take the initiative in improving their organization so as to better serve the interests of the public. We are especially gratified at the proposal to refashion the rules of the Exchange and to examine into the possibility of the establishment of a trust institution for the more adequate protection of customers of brokerage houses.

The SEC did criticize the Curb for not including public non-members of the securities industry on the board, as had the Stock Exchange.* But in all other respects, it endorsed the draft constitution.

The constitution was redrawn to include several minor SEC recommendations, including the equal division of board members between commission brokers, specialists, and outside members, with the last group not distributed as to exchange or over-the-counter affiliation. As had been the case in the original draft, the chairman was to be selected by the membership, while the president was to be selected by the board.

From the first all Curb factions recognized that under the terms the chairman and the president would have new powers. They were willing to accept this change as a price to be paid for increased SEC approval and perhaps additional business. At the same time all believed the real test of strength would come in the election of the new officers. Thus, while the constitution was approved in November without a fight, by December a vigorous struggle had begun over nominations and elections to the new board and the selection of the first chairman.

* Under the terms of an amendment in 1944, the board was divided into four categories. Fifteen members were to be either specialists or commission brokers, twelve to be associate members or non-member partners of regular or associate member firms, three representatives of the public not engaged in the securities business, and the chairman and president of the Exchange. The passage of this amendment indicated the end of the struggle between the commission brokers and the specialists.

Jerome Cuppia was discussed as a natural selection for the chairmanship. Some protested that the exchange would do better to choose him as its first paid president. Cuppia was one of the most contentious figures in Curb history, and for the next three years he would be the center of attention in the realm of internal politics. At first he would be the leader of the reform element, a role natural for one who had advocated constitutional changes since 1933. Then he would become the target for the new reformers, a symbol of what was wrong at the Curb. In 1939 he seemed the best man available to save the Curb; two years later he almost brought it to its doom.

There was little about Cuppia that was ordinary in either the financial district's use of the word or that of the general public. Born in Westchester county in 1890 of a French father and a Spanish mother, he was forty-eight years old when he rose to prominence at the Curb. He was educated in New Jersey public schools, and had ambitions to enter Princeton; family reverses during the 1907 panic forced him to give up the idea of college. Instead he went to Wall Street, where he found employment as a runner at the securities and commodities house of Craig & Jenks. Cuppia was interested in securities, but commodities fascinated him. He began to speculate, making more than $10,000 in a matter of months, only to lose it in three days of downward activity. Then his father died, leaving him an inheritance of $5,000, which he lost in a day. But Cuppia had learned his lesson. Transferring his activities to Hubbell, Figgat & Co., a firm with a reputation for shrewd commodities dealings, and hedging his bets carefully, Cuppia was able to make a small fortune through several swift deals after war was declared in 1914. By 1917, he was said to be worth over half a million dollars.

Cuppia enlisted in 1917, joining the Navy as a stoker on the U.S.S. *Massachusetts*. After the war he returned to commodities, this time at Taylor Cotton Co. in Macon, Georgia. In 1922 he returned to New York, where he opened his own house. Just before the 1929 crash he merged with E. A. Pierce & Co. and became a partner, specializing in commodities.

Cuppia boasted that he was a direct descendant of an aide

to the Mexican Emperor Maximilian. As though to substantiate this claim, he had three replicas of the coffin in which Maximilian was buried constructed and installed in the attic of his
home. In one lay a wax effigy of the Emperor wearing a loin-
cloth; in another, an effigy was dressed in a field marshal's uniform; in the third Maximilian was outfitted in the uniform
worn when he was executed. Nearby were hung all sorts of mem-
orabilia of the period, including what Cuppia claimed was
the Emperor's favorite sword.

There is little evidence to indicate Cuppia's claims were
correct, but he was no man to approach on the subject. Cuppia
was a well-built, athletic man with a fast-receding hairline and
a piercing look. As if to enforce his claims, he wore a large
waxed moustache of the type favored by officers during the
1870s, which he would twirl when angered.

Cuppia was one of the district's leading sportsmen as well.
He favored the racing of fast automobiles and, in his youth,
football. During the 1920s he took up polo, and was one of the
nation's finest amateur players. He engaged in all these pur-
suits with a ferocious abandon, witnessed by a fractured skull, a
broken collar bone, two broken fingers, two teeth knocked out,
a compound fracture of the nose, and a leg once broken in
eight places.

At first Cuppia concentrated his activities at the cotton exchange, but then turned to other markets. He purchased a seat
at the Curb in 1925, and four years later obtained one at the
Stock Exchange as well. At the time he held membership in
ten different exchanges; the number would reach fourteen in
1938, a record. He was determined to excel and have the most
of any man he knew. As the best-known vice-president of the
leading commission house in New York, his ambitions seemed
justified.

Cuppia did not suffer great losses in the 1929 crash, as he
had hedged wisely in commodities, and probably was worth
more in 1933 than he had been four years earlier. While other
brokers at the Curb were worried about meeting the rent, Cuppia would rise at five o'clock to get in an hour or so of horse-
back riding before going down to his office. Often he would

skip lunch to play a game or two of tennis with the best opponent he could find. He tried to form a Curb Exchange polo team in 1938, and was disgusted when he found few brokers who could ride and, of those who did, fewer who could afford the costs.

Cuppia had wealth, prestige, and the admiration of his fellows. He belonged to fourteen exclusive clubs, had homes on Cape Cod and in Montclair, as well as a luxurious apartment in Manhattan and a villa on Lake Como. Yet he remained ambitious. Cuppia became active in Democratic politics in the early 1930s, supporting Roosevelt in 1932. Along with E. A. Pierce he was considered an "enlightened capitalist." Roosevelt considered Cuppia for a post at the SEC, perhaps as one of the commissioners. But Cuppia was uninterested in the job. Instead, he intended to become a leader of a revitalized and reformed securities industry, one that would encompass all the exchanges as well as the over-the-counter and commodities markets. He believed this was coming, and that he was best equipped for the task. If and when F.D.R. looked for a man who knew all aspects of the industry, he would turn to him, or so Cuppia believed.

Cuppia had been elected to the Curb board in 1929, and was reelected in 1932 and 1935. In 1933 he had urged the board to go along with the New Deal, and his was one of the first voices at Trinity Place to advocate cooperation with the New Deal. Just as E. A. Pierce worked to obtain Big Board acceptance of the New Deal measures affecting Wall Street, so Cuppia did the same at Trinity Place. His words and deeds made him unpopular with many Curb leaders, who came to consider Cuppia a dangerous reformer. In 1938 he spoke out vigorously for a new constitution at a time when Moffatt and his group were still undecided on the issue. Because of this, he lost his re-election bid that year to Henry Parish 2d, a Moffatt ally. But Cuppia remained powerful as a leading commission broker and close personal friend of Pierce, as well as the leader of the commission brokers at the Curb. As he saw it, reform would come first to the Stock Exchange, since it was being singled out for such by the SEC. Then it would evolve at the Curb, in the face of opposition from the specialists. Yet come it must, and the natural vehicle for its arrival would be the commission brokers of Stock Exchange member firms. After leading the fight, he would take command of the Curb itself.

The first step in this struggle came in supporting Grubb for the Curb presidency in 1934, and in working with him and Lockwood for acceptance of regulation that year and in 1935. Cuppia did not favor Moffatt as Grubb's successor; he felt him to be a weak and indecisive man, as well as one in the control of the specialists. But he worked with Moffatt, always trying to turn him in the direction of reform. It was Cuppia who pressed for acceptance of the Conway Report, in a struggle in which he was pitted against Muller, the spokesman for the specialists. His victory in this fight was signaled in Myles' draft constitution, and in the fact that Cuppia was selected to go with Moffatt, Lockwood, Sykes, and the others to Washington to present it to the SEC. By then, too, Cuppia had the confidence of men like Douglas, and one of the reasons the SEC Chairman was so enthusiastic about the plan was his assumption that Cuppia would be the first chairman or president under the revised or rewritten constitution.

In early November the financial pages carried articles on the Curb constitution and the forthcoming election. Lines of conflict had developed, based on personality as well as program, but for the most part these were unclear to both the financial writers and the general public. For example, several news writers spoke of the "old guard" at the Curb. By this they meant the men who had power at the organization in the late 1930s, and who had been reluctant to accept constitutional changes. The old guard included those men antagonistic to the SEC, who had supported Whitney at the Stock Exchange, and who resisted reform at the Curb. The power of these men was being challenged by the "Young Turks," a reform faction that supported the constitution, believed the SEC was generally operating in the public interest, and worked for fuller disclosure of operations formerly kept secret. None of the articles indicated who belonged to which group—not even those by writers who were believed "on the inside."

At the time Leslie Gould of the New York *Journal and American* was considered the financial writer most conversant with Curb affairs, and a leader in the movement among the city's newspapers to reform the market. Gould was on good terms with many reformers, but most particularly with Cuppia. They corresponded regularly during this period, with Cuppia serving as Gould's guide to Curb politics. As one who considered himself sympathetic to the Young Turks, Gould supported Cuppia for the chairmanship. At the time Cuppia was saying he didn't want that job or the presidency, but it was clear from his actions that he could be persuaded to take either post. Gould implied that the old guard opposed Cuppia; it included Howard Sykes, Edwin Posner, and Mortimer Landsberg among its number, along with Moffatt and Grubb. Indeed, almost any broker who had held an important Curb office from 1928 to 1938 was labeled "old guard." Gould and other reform newsmen didn't take note of the fact that in the past many of these men had opposed one another, and that most had been willing to accept a constitution, although differing on details. Posner had worked with Miles in helping frame the document that Douglas thought admirable, and although Moffatt had some misgivings about it, he had done nothing to prevent its adoption.

In writing to Gould on November 17, Cuppia argued that Sykes would "make a worthy and efficient chairman of the board." Cuppia rejected Gould's rather arbitrary divisions. Instead, he insisted the real battle was between commission brokers (Young Turks) and specialists (Old Guard). Cuppia noted that Sykes was "at the moment" a specialist, but "he possesses the commission house point of view gained largely through his close association with Post & Flagg."

Cuppia went on to indicate that the division made by reporters was unreal, and certainly clouded the issues insofar as Sykes was concerned:

> His only disqualifying point, as I understand you view it, is the fact that for a long time he has been associated with the so-called Old Guard faction of the Curb Exchange. If the fact that he served with the so-called Old Guard would arbitrarily make him one of them, then I too must be an Old Guard as I served

until kicked off, for nine years steadily with the same Old Guard members with which Sykes served.

Cuppia then characterized Landsberg as one who represented "the best brains that Wall Street has to offer in security analysis," while Posner knew "every phase of the security market and unquestionably would be a tremendous help to the new Board." He claimed neither man was "extremely popular with the so-called old faction," but did not name the members of that faction. Could Cuppia mean Moffatt and Grubb? If so, it would be hard to explain Grubb's popularity with Posner and Landsberg, or Moffatt's with other members of the reform group.

In mid-December a movement was launched to draft Cuppia for the chairmanship. Commission brokers asked him to reconsider his decision not to run for office. On December 16, Gould helped fan the flames by writing, "The most likely candidate for the job—if he can be persuaded to accept—is Jerome C. Cuppia, partner in E. A. Pierce & Co. This writer some time ago suggested his name for the post." During the following week the movement grew. Then, on December 24, Cuppia wrote to William A. Hassinger, chairman of the Curb's nominating committee: *

Some months ago, in connection with ill-founded gossip arising out of activities attendant upon the proposed reorganization of the Curb, I stated, in good faith, definitely and repeatedly— once in a letter to Mr. Sykes—that I would not permit my name to be put forward as that of a candidate for office under the new regime. At the risk of appearing ungracious, which is far from my wish, my personal inclination still is to adhere to that determination.

It now appears, if one may rely upon the petitions, letters and oral representations that have been pouring in on me for the past few days, that, by some strange quirk of circumstance, a substantial majority of the members have become imbued with the idea that I am the one Moses to lead them out of the wilderness—an idea to which I certainly cannot subscribe.

* Cuppia sent a carbon copy of this letter to Leslie Gould, and it may be found in the Gould Papers at Hofstra University.

In this fashion, Cuppia entered the race.

At the time it was assumed that Cuppia had the support of the membership. At least, he convinced the newsmen that such was the case. The *Journal and American* article on the subject was entitled "J. Chester Cuppia Slated for Curb Post," and a later story began with "J. Chester Cuppia, partner in the Stock Exchange firm of E. A. Pierce & Co., has accepted the proffered chairmanship of the Curb Exchange in that market's reorganization plan." A picture of Cuppia appeared on the financial page on December 24 with the caption "J. Chester Cuppia: Partner in E. A. Pierce & Co., who will become chairman of the Curb in the reorganization plan."

But Cuppia did not have the support of a majority of Curb members or, for that matter, of commission brokers. More important, despite obvious attempts to shore up former enemies, he could not hope for a clear majority of nominees to Board positions. His activities over the past decade, as well as his belief that the constitution was only a starting point for reform and not its end, alienated many conservative brokers.

Prior to the Cuppia announcement, it appeared that Sykes might become the chairman, with Posner and Landsberg in important board positions. Many names had been bandied about for the presidency, with the most prominent support given to Ganson Purcell, chief of the trading and exchange division of the SEC. The Purcell nomination seemed to make sense, since the Curb officers had told Douglas they would see him prior to releasing the names to the press—apparently to gain his approval for the slate. The combination of old-guard members like Sykes, Posner, and Landsberg with a former SEC leader like Purcell seemed good politics.

Cuppia's entry into the race upset this plan. Sykes, who had never been very much interested in a return to management, withdrew and indicated support for Cuppia. His place as leader of the old guard was taken by outgoing president Fred Moffatt. Like Sykes, Moffatt was tired of administration and eager to return to the business of brokerage. But in order to prevent Cuppia's election, Moffatt let it be known that he would accept the chairmanship if drafted. Nor was he the only member of the old guard interested in stopping Cuppia in this way. Posner, Harold Brown, Floyd Keeler, and James Dyer, all considered old guard, were talked about as potential nominees in December.

The new board's first business would be to elect the president, and the old guard had a candidate for the position. E. Burd Grubb, still one of the most popular men at the Curb, entered the race late in 1938. At the time Grubb was a governor at the New York Stock Exchange and a partner at Coggeshall & Hicks. He had been considered a moderate reformer in 1934, but by 1938 Grubb clearly was a member of the Establishment. Like Moffatt, he was willing to work with the SEC even though he distrusted the agency, and to accept the new constitution without wanting to expand upon it.

As late as New Year's Day it appeared that Cuppia would win the chairmanship and then go on to lead a movement to elect Purcell to the presidency. But the old guard jockeyed for positions on the list of nominees to the board, and succeeded in placing several key men in position for election, among them Posner, Sykes, Parish, Grubb, and Dyer. By that time Sykes had left the Cuppia camp, and threw his weight behind the old guard. Alpheus Beane, Jr., was one of the few nominees enthusiastically in favor of Cuppia. Douglas seemed unaware of this development. He approved the list on January 5, still believing Cuppia would win election. At that time it appeared that the old guard would win a sweeping victory.

Purcell knew what was happening. On January 9 he announced his withdrawal as a candidate for the presidency. And that same day Cuppia, who suffered from ailments related to his sports activities, was admitted to Montclair Hospital "in serious condition." He did not withdraw from the race, but it seemed the reform slate had no chance of winning a majority on the new board.

Now that it was apparent Cuppia would not be elected, Moffatt withdrew from the race. A struggle then developed between the Cuppia backers and the various remaining old-guard candidates. The result was a draw, followed by a search for a compromise candidate. After several hours of bickering and name calling, the two factions agreed to support Clarence Bettman, head of Connell & Bettman, and a person who had remained aloof from the struggle from the start. Bettman was a conservative broker, but at the same time he had never belonged to the old guard as an insider. He had served on the board since 1933, and had been chairman of the finance committee since 1936. Bettman could best be described as a technician. He knew the market and was respected as an honest arbiter. Clearly he would offer the Curb little in the way of forceful leadership. At the same time, Bettman would not be a divisive leader, as Cuppia or Posner might have been at that time.

Bettman's selection was made public on January 10. At a press conference following his selection he said:

> We shall have nine days between the election and the time we take office on February 23. If the slate is unopposed we shall have even more time. I know but ten of my twenty-seven colleagues. We shall have a lot to discuss, including appointments to the committees controlled by the chairman of the board.

Bettman was asked of his choice for the presidency, and refused to answer. "After all, there aren't so many men qualified for the job, and we certainly ought to be able to canvass the field in the time we'll have," he said. He would not say whether he supported Grubb. There seemed little doubt at the time, however, that Grubb would be selected for the job. A majority of the new board had indicated prior to election they wanted him, and with Purcell's withdrawal, Grubb was the sole candidate in the field.

Then the unexpected happened. Rumors reached the Curb that Grubb was already assured of election, and that once in office he would quietly but firmly remove reformers from key posts. There was also talk of new faces in the administration, all of them from the old guard. These rumors did not originate at the Curb itself, but rather in suburban country clubs and New York private clubs. It was said that Grubb had been indiscreet in his statements on the subject. Support for his candidacy diminished.

Grubb could not muster sufficient support to win election, but there was no other candidate discussed seriously at the first meeting of the new board on February 23. As a result, Bettman was named president *pro tem* and charged with leading the search for the first paid president.

Bettman's first step was the selection of a committee that included all factions at the Curb. Alpheus Beane, Jr., spoke for the Cuppia group, while Edward J. Shean was in the Moffatt camp. The other committee members were Jacques Cohen of Baer, Cohen & Co., Morton Stern of J. S. Bache & Co., and Austin K. Neftel.

The search took the better part of two months, during which time dozens of men were considered and rejected by one faction or another. Soon it became clear that the new president could not be too closely affiliated with the Stock Exchange, could not be a New Dealer or a reformer from the SEC, and could not be a present or even past member of the Curb. This narrowed the field considerably. The Curb would not accept a man who knew little or nothing of the industry; it needed a president with the ability and personality to seek and obtain new listings, and one above reproach in his business life. Few men who could fill all of these requirements were willing to take the post.

In the end the Curb committee found such a man in George P. Rea. At the time the forty-five-year-old Rea was president of the Bishop National Bank in Honolulu, far from the Wall Street and Trinity Place scene. The bank had almost gone under during the early years of the depression, and was on the verge of collapse in 1931 when Rea arrived. Through careful husbanding of resources and a campaign to bring in new deposits, Rea had managed to increase deposits from $30 million in 1931 to $50 million in 1939. The Curb hoped he could transfer these talents to the securities area.

Nor was Rea a novice at finance. After graduating from Cornell in 1915 he had taken a position in the bond department of the Guaranty Trust Company, and from there he went on to become office manager at Keen Taylor & Co. Rea enlisted in the army in 1917, rising to the rank of captain and serving in France. After the war he returned to his home in Buffalo and formed the investment banking company of Victor, Hubbell, Rea, and Common, where he remained for six years. During part of the time he also served as vice-president of the Fidelity Trust Company of Buffalo, and both these activities had brought him into close contact with Wall Street underwriters.

Rea organized the Buffalo Stock Exchange in 1928 and was its first president. The following year he moved to New York, where he joined Goldman, Sachs & Co., and in 1930 he became president of North American Securities Co. He was there when the Bishop National Bank job was offered him. Rea accepted and was, therefore, out of the country during the hectic years of the early SEC.

Rea had a good reputation in the district, and seemed an excellent choice for the presidency. His sponsors at the Curb were Sykes and Posner, and although both men were associated with the old guard, neither was its leader. It was expected that they would guide Rea during his first months in office, and the new President said as much. The major task he faced, he said, was to learn more about the market and its problems.

Rea had two major tasks his first year on the job. He had to make certain the new constitution was accepted, by both the Curb and the SEC, and at the same time find additional business for the market.

Rea had little trouble at the Curb, since he had no connection with the Cuppia faction and only peripheral friendships with the Moffatt group. His relations with the SEC were correct yet guarded; Douglas wasn't impressed by him, but the Chairman was soon leaving for the Supreme Court in any event.

In May the SEC issued a report suggesting that specialists be forbidden from speculating for their private accounts in securities to which they were assigned. At the time he could act as a market maker for his securities, and also might buy and sell these same securities for his private account. If he wished he could transfer them from one account to the other. In effect, then, his business and personal investments were commingled. The situation provided opportunities for manipulation, and for this reason the SEC proposed to end it.

Rea claimed such a rule would be difficult to enforce. For example, a specialist would be asked either to abandon his stock or stop holding it in his private account. If he opted for the latter course of action, he would in effect be lowering the amount of reserves he had committed to making an orderly market in the stock, and this would hardly be in the best interests of the public. Furthermore, how could the SEC run checks on such a rule, given the small staff it had at the time? Finally, the rule was not necessary. Should a specialist use his private account as a vehicle to make profits from his public business, he could be prosecuted under the law, in addition to being in violation of Curb statutes.

Rea's case was weak; manipulations of the kind the SEC described had gone on throughout the 1920s and well into the 1930s, and had been discussed by many reporters and admitted by some specialists after the 1929 crash. But the SEC proposal was dropped, more due to its unworkability than to Rea's persuasiveness. The President was credited by the specialists with having done a good job, and his popularity rose.

As had Moffatt and Grubb before him, Rea urged the members to seek new listings, and he himself did all he could to attract new companies to the Curb. The committees on transactions and quotations, on formal listing, and on unlisted securities were mobilized for the task, while the public relations budget was increased. The executive committee proved ineffectual, however, and was bypassed. As though to inspire the members, Rea would appear on the floor from time to time to hold informal "pep rallies" during which he would report on his activities and try to exhort the members to greater efforts.

Rea also acted in a more practical way to increase business. He launched a study into the relationships between the Curb and the over-the-counter market. The financial problems of some marginal Curb specialists had resulted in a loss of volume, rather than an increase. Some specialists were no longer able to assume the risks of buying or selling large blocks of stock; their limited financial resources would not permit it. Under the terms of a state law, the commission broker was obliged to find the best market for his customer and execute his order there. Given a block of stock listed at the Curb to sell, or an order to buy, most brokers would go to the Curb first. But if the specialist there could not handle the order, or could not offer a good quotation, the commission broker might seek to buy or sell the stock over the counter. There was a rise in such activity in 1938 and 1939, and Rea meant to end it as quickly as possible.

He did so by demanding that the SEC police the over-the-counter market more than it had in the past. He stressed that all sales at the Curb were public, while those on the over-the-counter market went unreported. Surely the SEC, charged with full disclosure, should investigate the situation. Further, Rea asked the SEC to simplify some of its procedures (especially those involving reporting) to lower brokers' costs, in the hope that with additional capital obtained in this way, the Curb specialists would become more competitive. Finally, Rea called for "a general survey of the functional similarities and differences in the position of the Exchanges and the over-the-counter markets," to discover which areas each operated best in the public interest. All of this was designed to bring large block transactions back to the Curb Exchange.

The Rea program did not meet with success. Not until after the war, when Curb brokers revived financially, were they able to compete successfully with large block operators on the over-the-counter market.

Within six months Rea had been able to win the confidence of most Curb specialists and commission brokers. He had not proved the dynamic gatherer of new listings, as had been claimed by his sponsors, but at least he was making the effort. Rea's relations with the board, and especially with Bettman, were good. And if the SEC was not delighted with the new president, at least he seemed to have the staff's respect.

Yet the old antagonisms were not dead; some brokers no longer spoke to others as a result of the politics of 1938–39, and would remain estranged for the rest of their lives. Grubb was a member of the board and cooperated with Rea, although he never respected the President and was convinced that if he had been elected, he could have done a better job. Moffatt was back on the floor, still a power in Exchange politics, willing to work with the new administration but watching it warily for signs of irresponsibility. Moffatt had no ambitions for the presidency, but by mid-1939 he showed signs of willingness to be considered as Bettman's replacement as Chairman. Then there was Cuppia, who returned to the Curb in the spring of 1940.

Many brokers believed that Cuppia's illness had been political; that he had entered the hospital and withdrawn from the Curb when he realized he would not win the election as chairman. Such was not the case; the illnesses were real enough to cause additional confinements in 1939. Furthermore, if Cuppia had been rebuffed, he had not been disgraced, and he showed no signs of hurt feelings. Instead, he spoke out vigorously on Curb issues. Generally speaking, Cuppia supported Rea's policies vis-à-vis the SEC and the over-the-counter market, and he did all he could to obtain new listings. Cuppia was a far more personable man than Rea, and better equipped for the banquet circuit and the round of firms interested in listing. His speeches were better prepared and delivered, he knew the district and the Curb better than the President, and his contacts with the press were superior to those of any other man at the market.

Cuppia traveled throughout the East and Midwest during much of the fall of 1939, always at his own expense, giving talks about the Curb and the advantages of a listing. He had little contact with the administration during this period; as a result, rumors flew that he was preparing to mount a major campaign for the chairmanship in 1940.

In November, stories appeared to the effect that Cuppia would challenge Bettman in the February 1940 election. Then he would go on to replace Rea with a new man who would lead a reform effort and obtain many new stocks. There was talk that Cuppia wanted to unite with the regionals to form a nationwide securities network that might in time include the over-the-counter market as well. Then came another rumor:

merger with the Big Board, with the Curb members receiving full membership in the senior market. None of these rumors had much substance; they may have been planted to obtain greater support for the Cuppia candidacy.

The rumors convinced Moffatt that he would have to make the race to block Cuppia. Accordingly, he let it be known that he would be willing to replace Bettman in 1940. But Bettman would not step down; he announced in December that he would be a candidate for reelection.

The Cuppia candidacy never got off the ground. By late January it was clear that between them Bettman and Moffatt had a large majority of votes. With this, Moffatt announced his support of Bettman, who won reelection with no difficulty.

Cuppia retired gracefully from the contest, and continued his activities in search of new listings. There would be another election in 1941, and he wanted to be ready for it. If sufficient specialists received Cuppia's favors in the form of new listings, they and the commission brokers already in his corner might provide the margin of victory. Bettman seemed uninterested in serving beyond two years, so 1941 seemed a reasonable time for Cuppia's next drive for Curb leadership.

By 1941 Cuppia would become the most talked-about figure at the Curb, if not in the entire financial district. But this did not occur in the way Wall Street might have expected it to. Instead, Cuppia was the subject of the biggest Curb scandal in a decade, the greatest personal disaster in the district since the decline and fall from Big Board grace of Richard Whitney.

NINE

Plate v. Cuppia

Jerome Cuppia spent a leisurely six weeks in the Bahamas early in 1939, the guest of his friend (and boss) E. A. Pierce. The vacation was for rest and recovery after a heart attack, but Cuppia returned to Trinity Place more haggard than when he had left. Clearly, the powerful Curb figure was ill; friends thought he might soon die.* It was not surprising, then, that Cuppia began selling off his memberships in various commodities markets in mid-year. Few believed he needed the money. The sales were made, it was believed, to prepare his estate and put his financial affairs in order.

On March 28, 1940, Cuppia was served with a warrant of attachment signed by New Jersey Supreme Court Judge Aaron Levy, on application of William J. Plate of New York, a fellow-member of the Curb Exchange and a broker at Pierce & Co. Plate alleged that Cuppia had obtained $101,647 from him in the 1932–39 period, and had done so fraudulently. The thought seemed preposterous, but Judge Levy's signature on the warrant impressed many brokers. Under the court order, certain of Cuppia's assets were held until final disposition of the case.

* Though ill for the rest of his life, Cuppia had a strong constitution, and he lived until 1966, when he was seventy-five years old.

Plate v. Cuppia — 157 +

According to Plate, Cuppia had forwarded him $22,500 in 1932 to enable him to purchase a Curb seat. In return for this loan, Plate had opened a checking account, giving Maurice P. Shade, Cuppia's secretary, power of attorney to draw upon it. Since 1932, Plate had earned $159,852 in commissions, all of which went into the account. Of this amount, $101,647 had been withdrawn by Shade for Cuppia's uses. Plate had used the rest of the money—at a rate of approximately $65 a week for most of the time—to support his family. At the time the warrant was issued, the account contained less than a thousand dollars.

Cuppia denied any wrongdoing:

> My only comment at this time with reference to the action instituted by William J. Plate against me is that at the proper time it will be clearly demonstrated by documentary evidence that the suit is wholly without merit and that same is brought solely for ulterior purposes.

"Ulterior purposes?" Was Cuppia suggesting that Plate was merely a front for his enemies? Was the suit a means of denying him the Curb presidency in 1941? And what was behind the Plate charges? Why did he permit his commissions to be controlled by Cuppia and Shade? Cuppia was believed a wealthy man. Why would he have owed money to someone like Plate, who only a dozen years earlier had been a clerk, who now was thought by many to be an ingrate and a troublemaker, and who certainly had none of the polish and grace of a man like Cuppia?

Cuppia realized he would have to answer the charge, and quickly. To wait would be to admit there might be substance to the allegation. A counter-suit might be the best answer; charge Plate at least with libel and slander, Cuppia's friends urged. But Cuppia decided against it; his reputation had been challenged, and no amount of damages awarded by the courts could compensate for his loss of prestige. Far more important would be vindication by the Curb itself. Besides, suits took time, during which some of the charges might take on the coloration of truth. Cuppia wanted a chance to be heard as soon as possible, and in an arena of his selection.

Accordingly, Cuppia told reporters that he would ask the Curb's arbitration or business conduct committee to take action, and to expel Plate under terms of Article VIII, Section 1, of the constitution, which stated that when two members had business differences, they had to use the arbitration procedures of the Exchange. Failure to use these procedures would be deemed "an act contrary to just and equitable principles of trade."

Although Cuppia seemed to be suggesting that Plate's charge was merely a difference between two brokers (in which case the Curb could handle the matter itself) the warrant of attachment indicated that more was involved, perhaps even criminal charges.

Nevertheless, Cuppia sent a registered letter to the board in which he responded to the charge and asked for a meeting of the committee on business conduct to hear testimony. He also called in the financial district press corps and read the letter to the reporters. In it he outlined his case against Plate, saying, "I deny absolutely the truth of these allegations, or that I am indebted to said William J. Plate in any amount whatsoever."

Cuppia sent a second letter to the Curb, one he did not release to the press. Its existence remained a secret until an SEC investigation the following year. The tone and some of the content of this second letter were quite different from the first. Where the first letter was confident, the second was wary and circumspect. "I charge that the allegations in said affidavit by William J. Plate that I am indebted to him in the sum of $101,647 *are not wholly untrue* [emphasis added]," he wrote, "but by the institution of said suit and the making of said affidavit, said William J. Plate has deliberately sought to injure my name and reputation as a member of this Exchange . . ."

Here Cuppia indicated that there was merit in Plate's allegation, but that Plate had acted badly in instituting the civil action. He suggested that the matter could best be handled within the confines of the committee on business conduct. Not only was there no need for Curb members to air their grievances before the public, but Cuppia must have known he

Plate v. Cuppia — 159+

would receive a more favorable hearing at Trinity Place than in a court of law.

Cuppia's letters were dated April 1, 1940. On that same day the committee notified Plate of his requested appearance at hearing concerning "the question of whether or not the institution of aforesaid suit by you constitutes a violation of the arbitration provisions of the Exchange Constitution." No mention was made of Cuppia's letters or the fact that he, and not the committee, had instituted the action.*

In this, the first phase of the Cuppia-Plate conflict, three interests seemed in contention, jockeying for position. According to Plate, his money had been taken wrongfully. All he wanted was the return of his funds. As for Cuppia, he hoped to preserve his reputation; the money meant little compared with that. The Curb's interest was even more delicate, and its situation at least as sensitive as that of Cuppia. If Plate were upheld, then Cuppia would be dishonored and expelled from the Curb. An SEC investigation would surely follow, one in which the entire range of Curb activities during the 1930s might be investigated. Who could tell what would turn up in such an inquiry? The publicity attending the hearings would be bad for the Curb as an institution, and this was in the minds of all at Trinity Place. On the other hand, Cuppia had enemies at the Curb, men who had opposed him and his ideas for a number of years. They would have welcomed Cuppia's disgrace, some even to the point of accepting an inquiry as its price.

The Curb's leaders wished that the matter had never been

---

* A copy of the letter was introduced at the SEC hearings later. At that time it was alleged that the Curb was beginning to make a case for itself even then. By acting promptly, it was safeguarding the integrity of the market. Plate's charges would be investigated, and if they were substantiated, Cuppia would be expelled. But if the charges were untrue, then Plate would be forced from the district. Considering the language used by Cuppia in this letter to the Board, it would appear that he was prepared to concede at least part of Plate's charges. He must have thought he would win the case. Whatever the situation, Cuppia would not admit the charge had substance until the SEC hearings.

raised. But they were stuck with what had the aroma of a full-blown scandal. It was in the interests of the institution to keep the matter as quiet as possible, to work out some kind of an arrangement acceptable to both Plate and Cuppia, one that would not arouse the suspicions of the SEC or lead to further legal action. The Whitney scandal had shaken the Stock Exchange to its foundations; a scandal, scarcely two years later, involving a man of Cuppia's prominence, could very well do the same for the Curb.

The Cuppia-Plate contest had even broader implications, and these were recognized at the Curb. According to Plate, Cuppia had been taking money from him for a decade. Even while he led the reform movement and enjoyed the confidence and support of key men at the SEC, Cuppia was engaged in what amounted to criminal practices, said Plate. If this were so, then what was the use of an SEC? If, after six years of having a policeman at the corner of Broad and Wall—and Trinity Place, too—such chicanery took place, then perhaps a revamped and revitalized regulatory commission was needed. Or perhaps the answer was nationalization of the exchanges. The Cuppia affair could blossom into a full-scale investigation of the financial district. There was no guarantee that the Big Board would not be discussed and the Whitney scandal revived. And the SEC could be made to appear blind or inept or both. Whatever the case, the regulatory agency would be on trial too.

The hearings began on April 3, only two days after the exchanges of letters.* Ten brokers in addition to Cuppia and Plate would appear before the committee on business conduct, as well as four non-members. The testimony would be completed in mid-July, and the final report delivered on July 31.

* The full record of the hearings before the committee on business conduct was delivered to the Securities and Exchange Commission on August 23, 1941. Although the committee's records were referred to during the SEC investigation and parts read into the record, the full transcript was not made public then or since. The transcripts are in the SEC offices in Washington today.

Plate v. Cuppia — 161 +

All of the meetings were held *in camera;* great care was taken to see to it the press did not learn of the matter.*

The committee on business conduct, before which the hearings took place, was one of the more important branches of Curb administration. Few newcomers were named to the committee, which was reserved for experienced brokers and men of known integrity. Its chairman was Sherman M. Bijur, a middle-aged specialist with a reputation for honesty and great loyalty to the Curb. During the next year these attributes would operate at cross-purposes. Bijur was an intelligent and hardworking chairman; he could be counted upon to dig out the full factual record of what happened. He would show no favoritism between Plate and Cuppia, and would speak harshly to each as the occasion demanded. But what would he do with the information once it had been gathered? At this point his loyalty to the Curb would clash with his dedication to truth. Bijur was the biggest question mark on the committee. He would be the only person present at all the meetings; he would ask most of the questions, rarely relinquishing the floor to other members of the committee. More than any other member, Bijur knew the full record of what transpired between Plate and Cuppia.

John Goodbody, another committee member, appeared at a few meetings, and asked fewer questions. Goodbody had no clear idea of what was happening, although he realized the importance of the hearings. Morton Stern, a commission broker, likewise appeared irregularly at the sessions. Like Goodbody, he could be counted upon to follow Bijur's lead and those of the other two members, Rea and Bettman.

Rea was in a difficult position. As Curb President, he was expected to speak for the Exchange and be its public symbol. He had been appointed to foster business, defend the institu-

---

* The press blackout was complete, although Leslie Gould wrote several columns in which he referred to the hearings during this period. From material in the Gould collection it appears someone at the Curb leaked information to the columnist. In any case, Gould protected his source and did not write of what was happening during the summer of 1940.

tion against its enemies, and make certain it maintained an honest market. Clearly, a scandal would operate against his first task, while any attempt to mask wrongdoing, if discovered, would do the Curb irreparable damage. Also, Rea had been selected after Cuppia's withdrawal, and it was no secret that Cuppia planned to challenge Rea for the presidency in 1941. This must also have occupied Rea's thoughts during the hearings. The same problems beset Bettman, who liked to say he belonged to no faction but remained free to decide for himself what was best for the Curb as a whole. Such decisions would be hard ones in the months that followed.

Ezra Frost was in a quandary. He was a two-dollar broker whose firm did considerable business with E. A. Pierce & Co. If the investigation broadened into an inquiry into that company's affairs, Frost might be called to testify as a witness as well as judge the matter as a committee member. If Cuppia were cleared of all charges after Frost voted against him, Frost's business would suffer. Had this been a trial, Frost might have absented himself as an interested party. But it was not a trial, only a hearing, and so Frost remained on the committee. He was considered friendly to Cuppia, a known supporter of his presidential ambitions, and a man whose livelihood depended on the good will of men like Cuppia.

Young Alpheus Beane, Jr., was in a similar situation. E. A. Pierce & Co.'s business had declined in 1939, and the firm almost failed. Winthrop Smith, one of the partners, invited Charles Merrill to join the firm and revamp its structure. After consulting with friends—including Alpheus Beane, Sr., of Fenner & Beane—Merrill accepted the offer, and he joined the firm early in 1940. Soon after, the firm was reorganized as Merrill Lynch, E. A. Pierce and Cassatt, and was so called at the time the investigation ended. Thus, Beane and Cuppia were partners in the same firm.

At first blush this might seem an indication that Beane would favor Cuppia. Such was not necessarily the case. If Cuppia emerged with even a hint of scandal, it would reflect on Merrill Lynch, E. A. Pierce and Cassatt. This could not be permitted. Too, Beane was a rising star at the Curb, a man with a

Plate v. Cuppia — 163 +

bright future. He could not afford to leave the hearings with even a suspicion of favoritism.

Finally, there was E. Burd Grubb, now at the Stock Exchange but still interested in Curb affairs. The Moffatt-Grubb group had long opposed Cuppia, and harsh words had passed between the two men. The wounds had not healed by 1940. If Cuppia were guilty of any wrongdoing, Grubb would be the man to press for Curb action.

Plate was the first witness to appear before the committee. It was his task to explain what had transpired between himself and Cuppia.

The story seemed simple enough. Plate said he had been employed as a clerk at the firm of Dyer, Hudson & Co. from 1917 to 1928. As such he worked at both the New York Stock Exchange and the Curb. In 1928 he was at the Curb, representing his firm as its chief clerk.

It was then that he met Cuppia, E. A. Pierce's representative and a well-known and respected Curb figure. Cuppia approached Plate and told him that he would like the clerk to join his organization. If he did so, Cuppia would see to it that Plate received a good deal of business. There was nothing unusual in such an offer; similar ones had been made to clerks in the past. Plate accepted and joined E. A. Pierce, where his work apparently fulfilled all of Cuppia's expectations.

In 1932 Cuppia approached Plate with another offer. In view of his good work, he would advance Plate $22,500 for the purchase of a seat at the Curb. Plate accepted, and the seat was purchased in August. Again, there was nothing unusual about this transaction, which was approved by the Curb administration.

The next arrangement between the two men was irregular. At the time, Cuppia's secretary was Marion Shade, also a well-known Curb figure. Shade, who kept Cuppia's books, was rumored to know as much about E. A. Pierce & Co. as anyone. Cuppia told Plate that he would open an account for him at the Manufacturers Trust Company, and that Shade would have power to draw checks on that account. All of Plate's earnings would be deposited there. Each week Plate would be permitted to draw a small sum from the account for living expenses. It was $65 at first. The rest, said Plate, would remain in the account to be used to provide for his financial future. Later Plate claimed that Cuppia promised to use the money to purchase a partnership for him at E. A. Pierce & Co., or help him open his own firm.

Plate signed the agreement, which continued into 1939. In August of that year he asked the bank for a statement, and learned he had only $692.03 in the account. Plate was shocked. He investigated further, and learned that Shade and Cuppia had made withdrawals for their own uses. Money had been spent to pay for Cuppia's lawyers; several large checks had been made out to Mrs. Helen Cuppia. There was one to the British Colonial Hotel in Nassau, to pay for Cuppia's vacation in 1937; two checks for a total of over $5,000 paid for two of Cuppia's automobiles; and so it went. Plate claimed these checks indicated a misuse of funds, and he wanted restitution.

The story sounded rather strange, and Bijur examined Plate on its particulars. Why had Plate permitted Shade and Cuppia power of attorney over his account? Plate replied that he had seen nothing wrong with it; Cuppia had told him it was a normal way for money to be handled. He added that later on Cuppia repeated his promises of a partnership at E. A. Pierce, and the hope sufficed to end any fears Plate had that the money was in danger. In 1939, however, Plate asked Cuppia for an accounting, and suggested the agreement might be terminated. At that time, said Plate, Cuppia warned him that if he persisted in his request, he would be hounded from the Curb.

These explanations sounded rather weak, but Plate did produce cancelled checks signed by Cuppia and Shade; there seemed some substance to his charges. If the case ever got to open court, Cuppia could be made to appear a wrongdoer, and the entire matter would reflect poorly on the Curb.

Bijur recognized this, and asked Plate why he had taken the matter to court. Plate replied that he had done so on advice of his attorney. Didn't Plate realized that the committee could take care of his interests? Did Plate know how much

Plate v. Cuppia — 165 +

money a court case could cost? Was Plate aware of the bad publicity such a case would cause? Bijur asked Plate to withdraw his case and permit the committee to find justice for him. He hinted that if Plate did not use the Curb's grievance machinery, he could be charged with actions detrimental to the interests of the Exchange and face possible suspension or even expulsion.

Plate hesitated; he was not certain what to do at that time. And with this, Bijur opened a new line of questioning.

Bijur asked Plate if it were true that he had owed Cuppia $22,500 for his seat on the Curb. Plate said that he did, but that the sum had long been paid back out of his earnings. Did Plate owe Cuppia additional funds? Did the checks drawn by Shade and Cuppia represent the repayment of these sums, and not what Plate considered theft?

This raised a key question. It seemed strange that Cuppia would risk his position in the way Plate claimed he did. He must have realized that Plate would have access to the cancelled checks and, if the money indeed had been misappropriated, have recourse against him in a court of law. Cuppia was no fool, and to misappropriate funds in this way would be most foolish.

But what if Cuppia and Plate had entered into an agreement whereby they would split fees, and Plate would give Cuppia rebates for business brought him? Such actions would be a violation of both law and Curb regulations. Cuppia might then spend the money, safe in the knowledge that Plate could not bring action without implicating himself.

The testimony began with Bijur and the rest of the committee almost convinced Cuppia was guilty of misappropriation. Now the committee was exploring the question of whether or not Plate was involved in fee-splitting and rebates. Naturally, Plate denied this. But if he were—and, more to the point, if Plate felt the committee believed he was so guilty— then perhaps he might reconsider his court case.

Bijur pressed on. He had been given copies of the agreement Cuppia and Plate had signed in 1932, when Plate's Curb seat had been purchased. There was no mention of the $22,500 price Plate had named. Instead, the agreement read that Plate owed Mrs. Helen Cuppia $164,500. How could Plate explain this figure? The now-weary Plate replied he hadn't any idea, and denied knowledge of the clause. This seemed beyond the realm of belief, and Bijur hammered at Plate, catching him in one inconsistency after another. Earlier Plate had insisted that his earnings were to be placed in the fund, to be used for his own purposes. Thus, Cuppia and Shade had misappropriated the money. Now he changed his story: when Cuppia and he met in 1939 to discuss the termination of the agreement, the two decided to draw up a document giving Cuppia rights to the account, up to $164,500, with the money to be used to purchase his own firm or the membership in E. A. Pierce. Then Plate backtracked on this testimony, and claimed no knowledge of the clause.

Clearly, Plate was either confused or a liar, and perhaps both. Bijur had destroyed his testimony, and Plate must have realized this. Bijur repeated his question: Would Plate agree to withdraw his court case and submit the matter to the committee for arbitration? Plate agreed to do so.

The Curb had won the first round. The matter would be kept out of the courts—and, more important, the newspapers. It would be decided within the family, so to speak. Hopefully, scandal would be avoided. But in destroying Plate's testimony, Bijur had opened the question of kickbacks and rebates, and that question had to be answered. For if Plate and Cuppia were not engaged in some kind of illegal or at least unconstitutional action, then Plate's behavior in assigning power over his account and signing an agreement to pay Mrs. Cuppia the $164,500 made no sense.

Now Cuppia took the witness stand to give his version of the story. He came well-prepared for the encounter, having gone over every one of Plate's charges. Step by step he answered them.

First of all, what of Plate's contention that Cuppia had lent him money in 1932 for the purchase of a Curb seat? Cuppia replied that the loan had been made, but not by him. Rather, Mrs. Cuppia had handled the transaction.

Plate v. Cuppia — 167 +

In many matters the distinction between Jerome and Helen Cuppia as lender would have appeared unimportant, but it was vital in the development of Cuppia's statement. It also explained the large sum Plate owed Mrs. Cuppia. Finally, it absolved Cuppia of wrongdoing or the breaking of a Curb regulation.

According to Cuppia, his wife and the wife of another broker, Ralph Hubbard, had been partial owners of the brokerage firm of Locke, Andrews, and Pierce. Each woman had invested $50,000 in 1929, at which time brokerage seemed a good investment. Then came the crash. By 1932, the firm was on the edge of bankruptcy. But it did have some valuable assets, including seats on the New York and Curb exchanges. Cuppia thought Plate might be interested in purchasing one of the Curb seats. He offered to have his wife lend him the money for the purchase, on condition that Plate assume some of the liabilities of Locke, Andrews, and Pierce. Plate agreed to the arrangement, and this explained his willingness to sign the note in which he accepted his liabilities to Mrs. Cuppia. It also meant that Plate and Jerome Cuppia had no direct business connection; Plate's deal had been with Mrs. Cuppia. In this way, Cuppia tried to end suspicion of any business relationship with Plate, especially ones that might lead to kickbacks and rebates. Since Cuppia had no direct ownership of the firm, he had not violated the Curb rule that forbade a member from owning seats in two firms. And this would explain the many checks made out to Mrs. Cuppia: they were in repayment of the indebtedness.

What of the account at Manufacturers Trust? Plate had claimed that it had been established to provide him with a fortune. Cuppia denied this, and noted that he couldn't very well have promised Plate a partnership in E. A. Pierce as the firm had twenty-five partners, and he couldn't have committed them in any way. As for the account, it was Plate's own idea. Plate had told him that he had no head for figures. Would Cuppia find someone to handle his books for him? Cuppia replied that Shade had been his accountant for many years, and also performed the same duties for Ralph Hubbard and other brokers. Did Plate want Shade to handle his account? Plate did, and the agreement was made. Shade kept Plate's books from 1932 to 1939, and on several occasions Plate had remarked on how pleased he was with the arrangement.

Over the years, the money in the account was used to pay off the indebtedness. And all the time, according to Cuppia, he and his wife stood ready to help Plate in whatever way they could. As for the checks made out to Cuppia's automobile dealers and to Mrs. Cuppia—these were to repay part of the indebtedness. Plate said at the time that he understood this; Cuppia was surprised to learn that it had been dragged into question.

Was this testimony as implausible as Plate's? For a person of Plate's background, money was power and status; the committee found it difficult to believe he would be so cavalier in signing documents committing himself to large debts. But money meant something else to a man of Cuppia's position. It seemed possible he would help Plate in that way, even to the tune of more than $164,000. Besides, the money had been tied up in Locke, Andrews, and Pierce. Perhaps the Plate deal was the only way the Cuppias could have recovered their loss.

Bijur now turned to a crucial question. How could Cuppia be certain the loan would be repaid? The answer was simple: Plate was a floor broker, doing a considerable business, and he would repay the loan out of his earnings. Did E. A. Pierce do a great deal of business with Plate? Cuppia said his firm did. Did this mean that Cuppia favored Plate in his dealings on the floor, to insure the money would be earned and so repaid? Cuppia denied this was the case.

Kickbacks occurred when one broker returned a portion of the commissions earned to the broker who gave him the order. It was forbidden under the rules of both the Curb and the SEC. According to Cuppia, his arrangement with Plate did not involve kickbacks. But in receiving funds from Plate—even though through his wife—Cuppia had exposed himself to suspicions of having engaged in the practice.

Cuppia was asked whether he understood why the committee was questioning him on the matter. He was quick to defend himself. Only the previous year the Stock Exchange had had a

Plate v. Cuppia — 169+

similar case, in which it allowed the broker in question to recover funds from another broker by taking a portion of his floor earnings. If he was wrong, so was the Stock Exchange. Would the committee condemn him for so acting? If so, did it also condemn the Stock Exchange?

This was a big question, one Bijur preferred to ignore. Instead, he turned to the floor activities of E. A. Pierce and Co. Did Cuppia instruct his clerks to divert business to Plate? Cuppia denied that this was the case, maintaining his denial later in answer to similar questions.

Bijur might have dropped the matter at this point and returned to the questions directly involved in the Plate-Cuppia controversy. There was no need to go into depth on the questions of rebates and kickbacks. Neither man had raised the issue, and both denied having participated in them.

A lesser man might have taken this course of action. But Bijur was determined to find out whether or not the two brokers had engaged in the practices or, for that matter, were in violation of any other code of business conduct. In so doing, Bijur served the cause of honesty in a way seldom found at that time in the financial district. The Stock Exchange had gone to some lengths in covering up wrongdoing and potential scandal. Bijur, speaking for the Curb, would not engage in such practices. He persisted in his inquiry, always aware of several nagging questions.

If it indeed was true that Cuppia had violated the constitution, what of the dozens of brokers with whom he had done business? They too might be guilty of violations. And if Cuppia—the most powerful and influential commission broker at the Curb—split commissions, might not other brokers, less wealthy and more desperate, have done the same? In other words, the Cuppia testimony opened the door to the question of whether the Curb's regulatory arm was doing its job properly—and, for that matter, whether the SEC was performing as its supporters claimed it did. The Curb would deserve credit if it exposed wrongdoing on the floor, but the public and the SEC would soon forget the source of that knowledge, and concentrate instead on the scandal.

On March 28, *Plate v. Cuppia* was a relatively simple case involving the question of misappropriation of funds. By April 11, *Cuppia v. Plate* brought into issue the problems of Curb regulation, honesty, and other questions of Curb operations. The Exchange's leaders had acted originally to keep the matter within the family, as it were, but in so doing—by exercising self-regulation—they were in a position to demonstrate to Washington and the rest of the country that they were willing to punish a most powerful and influential man if it were warranted. But would they? A move that had been taken to defend the Curb as an institution against outside interference had resulted in an investigation of Curb procedures. By April 12, the leadership knew it had a tiger by the tail.

The investigation moved more slowly from here on. Other witnesses were called to testify regarding Cuppia's floor operations (Plate was all but forgotten by then). Harry Mark, one of Cuppia's wire clerks, proved most uncooperative, but in the end he conceded that fee-splitting and rebates did exist at E. A. Pierce, and with Cuppia's knowledge. Joseph Reardon, a broker, said that he had been in the practice of giving Mark money for business. Both men indicated that Cuppia knew of the deals and approved of them. Mark said Cuppia had told him to give Reardon the extra business. Other brokers corroborated the story, and told similar ones.

Ezra Frost also offered testimony. He denied having engaged in kickbacks or rebates. Frost said he thought Cuppia was a genius, the salvation of the Curb. He still admired the man. At one time, however, his business from E. A. Pierce declined. He had written Cuppia, and never received a satisfactory reply. Frost did not say so, but the implication was that the business had vanished because he had not "paid his dues."

Although the hearings were secret, word of what was being said was whispered on the Street and at Trinity Place each afternoon. Secrets are difficult to keep in the financial district, especially those involving scandal. In early July dozens of people realized a strong case had been made against Cuppia; that several witnesses had testified to kickbacks and rebates. Many Curb members knew the names of the people who had been

Plate v. Cuppia — 171 +

called to testify. They simply put two and two together and got four. The details of the testimony were secret, but their substance was not.*

Cuppia knew what was happening, and realized he would not be exonerated. Because of this, he resigned from his firm and notified the committee that he was willing to cooperate in order to keep the matter as quiet as possible, as well as provide him with a graceful exit from the financial world. The best he could hope for was that the rumors would fade with time. Verification was another matter, and Cuppia wanted to avoid this.

Cuppia would transfer his membership and leave the financial district if assured no further action would be taken against him. He conceded he had broken Curb rules. If his resignation was accepted under these conditions, he would leave the country and take up residence in South America.

This concession and proposal complicated the committee's work. All the members felt Cuppia's offenses merited severe penalties; had Cuppia insisted on a decision, it would have been against him, and he would have been forced from the Curb. Under those conditions, the entire matter would have had to be aired. On the other hand, Cuppia's suggestion, if acted upon and accepted, could save the Curb great embarrassment. Unfavorable publicity could be avoided, and the matter might soon be forgotten.

Whether this hope was realistic is hard to say, but it certainly is understandable. Some members might have believed public castigation of Cuppia would indicate to the financial community and the SEC that the Curb was vigilant against wrongdoers. Grubb thought as much, as did Ezra Frost. Alpheus Beane, Jr., agreed. The others argued that Cuppia had violated rules, but that no member of the public had suffered thereby. Those brokers whom Cuppia had favored with business had benefited, while the others had to forego commissions. But no evidence had been introduced to indicate that

---

* Much of the information in this chapter has been based on interviews with brokers of the period, "hints" found in the New York press, and material uncovered in the Gould papers. But the bulk of the testimony was revealed by the SEC in its 1941 investigation of the Curb.

any of the trades had been carried out inefficiently, or to the detriment of the purchaser or seller of a security through E. A. Pierce and Company.

Then there were questions Cuppia had raised during his testimony that had never been resolved. Was the checking account set up for Plate a violation of curb rules? Could not one member recover funds from another in this fashion? Was Cuppia's advance of funds for Plate's seat—whether done through himself or through his wife—a violation of rules? Clearly, such a relationship might invite wrongdoing on the floor, but was the purchase itself barred by the constitution?

William Hennessy, another broker who testified, indicated that he had been helped by Cuppia to purchase a seat, and was paying him back through earnings, part of which came from Pierce business. Yet Hennessy had not complained. Indeed, he insisted he still owed Cuppia money and was willing to pay it. If Cuppia was to be condemned for his arrangement with Plate, should he not also be condemned for the one with Hennessy? And what of Plate and Hennessy? As parties to the agreement, were they not equally at fault? The entire matter required clarification, and the committee, unsure of its ground, was unwilling to explore the matter further. This was the view of the majority of the committee.

If Cuppia was to be exposed as a wrongdoer, then the others would have to be condemned with him. Plate, Hennessy, and Reardon would certainly suffer. Others, brokers named but not called to testify, might join them. Who could tell where the matter would end? By the time full disclosure had been made, the public might believe the entire Curb was implicated. What would the public think if four brokers were punished? Ten? Twenty? How many more had escaped punishment? The SEC's reaction would be strong and swift. For these reasons, it seemed wise to keep the matter quiet—at least, as quiet as possible. Cuppia's offer seemed a good way out. The majority's decision may not have been wise, but it was understandable.

Grubb and Frost wanted to punish the lot. They felt the

Plate v. Cuppia   — 173 +

committee should not be swayed by fear of publicity. The SEC would soon know much of what was happening in any event; already rumors had reached Washington. Other details would leak to the press. It would be far better for the Curb to release the news than for outside agencies to do so. But this view was rejected.

Even before the hearings concluded, Cuppia had begun winding up his affairs. On June 21 he retired from Merrill Lynch. The reason given was illness; the *New York Times* story said he planned to live in the Southwest, where the warmer weather would be good for his health. Cuppia's biography in the *Times* mentioned his candidacy for the Curb presidency in the late 1930s and his work at other exchanges; it excluded comment on the lawsuit, and there was no hint of the hearings.

The committee on business conduct submitted its final report on July 31. There was no further action taken. A few days later the matter of *Plate v. Cuppia* was concluded. Cuppia continued to deny the charges publicly and for the record, but he settled the claim by paying Plate $7,500. Such a settlement, said Cuppia, was simpler than going through the costs, anguish, and bother of litigation. After all, he was a sick man, and could not be bothered with such matters.

On August 9, Cuppia and his family boarded the liner *Argentina* and set out for Rio de Janiero, where he said he would make his home. Health reasons were given for the move. There was still no hint of possible scandal in the newspapers. Financial writer Lemuel F. Parton suspected that Cuppia was going for business reasons. "The clews to Mr. Cuppia's sudden departure would seem to be romantic rather than financial, as Mr. Cuppia always had a keener eye for the trappings of romance than for mere routine money-making."

The matter rested there for almost a week. Then, in the afternoon of August 15, stories of a possible scandal broke. The New York *World Telegram* ran a headline story entitled "Curb Probing Activities of Former E. A. Pierce & Co. Partners." Merrill Lynch, E. A. Pierce and Cassatt refused official comment, although Charles Merrill noted that Cuppia was not a member of his firm. Rea issued a statement late that day which appeared in the newspapers the following morning:

> I have been asked to comment on new stories concerning a recent inquiry by this exchange into possible violations of exchange rules. The stories apparently refer to an investigation completed some time ago by the exchange. The investigation dealt solely with questions of floor brokerage and no matters investigated involved customers or public transactions. No charges were preferred against any members as a result of the investigation and the matter has been closed by the exchange.

By that time Merrill Lynch also had a statement for release. "I know definitely that Mr. Cuppia, because of the condition of his health, had long ago planned to resign his partnership in E. A. Pierce & Co. and dispose of his Curb Exchange membership," said Charles Merrill.

These statements did not satisfy the SEC, which finally, on August 19, awoke to the affair. The agency announced that it was conducting a "routine investigation of the financial affairs of Jerome C. Cuppia." It would consist primarily of a study of reports made by the committee on business conduct. There was no suggestion at that time of business misconduct.

In the New York *Journal and American* of August 21, columnist Leslie Gould's article, "Inside of the Cuppia Case— The Curb Misses Again," blew the lid off the investigation. Ever since late July Gould had been writing of the affair, while no other newspaper or journalist thought to investigate. Gould was known to have good sources of information, especially at the Curb, but he was also something of a sensationalist, and was responsible for false alarms too. Now he took credit for breaking the story, which he said was no mere case of a technical violation of rules. Gould told of how Cuppia handled kickbacks and rebates, but most of the article concerned the committee's actions. He wrote that the final vote had been 5–3, and that the majority of the board decided to try to keep the matter secret.

Plate v. Cuppia — 175+

In this whole case the effort has been to "hush hush" every-thing, and take a general attitude that what goes on internally there is none of the public's business. Although it is the public from which the Curb gets its business.

In this particular case, though, there was no need for publicity if it had been handled right, and the proper disciplin-ary action taken.

This had been the attitude of the minority: Grubb, Frost, and Beane. It would appear one of these men had leaked the story to Gould; no one else, with the exception of the stenogra-pher, typist, and counsels Lockwood and Truslow, could have done so. Cuppia, who himself had leaked stories to Gould throughout the 1930s, was now the victim of a new source for the columnist. Gould admitted he had been wrong in sup-porting Cuppia during the previous decade. ("A great many people were wrong on him, including this writer.")

The SEC received the Curb's records on the Cuppia-Plate investigation in early September. The committee on business conduct's transcripts began on April 3 and ran until July 31; these were the key documents, which covered less than three months of testimony. Together with other documents, the tran-scripts could have been read in less than a week by a seasoned staff member. The transcripts indicated violations of Curb rules. Also, there was a clear violation of Section 6(b) of the Se-curities and Exchange Act of 1934, which provided that no reg-istration of a national securities exchange "shall be granted or remain in force unless the rules of the Exchange include provi-sion for the expulsion, suspension, or disciplining of a member for conduct or proceeding inconsistent with just and equitable principles of trade."

One might have expected, therefore, that the SEC would begin public hearings sometime in late September or early No-vember. Such was not the case. Instead, the Commission waited until January 24, 1941, before announcing hearings on the mat-ter. In the interim the case was tried in the financial columns, and rumors flew in the district. The fact that Cuppia and oth-ers could act as they had in the late 1930s without SEC knowledge was an indictment of the Commission's effectiveness. This was followed by an unexplained delay in probing the matter. The Curb appeared shabby by January, but the SEC seemed a toothless and inept tiger.

While the SEC was looking over its papers, the Curb's leaders took steps to prepare for the forthcoming investigation. Several members of the board offered to resign, but were dissuaded from so doing in order that the Curb could present a united front against the SEC. Yet Rea and Bettman had to indicate that steps were being taken by the Curb itself to clean house. On November 13, Rea announced the appointment of John Madden, Benjamin Namm, and Victor Ridder as public governors. These men, said Rea, would represent the public interest, and would be asked to prepare a report on ways in which that interest might better be served. On February 4, 1940, less than two weeks before SEC hearings were due to open, the public governors issued their report.

> We realize that it has been the policy of the Exchange to give full publicity to any and all disciplinary actions that the Exchange has taken to members, whenever the offense has involved any financial loss on the part of the public. We likewise understand, however, that the Exchange has not seen fit to publicize disciplinary action taken with members when it felt that the public interest was not directly involved. In this last respect, we believe that such failure to publicize has been a serious mistake.
>
> A national securities exchange is a quasi-public institution. If it is to continue to act in that capacity, it must render a full account of its stewardship to the public at all times. . . .
>
> It must be a fundamental requirement that the members of a national securities exchange, to whom orders are entrusted by the public, should so conduct themselves that the highest degree of confidence may be placed in their integrity. Once this high standard has been established, there is no reason for not apprising the public as to the commission of a material offense by any member of the Exchange. The public should receive full information so that it may decide for itself whether its interest has been affected, either directly or indirectly.
>
> We feel that there should be no exceptions to a uniform

Plate v. Cuppia   − 177 +

policy of public disclosure of all material offenses by
members. . . .

It is our opinion that a review of the actions taken by the
Exchange in this matter [the Cuppia case] will illustrate the
need for the adoption of the above-mentioned recommendations.

The recommendations were unanimously accepted by the
board. Rea praised the report. Thus, he aligned himself on the
side of reform shortly before the hearings were scheduled to
begin. In effect, the board accepted what amounted to the
Grubb-Frost-Beane minority position of July 31, 1940. It had
done so under pressure and reluctantly, but there seemed no
other choice.

Soon after, unnoticed by the press, Jerome Cuppia returned to North America and took up residence in his Montclair home. He testified before the SEC as its first witness—but
he managed to extract a price for his appearance. The SEC
would not make public any of his testimony before the committee on business conduct. For that matter, the Commission
would not release any of the testimony at the Curb. It may
have been the price paid to get Cuppia before the Commission.
If this was so, then Cuppia was able to pay back in part at least
the consideration shown him by the committee majority. Almost all the brokers and others who had appeared before the
committee on business conduct testified publicly before the
SEC. And in each case, their public testimony differed from
their private.

Cuppia spoke of how he had arranged to receive kickbacks
from other brokers. He admitted having purchased Curb seats
for Plate and Hennessy, and also for John Raymond, his
nephew, because he was "unemployed, and I wanted to make a
place for him." Cuppia said he always regarded Plate and Hennessy as "mere employees" and the funds in their accounts as his
own, "held in trust for me." He conceded that he had not told
the truth regarding his operations when he had appeared before the committee on business conduct, but he repeated on
several occasions that the public had never suffered as a result
of his operations on the floor. Further, he denied having vio-

lated Curb rules, since there was no rule regarding a broker recovering loans from other brokers in the way he had done with
Plate, Hennessy, and Raymond. Toward the end of his testimony he noted that the wages of his sins were meager: Cuppia,
thought a very wealthy man, was actually in dire straights. He
had paid some $600,000 in capital to E. A. Pierce while asso-
ciated with the firm, recovered only $80,000 when he sold out,
and much of this had been used to pay off debts.

Cuppia was asked how much money had been involved in
the commission business he had done on the Curb. He replied
that he had paid over a million dollars in commissions to 61
brokers in the period from January 2, 1932, to March 30, 1940.
Six brokers received 43.9 percent of the business. Plate was
paid $197,830, Hennessy received $124,630, and Raymond,
$18,512. Powers, with whom Cuppia had had a "straight fee-
splitting arrangement," received $77,341. Cuppia did not re-
veal his share in kickbacks, or say what he had done with the
money.

Then Reardon testified. He spoke of his relations with
E. A. Pierce and his work with Harry Mark. Reardon said he had
given Mark money—usually $25 or $50 at a time—but always
as loans, never as payoffs. These "loans" were never repaid. On
one occasion Mark asked for a loan of $150. Reardon refused,
because Mark hadn't given him enough Pierce business. The
distinction between loans and gifts was not explored by the
Commission.

The next witness was E. Burd Grubb, who told of tensions
within the committee on business conduct. He said he had opposed the majority action and had wanted full disclosure. He
would not go into the reasons for the majority position.

George Rea defended the Curb's position in the affair.
He denied emphatically that the board had acted wrongly or un-
wisely. Rea observed that the Curb itself, and not the SEC, had
investigated the Cuppia-Plate affair, and this to him indicated
the success of self-regulation. Why, then, had the board not
taken stronger action? Because, said Rea, Cuppia had not been
technically guilty. Had Cuppia been found guilty of fee-splitting, as the term was commonly understood in the district, he

Plate v. Cuppia   — 179+

would have been punished. By recovering funds from Plate, Hennessy, and Raymond through controlling their checking accounts, Cuppia lay himself open to suspicion of wrongdoing, but no more.

In this way, Rea chose to ignore other evidence, such as that offered by Mark and Reardon, and concentrate on the major shadowy area as defined by Cuppia during his testimony. In his appearance before the committee on business conduct, Cuppia had claimed he had done no wrong and had cited the loophole in the regulations. He had abandoned this position before the SEC, but his old stance was being defended by Rea.

EXAMINER: Mr. Rea, you testified on cross-examination to the unwritten exception to the rule as to commission splitting?
WITNESS: Yes.
EXAMINER: Are there other unwritten exceptions to other rules?
WITNESS: I personally don't adhere to your characterization of "unwritten exceptions to the rule." The circumstances which you are discussing were simply not in violation of any rule.

Colonel Lockwood, who directed the Curb's defense, sat by Rea's side as the President testified. On cross-examination he explored the matter further.

MR. LOCKWOOD: Mr. Rea, did not Mr. Cuppia contend, before the Business Conduct Committee, that it was a practice on the New York Stock Exchange, a permissible practice on which he relied and which he claimed he had discussed with the president of the Curb Exchange, to allow a man who purchased a membership on money borrowed from a member, to assume a greater liability than the amount actually borrowed?

This would account for Plate's assumption of the liabilities of Locke, Andrews, and Pierce. Rea's answer was "Yes, indeed."

MR. LOCKWOOD: And was there not considerable doubt in the minds of the Committee as to that situation?
WITNESS: Well, I can't speak for the rest of the Committee, but I believe that your statement is correct. It certainly was so in my mind.

MR. LOCKWOOD: Referring to Mr. Hennessy, did not Mr. Hennessy, despite the payments which he made, still take the position that he owed more money to Mr. Cuppia?

WITNESS: He did.

MR. LOCKWOOD: And do you recall, in connection with the release of the subordination agreement—and this is my recollection only —that he stated that the release that was given by reason of some partnership relationship he expected to enter into, but that he still considered he owed the money?

WITNESS: I don't remember or have any recollection of the reference to partnership relationship, but I do recall that Mr. Hennessy testified that he felt he still owed money to Mr. Cuppia.

MR. LOCKWOOD: That is all.

Now the examiner explored the meaning of the testimony.

EXAMINER: In addition to the general rules and regulations which are in evidence here, of the New York Curb Exchange, are there unwritten rules?

WITNESS: I would not say so—there are policies.

EXAMINER: And this exception to this commission-splitting rule, you regard as a policy, do you?

WITNESS: I do not. As I have stated before, I regard it neither as an unwritten rule nor as a policy. It simply is not in violation of any rule.

EXAMINER: Then it is an exception?

MR. LOCKWOOD: In other words, this is not an exception, it is merely a way in which a man who borrows money may, in the opinion of the Exchange, properly repay it?

WITNESS: That is right.

In this way, Lockwood and Rea shifted the question from one of whether or not the Curb was implicated indirectly in fee-splitting, to that of a gap in the constitution. Rea conceded that fee-splitting was a violation, for which any broker should be punished. The arrangements between Cuppia and Plate, Hennessy, and Raymond did not involve fee-splitting, at least not technically. If the SEC insisted that the arrangement was indeed fee-splitting in practice, but conceded that the constitution was unclear on the point, it could condemn the constitution for sloppy wording. But this was the very constitution the

Plate v. Cuppia —181+

SEC had praised in 1939 as a model of its kind! Rea and Lockwood knew this, and presumably the SEC examiners—especially Ganson Purcell—knew it too.

What was unusual was the SEC's willingness to be led up this blind alley. Would it not have been wiser for the examiners to ignore the Plate-Cuppia arrangements and concentrate instead on Cuppia's admitted fee-splitting and rebates with other brokers—violations that Cuppia himself had admitted to in previous testimony? Yet for some reason the examiners did not do this, and instead followed Rea and Lockwood into the fruitless question of interpretation of the constitution.

MR. PURCELL: Mr. Rea, am I to gather from your most recent testimony, that it is a permissible practice on the New York Curb Exchange for a member to obtain an arrangement for splitting commissions with another member in order to reimburse himself for losses he has sustained?

WITNESS: I didn't say that, Mr. Purcell.

MR. PURCELL: I didn't say you did, I just wanted to be clear. I said —am I correct in understanding that from your testimony?

WITNESS: I don't know that it has ever come up, and I wouldn't want to answer that. I don't know.

MR. PURCELL: It might be?

WITNESS: I just don't know. As a matter of fact, it has been a matter of great discussion at the New York Stock Exchange particularly, in connection with the memberships of the odd-lot houses particularly. My mind, frankly, is not clear on the answer to your question.

MR. PURCELL: Suppose a man, a member of the New York Curb Exchange sustained losses over a period of time of, say, $1,000,000—would it be permissible on the Curb Exchange for that member to purchase a seat for another member, and split commissions with that other member, and thus reimburse himself for his losses?

WITNESS: Not as you phrase it, at all, but if a member enters into a voluntary obligation to somebody who advances the money for his purpose, I do not know whether that would be in violation of the rule or not.

MR. PURCELL: Mr. Lockwood, would you have any objection to helping us out on this point? You heard my question, and I wonder if you could state your understanding?

Lockwood and Purcell then entered into a discussion that resulted in a rephrasing of the question much more to the liking of Rea and Lockwood.

MR. LOCKWOOD: Mr. Rea, if a member borrowed from another member the purchase price of his membership, would we have any objection to the borrower paying that back?

WITNESS: None whatsoever.

MR. LOCKWOOD: And paying it back from business received from the man who had loaned him the money?

WITNESS: We would have no objection to that.

MR. PURCELL: Now I would like to add on the one-million-dollar losses to the case you have just given, Mr. Rea, and ask you whether in your opinion under the rules or policy of the Curb Exchange it would be permissible for the lender, that is, the person who furnished the funds for the purchase of the seat, to be reimbursed by that same method for the one million dollars in addition to the price of the seat?

MR. LOCKWOOD: No.

So it went. The examiners never did get to the crux of the problem: the need for reform at the Curb, and the reasoning behind the committee's refusal to punish Cuppia for admitted cases of kickbacks and fee-splitting. Rea went on to claim that he and other members of the committee had never received sufficient evidence to support a formal charge of fee-splitting. This too was not challenged by the SEC. The Commission adjourned on February 19 without having come to a conclusion, without calling for additional hearings, and without promising a report.

This abdication of responsibility permitted the Curb to clean its own house, which it proceeded to do. By then, too, some of the work of reform had been already accomplished. The public governors' report pointed the way. In addition, others involved in the scandal had either sold their seats or were preparing to do so. In March Charles Powers was expelled from the Curb, as was Edward F. McCormick, another broker who admitted to fee-splitting. James Reardon and William Hennessy were expelled in early April, and this cleared the slate.

Plate v. Cuppia   −183+

Cuppia's disgrace remained the key element in the case. For it was not only the failure of the man, but the end of an important movement in Curb history. For the first and only time in the Exchange's life, a reform challenge had been mounted by the big commission houses, represented by Cuppia. Had they succeeded, the powers of the Curb specialists would have declined, and at the same time the Exchange would have been drawn closer to the Big Board, since its base of independent power would have been crippled. In the late 1930s Jerome Cuppia planned for a unified securities market with government regulation, which would eliminate duplication of effort, inefficiencies, and parochialism. A similar plan would be considered seriously by the industry thirty years later. By then, however, those who remembered Cuppia recalled the scandal and not his dreams.

A similar though quieter leave-taking took place from the Curb Exchange's management. Those men involved in attempting to cover up the Cuppia Scandal began to leave administrative posts. Bettman did not run for reelection as chairman. He was replaced by Fred Moffatt, who throughout the hearings had criticized the way the Curb had handled the affair. Moffatt and Grubb had led the old guard in the late 1930s, and had been defeated after the new constitution had been adopted. The selection of Moffatt as chairman was a vindication of their position, or at least so it seemed at the time. It also signaled the triumph of the big specialists, who, although not particularly fond of Moffatt personally, recognized in him a defender of their power.

Sherman Bijur, Morton Stern, and John Goodbody did not seek reelection to the board. Their places and those of others were taken by such old-guard members as Posner, Howard Sykes, Joseph Cole, and William Steinhardt. Their return represented the collapse of the Young Turk movement. The old guard may have opposed the SEC originally as an unwarranted interference with normal activities in the district, but by 1941 they could claim that the Commission had proved a very inept organization, and so justify their opposition on that ground too. The old guard may have been closed to new ideas and wedded to the past, but the group was also honest, and this seemed refreshing in February of 1941. The kinds of changes the Curb perhaps needed would have to wait, but there would be no scandal while men like these were in command. Even Leslie Gould, the old enemy of the Moffatt-Posner group, conceded that "almost to a man it can be said that they would have taken stronger action in the Cuppia case than the Curb did under Mr. Rea."

Rea was the only person involved in the Cuppia case remaining. He served at the pleasure of the board, and clearly the new board would not want him to continue. Rea knew this, and made preparations to leave. He would not be forced from office; to do so would be unwise, for then it would appear that he too had been implicated in wrongdoing, and rumors of that sort would have destroyed any credibility the market had.

Rea announced his resignation on April 8, 1941, to take effect on June 30. He would not say why he was leaving, but rumor had it he would take a job in Washington connected in some way with the war effort. Later on it was learned that he was leaving to assume the presidency of Drexel Institute in Philadelphia. The board accepted the resignation with these words:

> Resolved, That this board accepts with regret the resignation of Mr. George Rea as president of the Exchange, which he has tendered to it upon the conclusion of three years in that office; Resolved further, That this board hereby expresses to Mr. Rea its deep appreciation for the energy and diligence which he has devoted to the discharge of the duties of the office during the difficult times through which he has served.

The search to replace Rea began. Grubb would have been the natural choice, but by then he was deeply involved in matters at the Stock Exchange, and in any case could not have accepted the loss of income the position would have entailed. A few other candidates were considered, and all were rejected for one reason or another. In the end the position went to Moffatt, who served as president pro tem, as well as chairman. The official reason given for this decision was to allow the Curb more

Plate v. Cuppia — 185 +

time to seek a successor. But there was a more pressing reason for Moffatt's selection as pro tem president. As such, he would receive no salary, and this was important at a time when the president received $25,000 a year. In 1942, the Curb was unable to afford a salaried president, for it teetered on the edge of bankruptcy.

+T E N−

Drift and Decay

The Cuppia Scandal coincided with the worst business period in Curb Exchange history. The combination of a continuing depression (by 1940 it seemed incapable of solution) and a
European war that at the time appeared on the verge of being
won by Nazi Germany caused further dips in securities prices
and trading volume.*

A few brokers argued that conditions were not much
worse than they had been in the mid-1930s. Some, though not
all, of the statistics would bear this out. For example, the trading volume in 1932, the worst year of the depression on the
Curb, was 57.1 million shares; in 1940, the figure was 42.9 million shares; it would drop to 34.7 million in 1941 and to an
all-time low of 22.3 million shares in 1942. On the other hand,
stock prices were higher in 1940–42 than they had been in the
mid-1930s. The Dow-Jones average of Stock Exchange in-

* Today we realize that the depression was ending in 1939, in large part
due to purchases of war supplies. To people of that period, however, the
depression seemed to be continuing. The economic upswing of 1939–40
was no greater than that of 1936–37. If the latter had not lasted, why
should the former? The same was true for the war. Newspaper headlines
of 1939–40 led readers to believe a German victory was in sight, and this
situation continued even after the Battle of Britain had ended.

dustrial issues hit a bottom of 41.22 in 1932; the low for 1940–42 was 92.92, reached in early 1942. But there was little price movement in 1942, a year in which the average fluctuated between 92.92 and 119.71, one of the smallest percentage ranges in the history of the averages.

The price declines of the mid-1930s, sharp and often violent, indicated a rejection of the district, accompanied by disgust, anger, and fear. The relative price stability of the early 1940s along with the volume decline was another matter. It seemed to show that investors were numbed, disinterested in securities, not caring one way or another about Wall Street and Trinity Place happenings. In 1934 the district was considered the villain, the scapegoat for the depression. By 1942 the financial community was being ignored; the former investors had learned to live without the markets, and were putting their funds into government bonds and savings accounts instead.

Fear and rejection often can be transformed into great upward sweeps on Wall Street. Such had been the case throughout the nineteenth century and into the twentieth. Disinterest and rejection were other matters. Before the district could prosper, investors would have to be lured back, and in large numbers. This would be the task not of a season, but of many years.

The nation would emerge from the depression in the late 1930s and early 1940s and enter a new period of prosperity, fueled by the war and, later on, post-war purchases and production. The gross national product in 1939 was $91.1 billion; it would reach $258.1 billion ten years later, in 1949. This economic growth was not translated into activity at the New York Stock Exchange. The Dow-Jones Industrials hit a high of 155.92 in 1939. The low for 1949 was 161.60, and the high that year was only 200.52. Faith in the economy had been largely restored by 1949, but faith in investment-grade securities at the Stock Exchange was still lacking.

The Curb Exchange fared badly in this period, but in some ways was better off than the Stock Exchange. In the first place, Curb brokers had lower expectations than their Stock Exchange counterparts; they could live more easily with relative deprivation. In this period the Stock Exchange was concerned with prosperity, while the Curb worried about survival.

More important, however, was the role speculation played in America. America has always been a nation of gamblers, and even during the mid-1930s there were speculators willing to "take a flyer" on a low-priced stock. Many of them could be found at the Curb Exchange. While investors stayed away from the Stock Exchange, speculators nibbled at Curb issues, especially after fear of an Allied defeat in the war had ended. The result was an increase in trading volume. By that yardstick, 1945 would be the best year since 1930.

Stock Volume at the Curb Exchange, 1939–49

Year	Shares Traded	Turnover Ratio	Daily Average	Dollar Volume
1939	45,729,888	6.7	183,654	$ 749,892,033
1940	42,928,377	6.3	171,029	646,146,547
1941	34,656,354	5.2	139,182	465,340,082
1942	22,301,852	3.6	89,566	284,804,875
1943	71,374,283	11.1	286,644	803,639,346
1944	71,061,713	11.4	285,389	911,447,710
1945	143,309,292	22.7	582,558	1,759,899,715
1946	137,313,214	20.5	549,253	2,021,047,018
1947	72,376,027	11.1	289,504	1,016,933,852
1948	75,016,108	11.4	297,683	1,041,778,268
1949	66,201,828	10.6	264,807	906,909,867

Source: *Amex Databook,* p. 30

The wartime and early post-war speculative enthusiasms helped the Curb brokers, but even this boom seemed the last bloom of the rose. Throughout this period stocks and bonds continued to leave the Curb, mostly due to their "moving up" to the Big Board or, in the case of bonds, maturity.

The situation, then, was one of speculative interest in a few issues. In the past, speculation had been accompanied by petty and large-scale thievery. Such could not be allowed in the aftermath of the Cuppia Scandal, and would not be permitted so long as members of the old guard controlled Curb administration. Honest speculation had meager rewards in this period,

Issues Gained and Removed at the
Curb Exchange, 1941–49

| | | *Stocks* | | |
Year	*Issues Admitted*	*Issues Removed*	*All Issues*	*Net Loss*
1941	8	55	1,023	47
1942	6	45	984	39
1943	11	49	946	38
1944	10	53	903	43
1945	38	61	880	23
1946	52	76	856	24
1947	31	51	836	20
1948	21	38	819	17
1949	16	39	796	23

| | | *Bonds* | | |
Year	*Issues Admitted*	*Issues Removed*	*All Issues*	*Net Loss*
1941	18	31	269	13
1942	0	32	237	32
1943	4	17	224	13
1944	0	34	190	34
1945	3	29	164	26
1946	1	32	133	31
1947	4	23	114	19
1948	3	7	110	4
1949	3	9	104	6

Source: *Amex Databook,* p. 24

and Curb brokers, seeing little future in the business, either sold their seats or at least considered doing so. Some went into the armed services; others found positions in the newly invigorated business world. Whatever the reason, the leave-taking was reflected in the price of a Curb seat. Toward the end of the war, when speculation seemed on the verge of a takeoff, seat prices rose. They declined soon after, reaching their 1939 levels by mid-1949.

Actually, the situation regarding seat prices was worse in 1941 and 1942 than the prices indicated. Reeling from the double blow of a lackadaisical market and the Cuppia Scandal, the Curb seemed doomed. A few brokers simply abandoned the

Price of a Seat at the Curb Market, 1939–49

Year	First	High	Low	Last	Number of Transfers
1939	$12,000	$12,000	$ 7,000	$ 8,500	25
1940	7,000	7,250	6,900	6,900	14
1941	2,600	2,600	1,000	1,000	27
1942	1,000	1,700	650	1,700	25
1943	1,600	8,500	1,600	6,300	20
1944	7,500	16,000	7,500	14,000	20
1945	15,000	32,000	12,000	32,000	35
1946	32,000	37,500	19,000	19,000	25
1947	25,000	25,000	13,500	16,000	35
1948	15,000	23,000	12,500	15,500	19
1949	10,000	10,000	5,500	8,000	16

Source: *Amex Databook*, p. 12

market, not even bothering to sell their seats, allowing their dues and assessments to lapse. Seats of deceased brokers, put on the market to help liquidate their estates, went begging, and while they did, dues and assessments went unpaid. Brokers on the floor knew of this situation; morale was at an all-time low.

In order both to deal with the problems of unpaid assessments and to maintain the price of Curb seats, the board began purchasing seats at a fixed price of $1,000. In effect, the Curb supported prices at that level, realizing they would fall to a fraction of that figure if this were not done. The Curb purchased fifty-one seats for these reasons in 1941–42.

In a way, these purchases made sense. Given the assets of the Curb in the form of land and buildings, as well as money in the cash account, the liquidating value of a seat was somewhat higher than $1,000. So the board, by purchasing seats at that price, actually enhanced the value of each remaining seat should liquidation of the Curb be necessary. In 1942 liquidation seemed more realistic than it had at any previous time.

Curb seats had sold for as high as a quarter of a million dollars in 1929. In October 1941, Francis Connolly's seat was sold to recover $755.79 in back dues and assessments. Others followed. On July 1, 1942, William Freeman, Harold Hart, and Laurence Rupp, and the estates of Ernest Meinken, Walter

Levenson, and John Kastner were notified of the pending sales of their seats, in order to recover back dues and assessments running from $278.15 to $905.87.

The Curb took these actions reluctantly, out of both humanitarian and practical reasons. Some of the men whose seats were sold had been old-time brokers fallen on bad days; to sell their seats seemed cruel. News of the sales disheartened the others. Whenever possible, the board tried to keep these men at the Curb. On several occasions a broker would be notified that his seat was up for sale; he would be given a period of time to meet back dues. In almost all cases requests for extensions were granted, as brokers tried to borrow sufficient funds—often less than $500—to remain in business.

The Curb bent over backward in permitting substitutions of registered representatives during the war. Several brokers were members of the New York, New Jersey, and Connecticut State Guards. As such they had to be away from their duties several days a month and, in the case of some, for weeks at a time. These men applied for permission to have authorized representatives take their places during these periods. By necessity most of these substitutes were part-time brokers. Some had left the district during the depression and were working full-time at jobs not related to brokerage. Yet the Curb permitted these substitutes to take the floor. It meant, for example, that one substitute broker would work on the floor until 3 P.M. and then rush off to his full-time job, that of special guard at the Pennsylvania Railroad.

This view of brokerage as a part-time occupation was not new; as we have seen, many brokers held two jobs during the depression, leaving the Curb for the night shift at Railway Express or the Post Office. This practice increased during the war. Brokers and salaried employees would work at defense plants, as longshoremen, teamsters, and at similar jobs. Years earlier such work had been looked upon as part-time employment, to last until times got better. The economy was robust by 1942, with war-related jobs plentiful and well paid. By then a dockworker received a higher salary than a senior clerk at the Curb. Little wonder, then, that such clerks came to view their work at Trinity Place as marginal, while their "real job" was on the docks. Or that a broker, making over $200 a week at the Brooklyn Navy Yard and less than half that amount at the Curb, took a similar view of his situation.

There are no available records of the personal finances of brokers and clerks of this period. Most who recall their lives at the Curb during the war speak of the temptation to leave the Exchange and seek better pay elsewhere. Many of these men had accumulated debts during the depression and saw in the labor shortage of the early 1940s a chance to clean their personal slates. Why did they remain at the Curb? Some of the older men felt secure at the Curb, where they worked as clerks. They were too old to change positions. And what would happen to them when the war ended? At that time, they were sure, returning veterans would take the jobs, leaving them unemployed. Such men had not survived the depression only to be jobless in post-war America. The more adventurous of the younger men might leave the Curb, but the rest remained, in what they hoped would be a secure position. Security was the key for men like these, not opportunity. There were others who liked the idea of a three-o'clock quitting time, unavailable at other jobs.

From discussions and scanty records, it is possible to reconstruct the finances of a Curb clerk. If he had been at work for more than a decade, if he was one of the many middle-aged clerks who had survived the depression, such a man might receive a salary of approximately $50 a week in 1942. Few such men lived in Manhattan. A number of them could be found in the east Bronx, but the largest group lived in Brooklyn. The lower-middle-class areas of that borough had several neighborhoods of two-family houses, most of them constructed in the 1920s. It was in neighborhoods such as these that the clerks and their families lived, renting upstairs apartments for approximately $50 to $65 a month.

The food bill for such a family would come to slightly less than $100 a month. Clothing was a small item, but dry-cleaning of work suits was a necessity. The clothing costs for the family came to another $20 or so a month. This left around $20 of the

$50 salary for medical expenses, insurance, and the like. Few clerks could afford even the most modest vacation. Social life revolved around the family, and entertainment consisted of the radio.

It was little wonder, then, that such men jumped at the chance for extra work, or that their wives took jobs during the war. It was understandable, too, that such men were tempted to take small bribes—$5 or $10—from brokers who wanted their favors when orders were distributed. After all, they reasoned, the order had to be executed by someone. If two brokers could do the job equally well, and one is my "friend," to whom I give the order, who is the loser?

If Curb brokers and employees were in bad financial shape during the early 1940s, the Exchange itself was in worse. Brokers and clerks could find part-time jobs to augment incomes, but the Curb Exchange could not take similar steps; it could not lease its facilities to other business or take in non-Curb work with which to earn money.* Instead, it was obliged to look to old methods of raising earnings, such as cutting costs and increasing business, as well as one new way: liquidation of assets.

Cutting costs was out of the question in the early 1940s. In the first place, the economy drive of the late 1930s had been most effective, and there remained little fat to be carved from the frame during the war. Clerks and other employees already were underpaid and overworked compared with other employees of the time. The wartime labor shortage made it difficult to attract new men and women to the Curb, where they were needed to replace those who entered the armed services, left the Curb for other employment, died, or retired. Yet the Curb could not raise salaries, due to both government regulations and its own inability to pay.

In earlier days the somewhat lower pay of Curb employees, and the low returns of brokers, might have been borne.

* In June 1944 the Curb offered four floors of its building to tenants, in a drive for additional earnings. Some offices were rented at the time, but the main Exchange facility, of course, could not be used for other purposes.

Like other financial markets, the Curb offered both glamour and the promise of future riches, if not present luxury. This was not the case during the war. Instead, glamour was found in war-related work of one kind or another, while finance seemed a dying profession at the time, a remnant of a bygone age. So the Curb was forced to limp along with the help of what amounted to a part-time staff and loyal employees who preferred to remain at the Exchange rather than take better-paying positions elsewhere. The thought of attracting new personnel was unrealistic given the problems of the period. Equally unthinkable was a cost-cutting program. It was rarely tried and, when attempted, was done in a half-hearted and dispirited fashion. Indeed, the pressures of higher wages elsewhere obliged the administration to revive the practice of year-end bonuses for employees as soon as possible. In 1945, when Curb finances were somewhat better than they had been earlier in the decade, the administration declared a bonus of 12.1 percent of total compensation for full-time employees who worked during the first quarter of the year, 9.4 percent for the second quarter, and 4.2 percent for the third. The fourth-quarter bonus was 8.5 percent, and the administration wrote that it hoped to maintain that figure in the future. (It did not always succeed.)

The second method of raising earnings was to increase business. Here too the men of the early forties were building on a strong drive taken by leaders during the late 1930s. In other words, that territory had been well-plowed, and little in the way of new business could be found.

The attempt was made. In mid-1942 a special committee of five was established "for the purpose of investigating the possibilities of increasing the business of the Exchange." Mortimer Landsberg chaired the committee, which was to consider changes in Curb organization and practices as well as to seek new listings. The committee made no recommendations for change, and there was no dramatic increase in either listings or floor activity. The increase could come only when fresh companies became interested in what the Curb had to offer, and when good "salesmen" for the Curb would take to the field. Small firms were unconcerned with listing in 1942, and Landsberg and others of the committee were poor salesmen in any event. Not for almost a decade would the right salesman find the right market for the Curb.

If small companies could not be attracted to the Curb, perhaps they could be traded against their will. Under provisions of Section 12(f) of the Securities and Exchange Law, stocks could be admitted to unlisted trading if such would be in the public interest. As we have seen, this meant the company's stocks had to be traded within the area of the exchange, and general interest in such trading had to be evinced.

In the past the Curb had raided the regional exchanges just as the Big Board had raided the Curb in the 1930s. Now, in 1943, the Curb mounted an invasion of the over-the-counter-market.

In early 1943 the Landsberg committee selected six of the most active over-the-counter stocks it could locate, and began studying them. The committee found out how many shares had been traded during the past few months, and the location of their shareholders. The hope was that each—or at least some —of the securities would meet the technical requirements of Section 12(f).

Several securities did fill the requirements. The Curb then asked the SEC for permission to place them in the unlisted section under the terms of the Act.

As might have been expected, this action brought prompt response from the National Association of Securities Dealers, which represented the over-the-counter brokers. The NASD charged that while the securities did meet the technical provisions of Section 12(f), they could not fulfill certain legal requirements. For example, the companies involved had not filed proper papers with the SEC, and were not reporting earnings, sales, and other required figures on a regular basis. The Curb admitted that such was the case, and it rested its hopes on the public-interest provision of the law.

Both the Curb and the NASD appealed to the Securities and Exchange Commission for support. At the time the SEC was somewhat moribund. As was the case with most federal agencies, the vitality of the first generation of administrators had been replaced by the placidity of the second; by 1943 the SEC was an integral part of the financial community, accepted by most leading businessmen, who no longer viewed it as a threat. In other words, the Commission had melded into the Wall Street Establishment; its crusading days were ended. Furthermore, the need for wartime harmony blunted any programs of reform the agency might have considered. In 1937 the Cuppia Scandal could have led to an SEC suggestion of federal control. By 1941–43, however, all the agency would recommend was greater power to oblige the exchanges to live up to their own rules and regulations. The SEC was not interested in radical reform at the Curb. Rather, the Cuppia Scandal convinced some administrators that the Curb had to be strengthened in order to prevent future scandals. For this reason, the agency was interested in the Curb's plan, much to the chagrin of the NASD.

In response to the appeals, the SEC undertook a study of over-the-counter trading in the six stocks involved. Questionnaires were sent to every over-the-counter dealer in the issues, requiring them to submit records of each transaction made during the previous six months. The results were then turned over to both the Curb and the NASD, which were told to use the material to present cases before the Commission.

The Curb's brief argued that the Exchange could make a better market in the six stocks than existed in the over-the-counter market. The spreads between bid and ask prices would be lower at the Curb, while commissions to brokers would be roughly the same. This meant that the buyer or seller of the security could do better if the stocks were listed on the Curb than they did at the over-the-counter market.* In this way, the public interest would be served by having the stocks listed at the

---

* Although neither the Curb or the NASD realized it at the time, this question was the beginning of a debate between the virtues of organized and unorganized markets, which would become of vital concern to both in the middle and late 1960s and early 1970s. In 1943 the NASD was on the defensive; a generation later it would take the offensive, claiming it made better markets than either the Big Board or the American Stock Exchange.

Curb. The Curb distinguished between active and inactive stocks in its presentation. Conceding that inactive stocks might best be retained by the over-the-counter traders, it contended that, at one point, activity in a stock should qualify it for trading on an organized auction market.

The NASD stressed the point that the six stocks involved did not fall under the purview of SEC requirements; they were not registered with the SEC.

The agency agreed with the NASD; the stocks remained on the over-the-counter market. (Although shortly thereafter one of the six went to the Curb, it was a public utilities holding company security, and so was registered under different provisions of the 1934 act.) This ended the Curb's most important attempt of this period to increase listings. It also meant that the Curb would be limited to the old methods of obtaining new issues: salesmanship combined with increased public interest in securities markets in general.

The final method of restoring liquidity to the Curb Exchange was the sale of assets. Such a method had to be handled with great delicacy in order to assure both the public and the brokers that it didn't signify the beginning of the end for the Curb Exchange.

The asset involved was the Hamilton Building at 22 Thames Street, which had been purchased to house Curb and member offices and handle other overflow operations of the Curb Exchange. Negotiations for the Hamilton Building had begun in early 1929, at which time several floors had been rented by the Curb. Purchase seemed a good idea at the time, for it was clear that even the addition to the original 1921 building, scheduled for completion in 1931, would be insufficient for the Curb's needs if the bull market continued.

Of course, the bull period soon ended. By the time title to the building had been transferred to the Curb in 1930, the beginnings of the Great Depression were in sight. During the 1930s the Curb would not need the additional space. Indeed, operations were such that some of the rooms in the new building were rented out at low costs to whomever wanted them. The Hamilton Building was a white elephant. Yet the Curb held on to it. Hopes for a business revival did not die during the 1930s, and additional office space would be needed when it came.

According to the Curb's accountants, the Hamilton Building was carried at a cost of $1,195,933.66. This figure included the original purchase price and the costs of improvements and additions, minus depreciation. In October 1943, Moffatt told the board that the New York Curb Realty Associates had received a bid of $250,000 in cash for the building. The previous February the board had instructed the Realty Associates that the building could be sold for a price of $350,000 in cash. The October bid represented the best the Associates could get. Such was the market for financial district real estate at the time.

The board considered the offer seriously, and in the end decided to reject it. Realty Associates was asked to try to get a higher price.

Moffatt reported a new offer the following month. A purchaser had been found who would be willing to pay a total of $375,000 for the building, on the basis of $75,000 in cash and a mortgage of $300,000 at 4 percent interest. Some members protested the offer—they wanted the cash—and wanted to withdraw the building from the market until conditions improved. They were voted down by a margin of 10–7. Instead, the board declared it would accept an offer of $100,000 in cash and a $300,000 mortgage at 4 percent. Such an offer was not forthcoming. In fact, the Curb received no serious offer for another year.

In December 1944 Realty Associates informed the board of an offer of $90,000 in cash and $310,000 in the form of a 4 percent mortgage. The board was most interested, but decided to hold out for an additional $10,000 in cash. This counter-offer was rejected.

Within a year the war would be over and the post-war boom would begin. At the same time, business at the Curb picked up, so the sale of the Hamilton Building was no longer of pressing importance. The price of financial district real estate was rising, and it appeared that the building might become more valuable as time went on. For this reason the board voted in April 1946 not to sell the building at that time. Instead, Realty Associates was asked to prepare a study of the situation and to make recommendations as to what should be done.

The recommendations, reported to the board on May 1, were most interesting, for they indicated not only an attitude toward the building, but a view shared by most brokers as to the future of their business, and of the district in general. In May, business was good, and gave promise of becoming better. Yet Realty Associates' first reason for not selling was that bids were too low; Realty quoted the findings of Charles F. Noyes Co., its consultant, which read in part that "you should not at this time accept an offer of $425,000.00 to purchase the property. We advise that you put a price of $500,000.00 on it because we think in this present market that you have a very good possibility of getting at least $450,000.00." Realty Associates added that the inflationary climate of the time might make the building an even better investment. To this they added the fact that the new Brooklyn-Manhattan tunnel, when underway, would cause the demolition of many buildings in the area, and would cause the price of real estate to rise. Finally, Realty Associates noted that the Curb "has an excellent cash position and does not need additional cash."

The board took the question of increased business into consideration. "There is a possibility that at some time in the future the Exchange or its Clearing Corporation may need additional space for expansion and the street floor and second floor could be available within a year." But this statement was made in order to consider all the possible reasons why the building might be retained; it was not presented as a serious argument. More indicative of the board's thinking at the time was the following statement: "Considering experience of the N.Y. Stock Exchange and to a lesser extent our own experience in real estate operation during the depression, we should not hold the Hamilton Building through another depression." It would appear the board thought a new depression more likely than a revived prosperity.

Austin Neftel, vice-president of Realty Associates, recommended selling for a price of somewhere between $450,000 and $600,000. His attitude seemed to be that it would be wise to get rid of the property at a time when the market was holding. He and many others could not believe conditions would improve much beyond what they already had.

A lengthy debate followed, and in the end it was decided to keep the building off the market for the time being. Realty Associates was asked to inform the board of new bids if and when they arrived.

One such bid was made in July 1946. A local real estate dealer offered $450,000 in cash for the structure, on condition that all present tenants would agree to the sale. The board voted to accept the offer. But the conditions could not be met, and once again the building went on the market.

Finally, in late August, the bid was remade, with present tenants remaining where they were. The price, as stated, was $450,000 in cash. This meant the Curb took a loss of $745,933.66 on the sale. Title was transferred to the new owners on February 28, 1947.

By itself the sale of the Hamilton Building would not be important. It does signify that, as late as 1947, the Curb's Board of Governors had little confidence in its future at least, and did not believe business could return to its pre-1929 levels. The Dow-Jones Industrials reached a high of 212.50 in 1946, and this was followed by a slump to 163.21 in 1947. The 1946 high would not be bettered until 1950.

In 1946 stock volume at the Curb reached 137,313,214 shares, slightly lower than the 143,309,292 shares of the previous year, but still respectable. Volume would fall to 72,376,027 shares in 1947. The 1946 figure would not be exceeded until 1954.

The sale of the Hamilton Building made good sense to Curb brokers in the late 1940s, who at that time still were betting on a new depression, or at least a recession. The board could not foresee that within five years of its sale the Curb brokers would be searching for new office space in the area, and pay record prices for small, dingy rooms in the Hamilton

The Curbstone Brokers, shortly before they moved indoors in 1921.

The Original Curb Market Building, in 1921.

The Curb Market Trading Floor in 1921. Note the posts, constructed as to resemble street light posts on Broad Street.

The Trading Floor in the 1930s. The overhead displays were soon removed, as they interfered with visibility.

The American Stock
Exchange today.

Trading on an average day in the late 1950s.

Edward R. McCormick, Curb President, 1914-1923. The founder of the Indoor Market, McCormick led the Curbstone Brokers indoors and established high standards.

Facing page

The Trading Floor today.

John Curtis (1923-1925) succeeded McCormick, inaugurating
an era of weak presidents.

David Page (1925-1928) served as president
during the bonanza years of the Great
Bull Market.

William Muller (1928-1932) attempted to
steer the Curb through the crash and early
depression, during which time he followed
the lead of the NYSE.

Howard Sykes (1932-1934), one of the most contentious figures in Curb history, faced rebellion on the floor and criticism from Washington.

E. Burd Grubb (1934-1935) led the reform element for a single term, and helped restore confidence in the Curb.

Clarence Bettman, a powerful specialist, became the Curb's first chairman under the new constitution in 1939.

J. Chester Cuppia at the height of his power. Cuppia, a reformer and leader of the commission houses, was the center of contention during the late 1930s and early 1940s.
(Photo courtesy of Mrs. J. Chester Cuppia)

In 1939, past and present Curb leaders posed for a group picture. Standing (l. to r.), Fred Moffatt, Edward McCormick, William Muller, and David Page. Seated (l. to r.), Col. William Lockwood, Clarence Bettman, President George Rea (1939-1942), Howard Sykes, and E. Burd Grubb.

James Dyer, who served as chairman from 1956 to 1960, and John Mann, chairman from 1951 to 1956, flank Edward T. McCormick, Amex President (1951-1961). McCormick would be at the center of the biggest scandal in Amex history.

Joseph Reilly, chairman from 1960 to 1962, was a moderate who was crushed during the reforms that followed the scandals.

David Jackson, chairman from 1965 to 1968, led the "Young Turks" of the early 1960s, who demanded a thorough reform at the Amex.

Edwin Posner, president pro tem (1945-1947, 1962) and chairman (1962-1965), was a power at the Curb and Amex for more than forty years. Posner was a moderate reformer, who helped pave the way for the Amex of today.

Edwin D. Etherington (1962-1966) was the first president under the 1962 con-
stitution, who together with Posner and Jackson was the architect of today's
Amex. Etherington was responsible for the most dramatic upgrading of the
Amex in its history.

Posner discusses reforms with William Earle and Solomon Litt.

President Etherington and Chairman Jackson discuss matters on the Amex floor.

Ralph S. Saul (1966-1971) continued the reform effort. Under his leadership, the Amex became an integral part of the "Establishment" during the crisis of the late 1960s.

Paul Kolton (1971-   ) leads the Amex in its attempts to use new technologies and adapt to changing markets.

The Amex Administration (l. to r.): Executive Vice President Richard M. Burdge, President Kolton, Senior Vice President Winsor H. Watson, Jr., and Senior Vice President James W. Walker, Jr.

Building. In retrospect, the Curb's experience in real estate was most unfortunate. In effect, it had bought high in 1929–30, survived the bottom of the market through good fortune rather than knowledge in 1943–44, and sold before the great upward sweep in 1946.

The attitude of retrenchment at the Curb was typified by the way the Hamilton Building matter had been viewed. The market would be honest if unimaginative, conservative if not prosperous. SEC regulations would be followed to the letter; ironically, though the Curb was better prepared to follow the SEC than at any previous time, the agency showed little inclination to use its power in the district.

It was a period during which survival seemed the most important objective of the board. Clerks were granted permission to take outside jobs, and brokers to engage in other activities so long as they did not affect their performances on the floor. More than a few brokers engaged in work on the over-the-counter market, a prime target for the Curb, and yet this too was permitted, for to crack down on the practice might be to force the brokers from the Curb, or even the district.

Moffatt was a good symbol for the Curb at that time. Honest, forthright, decent, he was also not the man to lead the Curb into new ventures. In times of distress, however, organizations need men like him, and Moffatt, whose services as president lasted from 1935–39 and then from 1942–45, was the right man at the right time.

Moffatt resigned as both chairman and president *pro tem* in 1945. Apparently he felt he had spent sufficient time in the posts and should remove himself for another man—assuming, of course, a man of like mind. Also, Moffatt had suffered financially while in administration; he wished to recoup part of his small holdings through active and full-time brokerage.

Influenced by Moffatt, the board elected Edwin Posner its next chairman and president *pro tem*. He and Moffatt had worked well together in the aftermath of the Cuppia Scandal. Both were noted for their integrity and were respected at the SEC and the Big Board. Posner's angry bursts of temper, which had earned him enemies earlier, were held in check while he served as vice-chairman during the Moffatt years. He was accepted without a fight by even his opponents.

Posner served for two terms, stepping down in 1947. Like Moffatt, he was not a wealthy man, and had to return to full-time brokerage in order to make a living.

The Curb was becalmed during the Posner administration as we have noted. The biggest news of his two years was the sale of the Hamilton Building. But before retiring, Posner made efforts to "normalize" Curb leadership. He realized that neither Moffatt or himself was fitted by personality for the presidency, and that no one man could be both chairman and president at the same time. The offices had been combined for financial rather than administrative reasons. Although the financial squeeze still existed, Posner felt strongly that the Curb needed the services of a full-time paid president, and he said so late in 1945. The new president would have two tasks: he would have to seek new listings, as well as convince the public and Washington that the Curb was an honest and well-run market. In addition, he would have to be conversant with Curb affairs and be a person of some stature. Posner thought an increased salary—$40,000 a year—might attract such a man.

Several candidates were interviewed—politicians, brokers, college presidents, and newspapermen—but no one man seemed able to combine all the qualities needed for the position. In the end the Curb was forced to compromise. The board's choice for the position was Francis Adams Truslow, who was elected unanimously in December 1946.

Truslow, only forty-one years old in 1947, was a long-trusted and familiar figure at the Curb. A graduate of Yale and Harvard Law School, he had joined Colonel Lockwood's law firm in 1934, and immediately became junior counsel for the Curb. As such he helped prepare many of the briefs Lockwood used in the Curb's many battles with the SEC. Although the Colonel received much of the credit and publicity, he made certain Curb leaders understood and knew that Truslow deserved their respect. In many ways, Truslow became Lockwood's protégé and heir apparent. When Lockwood retired in 1942, Truslow was named senior counsel, at the age of thirty-six.

Five months after being elevated, Truslow resigned his post to become president of the Rubber Development Corporation, a government agency charged with developing new rubber plantations in South America. Truslow traveled extensively through Brazil during this period, so that by the end of the war he was considered one of the country's leading experts on that nation. In 1945 Truslow was named to the American delegation to the Inter-American Conference on War and Peace in Rio. At the time, he was convinced his future lay in government service.

There was much history in his name—Truslow, related to the Adams family of Boston, could qualify as a blueblood. He was young, ambitious, intelligent, and well-connected; there seemed no reason to believe his ambitions would not be satisfied. But Truslow was a Roosevelt appointee, a man who found little place in the Truman administration, and as new men came in to replace the old in 1945, he was passed by. In any case the State Department, like other branches of government, was faced with retrenchment after the war. Because of this, Truslow was prepared to resume his law career for the time being.

For these reasons Truslow accepted appointment as Curb President. He made no secret of the fact that his ultimate ambitions lay elsewhere. Truslow was forthright with the men who had selected him for the presidency, most of whom he had known for more than a decade. He would serve until government service beckoned. Then, with their help, he would engage in the search for an acceptable successor.

The transition of power was smooth. Posner stepped down in February 1947 and was succeeded as chairman by Edward Werle, a commission broker and partner in the firm of Johnson & Wood, who had been at the Curb since 1928 and was considered a member of the old guard. Werle also became president *pro tem,* a post he retained until March, when Truslow assumed the duties.* With this, Curb administration was regularized for the first time since Rea had resigned in 1942.

One of Posner's most important duties as chairman had been to prepare the way for this transition—including the selection of Truslow. Ironically, Truslow's most significant act as president would be the selection of his successor, while Posner would be called upon, as chairman and president *pro tem* again at a future date, to regularize administration once more by leading in the search for a new president.

* Werle subsequently became a member of the New York Stock Exchange, and soon after joined its board and became its chairman. This is the only instance in which a former board chairman of the American Stock Exchange became a board chairman of the New York Stock Exchange.

+E L E V E N–

The Right Man

Francis Adams Truslow was a respected and honored figure as Curb President. He worked well with Chairman Werle, and later on with Mortimer Landsberg, who replaced Werle in 1950. During his term, which lasted from 1947 to 1951, Truslow traveled extensively throughout the country, delivering speeches on topics ranging from the future of the financial district to the importance of Latin America. No previous president or chairman—not even Sykes or Grubb—had had such good personal relations with opposite numbers at the Stock Exchange, and there was no important difficulty with the SEC during the Truslow presidency. In part this was due to the Commission's inactivity in this period, but Truslow deserved part of the credit, too. His honesty and integrity were unquestioned.

But was this the first order of Curb business at that time? The hope was that Truslow could obtain new listings. These did not materialize. In the past even Moffatt had taken to the road to appear before business groups in attempts to promote listings. Truslow would have none of it. He would discuss the problems of the district, but could not find it in himself to propagandize for the Curb. In the beginning he made the effort, but then gave up completely, and Curb brokers saw his lack of missionary zeal as a major failure. By 1950 the number of stocks traded at the Curb was down to 767, the lowest point since such records had been kept.

What might Truslow have done to increase business? As has been noted, he might have pushed harder to obtain domestic listings, as had some of his predecessors. In the past, salesmanship at the Curb had been combined with a willingness to stretch rules, such as overlooking deficiencies in balance sheets insofar as earnings, assets, and shareholders were concerned. Truslow was intent on changing this situation, and hoped to establish hard and fast criteria for listing. Due to member opposition, such was not possible. Backed by Lockwood, he insisted on high standards for securities, and the committees followed his lead in this.*

Some specialists hoped Truslow would use his Latin American connections to aid the Curb. Ever since its founding, the Curb had been the largest market for foreign securities in the United States. During the late 1940s there was much talk about the glowing future of several South and Central American nations, most particularly Argentina, Brazil, Mexico, Chile, and Venezuela. Could not Truslow visit these countries, seeking new listings? Curb brokers would scan the stocks on Latin American exchanges, wondering which would find the best markets in New York. All Truslow had to do, they said, was to help them help themselves, and he was admirably connected for such a task.

Truslow made no such move. Few foreign securities were listed at the Curb during his administration. Truslow made only one visit to Latin America during this period, and that was not on Exchange business. Perhaps he lacked the personality for the task, or it might have been his unwillingness to take any step that might endanger a future career in government, but whatever the reason, Truslow did not expand listings in the one area in which he was well-qualified to do so.

* The Exchange did not have formal listing requirements in this period. Any stock acceptable to the committee, accompanied by the necessary papers, would be admitted. The first specific requirements in terms of earnings, assets, shareholders, etc., were set down in 1962.

Instead, Truslow continued the movement toward an honest market that had been initiated by Moffatt and continued by Posner. Since the Cuppia Scandal Curb administrations had been particularly sensitive to breaches of floor regulations. Surveillance was strict, and in this post-1942 period the floor transactions committee handed down severe penalties for infractions of rules. Findings were released to the press, serving not only to publicize the vigilance of the committee, but as a warning to brokers to follow the rules.

This practice began to change about midway through the Truslow administration. In part this was one sign of discontent with his policies, but it also reflected the influence of John Mann, chairman of the committee on floor transactions. Since his admission to the Curb in 1933, Mann had risen rapidly as both broker and Curb leader. A major specialist in 1948, when he won election to the board, Mann had served as a member of the committee on admissions before becoming chairman of the floor transactions committee. In 1949 he was elected vice-chairman of the board, and was spoken of as the logical successor to the chairmanship when Bettman stepped down.

As chairman of the committee on floor transactions, Mann held that as little publicity as possible should be given to admonitions and fines, especially when the public interest was not involved. A majority of the committee agreed. For the rest of his period on the committee a virtual news blackout was in effect, marking a return to the attitude taken by the board during the Plate-Cuppia hearings, and for which the Curb had been criticized by the SEC.

Unlike Truslow, Mann was willing and eager to speak on behalf of increased listings. As an official better suited than Truslow to a market that needed business, Mann's prestige rose during the latter years of the Truslow administration. If such activism implied risks, then risks would have to be taken. To many, Mann's attitude toward the market place seemed more realistic than that of the rather puritanical Truslow.

In the face of declining business during the late 1940s, Mann and other activist brokers worked with Truslow to streamline the Curb and save money. They advocated the establishment of a joint clearing house with the Stock Exchange, to be known as the Stock and Curb Clearing Corporation. Truslow claimed this would result in increased income for the Curb, and at first the Stock Exchange, with financial difficulties of its own, seemed agreeable.

In the end the plan was dropped. The Stock Exchange backed away, not wanting to associate so closely with an obviously junior market. Nevertheless, the idea indicated Truslow's methods of saving money for the Curb and strengthening the market. Like most of his proposals, it involved closer relationship with the Stock Exchange and an end to duplication of effort.*

Before he left office, Truslow also suggested that Saturday trading, already discontinued during the summer, be ended for the winter as well. In its place, weekday trading could be extended an extra half hour, to three-thirty P.M. This too would be done in full cooperation with the Stock Exchange. Although Truslow had first broached the idea, he was willing to have the announcement of it come from the Big Board. But, like the project for a joint clearing house, the Stock Exchange withdrew, and Saturday closing was killed.**

If Truslow disappointed some brokers because of his inability or unwillingness to seek new listings, he pleased others who considered him a fine administrator and a man who gave the Curb a good public image. But fallen hopes led to increased discontent by 1950, and to a major change in Curb ad-

* The idea for a joint clearing house was ignored during the 1950s, but was revived in the mid-1960s. Securities Industry Automation Corporation (SIAC) was formed in 1971, in part to accomplish joint clearings. The 1971 plan was quite different from that offered by Truslow three decades earlier, but such was to be expected with a new technology and new problems. Nevertheless, Truslow had first initiated the idea, although he has never been credited with it.
** Saturday trading ended in 1952, at which time all the credit for the change was given the Curb's president, Edward McCormick. None of the financial writers of the time mentioned that it was the fruition of Truslow's 1950 proposal. In this, as with the clearing house, Truslow remains a forgotten man.

ministration the following year. This came as a result of three unconnected developments.

The first of these was a revival of interest in securities. Until 1949 the post-war markets had been disappointing. The economy seemed in fine shape, as the anticipated depression had not developed in 1945–46. There was a minor recession in 1949, which some bears felt could be the beginning of the depression. Yet, in the summer of the year prices began to rise, with the advance spearheaded by three stock groups: gold issues, soft drinks, and television. The rise in gold stocks was considered a bearish move, and that in soft drinks an interest in stable securities on the part of conservative investors. But the sharp advances in television shares represented a new development: a recognition on the part of the investing public that the new technology might produce huge profits for some companies. In 1948 fewer than 3 percent of American homes had television sets; even the most pessimistic investors realized that the boom would not end until almost all Americans had receivers. Sales of television receivers soared as Americans dipped into their wartime savings and rushed to the appliance stores.

The television boom led to interest in other stock groups. Aircraft, automobiles, household appliances, and other consumer-related and new-technology firms received attention. Purchases of many securities in these fields made investment sense, since the leading firms had good balance sheets and increasing earnings.

At the same time fantasy—without which no major bull market is possible—also appeared in the district and nation. The market may rise as a result of better economic conditions, but it does not boom unless and until investors begin to hold what later on may appear unrealistic dreams of great wealth, to be gained from investment in small, speculative companies in "glamour industries." This also began in 1949, with interest centered on uranium stocks. One popular belief of that year was that within a decade most of the nation's electric power would be derived from atomic power plants, and that a nuclear-powered automobile engine would soon follow. This could mean that uranium would be in short supply, and the price of the metal would rise sharply. There were uranium mines in Africa, but these were difficult to invest in. Canada, which had known uranium reserves, was another matter. Almost overnight American and Canadian miners began to wildcat the Canadian north, equipped with geiger counters but in other ways resembling the gold miners of the Yukon a half century earlier. Others explored the American Southwest, also searching for uranium. Any new mining company claiming to have found uranium could count on eager speculators willing to purchase low-priced issues—known as "penny stocks"—in the hope of seeing them rise to become "another Anaconda" or "the Kennecott of the nuclear age."

The Canadian securities markets were booming in late 1949. Brokers on Toronto's Bay Street noted that a good deal of their orders were coming from the United States. By 1951 well over $50 million a year in American money had flowed to the Canadian markets in search of new penny stocks and other speculative ventures. At the time it was common to compare the Canada of the 1950s to the United States of the post–Civil War period. In other words, Canada, about to become a major economic giant, was entering a new and major growth phase. Market letters observed that small investments in young American corporations in the 1870s would have reaped large profits for investors and they recommended Canadian securities.

As has been noted, the Curb was always the major organized market for foreign securities in the United States. Surely there were many Canadian issues that would interest American investors, and their American depository receipts, or the securities themselves, should be listed at the Curb. Truslow was urged to make a major effort in that direction. But the man who would not search for Latin American securities in 1947–48 by going to an area he knew well was hardly likely to go to Canada and search for new listings there.

At a time when speculation was growing, the leader of what was recognized as a more speculative market than the Big Board appeared more concerned with internal reform than new business. This served to increase discontent with the President, and it led to calls for new leadership.

The second development was the growth of dissident power at the Curb. By 1951 the old guard had completed nine years in power, during which time there had been no organized opposition. The Cuppia Scandal had given reform a bad name. This is not to say that the dissidents of 1951 were reformers; on the contrary, they had no argument with the old guard, but chafed at the inability of independent brokers to crack it. Posner, Bettman, Landsberg, and others of the group ran a tight ship, but an exclusive one. And not all brokers were willing to put up with what they considered excessive conservatism in selecting nominees for the board.

In late December 1950, leading old-guard figures selected their choices for the board. All were men who had put in long apprenticeships as brokers and had won the confidence of the Posner-Bettman-Landsberg group. The most interesting of them was Joseph Reilly, a commission broker who had joined the Curb in 1936. Over the years Reilly had earned a reputation as an imaginative, able, and honest broker. He was also considered one of the hardest-working and most dedicated men on the floor.

The old guard also selected Mann for the chairmanship, as Landsberg indicated a desire to step down after a year in the post. Mann had served only one three-year term on the board, but his aggressive work for the Curb had earned him the confidence of the older brokers.

The dissidents did not challenge Mann, but selected a five-man slate to run against the regulars. Generally speaking, the slate consisted of younger men than the regulars, or older brokers sympathetic to the outsiders. James Dyer, who ran on the opposition ticket, was one of the latter group. Dyer had come to the Curb in 1929, and was considered a capable specialist. Like the others, he had ambitions insofar as Curb politics were concerned. They had been thwarted in the past, and now Dyer joined the dissidents in opposition.

The entire administration slate won election, along with Mann. In a way, the victory might be considered a vindication of Truslow's regime. On the other hand, the fact that a slate had been filed reflected badly on the President. The election of

Mann seemed another sign that Truslow's inactivity in seeking new listings was being criticized. The new board supported Truslow, but in early 1951 this support was not as strong as it had been four years earlier.

The third and final reason for Truslow's departure was his own ambitions. As has been mentioned, Truslow had for years been anxious to get a diplomatic post. Early in 1951 he was called to Washington and asked to consider an appointment as head of the United States–Brazil Joint Commission for Economic Development, with the rank of ambassador. The appointment came about through the intercession of Secretary of State Dean Acheson, who was a fellow-member with Truslow of the Council on Foreign Relations. Truslow accepted the post in February, although he had notified members of the board of his intention to do so in mid-January. The search for a successor began at that time. Truslow agreed that he would make no official announcement of his resignation until his replacement had been informally accepted by the board.

As had been the case in earlier, similar situations, many candidates were put forth for the position, while others recommended themselves. This time there was no prolonged search. Providing he would accept, the board wanted Edward T. McCormick for the post. And McCormick accepted.

McCormick was an unusual man, and seemed even more so in 1951. If one were to put together a composite of a perfect president for the Curb Exchange, he would arrive at someone very much like him. In every respect, McCormick seemed the right man at the right time for the right position.

All board members agreed that the new president would have to be strong in those areas where Truslow had been weakest, the most important of these being the aggressive selling of the Curb Exchange and the search for new listings. McCormick had a warm, outgoing nature, a fine command of the language, and genuinely liked people. He was a natural salesman, showing talent in that area throughout his life. In 1923, when only twelve years old, he built up one of the largest newspaper routes in Tucson, Arizona. Once, when he broke his leg, the Tucson *Citizen* complained editorially that fewer newspapers had been sold since "Teddy" left his route. When he recovered he revived the route, making enough money from it to help pay for his college education.

Some board members expressed the hope the new president would be a more colorful person than the rather drab Truslow. Here too, McCormick filled the qualification. He was born in Phoenix, Arizona, the son of a Spanish mother and Irish father, and his Rye, New York, home was done in Spanish-modern style, setting it off from the more conventional homes in the area. McCormick was a fabled host, the center of attention at any party. A fine raconteur, he could hold an audience spellbound while he sold them on the virtues of American finance, the solidity of the Curb, and the varied blessings to be realized through listing.

Some past presidents—Edward R. McCormick, Moffatt, and Posner—had the respect of the floor brokers, and Grubb had been popular with the membership. None of them was better equipped to engage the affection of the older men and the new, younger contingent than McCormick. The short, chunky man with the beaming smile seemed the image of the successful Irish-American broker, and there was a large number of such men at the Curb Exchange in 1951. McCormick would joke with these men, dine with them, swap stories with them, and in other ways be "one of the boys." * He seemed to understand their problems and sympathize with them.

McCormick also fit in well with their sons, young men who had graduated from college and respected learning and academic accomplishments as well as skill in brokerage. With a B.A. from the University of Arizona, McCormick then had gone to Northwestern, where he took sufficient courses to qualify as CPA. From there he went to the University of California for an M.A. in economics, and he received a Ph.D. from Duke. Never before had a man of such academic credentials been selected for the leadership of a major securities market.

The Curb needed a president who would understand the

---

* McCormick was a Protestant, a fact that many Amex brokers do not believe to this day.

SEC, and be able to work with it. McCormick's doctoral dissertation was entitled, "Understanding the Securities Act and the S.E.C.," and was one of the first scholarly efforts in the field. Soon after, McCormick joined the Commission as a securities analyst, and he rose rapidly, serving as assistant accountant, chief accountant, and assistant director. In 1949, McCormick had been named an SEC commissioner.

McCormick knew all the top men at the SEC and was on good terms with them. He was considered a liberal, a "Truman Democrat," and a New Dealer. Many leading congressional critics of the financial community, including Senator Paul Douglas of Illinois, himself a distinguished economist, lamented McCormick's resignation from the SEC, but expressed delight at having such a man at the Curb Exchange.

Prior to receiving a formal offer of the presidency, McCormick met with a three-man committee, consisting of past Chairman Werle, Chairman Landsberg, and Chairman-elect Mann. All were favorably impressed, and recommended his candidacy. McCormick was to be offered $40,000-a-year salary for a three-year term, plus inclusion in the pension plan.

Later several leading Curb Exchange figures would claim they had had misgivings about McCormick from the first. There is little indication that such was the case. The only board member to show disfavor with McCormick in the mid-1950s was Edwin Posner, who had had a falling out with the President in 1952. Posner left the board in early 1953, and represented the sole outpost of opposition for the rest of the decade.

Posner's disillusionment began in July, when McCormick recommended the retention of Michael Mooney as Curb counsel, at a salary of $17,500 a year. Mooney had been with McCormick at the SEC, where he had earned a reputation as a perceptive and clever lawyer. Like McCormick, he knew most of the leading figures at the SEC, and was considered an ambitious and personable attorney. McCormick wanted Mooney as his counsel because he knew from experience that close relations between the president and the counsel were vital for smooth administration of the Curb. At the time the SEC was discussing new regulations for the exchanges. The Senate Banking and Currency Committee had just completed hearings on the proposed Frear Bill, which would have the effect of making every company of a certain size in the United States, whether on an exchange or not, subject to registration requirements. According to the version reported out of committee, companies with $3 million in assets and 300 stockholders would have to register with the SEC. If the bill were passed, these firms would be excellent candidates for Curb listing. Both Mooney and McCormick were conversant with the bill and capable of lobbying for its passage. For this reason, as well as his desire to have an old friend by his side at the Curb, McCormick pressed for Mooney's selection. The board acceded to his desire, and Mooney was given the job.

The selection of Mooney meant the dismissal of Thomas McGovern, his predecessor. As we have seen, McGovern was a member of the same law firm as Truslow, who himself had been Lockwood's protégé. These men had held that office since 1923, and had been the backbone of the old guard. Mooney's elevation and McGovern's dismissal was more than a rotation in office; it was a symbol of a new era at the Curb, and a major manifestation of change. Posner, who by then had become the leader of the old guard, resented the change. His refusal to serve under McCormick was his way of indicating a vote of no confidence in the man. Thus, Posner left administration after an unbroken stretch of twenty-eight years.

McCormick took two moves during his first term that further symbolized the change in leadership, although both had been initiated by Truslow.* The first was the decision to end Saturday trading, which was discontinued after May 24, 1952. To make up the lost time, trading hours were extended to three-thirty beginning June 2. It was a break with tradition, although for many years the exchanges had closed down during the summer months on Saturdays. All McCormick did was to

---

* Truslow never filled his diplomatic post. He died of a heart attack on July 9, 1951, en route to Brazil. At the time he was forty-five years old. Ironically, Truslow died on board the *Argentina,* the same ship Cuppia had taken to Brazil on his way to exile in 1940.

close the Curb on Saturdays the year round, a realization of Truslow's plan of three years earlier.

McCormick carried it out in grand style. First of all, news of the change was carried prominently in all the city's newspapers and in many out-of-town financial pages. By then McCormick had developed excellent relations with the press, and Curb news now appeared regularly in featured positions, for the first time in history. McCormick was proving he was the man to bring the Curb to the public's attention. Next, McCormick made the closing seem a bold innovation: the Curb was keeping up with the times, and even leading the way. Finally, by indirection McCormick indicated the Curb would no longer follow the lead of the New York Stock Exchange. In the past, the Big Board would introduce changes, with the Curb following. Now the roles were reversed. On May 7, McCormick told the board that the Stock Exchange had voted to close down on Saturdays beginning May 31; he implied that it was following the Curb's lead. Needless to say, such a change in roles increased morale at the Curb, as well as McCormick's reputation.

In the months that followed, McCormick put forth ideas regarding trading hours that seemed in advance of anything before considered in the district. He thought the Curb might well remain open for trading one night a week. The department stores did it. Why not the securities markets? Ignoring the fact that there was quite a difference between the two kinds of establishments, the idea seemed novel, exciting, and perhaps a means of increasing business, and all of these factors intrigued not only Curb brokers but the general public as well. Then McCormick put forth the idea of "satellite markets" in the Midwest and Far West, where Curb securities might be traded. In this way, the Curb's influence would truly become nationwide. A Curb satellite on the West Coast would also enable trading to continue in New York longer than had previously been the case, due to time differences. McCormick noted this, and implied that round-the-clock trading might not be a bad idea. Certainly it would help volume and bring in new business. The Curb Exchange was the leading market for foreign securities in the United States, McCormick would say.

Such trading hours would encourage other foreign firms to seek listing, and help make New York the securities capital of the world in every respect.*

McCormick's second move grew out of this belief, but also reflected a tendency that existed during the Truslow years.

The name "New York Curb Exchange" had long bothered some brokers, while others nostalgically considered it as a link to the outdoor past. There had been talk of changing the name during the Truslow administration, but nothing had been done about it. Now McCormick raised the issue once more. The name "Curb Exchange" signified little to new investors, he said. "Did it mean the exchange traded in curbs?" he asked. While respecting the sentiments of old-timers, he insisted that the organization assume a new name, more dignified and in keeping with its role. He suggested the members select from three choices: International Stock Exchange, National Stock Exchange, and American Stock Exchange. The first, which would reflect the Curb's interest in foreign securities, was rejected as being not fully descriptive and somewhat deceptive. After all, the vast majority of Curb stocks were American, and this would be masked by the new name. Too, some brokers felt the term "international" might prove contentious in the early fifties, the beginning of the McCarthy era. The Big Board expressed displeasure (although indirectly) at the term "National Stock Exchange," since it would indicate that the New York Stock Exchange in some way was not a national institution.** This left the name "American Stock Exchange," which was adopted and went into effect on January 5, 1953.

During this period McCormick seemed in competition for

* The plan for national trading was not new, although McCormick was not aware of this. Officials at the Consolidated Stock Exchange had considered satellite exchanges in the late nineteenth and early twentieth centuries. The American Stock Exchange would revive the idea in the late 1960s, calling it "Amex West."
** In 1962 the New York Mercantile Exchange organized a securities market and named it the National Stock Exchange. Soon after, McCormick became its president. Thus, he served as head of the National Stock Exchange after all, although not in the way he had expected.

headlines with Stock Exchange President Keith Funston, who had succeeded Emil Schramm at the Big Board months after McCormick came to office. Like McCormick, Funston was far more a public figure than his predecessor. He had become president of Trinity College in 1944, at the age of thirty-three, and immediately gone into the service. Upon his return, Funston led in the reconstruction of Trinity's curriculum and helped make it a first-rate college financially as well as academically. Funston proved an excellent fund-raiser, more a salesman than an academician. All of Wall Street, the Stock Exchange included, cried out for new business in 1951. Just as the Curb hoped McCormick would increase its volume and listings, so the Big Board looked to Funston for the same.*

Both men agreed that something had to be done to attract the small investor to the securities markets, and each was willing to use promotional appeals to help in the work. The Big Board came up with the idea of the Monthly Investment Plan in 1953, and put it into effect early the following year.**

MIP was a failure. Fewer than 30,000 accounts were started in a year's time, and it never became very popular. The reasons for this were obvious. In the first place, MIP investors had no guidance except that offered by their brokers, who in

---

* Both men proved excellent promoters, but clearly McCormick had been better prepared for the job. Funston had had no previous Wall Street experience and had to undergo what amounted to on-the-job training. Even Big Board leaders admired McCormick, and this must have distressed Funston. By the late 1950s, there was serious talk of Funston stepping down and being replaced by McCormick. This had never happened before, and at the time was viewed as another sign of the Amex's having come of age. But such talk was not long-lasting, and in any case, there were enough powerful men at the Big Board opposed to McCormick to have blocked such a move.
** Under MIP, stockholders could set up special accounts with their brokers in a selected or several selected securities. Then, at regular intervals, they could put a fixed amount of money into the account—as low as $25—which would be used to purchase fractional shares in the selected issue. In time, the stockholder could amass a considerable holding. In addition, he could benefit from dollar-cost averaging. Finally, from the Big Board's point of view, the MIP could provide a useful alternative to mutual funds.

many cases cared little about such small accounts. Then there was the matter of commissions. The odd-lot differential, combined with large commissions on small purchases, meant that even if the price of an average stock rose by approximately 15 percent in the first year, the MIP owner would have securities worth less in dollars than the amount he had put into the plan. In other words, he would have been better off with a salesman-sold mutual fund, which charged around 8 percent commission. *Barron's*, the *Wall Street Journal*, and *Forbes* all pointed this out and recommended that MIP end; in 1955 *Barron's* called MIP an attempt "to lead the lamb back into Wall Street."

The Amex* under McCormick developed a different approach, one that worked better, was less expensive, and was longer-lasting: the investment clubs. The Amex had no direct link with investment clubs, but it publicized them just as the Big Board advertised investment in MIP. Small investors would join together, pooling their funds and knowledge, and invest as a group. The Amex would help them to organize and obtain information and guidance, and even helped arrange for the organization of a national body. Members of investment clubs saved on commissions by purchasing larger amounts of stock, often saved on odd-lot charges, and had better knowledge of what they were doing. In the late 1950s, as MIP faded, the investment clubs grew rapidly in number and purchases.

McCormick took great personal pride in the clubs, and in the Amex's role in helping them. Speaking before the National Association of Investment Clubs in 1953, he said, "You, not Wall Street, have found a practical answer to selling shares in our future." Needless to say, all of this enhanced the Amex's image in the nation.

McCormick was also able to cement good relations with Washington, at a time when the industry was being criticized for excesses. By the mid-1950s the great bull market of that decade was in full swing, with prices rising steadily, often spectac-

* From the start, the nickname "Amex" caught on, and is still used today. One financial columnist, Alan Abelson of *Barron's*, persists in calling it "the Curb," much to the chagrin of Amex officials.

ularly. The nation had not witnessed such a movement since the 1920s, and this bothered many congressmen and senators, as well as writers and the general public. There was bad economic news in 1954, and yet the rise continued. Although there was slow recovery in the first half of 1955, the market shot ahead, in the words of one analyst discounting not only the future but the hereafter. Professor John K. Galbraith of Harvard noted the similarities between 1929 and 1955, and warned of weaknesses that might lead to a worse crash than the one experienced a quarter of a century before. His account of the earlier period, *The Great Crash,* was published in 1955, and in it Galbraith elaborated on his fears. Others joined in the chorus, and echoes reached Washington.

This helped spark the first major investigation of the securities industry since the end of the war. A subcommittee of the House Committee on Interstate and Foreign Commerce held hearings early in the year. They were followed by hearings before the Senate Committee on Banking and Currency in March. Finally, the House subcommittee resumed its hearings in September. The hearings were held to explore new legislation considered by Congress to regulate the markets. Committee members visited the financial area and were shown around the exchanges by Funston and McCormick, and both men attempted to win support for their own plans and oppose those offered by congressmen and senators who wanted stronger regulation at the exchanges.

A large number of Wall Street leaders appeared to testify. Many did well, but McCormick's performance was outstanding. This was so for two reasons, one of which he could not control: the lack of knowledge and experience on the part of most congressmen and senators in Wall Street operations. The most basic procedures and terms had to be explained to committee and subcommittee members, often several times, before they understood their meanings. The only senator who asked sharp and incisive questions was Paul Douglas of Illinois, a former economics professor. Herbert Lehman of New York, who had been a member of a distinguished investment banking firm in the 1920s, also had experience in the field, but his was woefully outdated, and his questions showed it. To the others, the witnesses were as much teachers as anything else. McCormick did a good job of teaching.

The second reason for McCormick's fine performance was the obvious sympathy and admiration he inspired among the committeemen. They knew he had been a former SEC commissioner, and in 1955 McCormick was considered a reform leader in a district that did not want reform, and a liberal Democrat among conservative Republicans. Even J. William Fulbright of Arkansas, chairman of the Senate committee and an acknowledged foe of Wall Street, showed respect and deference to McCormick. On March 4, 1955, he called the committee into session, and introduced McCormick as the first witness.

CHAIRMAN: This morning we have as our witness the president of the American Stock Exchange, Mr. Edward T. McCormick. Mr. McCormick has supplied the committee with a statement.

Mr. McCormick, we are very happy to have you here.

He has had long experience in Washington. He is thoroughly at home here. For the information of the committee, Mr. McCormick used to be with the SEC.

I believe you originally came from Arizona, did you not?

MR. MC CORMICK: That is correct, Senator.

CHAIRMAN: Some place in the Far West. He is a cowboy, I guess, who finally came down here and was on the SEC, so that he is a professional. He is a professional and probably will be a very difficult witness. He knows more about it than anybody else.

McCormick spent much of the morning explaining the composition of the Dow-Jones average, politely indicating to Lehman that procedures on Wall Street in 1955 were different from what they had been in the 1920s when he had been a banker, and describing the functions of a specialist to Senator Mike Monroney of Oklahoma. McCormick was confident in the future of the economy, and he discounted talk of depression. At the same time, he supported the investigation and the committee's call for greater regulation of securities and trading. It is important, he said, for the public to have confidence in the markets, and this could be accomplished best by a strong SEC. Not all stocks were good investments, he conceded. "Let's not kid ourselves. There are dogs on both exchanges." For that reason, standards had to be maintained, and bettered. But the major problem, said McCormick, was in the over-the-counter market, so difficult to regulate since there was no trading floor, and whose securities did not provide the same public information as those on the Amex or the Big Board. McCormick strongly urged greater supervision of the over-the-counter market. He implied, but did not say, that the public would be safer if such securities were listed on an exchange—perhaps the Amex.

Fulbright was pleased with this testimony, but he chided McCormick for what he considered excessive optimism.

CHAIRMAN: I take it from your last comment that you think that a new era has been achieved in our economy and that we are about to abolish poverty, and that we can expect three cars in every garage.

MR. MC CORMICK: I would say, Senator, that never in the history of civilization have we had such progress as we are experiencing today, and if our capitalistic system cannot improve the standard of living of our people, there is something wrong.

CHAIRMAN: Is that statement reminiscent of anything at all that we have heard before?

MR. MC CORMICK: I was in college at that time and read those statements. You, sitting there, can do only but appraise the value of my statement based on my background and whatever knowledge you think I have. And I make the statement in the light of the fact I know those statements were made in 1929.

CHAIRMAN: Is there any activity of our people that would indicate great improvement in the level of our understanding? If you look about at politics or education or international relations, does it lead you to believe that the American people have made great progress in understanding of life, economy, or human relations?

MR. MC CORMICK: I think we have. I think the process of education is bearing fruit. I feel that it would be highly desirable to move faster, but we have to walk before we run. I think we are making progress.

CHAIRMAN: What I mean is that it is not just in this field of stocks and business that we have made this great progress. You feel that we have become a lot smarter than we used to be?

MR. MC CORMICK: I certainly agree with that.

CHAIRMAN: Do you? Well, that is encouraging. Is that because we have returned the same political party to the White House that we had in the Twenties?

MR. MC CORMICK: Well, now, of course, I am in a good position to answer that. I have been a lifelong Democrat in Arizona. As a matter of fact, I was appointed to the Commission of the SEC by Harry Truman.

CHAIRMAN: I know, but you have gotten rich. I have seen many examples of that.

MR. MC CORMICK: You would not say that was bad, would you?

CHAIRMAN: It's just human nature. I have lots of friends that used to be Democrats.

MR. MC CORMICK: Are you implying that I am not still a Democrat? I admit my vote is practically lost in Westchester County, but I still vote Democratic.

Senator Homer Capehart of Indiana exploded at this. What was Fulbright trying to suggest? That in some way it was wrong to be successful and a Republican? That the nation would have another depression because a Republican was in the White House? Fulbright tried to back down, to no avail. For the rest of the session and part of the next, Fulbright and the Republican members of the committee traded insults and engaged in political bantering, and the purpose of the hearings often was forgotten. In any case, all agreed that McCormick had done an outstanding job in his testimony.

McCormick also performed well in testimony before the subcommittee of the House committee on interstate and foreign commerce, where once again he led novices in Wall Street through the maze of regulations. Representative John Bennett of Michigan, who had known McCormick during the SEC days, was as flattering as Fulbright.

I have known Mr. McCormick for a long time. I do not believe there is any person better qualified by experience and training and background to speak with authority on this subject. I certainly respect your views. This is not only as president of the American Stock Exchange, but also the former member of the Securities and Exchange Commission, and one who I know has given this problem considerable study.

To this, Representative John McGuire of Connecticut added:

Mr. McCormick, it is a pleasure to have you before our committee and it was always a pleasure to have you before our committee in Washington. You always stand out like a lighthouse. I know when we asked some of the members of the Commission questions, they deferred to you as the omnipotent one of the Commission, and I want to congratulate the governors of the New York Curb Exchange for having such excellent judgement to elect you to be their top man.

So it went in all of McCormick's testimony before congressional committees during his presidency. Never before had a Curb representative received such a hearing from Washington. Not only that, but other Curb witnesses did better than before, in part the result of McCormick's coaching.

By the late 1950s McCormick had shown that those at the Amex who had supported his candidacy for the presidency in the hope of achieving better relations with Washington were correct. Although there were irregularities at the Amex, there was no congressional inquiry in this period. Even when it was clear to insiders on Wall Street that all was not well at the Amex, the SEC did not investigate it. Such might not have been the case had not McCormick won great respect at both Congress and the SEC.

Seldom was McCormick asked a probing question. At times Funston would be grilled; McCormick did not receive the same treatment. On occasion, he would be asked questions that might have been explored in depth, but they never were. One of these exchanges, between Fulbright and McCormick, would prove interesting reading in 1961, when McCormick's activities were under investigation.

CHAIRMAN: Are there any restrictions or controls upon trading in stock imposed upon officers of the American Stock Exchange?
MR. MC CORMICK: Employees? Is that—

CHAIRMAN: Officers.

MR. MC CORMICK: There is none except that a brokerage account cannot be opened without my permission, and as I pointed out, if anyone traded on margin they would have to get my approval.

CHAIRMAN: Well, do they trade?

MR. MC CORMICK: Do they trade?

CHAIRMAN: Yes.

MR. MC CORMICK: Yes.

CHAIRMAN: Do you trade?

MR. MC CORMICK: I do.

CHAIRMAN: Can you supply the committee with the same information regarding the trading of your officers, including yourself that Mr. Funston agreed to supply yesterday?

MR. MC CORMICK: I would be delighted to.

CHAIRMAN: For 2 years, I believe. The same period. Do you and your officers have any special privileges regarding trading?

MR. MC CORMICK: As a matter of fact, as I pointed out, we have less, in that we do not trade on margin unless we have special permission. I happen to have never bought any stock on margin. All my stock is now held on a cash basis.

The Promised Land

In 1955 Senator Fulbright asked McCormick whether he believed the Amex "has an obligation to advertise and to bring people into the marketplace." Was the President performing "a public service by inducing people to buy stocks who did not formerly buy stocks." McCormick thought this was the case.

> As president of the American Stock Exchange, I would say that I spend about half my time in management functions and so-called housekeeping duties and 50 percent as their ace salesman. The purpose of that salesmanship is to convince the American public that they can with confidence invest in securities traded on these exchanges.

McCormick went on to say that the ASE did not have an advertising budget; his speeches were the major effort in that direction made by the Exchange. During his first three and a half years in office, he made sixty speeches before public groups.

Few brokers would disagree with McCormick's statement that he spent only half his time in performing administrative duties. No previous president spent so little time attending to internal matters at the market. However, still fewer brokers would complain of this situation. McCormick had a large and able staff, qualified to handle administrative matters. The committees seemed to be functioning smoothly. Why should the President spend his time at Trinity Place when it could better be used on the road? *

It would be misleading to say that McCormick's sales efforts were directed primarily toward the public. Although he was more visible and accessible than previous presidents, his road trips were taken to secure additional listings for the Amex, and not new investors. According to one board member, McCormick was "constantly on the go working on listings." In 1960, Chairman Joseph Reilly told the board that McCormick had delivered on his pledge to obtain new listings. "Directly and indirectly, he has played the major role since 1951 in starting this trend as far as listings are concerned, which will set a new record for this Exchange during the last twenty-five years."

The statistics would appear to bear out Reilly's statement. McCormick had been brought to Trinity Place in the hopes that he would be able to attract new companies to the Exchange, and so far as the membership was concerned, he had delivered on his promise. Since 1934, Curb brokers had been convinced they could never equal in new listings those securities lost to the New York Stock Exchange through transfer and the dropping of discontinued unlisted securities. In almost every year since 1934 the number of listed issues had gone down; in every year since the establishment of the SEC, the total number of issues at the Curb had been lower than in the previous year. McCormick changed this trend in his first year in office, and had an unbroken skein of advances during his administration. In so doing he not only helped increase business, he gave the brokers confidence in their own futures. **

* In 1962 the SEC stated: "It is not unlikely that the Exchange's encouragement of McCormick's efforts to bring in new business precluded him from acting effectively as an administrator and prevented him from devoting a substantial amount of his time to the government of the Exchange." But the agency said nothing regarding his absences while McCormick was president, and generally maintained a "hands-off" policy toward the Amex.

** Total listings at the end of 1958 were no higher than they had been at the same time in 1957, but they reached a new high during the year.

Listed and Unlisted Issues at the Amex, 1949–61

| | Stocks | | | Bonds | | |
Year	Listed	Unlisted	Total	Listed	Unlisted	Total
1949	431	347	778	18	65	83
1950	424	333	757	11	58	69
1951	443	320	763	14	49	63
1952	470	308	778	16	47	63
1953	498	296	794	17	47	64
1954	520	288	808	19	60	79
1955	544	274	818	19	50	69
1956	588	261	849	21	47	68
1957	609	246	855	23	36	59
1958	618	237	855	24	35	59
1959	647	224	871	29	33	62
1960	726	216	942	33	30	63
1961	797	204	1001	45	28	73

Source: *Amex Databook,* p. 27

As expected, McCormick made a major effort to attract Canadian issues to the Amex. The President flew to Canada several times a year, speaking before business groups on the advantages of listing. His work in this direction bore fruit, as many Canadian mining, oil, and industrial issues applied for and received listing in the early 1950s. This number leveled off at mid-decade, however, as the Canadian boom fizzled.

Foreign Issues Traded at the Amex, 1951–61

Year	Canadian Issues	Other Foreign Issues	Total	Percent of List
1951	75	34	109	14.00
1952	90	35	125	15.70
1953	93	37	130	16.08
1954	95	39	134	16.26
1955	105	41	146	17.54
1956	108	44	152	25.82
1957	113	39	152	24.33
1958	109	39	148	24.04
1959	107	40	147	27.72
1960	107	41	148	25.68
1961	103	39	142	23.16

Source: American Stock Exchange

Certainly McCormick's efforts in the area of public relations helped bring companies to the Amex. The board showed its approval and support for his work in concrete fashion, rewarding the President with a series of pay raises that had boosted his salary to $75,000 at the time he left office. In addition, McCormick received substantial increases in his expense account.

An argument might be made, however, for concluding that McCormick's efforts in the promotional area were overrated. While it was true that he had attracted new listings to the Amex and in other ways publicized the market, the increase in volume and the public's interest in securities was not of his doing. Instead, they resulted from general peace and increased production and profits. McCormick's election coincided with the greatest bull market since the 1920s.

There were several reasons for the advance: a recognition on the part of investors that the post-war depression would not materialize, the winding down of the Korean conflict, confidence in President Eisenhower, a desire to seek protection against inflation through the purchase of equities, the appearance of new glamour industries such as computers, electronics, convenience foods, plastics, and space exploration, combined with sales efforts made by brokerages and news items written by analysts.

The last factor was important: the public was wooed to the market places by economists, journalists, and brokerages. Charles Merrill, head of Merrill Lynch, Pierce, Fenner and Smith, Wall Street's leading brokerage, became the apostle of "People's Capitalism" in the late 1940s, and continued in this role in the 1950s. As early as 1948 he ran advertisements such as this one in leading newspapers, in which Merrill combined politics, economics, and sociology:

> One campaign tactic did get us a little riled. That was when the motheaten bogey of a Wall Street tycoon was trotted out. . . . Mr. Truman knows as well as anybody that there isn't any Wall Street. That's just legend. Wall Street is Montgomery Street in San Francisco. Seventeenth Street in Denver. Marietta Street in Atlanta. Federal Street in Boston. Main Street in

Waco, Texas. And it's any spot in Independence, Missouri, where thrifty people go to invest their money, to buy and sell securities.

Merrill restructured his operations, appealing to the small investors, who in the past had received short shrift from brokerages interested in large accounts. Merrill Lynch brokers concentrated on investors with a few hundred dollars as well as servicing the larger accounts. By the late 1950s, the firm was spending well over $1.5 million a year on advertisements, market letters distributed free to interested people, and other forms of promotional activity. Other firms followed Merrill's lead, and it was these organizations, not McCormick and the Amex, that led investors to Wall Street—and Trinity Place too.

Others helped in the work. The market services—newsletters subscribed to by investors—expanded and proliferated during the 1950s. Most of these were bullish most of the time, since bears usually don't invest. These letters and services not only helped boost the bull market, they also encouraged investors and speculators to re-enter the market. So did economists and journalists. Professor Marcus Nadler, employed by the Hanover Bank, strongly supported stock purchases. "Through stock ownership the people own the means of production," he claimed. And hundreds of thousands of investors rushed to the securities market to get their share of the pie, clutching market reports written by men like James Dines, Edmund Tabell, Frank Schoembs, Armand Erpf, and others. Most of these investors probably never heard of McCormick. They purchased a security because *Value Line* recommended it, not because it was listed on the Amex.

The Dow-Jones Industrials rose steadily throughout the 1950s, adding fuel to a market noted for buying panics, when investors rushed to buy almost anything in the fear that they would miss out on the next rise. Speculative issues always do well in such markets, and since many of the Amex issues were in this category, their prices and volume increased substantially. This same factor helps explain the Amex's steadily increasing

Dow-Jones Industrial Average, 1949–61

Year	D-J High	D-J Low
1949	200.52	161.60
1950	235.47	196.81
1951	276.37	238.99
1952	292.00	256.35
1953	293.76	255.49
1954	404.39	279.87
1955	488.40	388.20
1956	521.05	462.35
1957	520.77	419.79
1958	583.65	436.89
1959	679.36	574.46
1960	685.47	566.05
1961	734.91	610.25

Source: *Barron's*, November 1, 1971

share of the percentage of stocks traded on all American securities exchanges. It rose steadily though slowly during the McCormick era, the result not so much of salesmanship as of increased interest in speculative securities.

These statistics indicate that the total number of shares

Common Stock Trading Statistics at the Amex, 1949–61

Year	Shares Traded	Shares Outstanding	Turnover Ratio	Daily Average
1949	66,201,828	621,932,235	10.6	264,807
1950	107,792,340	610,793,399	17.6	434,647
1951	111,629,218	689,238,088	16.2	448,310
1952	106,237,657	786,707,948	13.5	426,657
1953	102,378,937	844,744,650	12.1	407,884
1954	162,948,716	911,207,052	17.9	646,622
1955	228,956,315	1,073,466,189	21.3	912,177
1956	228,231,047	1,227,954,044	18.6	912,924
1957	214,011,566	1,375,038,202	15.6	845,896
1958	240,358,524	1,420,200,252	16.9	953,804
1959	374,058,546	1,474,999,267	25.4	1,478,492
1960	286,039,982	1,584,889,172	18.0	1,112,996
1961	488,831,037	1,799,444,094	27.2	1,947,534

Source: *Amex Databook*, p. 30

listed at the Amex increased substantially in the 1950s. Many new issues might have sought listing in such a boom period even without salesmanship, and McCormick never was very successful in preventing issues from leaving the Amex to go over to the Big Board. Volume depended even more on the turnover ratio, which McCormick's publicity did little to affect. General prosperity, not the work of McCormick's office, was responsible for this. It would be difficult to assess credit for the rise in Amex turnover and total sales, but at least as much credit belongs to President Eisenhower as to President McCormick.

Distinctions such as these mattered little to many Amex brokers. So far as they were concerned, business had been lackluster prior to McCormick's arrival. Then sales and profits at Trinity Place rose significantly. Just as they might have blamed McCormick for a decline, so they credited him for the advance, which was also reflected in the price of Amex seats.

Earlier a securities exchange was compared to a department store. If we may return to this analogy, we can say that McCormick may have increased the amount of goods sold, but could do little to attract customers. They came to buy for other rea-

Price of a Seat on the ASE, 1949–61

Year	First	High	Low	Last	Total Transferred
1949	$10,000	$10,000	$ 5,500	$ 8,000	16
1950	8,000	11,000	6,500	9,500	30
1951	10,000	15,500	9,500	11,500	26
1952	13,500	14,000	12,000	14,000	23
1953	14,500	15,000	10,100	10,100	12
1954	10,000	19,000	10,000	18,000	22
1955	18,000	22,000	17,500	20,500	26
1956	21,500	31,500	21,500	28,000	26
1957	26,000	26,000	21,500	22,000	23
1958	20,000	42,000	18,000	42,000	30
1959	44,000	65,000	44,000	60,000	31
1960	60,000	60,000	51,000	52,000	30
1961	52,000	80,000	52,000	65,000	51

Source: *Amex Databook*, p. 12

sons, which resulted in additional merchandise being stocked. This new increment in listings was due only in part to McCormick's efforts; it was partially his responsibility, but not necessarily his doing.

Even then, not all the new securities attracted to the Amex in the 1950s were lured by the President. Chairman Mann did a good deal of field work, as did other members of the board and individual brokers. In 1961 one such specialist testified:

> And then I proceeded to avail myself of the library of the exchange, namely, securing the complete information on advantages of listing and so forth.
>
> And I had in my favor the fact that I could read a balance sheet. I availed myself of prospectuses wherever I could and I also spent practically as much time as I possibly could in our library with all of Moody's books et cetera.
>
> I took down as many as ten, fifteen companies a week that I would write down . . . companies that would meet with the requirements of listing on the American Exchange.
>
> My weekends practically [were devoted] . . . to nothing but correspondence, sending out letters, trying to induce listings on the American Stock Exchange, which my files at one time I would assume contained almost 600 or 700 companies that I had contacted.

Another specialist said he "would crisscross around the country and on some occasions I would run into McCormick." Others attended professional conventions, seeking out corporation presidents and trying to interest them in listing. A few asked for permission to address boards of directors in the search for listings. According to Joseph Reilly, who became chairman in 1960, "Once they [specialists] became officials, they became high-powered salesmen."

So McCormick had much help in his efforts. As a salaried president and not a member of the Amex, he had no direct interest in obtaining new listings. Many of the specialists did, and it was his responsibility to see to it that a fair distribution of securities was made—that no specialist or group of specialists received undue "favors." In addition, McCormick had to make certain that the new issues represented more than a press agent's dream. On many occasions, he failed to do so.

New applications for listing were received by the Division of Securities, which checked to make certain that all the necessary papers had been filed, and then passed them on to the committee on securities. Once the new issues were approved there, they went to the board, which made final disposition of the application. In theory, the committee was to have screened the issues prior to sending them on, but in practice this rarely happened. As a result, firms not meeting the standards of economic viability were able to obtain listing. The quest for new listings was such that no member wanted the responsibility for having kept a security from a specialist who wanted it.

These activities were particularly evident in the case of the new Canadian issues. Of the 104 Canadian stocks on the Amex at the end of 1960, 77.3 percent had deficits in earnings for one year, 54.4 percent had earnings deficits for two of the prior three years, and 32.7 percent had earnings deficits for all three years.

The Amex was also charged with responsibility to see to it that unregistered shares were not traded on the floor, but on several occasions large blocks of unregistered shares were traded. Of course, McCormick could not oversee every aspect of floor trading, but he had the responsibility for the job, and therefore the blame. In both this and the decline of newly-listed issues, McCormick was ultimately responsible. Yet there is little evidence that during his administration he took steps to correct the situation. On the other hand, few brokers complained of these conditions. Indeed, they probably would have criticized McCormick for "taking the bread from their tables" had he taken action. Nor did the SEC do its job in the 1950s, for even regular surveillance would have uncovered these abuses. All—McCormick, the membership of the Amex, and the SEC—failed in their responsibilities. In so doing, McCormick received applause and recognition, the members obtained additional business, and the SEC was permitted to remain in its somnolent state.

Consider, for example, the case of Algemene Kunstzijde

Unie N.V., also known as AKU. This was a large Dutch chemical company that applied for Amex listing in 1953 and received it the following year. It met Amex requirements insofar as stockholders, earnings, and assets were concerned, but the listed shares had restricted voting rights. In a public statement, McCormick dealt with this situation, which violated both SEC and Amex rules for listing.

> It has for many years been the policy of the exchange to accept for listing certain stock issues meeting specified conditions even though they may have restricted voting rights. Our securities committee and Board of Governors accept such stocks if the distribution of the securities is sufficiently wide to assure the maintenance of a satisfactory auction market. This policy is believed to be in the public interest, and is predicated on the belief than an exchange market affords to the company and its stockholders certain advantages, including the immediate reporting on the ticker tape of all transactions and compliance with Securities Exchange Act annual reporting requirements.

While it was true this had been done in the past for American issues, there was no broad market for AKU in the United States at the time—the company hoped that listing would create a demand for the issue. Nor did McCormick's statement deal with violation of rules—instead, he spoke of "policy." Yet the AKU listing, open and aboveboard, stirred no interest at the SEC.

More to the point was an attempt on the part of some board members to enforce "an informal and unwritten practice . . . whereby it [the board] would not consider applications for the listing of stock issues selling below $1.00 a share." At first, McCormick favored enforcement of the practice, which had been ignored in the rush to obtain new listings and keep old ones on the list. Then he changed his mind, and joined the majority favoring the retention of the low-priced issues.

Several factors might have caused this change. A reconsideration of the problems involved with delisting or attempts to change rules could have done it. More important was the force exerted by James Gilligan in favor of retention of low-priced securities. "Department stores need volume to exist," said Gilligan. "I never heard of anyone refusing to buy a fur coat or a piano from them just because they had a bargain basement. Our Exchange needs the commission houses badly, and the only way a commission house can exist is on volume."

The argument was weak. Many stocks sold for low prices because they were in shaky condition, often so bad as to be near failure. Specialists as well as commission brokers would have lost business if they were delisted. Still, Gilligan had his way in this, as he would in most matters he was interested in during the McCormick era. He was one of the most powerful men at the Amex, and had greater influence over Amex affairs than any other specialist, and perhaps more than McCormick himself.

James Gilligan retained his reputation as one of the toughest brokers at the Curb. As we have seen, on several occasions in the 1920s he had been admonished for engaging in brawls on the trading floor. Other times he was called before committees for minor infractions of rules. If the old Curb was a jungle, Gilligan was one of the lions. Always ready for a struggle, he gave no quarter in a fight, and most of the time won.

Gilligan was not popular at the Curb. Other brokers feared and/or respected him, but few considered him a close friend. Gilligan did not seek popularity; he was more interested in power—in building the most powerful specialist firm at the Curb. He had served on the board in 1939–40, but left and never returned. The action was on the floor, and that was where he wanted to be.*

Gilligan prospered in the heady markets of the 1920s, survived the depressed markets of the 1930s, and made a comeback in the stagnant ones of the 1940s. In 1940 he joined with William Will to form Gilligan, Will & Co., and set about acquiring as many stocks as he could. By the time McCormick came to the Curb, Gilligan was well-positioned for a major advance. The great bull market of the 1950s, combined with lax administration at the Amex, was well-suited for his talents.

---

* Gilligan said he did not stand for reelection in 1940 because "it is a terrific headache. Only the people who want glory take it."

Now the brawling tactics of the 1920s no longer were necessary. Gilligan applied more than three decades of experience to the task of getting as much as he could. Others competed with him for listings and powers. If they were weak, Gilligan would brush them aside; if strong, he would ally himself with them. In one way or another, he would get to the top.

By the end of the decade he was there. In 1960, Gilligan, Will & Co. was specialist in 44 stocks. In addition, the firm acted as banker for eleven other specialist accounts handling 85 stocks. Thus, he had a hand in 129 individual securities, about 10 percent of the Amex's listings. Little wonder, then, that when Gilligan opposed the delisting of low-priced shaky issues, the administration listened and acted.

How had Gilligan obtained such power? Not through chicanery or breaking rules, but rather by following Amex listing policy insofar as allocations were concerned.

During the 1950s there were several categories into which newly listed securities fell, and each encouraged men like Gilligan. First of all, if a security were brought to listing through the efforts of a specialist, who could prove to the satisfaction of the committee that such was the case, he would receive that issue. The committee on securities rarely broke this policy, which in practice encouraged specialists to spend a good deal of their time off the Exchange floor, beating the bushes for new listings. As has been indicated, such was the case with Gilligan.

If an Amex member (usually an underwriter) could demonstrate to the committee on securities that a particular specialist had been instrumental in the filing of a listing application, that specialist could expect to be assigned the security. Ambitious specialists would make certain their contacts with leading underwriters were current and good, since the underwriters were in position to throw business their way. Here too, Gilligan was a master. One of his few close friends was Edward Elliott, a partner in the brokerage firm of Van Alstyne, Noel & Co., a leading underwriter of small, marginal firms in the 1950s. Later on Elliott formed his own underwriting firm, Elliott & Co. Both gave Gilligan a good deal of business, and Gilligan reciprocated. The same was true with Richard Pistell, who was with Elliott at both Van Alstyne, Noel and Elliott & Co., and then with his own firm, Pistell, Inc. Through Elliott, Gilligan met Richard Noel, who continued to help Gilligan, Wills after Elliott and Pistell left Van Alstyne, Noel. Between them, Elliott, Pistell, and Noel underwrote many small companies in the 1950s. More than sixteen of them wound up with Gilligan, Will as specialist. The firm also specialized in New Idria Mining and Chemical Co., the chairman of which was David Van Alstyne, Jr.

Apparently Gilligan had business contacts with many such individuals, who fed a steady stream of new listings to him, which were ratified by the committee on securities as a matter of course.

How did Gilligan repay these favors? By "taking care of them" in the matter of block sales. He would call them when a large block of stock was being offered for sale with few bids on the book. This was clearly contrary to Amex rules and law, and yet it went on throughout the decade. As Gilligan later said:

> Well, and because lots of times they may not care if it sells down an eighth or a quarter, but they don't want to see the stock break a half dollar, you know, because it might upset the whole market in the thing, so they have a right to—after all, they have got a lot of customers in it. They have a right to know what is going to happen just as well as I have.

These telephone calls meant that Van Alstyne, Noel and the other firms had privileged information, which could be used for their own benefit and that of their customers. Holders of the securities involved at other firms operated at a disadvantage in such cases. Such operations not only hurt brokers who were denied business, but the public itself. Gilligan's operations represented a far more serious breach of rules than had those of Cuppia in the 1930s; there was no loophole in the constitution involved in Gilligan's case. Rumors flew at the Amex regarding Gilligan's activities, and they must have reached the administration. Several brokers would later claim to have known details of Gilligan's activities with Van Alstyne, Noel. Yet the Amex took no action in the case.

A specialist might receive a stock if it was felt he was a "natural" for it. For example, a new issue, in which the public was clearly interested and which could expect a heavy volume of trading, would not be given to a novice or a small specialist unit, but to one of the bigger, more experienced units. Gilligan, Will certainly qualified as one of these, and received a good share of such issues. At times active stocks would be shifted to such specialists in the interests of trading continuity and "good markets." Here, too, Gilligan, Will benefited.

Gilligan made a great deal of money through specialization, but even more—and with less work—through stock dealing. He would purchase large blocks of a new stock prior to its being issued, usually at a price lower than the issue quotation. Then he would "distribute" it to interested parties. An example of this took place in 1955, when Guild Films sold 200,000 shares of its stock to Gilligan and two other parties, who immediately resold them at a substantial profit to 172 persons connected with Gilligan, Will or the other parties. Guild Films filed a listing application at the Amex the following year, and in its application noted that Gilligan had been instrumental in obtaining the listing. He and George De Martini visited the firm and suggested that its application would be better received if it had a better cash position. "In order to do this quickly and without any fuss," said Gilligan, "George and myself bought $500,000 worth of stock." In this way, Gilligan, Will became specialist in a stock in which Gilligan had a substantial interest. The temptation for manipulation was great.

Gilligan had similar arrangements in reference to the application and eventual listing of Chromalloy, Audion-Emenee, North Rankin Nickel Mines, Capital Cities Broadcasting, and Crowell-Collier. These firms also kept Gilligan notified about future developments before the news was released to the press. For example, officials at Guild Films advised Gilligan of the firm's financial difficulties, and told him of merger news before it was released to the public. On several occasions Gilligan loaned money to Guild, the loan secured by Guild stock, and he did the same with other firms in whose stock he specialized. Later on, Gilligan would claim he had a right to such information—a position contrary to Amex practice, and one no other specialist would support, at least openly.

QUESTION: Do you think a specialist is entitled to inside information about occurrences that are about to happen in a corporation?
ANSWER: Yes, I think he should be kept fully informed, because he has a duty to maintain a market.
QUESTION: This being fully informed would be prior to informing the general public?
ANSWER: Yes.

Even after the security was listed at the Amex and assigned to Gilligan, Will, the specialist would take positions in the stock, often through off-board purchases. Without using Amex facilities, Gilligan obtained large blocks of Guild Films, Occidental Petroleum, El-Tronics, and other stocks unknown to the public through the ticker tape. This too was in violation of Amex rules. Gilligan would purchase these blocks for sale at the Amex. Even a cursory examination would have disclosed what was going on. Yet none was made.*

If some of this was known in the late 1950s, and much of the rest suspected, why didn't the administration move against Gilligan, Will? Why wasn't Gilligan brought before the proper committees to answer for his activities, so many of which were in violation of rules? Brokers who knew of Gilligan's activities, but little more, suspected that the administration remained quiet for fear of a new scandal, one many times worse than the Plate-Cuppia affair. Some believed the rumors were exaggerated—that if Gilligan were indeed guilty of wrongdoing, he would have been punished. Those who knew more of Gilligan's actions and were privy to administration thinking

* There was one exception to this. In 1955, Gilligan, Will purchased $50,000 worth of Crowell-Collier debentures convertible into common stock, and later on took an additional $150,000 worth. These debentures were converted and sold at the Amex from May 1957 to October 1958. The SEC learned of the transaction, which was in violation of rules, and brought action against Gilligan. The firm's punishment was nominal: five days' suspension from membership in the National Association of Securities Dealers. Knowing of Gilligan's activities, however, the agency did not probe deeper, a rather surprising situation.

recognized that Gilligan was not the only person at the Amex who believed his actions acceptable. Several important administration leaders—McCormick included—were involved in Gilligan's transactions, and to expose him would be to destroy themselves. As John Brick, then chairman of the committee on business conduct, later testified, the Amex was a web of violations during the McCormick era.

> My own personal feeling was that somewhere along the road, Gilligan & Will had an interest in too many situations relating to the Exchange; that is, the individual members, not the management of the Exchange. That, in having that interest, say, in having financed seats, which I thought they were doing, financing books, which they possibly were doing, or at least, I thought they were doing, they were quite powerful over there. Having learned the nature of the man later, which I did not know when I had this feeling over there, I decided in my own mind that he would be the fellow to use whatever power he had.

So Brick believed Gilligan was guilty of violations similar to those of Cuppia in the 1930s. Yet the chairman of the committee on business conduct took no action. He said he thought Gilligan did not have power over the Amex's management, when even rumors of such should have been investigated by the committee. When faced with similar beliefs in the Cuppia case, Sherman Bijur led the committee in a thorough investigation, and was supported by the administration. But President George Rea had not been implicated in Cuppia's dealings, while President McCormick—one of the nation's leading experts on securities laws and regulations—not only knew of what Gilligan was doing but, as we shall see, profited and benefited therefrom.

The details of this cooperation and knowledge were unknown in the late 1950s. They would be spread before the district and the nation in 1961–62.

Gilligan's bending and breaking of rules indicated the Amex's administration was at best lax and at worst corrupt. If some members of the administration worked with Gilligan and his kind, then they too were guilty of violations. Some claimed that McCormick would have taken action against Gilligan if he had known more of what was going on, and had been a better administrator. The picture of McCormick as a super-salesman and indifferent administrator gained wide currency in the early 1960s.

If McCormick's reputation as a catalyst for the bull market was exaggerated, so was the impression that he had little impact on the Amex's internal workings. In fact, McCormick proved an imaginative leader in some areas. In others he could do little but prod the board and members into action.

Insofar as the internal workings of the Amex were concerned, the President had far less power than was commonly believed. He did not select the committees, which did much of the administrative work at the Exchange, and was only one member of the board, which had ultimate power. Committees could and did overrule presidential decisions and decide budgetary matters. McCormick could bring his ideas to the committees, but final disposition of all plans and proposals were made there. McCormick's ability to charm people enabled him to get some proposals through the committees and influence members on others, but the members were less willing to bend on bread-and-butter issues. On such occasions the Chairman, not the President, had more influence. Unlike the President, he was a member of the Amex, an old-timer and a man who could draw upon personal friendships. Too, he had a better knowledge than the President of "where the bodies were buried."

McCormick served with three chairmen. The first of these, John Mann, remained in office until 1956, at which time he was replaced by James Dyer, who previously had been vice-chairman. Mann, whose specialist business had grown considerably while he was chairman, was expected to return to the floor. He surprised the membership by running for the board as an independent, and winning a place. Soon after, Mann became chairman of the important committee on finance.

Mann continued his missionary work for the Amex, all the while adding to his specialist list. Dyer, whose interests were similar, spent more time than his predecessor at Amex business. Dyer, who served until 1960, was a member of Gilligan,

Will, giving that powerful firm access to one of the two highest offices at the Exchange.

Dyer was succeeded by Joseph Reilly, the former vice-chairman. In Reilly McCormick found his perfect chairman. He knew the Amex as well as any man. Reilly went from City College of New York to a page's post at the Curb in the late 1920s. In 1928 he was hired as a specialist's clerk, and during the depression became a floor order clerk. He went from job to job in this period—order room clerk, purchase and sales clerk, assistant cashier—learning all aspects of Curb operations.

Reilly purchased his seat in 1936, working as a floor trader for several firms. Then he joined a specialist unit, and for nine years presided over a small list of minor securities. Reilly was honest, refusing to enter into the kind of arrangements with clerks typified by men like Plate, Cuppia, and Mark. For this reason he was no match for other specialists, and as his list dwindled, he decided to become a commission broker and trader. Reilly never became a major commission broker, although he was by no means a failure.

Reilly was elected to the board in 1951, at which time he discovered his talents for administration. As chairman of the committee on floor transactions he helped transform a moribund group into one of the most efficient committees at the Amex. Meetings were held regularly, work was completed on time, and Reilly often asked for extra sessions in order to discuss reforms in procedure. Late meetings were the rule; Reilly insisted on going over all material carefully before votes were taken. Other members protested; they were not used to all this work. On the other hand, they conceded that Reilly was one of the few board members who took his job seriously enough to subordinate other interests to it.

As a commission broker, Reilly had no direct interest in new listings, as had Mann and Dyer. He spent far less time than they on the road giving speeches. Instead, he concentrated on Amex internal affairs, working weekends to teach himself about current and anticipated problems and opportunities. Amex guards learned to expect Reilly, often dressed in old clothes, to come to the Amex on Saturdays, searching through old records in order to have background information to present at board meetings.

McCormick, who was unwilling to do such work and in any case had other interests, came to rely on the Chairman for information and support in reform measures. The eighth chairman since ratification of the 1939 constitution, Reilly was the first to perform his tasks fully. And no president needed such a man as much as did McCormick.

McCormick, Mann, Dyer, Reilly: there were the Amex's leaders in the 1950s, while Mooney was its counsel and Gilligan its most powerful specialist. Little wonder, then, that the organization was dubbed "the Irish-American Stock Exchange."

Throughout the Mann and Dyer years, McCormick would suggest and recommend programs and ideas to the board. Some of these have already been discussed. Others included reviving Truslow's proposal for a central clearing house for all of Wall Street, in which the Big Board and Amex securities would be cleared. This would be modeled after the Amex's clearing house, considered more efficient than that of the Stock Exchange. The proposal made sense, and even seemed urgent at a time when volume was rising and losses of securities mounting. Big Board leaders were wary of the idea, since, as before, they had no desire to be led into anything by the junior market. Amex brokers were concerned that their securities would receive second-class treatment in any joint operation. Although McCormick's idea was debated by the board, little additional work was done. By mid-decade the proposal was dead.

McCormick wasn't prepared to push hard for his proposals. Mann and Dyer were interested in McCormick's regular dinners with Stock Exchange and over-the-counter leaders, and were willing to deliver speeches in behalf of the Amex, but they had little taste for the hard, tedious work of committees. Thus, many of McCormick's proposals met the same fate: death after a brief flurry of interest.

This situation changed somewhat when Reilly entered the chairmanship. Reilly was interested in the idea of a central depository for all securities, and he tried to kindle interest at both exchanges. By then, however, such plans received little consideration, and the Chairman dropped it.

Reilly had better fortune with another of McCormick's ideas: automation of the Amex. On one of his early visits to the Toronto securities community, the President visited that city's stock exchange, which had just installed a small electronic system to handle quotations. He learned that the innovation not only made sales work more efficient, but actually had paid for itself by lowering costs.

McCormick recommended that the Amex consider such a system, and studies were initiated in 1952. Mann and Dyer showed little interest in the idea, however, although they were willing to go along with additional studies. But McCormick was able to interest some board members in the work, and the most important of them was Reilly. In 1954, the President gave Reilly a series of short books on the subject of automation, which fascinated him. By the time Reilly became chairman of the committee on floor transactions, he was conversant with most of the problems and possibilities such systems presented. Through reading and other study, meeting with technicians and executives of automation companies, and simply asking questions, the self-educated Reilly became the Amex's expert in the field.

Beginning in 1956 and continuing for the next three years, Reilly reported regularly on his work in the field. He asked several automation firms to submit bids on installation and reports on capabilities of systems. In 1957 he told the board that one system, offered by Teleregister and costing $1,250,000, could provide brokers and other interested parties with stock quotations, ranges, and volume in a matter of seconds, produce a newspaper stock table every hour, and provide a résumé of the day's trading shortly after the closing bell at three-thirty. By 1960 the cost of the system had risen to $3 million, but its capabilities were also enlarged. According to Reilly, the improved system, with auxiliary computers, could handle most of the Amex's paperwork as well, permitting the Exchange to cut down considerably on the number of clerks and allied personnel then on the floor and in the back offices. Services could be offered to member firms, who would pay for them, and this too would bring in revenues. At no time did Reilly say or imply that the system would pay for itself, but he did make a good case for its being economical. As he saw it, the Amex could not function in the enlarged markets of the 1960s without a great degree of automation. It was not a question of buying a glamourous system for the sake of "progress"; unless the Amex automated, trading might grind to a halt and back-office pressures become insurmountable. Reilly urged the members to accept automation before a crisis situation developed.*

The Board accepted many of Reilly's proposals and suggestions, and plans were made to study a system developed by Teleregister. But some of his other important ideas were voted down. Although he did not say so, Reilly realized that the new sophisticated systems would not only make many clerks obsolete, but possibly could take over some specialist functions as well. Fearful of opening the door to a system that might in time make them redundant, many specialists looked upon automation with fear and suspicion. Mann, Dyer, and other specialists were not as enthusiastic about computers as was Reilly himself, who after all was not a specialist.**

In the midst of these automation debates, the Amex was hit by a new scandal, one more complex than anything previous, and once again the Exchange had to turn to the problems of internal policing. To some old-timers it seemed a replay of the Cuppia affair, but this new problem was to be to the Cuppia-Plate controversy what the atomic bomb was to TNT.

---

* Reilly's statements during the late 1950s anticipated most of the back-office problems of brokerages a decade later. Had his ideas been implemented by both exchanges, and some of the techniques accepted by the commission houses, part of the grief of the late 1960s might have been avoided.

** Here too, Reilly's ideas proved an omen of things to come. Although the merits of the specialist system had been debated for decades, and others preceded Reilly in suggesting reforms, the Amex Chairman was one of the first to demonstrate—without meaning to do so, perhaps—how the system might be improved. Of course, Reilly denied having a desire to bring about drastic changes, but these might well have evolved from the forces he hoped to put into motion in the late 1950s.

THIRTEEN

The New Speculation

No major bull market in American history has been unattended by scandal. The scandals differed in each, however, the result of the play of personality, the nature of the markets and opportunities presented, and outside economic and political forces. All of these factors figured importantly in the speculation and scandals of the 1950s and the first years of the 1960s.

The bull sweep of the 1950s was spectacular, in some ways even more so than that of the 1920s. Many Americans who bought and sold securities in the 1950s knew of what had happened in 1929, and they knew also that legislation had been passed in the 1930s to make certain a major crash would not take place again. Wall Streeters themselves remembered the markets of the 1920s, mistakes made and compounded; surely they would not permit the same thing to happen in the 1950s. Both the exchanges and the government policed the financial district during the Eisenhower era; neither had done much of anything in the days of Harding, Coolidge, and Hoover.

They did their work well in the 1950s, at least insofar as blatant manipulation was concerned. The pools and related devices used to push prices higher in the 1920s were hardly utilized in the 1950s. Men like Meehan, Livermore, and Arthur Cutten had been raiders who bought and sold securities in huge blocks and made fortunes on each turn in the market. They had dominated exchange floors, with no challenge from the institutions themselves or from any important outside force.

The situation differed considerably during the 1950s. The markets of that decade were too large for any group of individuals to control, and the lone raider had little chance on the exchange floors. Were power to be exercised, it would come from the heads of large institutional investors: the mutual funds, pension funds, foundations, and the like. These men were hardly the speculative type. From 1957 onward the pension funds invested over a billion dollars a year in stocks and almost twice that amount in bonds. By the end of the decade, the pension funds owned over 2 percent of all corporate stock in the nation. The mutual funds were not quite so powerful, but they had grown from $2.5 billion in value in 1950 to $17 billion at the decade's end. Men like Dwight Robinson, Joseph Fitzsimmons, Walter Morgan, and Cameron Reed controlled billions of dollars—all headed large funds. Their names were unknown outside the district, though they were many times more powerful than the Meehans and Livermores of the 1920s. As analyst Ragnar Naess put it, "The speculator and the general public are unimportant in shaping the trend of common stock prices. The speculator has been relegated to a minor position by legislation, and the general public is investing largely through mutual funds."

But illegal speculation arose in the 1950s, along with manipulations, which resulted in scandals. The manipulators of this period were far more sophisticated than those of the previous era, and, if as gaudy, at least were less powerful in determining the general direction of the market. The scandals of the late 1920s and early 1930s had made front-page news, and the men involved had been topics of conversation in small towns as well as on Wall Street. In contrast, most of the scandals of the late 1950s and early 1960s were relegated to the financial pages and, after they were over, were forgotten by most Americans.

The manipulators of the 1950s realized they could not operate in the open, and knew the content of the law and its implications. So they went underground. They would take control of a company, publicize it, make deals with insiders at the exchanges and elsewhere, and try to interest the institutions and the general public in buying the stock. Unlike Meehan, they would not be mere speculators and brokers. Instead, they were industrialists, operating as presidents of their firms, holding much of their own securities. The man who told reporters that his firm would become "another IBM" was not a stock speculator, but a seemingly responsible businessman whose securities were listed at either the Big Board or the Amex. Since it was believed that the exchanges were now well-policed, both internally and by the SEC, the investing public viewed such companies as sound and their presidents as capable and enlightened businessmen.

In most cases they were, but not in all. At a time when McCormick and Funston were assuring the SEC and the public of honesty in the district, many speculators, posing as innovative industrialists, were engaging in manipulations. They could not have managed without the cooperation of venal and corrupt brokers and investment bankers willing to bend rules or find loopholes in regulations. In some cases exchange officials had knowledge of such activities, but either did nothing or actually cooperated with the speculators. After more than two decades of the SEC there was important corruption in the financial district. This was not the work of outsiders, attracted to the district by dreams of easy money to be had in a bull market. Rather, it came from the district itself.

The major speculators of the 1920s operated as individuals or heads of pools. The individual pools had little contact with one another, and often were in competition. Such was not the case in the 1950s. The affairs of manipulators like Lowell Birrell and Alexander Guterma often were interrelated, if not directly, then through the medium of brokers, exchange officials, or investment bankers. The corruption of the 1920s was widespread, but, like sores on the body of a person with measles, isolated in spots. In contrast, the wheeling and dealing of the

1950s was weblike and convoluted, so that even those who understood it had difficulty in explaining the manipulations fully.*

One way to start would be with the career of Gerard A. "Jerry" Re, who was a key figure at the Amex throughout the 1950s.

Jerry Re was an old-timer, one of the men who had followed Edward McCormick indoors in 1921. Like so many of his fellow curbstone brokers, Re, the son of immigrants, left elementary school at an early age and received an education in survival on the streets of Greenwich Village. Along with dozens of other young men of his generation, he gravitated to the financial district seeking employment, and found it at the old pre–World War I Curb. Beginning as a runner, proceeding to a clerkship, and finally to brokerage, Re underwent a second kind of street education in the hectic markets of the wartime period. He soon learned how to make money by shaving points, making deals, and outwitting other brokers. It was each man for himself for the most part, and Re survived.

He prospered in the bull market of the 1920s. Although called before Curb committees for admonitions on several occasions, he was not very different from a majority of the brokers of the time—except in being tougher, shrewder, and more intelligent. Like his fellows, Re did badly during the 1930s, but he was never in danger of failure. At a time when other brokers were operating on shoestrings, Re was able to maintain a solid if not ornate life style. His rise as a specialist continued in the 1930s and into the next decade. If not as wealthy and prominent as Gilligan, Re was as successful in his own way. Gilligan was a single-minded man intent on dominating the specialist business at the Curb, while Re wanted more than just his share, and had wider aspirations, mostly of a social nature.

---

* Dozens of books have been written about the markets of the 1920s, but there is no major work on that of the 1950s. The reason is not difficult to find: the bull market of the earlier period was capped by the dramatic crash of 1929, and there was no such crash in the 1960s. If the institutional structure of securities capitalism has failed to eliminate corruption, at least it has succeeded in the far more important task of ending panics and major crashes.

A gregarious man, Re had a wide circle of friends and acquaintances, and he enjoyed their company even more than he did the accumulation of wealth.

Most of Re's friends were either politicians or baseball figures. He was a leading member of the Progressive Era Association, a Greenwich Village dinner club whose members included some of the city's leading Italian-American businessmen and politicians. Re tried to attend as many of the political testimonial dinners as he could, and often sat on the dias. He would also dine with members of the old Brooklyn Dodgers, such as Leo Durocher, Cookie Lavagetto, and Charlie Dressen, and was proud to be considered one of Toots Shor's friends. Such people would talk to Re of politics and sports, often telling him of inside information in both areas. At a time when the public was being drawn back to Wall Street, they expected Re's help. He usually obliged them. As the banquet manager of Cavanagh's, a leading gathering place for such individuals, put it, "When Mr. Re was at these here dinner parties, everybody seemed to be talking with him. He seemed to be such a constructive person that I thought he would give good advice. . . . I used to like to sit and talk to him because I thought it was constructive."

Re spent more time at such restaurants than on the road seeking listings. But plenty of business came his way as a result of such dinners and parties. Gilligan would search for new listings; Re was content to wait for them to come to him. He was on good terms with such men as Abraham Gellinoff, chairman of the law committee of Tammany Hall, and Vincent Albano, Republican leader of New York's East Side. Re was considered a man of importance, with proper connections. Businessmen sought him out; he didn't have to ingratiate himself with them.

Like many brokers of his age and experience, Re preferred the code of the old Curb to the laws of the New Deal. Re, Re & Co., his firm, had great influence among the Curb's leaders, and this continued at the Amex. No one who knew how the Amex operated dared cross his path. When the directors of one firm in which he specialized asked to have their stock switched to another specialist, they were told the change could not be made. "I inquired from friends of mine that were on the floor," explained one director, "and they said, 'Lay off. That guy owns this joint.'" When another director of a different firm tried the same thing, he also was refused. Later Re said, "Well, the Exchange told him in no uncertain words that I was one of the outstanding specialists and that I was doing an outstanding, excellent job." That job had little to do with the actual work of brokerage.

Re considered rules and regulations regarding the keeping of records as "confining," so he ignored them. He excused himself by saying that most brokers acted in the same fashion. "I have been down here a long time and I am not making excuses for myself, but I would wager that there is quite a number that don't do it that way."

Re relied on the old Curb maxim "One hand washes the other" for protection. His business friends took care of him by sending prospective clients to Re, Re & Co.,* and they received favors in return, in the form of stock tips and special distributions of securities. The same held true for Re's political friends.

So it was at the Amex. Re had an interest in American Leduc, a small mining firm that he hoped to have listed at the Exchange. To this end, he allowed President McCormick to purchase 2,000 shares for 36 cents a share in 1954; after the stock went public it reached a dollar a share.** Amex member Charles Foshko, who exchanged favors with Re, was sold 1,300 shares of Thompson-Starrett at 3⅞ on October 25, 1954. This Re, Re stock sold for a low of 4 on that date. Clearly, Foshko received preferential treatment, and his purchase had not appeared on the tape, a major violation of Amex rules. "If the sale wasn't recorded, it isn't my fault," explained Foshko later on. He suggested the possibility of an "oversight." There

* The firm later became Re, Re & Sagarese.
** But American Leduc was turned down for listing. Either McCormick didn't support listing, or the committee was not under his control. Later McCormick would claim he had little power over internal matters at the Amex. If this were the case, either Re had made a mistake, or he had permitted McCormick to participate for other reasons.

were four other "oversights" in Thompson-Starrett that day. Did Foshko think this unusual? "Well, five times, you would think that, yes," was his reply. All five cases involved Re's friends, and all paid him back in kind.

Re was a major specialist willing to break rules in order to obtain his ends. Clearly, such brokers were important to businessmen with the same moral code.

Lowell Birrell was one such person. The son of an impoverished Indiana minister, and one of five children, Birrell's childhood was every bit as hard as that of Re. Birrell managed to graduate from Syracuse University, and then went on to the University of Michigan Law School. An excellent student, he graduated at the top of his class in 1928.

Birrell entered the field of law at the worst time possible —the beginning of a depression. Yet he was an immediate success, joining the prestigious firm of Cadwalader, Wickersham & Taft at the age of twenty-one, and handling the accounts of some of the largest corporations in the nation. In 1935 Birrell formed his own firm, taking on the reorganization of several important depression-struck corporations. For a while he handled accounts of small breweries and distillers, freed from restrictions by the end of Prohibition.

In 1938 Birrell purchased the assets of Fidelio Brewery. To this he added other breweries, reorganizing the lot into a new firm called Greater New York Industries. By then Birrell was a wheeler-dealer, one of the most knowledgeable lawyers so far as the securities laws were concerned. He and other insiders sold unregistered shares of Greater New York and reaped a small fortune. Much of the money was used for possessions: a large mansion in Pennsylvania and a lavish home overlooking San Francisco Bay. The rest was put into the purchase of Claude Neon, which Birrell commanded in 1944. Jerry Re was Neon's specialist. Thus, the two men met.

During the next few years Birrell bought out, milked, and then dumped other companies, such as Rhode Island Insurance and United Dye & Chemical, the latter listed on the Big Board. He also began to move in new circles. His neighbors in Pennsylvania were writers Moss Hart and Budd Schulberg. Birrell took an apartment in Havana, where he entertained Jerry Re, who also vacationed there. He and Re often talked about business there, planning coups and new ventures at the Amex in which both would benefit.

Alexander Guterma also vacationed in Havana, and he and Birrell met and held many discussions. Guterma's past was shrouded in legend. He claimed to have been born in Siberia in 1915, the son of a czarist general. He traveled to China, Hawaii, and, on the eve of World War II, the Philippines. There he married the daughter of a prominent businessman. In 1950 Guterma entered the United States and applied for citizenship. He swiftly entered the financial world, organizing a holding company, Western Financial Corporation, which had great promise but few assets. Guterma convinced enough people of its worth to sell them stock, and with the money so obtained he created Shawano Development Corporation, a land-development concern. Guterma sold unregistered shares to the public and made a fortune. Other coups followed: McGrath Securities, Diversified Financial, Micro-Moisture Controls. By 1954, Guterma was in the big time.

The following year Guterma purchased control of United Dye from Birrell, and proceeded to loot the company. Then he took over control of F. L. Jacobs, a manufacturer of auto parts. With money derived from Jacobs, he obtained control of Bon Ami Company. All three firms—United Dye, Jacobs, and Bon Ami—were listed on the New York Stock Exchange. Guterma was the first and only man in history to be president of three so-listed companies. His explanation for his success? "I get up early and stay up late and . . . in between I put in a lot of hard work. Also, I've been very lucky."

Like both Re and Birrell, Guterma knew the importance of being on good terms with Exchange insiders. Listing would create a larger market for his shares and give them an aura of respectability. He wanted listing particularly for Shawano, which he saw as a natural for the Amex. Guterma met McCormick in Havana, and the two men went gambling together. McCormick lost $5,000, which Guterma then advanced to him. Later, when McCormick tried to repay the debt, Guterma refused. Foolishly, McCormick accepted what amounted to a gift from Guterma, who at the time was applying for Amex listing for Shawano. The firm was not accepted for listing, but the veto was exercised by the Amex committee, not the President.

There were ties, then, between Re, Birrell, Guterma, and McCormick in the early and mid-1950s. Guterma paid McCormick's debt, and Re helped the President make money in low-priced securities. Re violated SEC and Amex rules with impunity. Birrell and Guterma ignored SEC regulations regarding the sale of unregistered securities, and hoped to use the Amex as their vehicle for profits, while McCormick said nothing, guilty of negligence if nothing else.*

A network as complicated and interwoven as this is delicate and liable to rupture at weak points. At the same time, the participants often get careless, or take great risks in the belief that they cannot be stopped. Such a situation caused the downfall of the complex.

It began in 1954, after Birrell sold his United Dye holdings to Guterma. Seeking a new vehicle for his operations, he came upon Swan-Finch Oil Corporation, an unlisted Amex company. Swan-Finch was an old firm, having been founded more than a century before by the Standard Oil Company. It had been spun off in 1911, at which time it received unlisted rights at the Curb. It wasn't much of an operating firm at the time, so Birrell was able to take control of 40 percent of its stock for $250,000. It was a perfect vehicle for manipulation.

As soon as he had obtained control, Birrell had the board authorize additional shares of stock, raising the number of shares from 34,793 to 2.8 million within two and a half years. This stock was used to purchase oil and gas companies, a grain-storage warehouse, and several other properties. Birrell touted Swan-Finch as a glamourous conglomorate, a firm that would be doing over a billion dollars worth of business with-

---

* The details of the Birrell and Guterma activities are fascinating and complex, but in this work we will deal only in those operations connected with the Amex. For fuller accounts of their manipulations, see Hillel Black, *The Watchdogs of Wall Street* (Morrow, 1962) and Frank Cormier, *Wall Street's Shady Side* (Public Affairs, 1962).

in a decade. Interest in the firm grew, and the price of its stock rose.

In January 1956, Birrell used 527,427 shares of Swan-Finch to purchase Doeskin Products, a manufacturer of paper tissues, which he also controlled through Greater New York Industries. The Swan-Finch shares never reached the Doeskin owners. Instead, they were turned over to Greater New York Industries and from there to other Birrell-controlled firms. Clearly, Birrell was preparing for some master stroke.

Jerry Re would be Birrell's partner in the Swan-Finch deal. Soon after Birrell took over at the company, Re invited a large group of his friends to a dinner at the Bankers Club, the purpose of which was to furnish them with information about a "bright new company": Swan-Finch, of course. The investors had benefited from Re's tips in the past, and they purchased large amounts of the stock. Through their efforts, Swan-Finch rose from pennies in 1944 to dollars in 1956 and Re, its specialist, benefited greatly.

On December 7, 1956, Birrell called Jerry Re to his office to tell him that he was in serious financial difficulties. Money lenders were calling in several large loans, and he needed a great deal of cash quickly. Swan-Finch stock, used to collateralize the loans, would have to be sold. He wanted Re to sell as many shares as he could.

Re agreed to do this, enlisting the aid of his old friend Charles Grande. The two had known each other in Greenwich Village before World War I. Grande had held a variety of jobs, from horse trainer to chauffeur to broker. For several years he had maintained an account at a brokerage through which Re funneled securities, some of them unregistered, to the public. The securities were deposited in Grande's account, and from there sold on the Amex. Now Re wanted to dump Swan-Finch stock in the same manner, and Grande was agreeable. "I told Jerry Re that I would be interested in the speculation," he later testified.

During the next three months some 470,000 shares of Swan-Finch—approximately 20 percent of the outstanding stock—went into Grande's account, to be sold at the Amex and the over-the-counter markets. About 388,000 shares went to the Amex, where Re, as their specialist, handled the trades. Meanwhile, Birrell used other intermediaries to get rid of additional Swan-Finch stock as well as a large block of Doeskin, much of which was unregistered. Birrell's firms eventually sold 1.2 million shares of Swan-Finch at an average price of $4 and 400,000 shares of Doeskin at an average price of $8. The sale of all this stock, for which Birrell had paid pennies, served not only to pay off all his debts, but meant another fortune for the financier.

It also meant additional business for the brokerages at which the dummy accounts were situated. Throughout this period most were at Josephthal & Co. The firm's floor representative, Anthony Cordano, was an old friend of Jerry Re's, and was happy to cooperate and receive such a landslide business. Cordano did not think to question the source of the large blocks placed with him, although he would later testify that he always asked Grande whether they were control shares, and was told they were not.

The Re-Grande-Birrell nexus was in violation of Amex rules, while Cordano was guilty at the least of amazing credulity. The sale of unregistered shares at the Exchange was a violation, as was the sale of control shares without prior notification.*

The unusually large volume of trading in Swan-Finch interested the Amex's committee on floor transactions, which ordered an investigation. The committee compiled a list of all purchases and sales, as well as a second list, which consisted of the largest transactions. The second list indicated that Grande had sold 256,200 shares of the stock during the previous three months. Investigation indicated no way by which Grande could have come into possession of such stock. It further indicated that Josephthal had not questioned any of the transactions. But the committee went no further with its investigation, nor did it

* Later Birrell would claim that since the shares were unregistered, they were not control shares. And since they were not control shares, they need not have been registered. This circular reasoning did not impress the SEC.

bring charges against any of the people involved. Instead, the full report was sent to Paul Windels, Jr., head of the SEC's New York office.

Unknown to the committee, Windels had already begun a study of Birrell's activities. The Amex report confirmed his suspicions that Birrell had been looting Swan-Finch and other companies under his control. Later on, Windels said:

> Even though Birrell was in effect embezzling Swan-Finch, we could not get him on a charge of failing to file a report exposing what he was doing to the company. Although the stock was traded on the American Stock Exchange, the fact that it was in the unlisted category meant that Birrell did not have to file the usual reports. Furthermore, while the assets were being removed from Swan-Finch, the stock was increasing in price. I knew that Birrell had to be unloading against a manipulated market. That's when I ordered a full probe.

Windels confirmed that Birrell's activities had interested his office for several months prior to the Amex investigation. Why, then, had he not ordered an investigation of his own? Part of the reason might have been the understaffed condition of the New York office. Another could have been that the SEC simply did not know how to unravel the complicated dealings of men like Birrell. Finally, the investigators were not certain they had the power and authority to act in this unusual case. The securities laws had been written a generation earlier, and were very much out of date. They were geared to the workings of men like Mike Meehan, not those of a Lowell Birrell. As Windels put it:

> It appeared that Swan-Finch was being sold by moneylending groups which obtained the shares as the result of defaulted loans. The moneylenders, in turn, claimed that registration was not necessary because of the 'bona fide loan exemptions.' They and Birrell seemed to have an excellent defense. It looked pretty grim. Then we hit upon the idea of making a frontal attack. Our case would be the simple truth, that the so-called sale of 'distressed shares' was just a subterfuge to sell stock without registering it. In effect, Birrell was hiding behind the bona fide loan exemption. Furthermore, we would claim that the

moneylenders were actually serving as underwriters and that the two percent monthly interest charge on the loans to Birrell was their commission for selling the stock. But the going promised to be rough. There was simply no legal precedent.

Clearly, then, the SEC was concentrating its fire on Birrell, not the Amex. Windels may have suspected Re's role in the sales, but even if he did, he was after Birrell and not the specialist.

On April 15, 1957, the SEC obtained a temporary restraining order to halt the sale of Swan-Finch stock unless and until it was registered with the agency. With this the Amex acted. Swan-Finch had not filed reports for several years, a violation even though the stock was unlisted. The following day the Amex suspended trading in the security. The Amex moved less swiftly against Re, even though he and Grande had been named in the order.

A week later one of the money lenders submitted a motion to lift the order. Judge Sidney Sugarman agreed, and the order was vacated. With this, Birrell and Re sprang into action, dumping their remaining shares on the market. Windels also acted. Recovering from his surprise, he appealed the Sugarman order to Judge Harold Medina of the Circuit Court of Appeals, telling him of the high volume in Swan-Finch and what it meant. Medina reinstated the order, and on June 27, when the case was called for trial, Birrell and most of the others named consented to a permanent injunction. Thus, trading ended in Swan-Finch as Birrell and Re prepared for their next move.

It remained for the SEC to serve the two men with subpoenas and have them testify about their activities in Swan-Finch. Re accepted his with no difficulty, but the key man, Birrell, was more difficult to locate. Rumors of a flight to Canada, to Cuba, and even of his death, appeared in the newspapers. Finally, Birrell was located at a party at his Pennsylvania home, and he took the subpoena in good grace. Then he disappeared once more—the talk was that he had gone to Venezuela, but others had him in Paris. The trial was set for the fall, and Birrell was under an order not to travel. Still, Windels had him served with a second subpoena in July, this one delivered at the Idlewild airport. As it turned out, at the time Birrell was on his way out of the country, winding up in Brazil after long stays in Cuba and Europe.*

Without Birrell there could be no trial, and there the matter rested. In effect, this took Re off the hook. Although the SEC continued its investigation of his pre-1957 activities, there was insufficient evidence to bring charges against him. Had Re heeded this clear warning—had he been a more prudent man —he might have remained a power at the Amex, retiring in the 1960s after a long and successful career. But Re was not the man for inactivity. He had broken rules for his own benefit before meeting Birrell, and would continue doing so until stopped by some outside agency. His modus operandi in the post-Birrell period was interesting, but hardly original. Either Re secretly wanted to be caught (not very likely), or he was not as clever as his Amex contemporaries believed him to be.

In July 1957—about the same time Birrell was accepting his second subpoena—an account was established in the Swiss Credit Bank in Zurich in the name of Jose Miranda. This was a common Cuban name, somewhat akin to John Doe or Richard Smith in America. The account was opened at a time when Jerry Re was visiting Zurich. Simultaneously, an account for Miranda was opened at the Swiss American Corporation in New York, and the Zurich bank was informed that from time to time it would receive orders for deposits and withdrawals from Miranda through Swiss American. One of the first such cables was signed "Jose et Gerardo Miranda." Jerry Re's son and partner was Gerard—the initials matched.

Did Jose Miranda exist? Who was Gerardo? Why did supposed Cubans sign their names "Jose et Gerardo" instead of "Jose y Gerardo," a more common usage? Charles Grande later testified to having met Miranda at a racetrack in Havana. Benjamin Wheeler, president of Rokeach, Inc., a Re stock, as well as a close friend of both Res, said he too had met Miranda—a

---

* The financial manipulators of the 1920s wound up in jail, on Wall Street, or, in the case of Joseph Kennedy, on the SEC. In contrast, most of their counterparts of the 1950s went into exile in Brazil, which had no extradition treaty with the United States.

dark man of medium height with a black mustache. "He seemed to be a very personable kind of guy, very free with money." But Miranda was seen only by Re's friends; otherwise, he left no trace.

According to Wheeler, Miranda suggested that certain of his business transactions might be conducted through Wheeler's accounts, and he implied that Jerry Re would like it that way. Wheeler was willing to do this, but only after a written agreement listing all details was signed by Miranda. Although Miranda rejected the idea, Wheeler handled dealings for him on several occasions. But he had no documents signed by Miranda. According to Wheeler, all orders came through Jerry Re, or by telephone from a man with a "thick Spanish accent." Wheeler thought the voice might be Miranda's, but conceded that Miranda sounded a bit like Charles Grande at times.

During the next two years some $3.3 million worth of securities were sold through the Miranda and Wheeler accounts. Many of these were unregistered shares that found ultimate destinations in the hands of Re's friends. A pattern soon developed. The distribution through the Miranda and Wheeler accounts would be made, and Re would push the price of the stock to a new high. Then the Miranda and Wheeler stocks would be dumped on the market and sold for high profits. Sometimes Re would take the stock himself and then transfer the shares to clients who had gone short on the issue, but most of the transactions were handled as straight buy or sell orders.

Since there was no way of knowing exactly how much of Re's business was handled off the floor, only his "legitimate" floor dealings could have been calculated. By mid-1949, he was a major figure on the Amex floor, doing almost 4 percent of the total volume of business at the Exchange.*

The Amex leaders were informed that the SEC was looking into all of Re's dealings. Since mid-1957 the committee on business conduct had been reviewing his floor activities to as-

* It should be noted that although Re did a large volume of business in this period, the *dollar value* of his dealings was not nearly as high as that of other brokers who specialized in higher-priced issues. As before, Gilligan, Will was the leader here.

certain whether regulations had been violated. However, Re's activities were so neatly executed that no breach could be uncovered for over a year. Then, in mid-1959, the committee charged Re, Re with price manipulations in several issues. In particular the committee stated that the firm had violated Amex rules in the methods by which they shorted Trans Continental Industries.

Re denied all charges and defended himself vigorously before the committee. He denied he was ever short in Trans Continental Industries, accused the committee of trying to read his mind rather than judge his actions, and denied every charge made against his firm. The committee, which was led by John Brick, did not dig as deeply into the evidence as had previous groups faced with similar problems, but it did find sufficient evidence of manipulation to take action against the firm and its partners. As a result, it found them guilty of illegal short sales and recommended punishment.

The case was then reheard before the full Board of Governors, which met for that purpose in mid-December. Once again the Res entered strong defenses and claimed that at no time had they been short of the stock, although they conceded that such might have appeared the case. At the same time as they had been selling, they claimed, purchases had been made to cover the sales. The largest of these was for 57,000 shares, from David Haber, whom they described as a man of high integrity. Haber failed to deliver all of his shares, leaving the Res in a short position. The fault was not theirs, but Haber's. They were the victims of the violation, not the perpetrators.

Brick also appeared to testify. He indicated that he had checked the Res's story and found it to be true in its essentials. If the board found the Res and Sagarese guilty, his committee was prepared to make recommendations as to penalties. But Brick would not make recommendations on his own, despite the fact that earlier he had led the committee in finding the three brokers guilty of manipulations.

The board was in a strange position. It had little doubt that the defendants were manipulators. Yet the evidence presented at the hearings was inconclusive. To find them innocent would be to fly in the face of common knowledge, but at the same time be consistent with the principle that a man was innocent until proven guilty. Such a decision surely would provoke SEC reactions, perhaps in the form of an all-out investigation of the Amex. Should the brokers be found guilty, might it not have been as much the result of what amounted to hearsay as of evidence and testimony? Might not the board then stand accused of throwing the Res to the wolves in order to save the Amex? *

There was no easy way out of this situation. Whatever the board decided, it would be accused by some of expedient behavior and praised by others for bravery.

In the end, the board voted to dismiss the charges. The margin was eighteen to five. Among those voting for acquittal were former chairman John Mann, vice-chairman of the board Charles Bocklet, and William Zeckendorf, one of the governors representing the public and also president of Webb & Knapp, a listed Amex stock.** Among the five voting for conviction were future chairman of the board Joseph Reilly and Mrs. Mary Roebling, who, like Zeckendorf, was a public governor.

Yet some of those voting to exonerate the three did so with feelings of remorse. Zeckendorf put it this way:

> I think that there has been evidence brought forth here that, while it does not make them guilty as charged, did indicate a

---

* News of the board hearings leaked to the press. Leslie Gould had an almost daily report as to what was happening. At one point he told Reilly he would print what he had, but asked Reilly to add to the material to make certain the full story was told. Reilly notified the board of this situation, and asked whether it would approve of such action. The board rejected it. Reilly did meet with Gould on several occasions to discuss the matter. Within weeks, news of the hearings, the votes, and positions taken by leading figures was in the Gould columns.

** Zeckendorf, Roebling, and the other public governor, George Collins, rarely attended Board meetings. As the SEC later wrote, "Even by the unexacting standards set by the Exchange, the attendance of the public governors at Board meetings has been poor. During the two and a half years beginning January 1, 1959, Collins attended one meeting and Mrs. Roebling and Zeckendorf each attended four." Collins was not present for the Re, Re & Sagarese vote on December 16, 1969.

certain type of omission and other sloppiness of procedure that, even as a layman, not knowing much about the securities business, calls for further consideration or for possible reprimand or some sort of penalty notwithstanding. That's how I feel about the matter.

Zeckendorf took this stand not because of feeling the Res and Sagarese were guilty, but in the hope of salvaging the Amex's reputation.

I said I thought it was in the interests of the Exchange from the standpoint of public relations and relations with the SEC that some action be taken of a punitive nature against these people so that we do not accept all these explanations and take everything carte blanche. There definitely have been acts of omission and commission here that are susceptible to severe criticism and I hope that they are dealt with with promptness so that we can have on the record that we do not accept this type of thing carte blanch.

We are on notice in the records here, and I think we have got to do something about it.

By deciding in favor of acquittal, however, the Amex made certain the SEC would enter the affair. The board must have realized that this would take place. Later the majority would be accused of attempting to cover up the Re situation. This was not so: by December, 1959, a coverup would have been impossible, and all board members knew this. Why, then, did the eighteen take the stand they did? Each person must have had a different set of reasons. One reason might have included the belief that insufficient evidence for a guilty verdict had been introduced.*

The exoneration shocked some brokers and disgusted others. Only twenty-three of the thirty-two governors had voted at that important meeting. Three of the remaining nine, members of the committee on business conduct, could not vote under terms of the constitution, and the chairman—Dyer—

* It was later suggested that McCormick influenced some of the eighteen to vote as they did. Such an analysis makes little sense. McCormick had every reason to fear an investigation, and knew that acquittal would result in one. If anything, he favored a guilty verdict.

could vote only in case of a tie. Five were not present. One of them, Paul Porzelt, later recalled that the verdict "left a bad taste in my mouth." Yet even if he and the other four had voted against the Res, they would have been found innocent.

Joseph Reilly, at the time chairman of the committee on floor transactions, was angry at the vote. He considered the Res and Sagarese guilty, and had hoped that the board would agree. But what could he do under the circumstances? He called a special session of his committee, which then found Jerry Re guilty of several technical violations and suspended him from membership for thirty days. The committee blunted the impact of the action by suspending the verdict for a month, so Re's absence could coincide with his annual Florida vacation. And the committee took no action against Gerard Re and Sagarese.

As expected, the board's verdict triggered a reaction at the SEC. Ralph Saul, the Associate Director of the Division of Trading and Exchanges, led an investigation of the affair that lasted four months. On the morning of May 12, 1960, Saul and his colleagues released the first of several bombshells directed at the Amex.*

Saul charged the Res with technical violations and abuses of their positions as specialists. They had engaged in eleven major "distributions," involving some $6 million worth of securities, without disclosing that they were the distributor or registering as such. Between 1954 and 1960 they had illegally sold over one million shares of stock in nine corporations, worth some $10 million, in violation of Amex and SEC rules. Saul promised to release details and proof of these allegations as soon as a brief could be prepared.

Some of the manipulation was done with the full knowledge and even cooperation of Amex officials. For example, when the Res sponsored I. Rokeach's application for listing in

---

* On April 20—less than a month before Saul's first investigation was completed—Chairman Dyer said "with great pleasure that the American Stock Exchange relationship with the Securities and Exchange Commission is at its highest peak since that agency was formed." Dyer did not eleborate on what he had in mind.

December, 1955, they had effective control of the corporation. A specialist was not permitted to take on a firm if such were the case, and yet the brokers wanted to do just that. They did not attempt to hide the fact. In a letter to the committee, Gerard Re wrote, "We helped to achieve this application for list-ing in another significant manner. Namely, we joined the syndicate in purchasing control of the company." Despite this admission, Re, Re was assigned the stock. This served to substantiate the rumor that Jerry Re was the most feared man at the Amex, a situation he exploited skilfully and often.

Later on, the Res sold their stock illegally, netting a profit of some $400,000 on the deal. This money was deposited in the Miranda account. At the time of the first Saul report, it was assumed that Miranda actually existed, and a search was begun for both him and Charles Grande.

That afternoon Ira Pearce, one of Saul's colleagues, approached Jerry Re on the Amex floor. Re knew Pearce from the days of the Birrell inquiry, and assumed he was there on related business. He led Pearce to a corner of the floor, and asked, "Have you got some sort of subpoena for me there, Ira?" "No, Gerard," was the reply. "It's something more than that." Pearce then presented Re with nine pages of detailed accusations regarding his dealings in the 1950s.

That was the last day Jerry Re appeared on the Amex floor as a specialist. This fact alone would have marked the end of an era for the Exchange. But it represented far more than that. As Saul and his colleagues unraveled Re's dealings, the nation learned of the most widespread scandal in the history of the American securities industry, one that involved more investors and speculators than any other, before or since. The Re scandal would drag down not only the powerful and feared Jerry Re, but the Amex administration itself.

FOURTEEN

Denouement

Joseph Reilly assumed the Amex chairmanship in February of 1960, less than two months after the board had voted to exonerate the Res and his committee suspended Jerry Re. For him the chairmanship represented not only the pinnacle of success, but a vehicle to be used to carry out the final phases of the automation program on which he had worked for six years. Were it not for the scandals then developing, Reilly might have completed the task in little more than a year. He could then have left office with that major project completed, and the Amex thereby prepared for what everyone expected to be the hectic markets of the 1960s and 1970s.

Time and again during his first year in office, Reilly raised the automation issue, but on each occasion new revelations in the Re story would capture the attention of the board. Reluctantly, the Chairman had to forego questions on the internal development of the Exchange to concentrate on outside attacks by the SEC and on internal dissension, from both those who wanted to defend the Amex from change and others who insisted that he move swiftly in the direction of reform. Much of the time Reilly was the man in the middle, and in 1960–62 that was an uncomfortable, tenuous position.

On learning of Saul's report on the Res, Reilly called a

special meeting of the board to consider the situation. The board suspended the brokers, pending a final decision by the SEC. Members who had found the Res innocent in December now called for their heads; they wanted the Amex to expel the brokers as soon as possible, condemning them in strong terms, in the hope that this might convince the SEC that the Exchange was capable of self-policing. Reilly, who had voted against the Res in December, opposed such action. Instead he insisted that the brokers had certain constitutional protections that could not be overlooked. For example, they could appeal the decision within five days. Until then, the board could do no more than it already had. Reilly assured the board that he did not take the matter lightly. He would initiate an investigation of the affair and report his findings on June 2, when the board would meet for its next regular session. Reilly concluded by asking the members to close ranks. What had happened, he insisted, had been far beyond the power of the Amex to control. The Exchange mechanism was sound, and manned by able and dedicated brokers. All that was needed was to remove those few negative factors that were causing temporary trouble.

Reilly reported to the board on June 2. So far as he was concerned, the key question the members had to consider was the Amex's role in the situation. The committee on floor transactions had looked into the Swan-Finch affair as early as 1957, at which time it had submitted a report to the SEC on the selling of unregistered shares. Since the Amex lacked the power to subpoena non-members, such as Grande and Miranda, it could have gone no further than it did. But why did the SEC wait until 1960 to take action? Reilly thought the Commission would have to explain this when the time came.* The Chairman also thought that the wording of the Securities Act of 1933 regarding the sale of controlled or unregistered stock by officers, directors, or controlling stockholders was unclear, and had never been fully ruled upon by the SEC. Yet it would appear the Commission was insisting that a prima facie case existed.

---

* The SEC never stated why the investigation did not begin in 1957, or allude to the Amex report in its final brief.

Without mentioning the Res by name, Reilly asked how specialists could be expected to check on the stock they handled —how could they find out whether the stock was control stock or not, or the shares unregistered? In other words, the SEC was making grave charges against the Res, and now would have to prove them. In effect, Reilly was defending the specialist system at the Amex, and in so doing had to offer a partial defense of the Res, no matter how that action must have troubled him. The Chairman, who had voted to find the Res guilty in December, now used arguments put forth at that time to support votes for acquittal.

The SEC investigation took almost a year, during which time news of the closed hearings leaked to the Amex. Long before the final report was handed down on April 28, 1961, the board knew the Res would stand condemned of major manipulations, along with others at the Amex. Such a situation could not help but reflect badly on the administration, and would result in demands for sweeping reforms. If the Res were guilty, then perhaps other major brokers, such as Gilligan, would also be investigated. During the preceding decade several important administration figures, such as John Mann, Charles Bocklet, and James Dyer had increased their business and grown wealthy and powerful. Had they used their Amex positions to enlarge their specialist business? And what of McCormick's connections with the Res, and rumors of stock deals he had entered into, and from which he was supposed to have profited?

Had the board investigated these situations and sought answers to these questions, it might have presented a better face when the final report on the Res was handed down. But there was little of this in the year prior to April 1961. Responsibility for this inaction rested with the board, and Reilly was supposed to lead it, to give the other members direction. McCormick, under suspicion at the time, could hardly have been expected to act in this manner, and there was no other person of stature in office to undertake the task. Yet Reilly did little in the way of reform during this period, and this was his chief failure.

He did not refrain from action for personal reasons. Almost alone of the major Amex figures on the floor, Reilly was not a specialist, and so could not have benefited from allocations. Neither had he done a large business in brokerage, and his commission had not increased substantially as a result of his administrative work. Reilly had nothing to hide, a fact that most of those in administration knew. It was one reason for the respect he carried, and this gave him some of the power—which he did not exercise—in 1960–62.

Reilly was an emotional man, and one with a great sense of institutional loyalty. As he saw it, one of his tasks as chairman was to defend the Amex against those who attacked it. This may be an admirable trait, but it led Reilly to defend what in other contexts he would have recognized as indefensible. At times he would resist change and reform, not so much because he opposed it but as a reaction against men who made the recommendations, whom he viewed as those who would harm the Amex.

Throughout 1960 and early 1961, Reilly praised the work of McCormick and Mooney. He thought the President had done an admirable job in bringing new issues to the Exchange, and he said so on several occasions—without going into the quality of the issues, and ignoring the fact that the SEC was investigating that very point, if not in regard to McCormick's work, then to the role played by Re. Reilly thought McCormick's testimony before the SEC was "outstanding," and considered Mooney's mastery of securities regulations "complete." Reilly initiated no study of his own on Amex policies; neither did he try in any way to investigate the matters before the SEC.

John Mann, chairman of the committee on floor transactions, did not increase his surveillance in this period; there was no dramatic increase in the number of cases brought before him. Only one case exclusive of that involving the Res was brought before the board: Michael Horowitz, a two-dollar broker, was charged with failing to pay transactions fees, keeping improper records, and making gifts to Amex employees without first obtaining the required permission. Horowitz also admitted to faking entries to avoid income taxes, and in other ways manipulating his accounts to lower his gross income. Horowitz's case was concluded in September, and he was found guilty of all charges. No attempt was made to discover exactly how much he had cheated the Amex, or the full extent of his operations. But his guilt was obvious. Horowitz received a three-month suspension and a fine of $5,000. At the time, Horowitz admitted to earning approximately $200,000 a year in commissions. A man with that amount of earnings, in trouble with the Internal Revenue Service, at a time when the SEC was investigating floor operations, might have expected a more severe penalty. By being lenient, the board was practically begging for criticism. That would come in 1962, when the SEC, writing of the Horowitz case, said: "The penalty, although serious, hardly seems adequate in view of the offenses involved, especially since the constitution of the Exchange provides expulsion as the penalty for fraud."

On April 27, 1961, the SEC handed down its brief, in which it charged the Res with violations of at least eight Amex rules designed to assure fair dealings between specialists and the public. The brief claimed that the Res had been operating "an underground business combine" whose goal it was not only to enrich themselves, but to take care of a host of others, many at the Amex, some on the outside. They did this by acting as "market riggers."

> Although these violations are deliberate, numerous, and gross in character, they do not form the core of this case. Rather, the core of this case is the willful and planned violation by the Res of their fiduciary duties as Exchange specialists. . . . Statute, common law and custom place immense trust and responsibility and a correlative potential for harm in the hands of specialists. It is the prostitution of the specialists' important role, at the heart of the market mechanism, which provides the *modus operandi* for the operations described in this brief, and resulted in many millions of dollars of harm to thousands of unsuspecting investors who had every reason to expect that the exchange market in which they dealt was honest and fair in accord with the laws administered by this Commission.

Specifically, the Res were accused of using their specialists' positions to distribute control stock to the public, of handling discretionary orders which were prohibited under the Securities Act of 1934, and of using non-members to close certain deals in the stocks in which they specialized. These stocks, ten of which were named, included Rokeach, Swan-Finch, and Trans Continental. According to the brief, officials of these companies would deposit blocks of securities in the Grande and Miranda accounts, from which they were sold, either at the Amex or on the over-the-counter market. In all cases, the Res were in full command.*

The report made public knowledge what many Amex brokers had known for years. It told of Re's connections with sports and political figures, his background and rise to power, and his influence on the floor. It went into Re's testimony before the Board of Governors, his relations with Grande, the secret account set up in Miranda's name—and the brief questioned whether Miranda actually existed. Although additional information regarding Re's dealings would be uncovered by future investigation, the brief was well-drawn and damning. A good deal of what was disclosed had been known to board members almost a year earlier; only the details, the statistics, and the dates were really new.

The Res did not dispute the Commission's findings or challenge any of the testimony offered during the closed hearings that resulted in the final brief. Indeed, two months earlier they had entered voluntarily into a stipulation of facts in connection with the proceedings. They did not deny any of the charges at that time, either of abuses of Amex rules or of federal laws. But both men reserved the right to make oral arguments before the Commission when it met again. All indications at the time were that the Res would say that there were mitigating and extenuating circumstances. Notwithstanding this, the Res conceded that "the facts plainly justify sanctions" against them.

The Re brief, delivered to the SEC at that time, placed most

---

* Sagarese, who had a very small share of the firm, was excluded from the charge. In any case, he had entered the firm after many of the manipulations set forth in the brief had been concluded.

of the blame for violations on the elder Re, and held that the son "has already been severely penalized by his suspension at the Amex." Apparently Jerry Re wanted to sacrifice himself in order to save his son.

> We respectfully submit that on the evidence here, he should be given an opportunity to engage in his profession in circumstances where he would be free of the unfortunate influence which his father exercised over him. . . . It is appropriate to appeal to the discretion of the commission that the younger Re should not be subjected to commercial extinction.

The Res, who were among the wealthiest brokers at the Amex, were hardly in danger of "commercial extinction." As further testimony would indicate, the younger Re was involved willingly and knowingly in almost all his father's operations.* The appeal was rejected. On May 4, the SEC revoked the registration of Re, Re & Sagarese, and ordered the Res expelled from the American Stock Exchange. The Res did not challenge either move.

Why had not the Amex suspended the Res on its own? Why did it wait for SEC action—a week after the brief was filed and released? Such questions were asked by reporters in the weeks to follow, with no comment from the board. Leslie Gould and others reported that the list of people dealing with the Res was incomplete, that it should have included Amex President McCormick, who was rapidly becoming a focus of public ire. What of McCormick's role in the Re story?

Reilly took the position that McCormick was just one of many who had been victimized by the Res. In 1954 the President had purchased 100 shares of Thompson-Starrett, preferred, one of the stocks in which the Res specialized. Perhaps he had done so after speaking of the security with Jerry Re. But he had sold it at a loss: $25. Reilly also conceded that

---

* One Amex broker, in a conversation with the author, said he was not surprised the Res tried to separate Gerard from his father in the case. He was encouraged when he learned that the motion was rejected. At the time, he said, he believed the Res' power extended to the SEC itself, and that "the fix was in."

McCormick had purchased shares of American Leduc, and added that he had owned 2,500 shares of Virginia Mining, both over-the-counter issues. The total cost of these two transactions came to $1,369, the full extent of his dealings with the Res.

Was it wrong for McCormick to accept tips from members? Reilly defended the President by noting that Funston admitted to having traded in Stock Exchange securities (although the cases were hardly similar, since Funston did not concede to having done so as a result of inside information. Neither did Funston deal in over-the-counter issues that might have had difficulty qualifying for listing but planned to make application in the near future). Reilly concluded by saying that McCormick hadn't traded in Amex stocks since 1957. He hoped the matter would not be raised again.

Reilly went on to state that Amex rules were sufficient to take care of wrongdoers, and that no new regulations need be considered as a result of the Re disclosures. In particular he cited rules 188, 189, and 190, all adopted in 1959 and 1960.* These would take care of problems like those of the Res should they appear in the future.

In condemning the Res and rejecting the plea for Gerard Re, the SEC stated:

> The securities laws arose from events which occurred over
> thirty years ago. Since that time and after the disclosure which

---

* Rule 188 stated: "No specialist shall effect a transaction, for any account in which he is directly or indirectly interested, in any security traded at any section of the post to which he is assigned as specialist except in a security in which he is registered as a specialist." Rule 189 stated: "No specialist, either during or outside of regular trading hours, may purchase, directly or indirectly, off the floor of the Exchange, any security in which he is registered for the account of a customer; provided, however, that the provisions of this rule shall not prohibit a transaction made to offset another transaction made in error." Rule 190 stated: "No specialist, either during or outside of regular trading hours, may purchase or otherwise acquire, for an account in which he is directly or indirectly interested, a block of stock in which he is registered and which is part of all or a private placement by the issuer or by any person controlling, controlled by, or under common control with the issuer." These might be called "the Re Rules," since they were written with him in mind.

resulted from both private and public investigation, the confidence of the public in the operation of the exchange markets has been slowly rebuilt. The Res, who . . . stood at the very heart of an exchange market, have struck a heavy blow at that market.

This strong statement should have been sufficient indication that Amex action was necessary. At least one large brokerage took it as such, and issued the following statement to its employees: ". . . To those of you who have recently entered this profession, I will tell you flatly that the warning flags are flying, and it behooves every one of you to recognize this signal and to conduct yourself accordingly." Representative Peter Mack, head of the House Subcommittee on Commerce and Finance, noted that more than two decades had passed since the last major investigation of the entire securities industry. He suggested that the SEC undertake such an inquiry, and he introduced a resolution directing the SEC "to make a study and investigation of the adequacy, for the protection of investors, of the rules for the expulsion, suspension, or disciplining of a member for conduct inconsistent with just and equitable principles of trade."

No move in the direction of reform came from the Amex Board of Governors. Instead, the board ordered a reallocation of the Re, Re & Sagarese securities. Even this was bungled. The Re stocks were assigned to Schweickart & Co. The following day the president of Thompson-Starrett protested, noting that Schweickart had acted as clearing agent for the Res both before and after their suspension. In effect, he suggested, the Amex had taken his stock from Re only to give it to a partner. The board replied it would take his request for a different specialist "under advisement."

So far as the SEC was concerned, the Re case, important though it was, marked the beginning of an even more significant examination of the American Stock Exchange. Although the case was reported upon, it was soon replaced by other, more damaging revelations.*

* The Res were indicted on stock manipulation charges on April 2, 1962, and they pleaded innocent. They were found guilty of conspiring to rig

Although the Res were major Amex figures and men of substance, they were not as powerful or influential as James Gilligan, who in 1961 was the most important specialist at the Exchange. Gilligan, Will & Co. was not only the largest specialist firm at the Amex, but it also handled some of its most active and prominent stocks, such as Kaiser Industries, Hazel Bishop, Lefcourt Realty, Cenco Instruments, and Parker Pen. Gilligan's ability to attract new listings was unquestioned; of the 139 new allocations in the period from July 1, 1956, to September 30, 1961, Gilligan, Will received seventeen, more than any other unit. Seven other specialist units cleared their transactions through Gilligan, Will, and four were financed by the firm. Many major commission brokers gave Gilligan, Will most of their business, and the most important of them, George De Martini and Louis Alter, worked in harmony with the firm in obtaining new listings and business. These two were major figures in their own right, as the third and fourth most active floor traders at the Amex. In 1959 Alter accounted for 8.2 percent of all sales at the Amex and 7.6 percent of all purchases, while De Martini did 7.9 percent of the Amex's sales that year and 6.2 percent of its purchases. Through his connections at the corporate headquarters of the firms in which he specialized, Gilligan had entry to several important executives who were willing to cooperate with him in areas of mutual interest. Several mutual funds, among them Value Line Special Situations Fund, learned the worth of having an account with Gilligan, Will. This nexus of corporation executives—mutual funds—commission brokers—specialists was in effect a trading empire, one that made the Res' operation seem somewhat minor league

the price of Swan-Finch and of conspiring to sell one million unregistered Swan-Finch shares. Each received a five-month sentence and a fine of $15,000. After being released from jail they were indicted on charges of having evaded nearly one million dollars' worth of taxes on profits derived from their dealings in 1958 and 1959. The Res contested this charge, and at the same time asked the courts to void their conviction. As they fought these battles in 1967, however, they were all but forgotten, except for those at the Amex whose lives were affected so deeply by their actions.

in comparison. The Amex administration knew this—the executives could scarcely not know of such an array of power. So much influence in the hands of one man could be dangerous. Gilligan often threw his weight around on the floor, fearing no man or official, appearing to take and do what he wished. Yet the administration took no steps to curb him.

Considering his position at the time, it is doubtful whether it could have acted even had it so desired. Gilligan could not be dealt with by the Exchange. Only the SEC had th ˋ power for such a task.

Gilligan knew all this. He must have watched the Re case with great interest, seeing how it would develop and what actions the government would take in the matter. The SEC report on the Res, released on April 28, 1961, might have convinced him that an investigation of the Amex was due and that such an inquiry might prove embarrassing. Never a man to hesitate, Gilligan acted at once. On that same day, he resigned as senior partner of Gilligan, Will. Little more than a month later he sold his Amex seat—as did his friend and associate Louis Alter.

Ted McCormick marked his tenth anniversary as Amex President in March of that year. This eclipsed the record of Edward R. McCormick, who had been president of the old Curb from 1914 to 1923. Ted McCormick was congratulated for his efforts on behalf of the Amex by many leading officials and brokers, including Reilly, Mann, Bocklet, Dyer—and Gilligan. McCormick had developed close and warm relations with all these men. The brokers who were in the President's inner circle had a great deal in common. All had been born in humble circumstances, had survived the tough education of the streets, were veterans of the old Curb, had risen at the Exchange by being tougher than the next fellow, and were at the height of their powers. If one were to eliminate the pushing and the shoving, the wheeling and the dealing, their stories would appear to vindicate the Horatio Alger epic; a synthesis of their life stories might have been subtitled "From Slum Boy to Financier." Jerry Re, who understandably was not there to congratulate McCormick, came from the same mold, as did other old-timers.

Two years earlier this group had appeared invulnerable. Although they often competed with one another for business, each respected the others as contemporaries and colleagues. Their man, McCormick, was in the presidency, while Mooney, who also fit in well with the old-timers, was counsel. There were a few dissidents, but they appeared isolated; most of the brokers seemed willing to work with these powerful men. In 1961 the Amex was under attack, with the Re episode clearly only the first round in a long battle. No longer was McCormick talked of as the next president of the Big Board, the favorite of senators and congressmen, the nation's leading expert on securities laws. Still, the ruling group seemed secure at the Amex in March, as it met to congratulate the President on his record tenure.

Gilligan would resign from his firm less than two months after the anniversary. It was the beginning of the end for the old inner group, although none could have known it at the time. Within a year their power would be crushed, even though the men themselves would remain at the Amex. The tenth year of the McCormick era, just short of the fortieth anniversary of the move indoors, marked the last hurrah for the men of the old Curb.

McCormick had reason to be grateful to this group. Not only had the men supported him throughout his administration and defended him against critics that past year, but some had given him assistance with his stock portfolio. The purchases made through Re's tip have already been mentioned. These were small compared with those achieved through the assistance of James Gilligan.

McCormick's portfolio was quite active in the mid-1950s, and a majority of his purchases were in Gilligan stocks. McCormick bought and sold Consolidated Diesel Electric Corporation, Continental Uranium, Inc., Guild Films, Inc., New Idria Mining and Chemical Co., and New Pacific Coal & Oils Ltd. McCormick had purchased $15,000 worth of Crowell-Collier debentures from one of Gilligan's friends in 1955, and so was involved in the illegal distribution referred to earlier.*

McCormick also purchased shares in over-the-counter issues that were soon to apply for listing. Among these were American Tractor, Chromalloy, El-Tronics, Prairie Oil Royalites, and F. C. Russell, all of which he purchased in 1954–55. With the exception of Prairie Oil Royalties, each of these securities was assigned to Gilligan, Will on listing.

Such transactions on the part of an ordinary speculator would indicate he had inside information, a not uncommon situation in the district at that time. For an Exchange official to have used such information in the way McCormick apparently did was, at best, foolhardy. Of all people, McCormick, with an SEC background, should have realized the criticism such activities would provoke should the news become public. It would appear to most that the risk was not worth whatever the profits might have been.

Why then had McCormick speculated in Gilligan and Re stocks? Why had he permitted Guterma to pay his gambling debt in Havana? What had happened in 1954 and 1955 that had led McCormick to take such risks, which eventually would lead to his downfall? The answers were not available in 1961. Nor would they appear later on, when McCormick was the center of inquiries. Even today the questions cannot be answered with certainty. All we can do is consider the man at the time, his position, and the view of him held by the outside world and the financial community.

McCormick was at the peak of his reputation in 1954–55. Hailed as an innovative force, a master salesman, the spirit of the new bull market, and the man who had saved the Amex from failure, it seemed nothing he could do would go wrong. Praise from congressmen and senators, specialists and commission brokers, editors and reporters, showered upon him. Some people can handle such fame. McCormick was not one of them.

The spirit of the bonanza was in the air at that time, and

* See p. 240.

the Amex President partook fully of it. He traveled too much, gambled too much, ate and drank too much. According to those who knew him, he became a man of excesses during a time of excesses. McCormick was called a symbol of the great bull market of the 1950s in 1955. This was so. He had its optimism, charm, aura of success—but also its lack of depth, its amorality, and its willingness to compromise standards. Perhaps he also had the ability to convince himself that there was nothing wrong with what he did. Shortly before his tenth anniversary, he told a visitor, "This is the best-policed stock exchange in the world." McCormick was an intelligent man. He must have known at the time that this was not the case. As he indicated, one of the functions of an Exchange president was to act as policeman. Ted McCormick was not cut out for that job.

On May 15, 1961—after Gilligan had left his firm but before he sold his seat—the SEC announced that it would begin an investigation of the securities industry, in which the American Stock Exchange would come under special scrutiny. The Amex study would go into the "rules, policies, practices and procedures" of the Exchange. Philip Loomis, director of the Division of Trading and Exchanges, wanted to know the background of the Re case to determine "why it was possible for a thing like that to happen and what should be done, if anything, to prevent it from happening again." Referring to the adoption of rules 188–190, Loomis noted that the Amex had already "changed its rules and procedures appreciably" since the Re case, but he wanted to discover what other changes might be necessary. Loomis also announced that the study would be conducted by Saul, who had prepared the original Re brief, and who knew more of the Amex than any other SEC official.*

* Alexander Guterma had been arrested on charges of stock fraud in 1959 and found guilty in 1960. He appealed the decision to a higher court. But on the day of the announcement of the SEC investigation, Guterma pleaded guilty to other stock fraud charges. On March 12, 1962, he testified that McCormick had been present at a meeting in Miami in 1955, when he and his co-conspirators planned to manipulate the stock of United Dye and Chemical Corporation, a Big Board security. But Guterma added, "to the best of my recollection, he was not present at any of these conversations."

McCormick and Reilly had conferred with the Commission heads prior to the announcement in Washington, and they issued a prompt reply. They noted that the SEC "has in the past reviewed the regulations and examined the procedures of the American Stock Exchange on a number of occasions."

> We welcome a thorough check of our operations at this time because of the unwarranted inferences which had been made as a result of the recent action taken by the commission against Mssrs. Re and Re. As in the past, we will offer the commission complete cooperation.

Now the committee on floor transactions and the board did what they should have done much earlier: they initiated a clean-up campaign on the trading floor. In a flurry of activity, several brokers were fined and suspended for violations of rules. One of these was Louis Alter, well-known for his dealings with Gilligan, who was fined for excessive trading in Electronics Corporation of America common stock and for confining his trading to one post, all of which took place on May 9, less than a week before the announcement of the SEC probe. Electronics Corporation of America was a Gilligan stock; the post involved was Gilligan's. Up to the end, then, Gilligan and Alter continued to exercise their dominant positions.

Then, as though to negate what appeared to be the beginning of a reform movement, the board voted to make no disclosure of the action, in view of the fact that the public was not directly affected.* The campaign continued throughout the summer, always without publicity. Some members thought this unwise. In the first place, news of an Amex campaign against wrongdoers would be well-received. Since there was no chance of a coverup in any event, it could do no harm. One member, Solomon Litt, thought the movement should be publicized. Furthermore, he didn't know how the board could claim that the public was not involved when commission brokers and specialists entered into deals with one another.

The matter was referred to the executive committee,

---

* The Amex records of this period were later turned over to the SEC, and so the material did become public information.

where it died. But Litt had raised an important question, one that indicated that some members realized that the Amex was a public institution, and that very little which occurred on the floor could be said not to involve the investing public.* This attitude would grow in time. It was one of the faint signs of rebirth that could be discerned in the summer of 1961.

Although the Amex leaders insisted their market was being attacked unduly, they cooperated fully with Saul and his investigators. Reilly thought that Congress hadn't appropriated sufficient funds for the inquiry. He went so far as to suggest the imposition of a temporary registration fee on all brokers, the proceeds of which would be used to defray expenses of the investigation. Both he and McCormick testified before the SEC and the House Commerce Subcommittee that summer, defending the Amex and the role of the administrations. McCormick was more defensive than Reilly in his testimony. He criticized the press for insinuating the Amex was corrupt.** McCormick defended past statements he had made in which he had recommended the purchase of securities. He always told investors to purchase stocks "intelligently, and know what you are buying." When asked to comment on Funston's call for better control of so-called "hot issues," McCormick spoke sharply: "I've no comment on Mr. Funston's authority [to speak as head of the Stock Exchange]. I'm the only spokesman of the American Stock Exchange, and when I have anything to say I say it," he replied, ignoring Reilly, who sat beside him. He added that when the governors of the American Stock Exchange "lose confidence in me, it's up to them to change it."

McCormick could count on Reilly's loyalty. "Like 98 percent of our active members on the floor, [I have] always admired our President, because of the outstanding job he has done in the interests of our Exchange . . ." Either Reilly had

* The reader will recall that the same attitude the board held in 1961—that in affairs in which the public was not directly involved no disclosure was necessary—had been held by all throughout the Cuppia Scandal.
** Leslie Gould was one of those to whom McCormick referred. His articles in the *Journal American* offer the best running commentary of inside happenings at board meetings we have. As in the past, the board tried to find out how Gould got his material, but failed.

lost touch with the membership, or he had allowed his emotions to rule his judgment. For even then, reform elements at the Amex were grouping, and their target was the President. Reilly also was criticized for not acting swiftly to bring about reforms. Corruption would have to be eliminated, said the reformers, and those who have permitted corruption to exist might have to be removed from office, decent and honorable as they may be in other respects. Such men made no secret of the fact that they were referring to McCormick and Reilly.

The Wall Street community in general and the brokerage houses in particular were unhappy with the Amex reaction to both the Re scandal and the SEC investigation. It seemed the board was doing little to bring about reform. If this were so, then needed changes would be mandated by the SEC or Congress. In either case, the reforms would be more drastic (and perhaps more painful) than those initiated by the Amex itself. Wall Street seemed convinced that its wound could best be healed by local doctors, and not general practitioners from Washington. Equally important was the attitude of investors and speculators. If they thought the Amex was a rigged market, they would avoid its securities, and perhaps Big Board stocks as well. This would affect not only the specialists at the exchanges, but the commission houses. One broker was quoted in the *Wall Street Journal* as saying, "The mess on the American Stock Exchange is so bad, it's apt to hurt all of Wall Street." This feeling was widely held. The senior partner of a large commission house added, "If I were running the American Exchange I'd be trying to clean house right now before the SEC delivers its second punch." The SEC had rid the district of the Res, a job the Amex should have done. Was the same thing to happen again? A third customer's man claimed that the Res were not an isolated case; other Amex brokers who hadn't been identified as yet were doing the same things. In speaking of one such specialist, he said, "He's touting a certain stock through some brokers I know. He's telling them, 'Help me support the market and I'll guarantee you four, five or ten points.'" Such "guarantees" could be offered only if the specialist violated Amex rules. He then told of a manipulation of which he claimed to have first-hand knowledge:

I was approached by the president of a company on the American Exchange and by his public relations man. We went out at four-thirty and had a few drinks. They told me what a good future the company had and how they'd like to see the price of the stock go up. The president had heavy holdings, and not much stock was in the public hands. They offered me ten thousand dollars for pushing the stock.

They said they'd arrange it so my customers could buy twenty-five thousand shares without pushing the price up substantially in the process. There's no question in my mind the specialist would have to be cut in on such a deal.

The accuracy of such stories is always difficult to trace; the genre usually appears at such times in rumor-rich Wall Street. Many believed them in the summer of 1961, and the SEC gave substance to them. The board's inaction served only to give additional verification to the rumors. The Amex seemed oblivious to criticisms such as these, which appeared regularly in the press. The *American Stock Exchange Investor,* a monthly publication of Amex news published by the Exchange, ignored the investigations. At a time when McCormick was coming under attack, the May issue spoke of his "devotion to duty during 10 years of A.S.E. progress." In responding to critics of the Amex, McCormick said, "I will stack the honesty and efficiency of our specialists against any other specialists or over-the-counter dealers in the country," and Reilly insisted that Amex specialists were subject to more frequent checks than those at the Big Board. This at a time when the SEC probe was indicating widespread dishonesty at the market!

Pressure for change, then, came from three groups either completely or partially outside of the Amex: the SEC, the commission houses, and the investing public. There was a fourth group, consisting of Amex brokers who hoped to overthrow the McCormick-Reilly administration, substitute one of their own, cooperate fully with the SEC after admitting the Exchange needed a housecleaning, and in this way win back both public confidence and that of the large commission brokers. As such groups had been called so often in the past, it was dubbed "the Young Turks."

FIFTEEN

The End of the Tunnel

Reporters identified David Jackson as the leader of the Young Turks of 1961. Such a designation was misleading. Jackson was fifty-nine years old at the time, a specialist of twenty-seven years standing. Still, he was a second-generation broker. His father, Emanuel, had become a curbstone broker in 1908 and, although never wealthy, was able to send his son to Peekskill Military Academy, Brown University, and St. John's Law School. Jackson did not graduate from college or law school. Instead, he quit to take a job as reporter for a small Brooklyn newspaper. Then, in 1925, he went to the Curb Market to join his brother Jack as a specialist.

It was a good time to become a broker, and Jackson learned quickly. He made money in the 1920s, lost most of it in the 1930s, suffered through the 1940s, and prospered once again with the coming of the Eisenhower bull market. In all of this he was fairly typical; his business fortunes were little different from those of a majority of brokers.

Jackson was not among those who scrimped and barely got along, but he was not a member of the aggressive group (which included Re and Gilligan) that sought power and wealth. Jackson was honest, a decided liability for one who might have aspired to such status. He had little desire for fame, and lacked the kind of drive that made Gilligan the leader on the floor. In fact, Jackson was always more *at* the Curb and the Amex than *of* it. As far as he was concerned, art, the theater, travel, and literature were more interesting than brokerage. Jackson had a reputation as a competent specialist, but not an outstanding one. The Amex was his place of business, not the center of his life.*

Jackson could have qualified for membership in the inner circle by virtue of age and longevity. Beyond that he had little in common with men like Gilligan, Mann, and Reilly. Unlike them, he had a middle-class upbringing and education, rather than one derived from the streets. The old leaders had come to the Curb as runners and then worked their way up to specialist status. Jackson had begun as a specialist. Amex affairs did not dominate Jackson's life, but were only a part of it. He had few outside interests in common with the inner group. Jackson might have been more comfortable at the Big Board, or in investment banking. As it was, he found he had more in common with the younger brokers—the second generation of indoor specialists—than with their fathers. His background and interests were not very different from theirs.

Jackson had the experience of the older generation and the attitude of the new men. In different circumstances he might have acted as a bridge between them, but such was not possible in the 1950s. The older brokers didn't care very much for Jackson, who always seemed rather out of place and foreign to them. Jackson's honesty meant he would not participate in deals, and they resented what they believed to be his lack of loyalty to the institution. Many of the younger brokers liked his ideas and the man himself, but were unprepared to risk

---

* This is not to say Jackson did not perform his duties well. In 1955, at a high point in speculative frenzy, Walter Winchell offered stock tips on his popular radio program. One of these involved Pantepec Oil. The next day there was great demand for Pantepec, one of Jackson's stocks. After a delay, Jackson opened Pantepec with an order to buy 357,500 shares at 8⅞, a record at the time. Jackson's handling of the situation made him famous for a while, and led to an appearance before the Fulbright Committee.

their careers by angering the men in power; they would not follow Jackson in any crusade he might wish to lead. Jackson, who was not young, or a Turk, also was not a leader in the late 1950s, for few would support him, and fewer still would do so openly.

Jackson was elected to the board in 1950, and so was there when it selected McCormick for the presidency. With the rest of the members, he considered McCormick an excellent choice for the position. He expected the new President to take more of an interest in the internal workings of the Amex than he did. Jackson was disturbed by McCormick's long absences, the appearance of marginal issues, and the increase of wheeling and dealing that took place. He spoke to McCormick about the situation, and these conversations served only to increase his apprehension. Jackson was on the executive committee and the committee on finance, and was chairman of the committee on floor transactions, all three of which were key bodies. He saw what was happening and protested. During this period he stood alone against not only the majority of the board but, in some cases, the entire board. Votes of twenty to one, twenty-two to one, and worse occurred in this period, when Jackson was the lone dissenter. He went so far as to oppose a salary increase for McCormick at a time when it was deemed necessary not only to keep him at the Exchange, but as a sign of gratitude for what he had done.

Jackson left the board in 1953 but returned in 1956, and once again was assigned to the committee on floor transactions. There he protested against shady deals and questionable securities—again a minority of one. Needless to say, prior to the Re disclosures, Jackson was one of the loneliest men on the floor.

He also was the only man of prominence capable and willing to lead a movement for widespread reforms at the Amex. Reilly had hoped to smooth things over, believing that in time the Re and Gilligan disclosures would be forgotten. The SEC probe changed all this; now major changes indeed were called for, and still Reilly held back. The Chairman rejected leadership of a reform movement, and so it passed to Jackson.

By late summer and early autumn of 1961, as it became evident that the SEC was discovering evidence of institutional corruption at the Amex, additional brokers appeared sympathetic to Jackson's call for change. In early October the number swelled to between fifty and seventy-five. Most of this group were young men, but there were a few veterans as well. Sylvester May, an Amex member for thirty-three years, joined with Jackson and held several "organizational meetings" in his office, after hours, to discuss what should be done. They were backed by some of Wall Street's most powerful commission houses, fearful of what might happen if reform were not undertaken. This was a small but substantial group, one that could not be ignored.

McCormick now realized that the opposition to his administration was growing. Earlier he had said that the dissident movement existed "mostly in Dave Jackson's own mind." Now he conceded that there might be discontent, "but it's all a very young group, and they don't have all of them." It was large enough, however, to cause grave concern at the board.

As always, Reilly hoped that any concession, to either the Young Turks or the SEC, would be made without a sense of urgency, and appear as normal procedure. His reaction was of a piece with his previous attitude. He recalled that in 1955 the Big Board had established the Vilas Committee, which looked into its administration and made recommendations for reform. It might be the time to have a similar committee for the Amex, he said. On October 12 he reported that one was being formed, to be headed by Gustave Levy, the powerful and prestigious head of Goldman, Sachs & Co. Eight of the members would represent the largest brokerages in the district: Merrill Lynch; Paine, Webber, Jackson & Curtis; Goodbody; and Shearson, Hammill & Co. among them. May would be the ninth member of the Levy Committee.

The selection of any committee charged with investigating the Amex would have been considered a sign of defeat for Reilly and McCormick. The fact that it consisted of leaders of major commission houses, as well as May, foreshadowed a highly critical report, one that would reflect some of the Young

Turk ideas. Earlier, one of the Young Turks had said, "If we can get the big houses, we've got a good chance; without them, we're sunk." Now the movement had not only the SEC on its side, but the major commission houses as well.* By mid-October, it seemed that McCormick and Reilly were in an untenable position. They were being attacked on all sides. Then, on October 13, came news that the Young Turks would put up a slate of candidates for the board elections in February.

Never before or since has the Amex been so divided—not during the outdoor days, the harsh 1930s, the Cuppia period, or even the Re investigations. The exchange had a fissure: the Reilly-McCormick group on one side and the Young Turks on the other, with most Amex brokers choosing one or the other. The tensions on the trading floor were almost unbearable, with men in their sixties and seventies leaving for work half expecting to have a fist fight before the day was over. Old friendships dissolved; brokers who had known one another for decades looked aside when passing on the floor.

On October 17, Jackson went to the board and talked with the members. Word leaked to the press (or was given to it by Jackson) of a confrontation between McCormick and Jackson. Apparently a crisis point had been reached even before the filing of the SEC report, the election, or the completion of the Levy Committee's work.

All of this crushed Reilly. Ever since assuming the chairmanship he had tried to bring harmony into a situation where none was possible. As an old friend of Jackson, he had pleaded with him to help keep the peace. Then he tried to convince Jackson to use the Amex grievance machinery as an arena for his attack.** Nothing seemed to work. The McCormick-Jackson

* The head of one major house said, "Until 1959, that exchange [the Amex] had about as much volume as the Midwest Stock Exchange has today. It just wasn't very important to our total business. Now, the picture has changed. The American Exchange is putting on long pants, and we're vitally concerned with what goes on there."
** Reilly's suggestion that Jackson use the grievance machinery was similar to Bijur's request that Plate use the committee system, during his fight against Cuppia. Plate had bowed in 1940; Jackson would not.

confrontation was almost more than Reilly could bear. Angered and hurt, he lashed out at Jackson. The following day he took the unprecedented step of addressing the members on the floor, over the loudspeaker system.

Reilly began by stating that he regretted what he had to do that day. If one member had complaints against another, or against the President, he had a mechanism through which he could be heard, and which would act for him. Yet one member had refused to use the committees. Instead, he had granted interviews to members of the press, and these had placed the Amex in a bad light. Not only that, but the stories were inaccurate.

> As long as he was so glib with his tongue, he should at least have checked his handiwork since these news articles shook the very foundation of our Exchange. I hope Mr. Jackson realizes now that the caption could have read: "Young Turks led by David Jackson publicly assassinates the American Stock Exchange."
>
> . . . Mr. Jackson has said on many occasions—I believe he will still say after this meeting in spite of the broad attack I make against his principles—that I am a very dedicated man. I agree with him. I am dedicated—so dedicated that any public attack on our officials reflects on our Exchange and, therefore, I take it as a personal attack.
>
> Now, it is time I straightened out the record.
>
> While Mr. Jackson, through a series of conjectures, has become a "self-appointed" hero, he has neglected to state that he served on the board during the years which are being covered by the present investigation. Unlike Mr. Jackson, I do not imply he or anyone else could have detected the Res' operation during this period. However, as he criticized officials and Board members for mismanagement, we must ask, "What is his excuse?". . . .
>
> At this time your Chairman wishes to state that he is very tired and, as you know, he has had quite a rough time for the last two years. It has been difficult enough to handle the routine duties of my office and at the same time devote the time necessary to fight the brush-fires created by the Re & Re case. I should not have to dissipate my strength to fight for our Ex-

change over arguments born of dissention by minority groups
aired in the newspapers which add so greatly to my burden,
particularly when I know their serious impact on the confidence of the public, investing public and issuers. . . .

I conclude by saying, "What has been done, let it be
done!"

I would also like it understood that I do not come before
you to seek praise as your Chairman. I hold no brief for Messrs.
McCormick, Mooney, or any Governor. All officials must stand
or fall on their own record before the majority thinking of our
members. However, I must insist that no member or group of
members in the future turn this Exchange into a public battleground. I am going on record as your Chairman that I will no
longer tolerate it.

Jackson was not on the floor when Reilly delivered his
broadside, having left to prepare for his forthcoming vacation,
but he learned of it soon after. He told reporters, "Mr. Reilly
must live with his conscience and I must live with mine." He
verified Reilly's claim that he had spoken to reporters, and insisted that that was his right as a citizen and an Amex member.
Jackson also told his version of what had precipitated Reilly's
attack. The previous day, as Reilly indicated in his speech, he
had gone to the board and asked for the resignations of McCormick and Mooney.

Ted slammed the desk and banged the walls of his room when
I asked for his resignation. But he neither frightened nor terri-
fied me. I told him I thought that he acted indiscreetly in his
dealings in various stock issues in which the Res were specialists and also for not having revoked the Res' franchise as specialists once we had learned of the injunction that had been
obtained against them in the Swan-Finch case.

That was the beginning of the end between Joe [Reilly]
and me.

Jackson was asked whether Reilly's attack meant that he
was going to challenge Reilly for the chairmanship. Jackson
denied having ambitions for office, or even for seeking publicity in the affair. He concluded by saying that he would not cancel his European vacation, but he would not drop the matter of

the Reilly attack either. Instead, he would deal with it on his return. By then he hoped to have a copy of the Reilly charges, which he would answer one at a time.

On December 11, Jackson told the board that he rejected the Reilly statement en toto: the document was "replete with utter falsehoods and half-truths conmingled with little that is factual." Jackson thought he could win a libel and slander action against Reilly, and his lawyers agreed. But he would not proceed with one because he did not want to involve others, as well as the Amex, in a long, drawn-out court battle.

Jackson's reply was not the most pressing problem Reilly had to face on December 11. A few days earlier he had met with Gustave Levy, who had learned of McCormick's relations with Guterma, including the matter of the gambling debt. Levy informed Reilly that McCormick would have to leave the Amex, and that his report would make that recommendation. Reilly had not known of the Guterma link until six weeks before, when he had said nothing, hoping the news could be kept out of the papers until sometime in 1962. This was no longer possible. Reilly spoke to McCormick and Mooney, and informed them of the situation. Clearly it would be better for both if they resigned before being fired. They agreed, and did so on December 11.

McCormick spoke to the board before resigning. He told the members of his gambling, and of how he had tried to pay the debt. He conceded his bad judgment, but insisted his motives had been pure. He denied having any connection with Birrell, as had been reported in the press.

Then Mooney appeared. He alluded to certain business he had had with the Res, such as giving them advice on a Rokeach transaction, and he admitted to having purchased stock for speculation. Mooney insisted that part of his understanding with the Amex on taking his position was that he would be free to engage in private practice. Like McCormick, Mooney denied having consciously done anything wrong.

Then Reilly spoke. He told of his conversation with Levy, adding that both he and the committee chairman agreed that neither McCormick or Mooney was guilty of anything but indiscretions. But the Amex was in a situation where indiscretions could not be forgiven. Reilly wanted the resignations, and was ready to accept them.

The resignations were accepted unanimously. The board, which a year before had rallied around McCormick, now had to accept the fact that support of the President was no longer possible.

Reilly then told the board he would inform both the SEC and the Levy Committee of the resignations, and would release the news to the press. Secrecy—the crux of his argument with Jackson—was no longer possible. Shaken, pale, and weary, Reilly closed the meeting by noting that it was a dark hour, adding that the Amex had come through bad times before and would survive this blow.

The McCormick era was ended.

Reilly had defended McCormick for as long as he could, not because he admired the President (although he did), but rather to preserve the Amex, and to guard against what he considered radical and undesirable changes. At first almost all board members had supported his position. Now he was alone in it, at least publicly. Until a new election could be held, he said, he would assume the post of president *pro tem.*

As the board members left the room that December 11, most were certain that the elections would result in a sweep for the Young Turks. David Jackson, despite his public statements about not wanting the post, could easily be the next president, or chairman. As the first to speak out against McCormick, he seemed the logical candidate. His election, so the thinking went, would precipitate a thorough housecleaning at Trinity Place—a "night of the long knives." The Amex would be scoured, but after the job had been completed, what would be left?

There was little time to consider such hypothetical questions, since events were moving so swiftly. The Levy Committee issued its first report on December 21. As expected, it called for sweeping reforms of the Amex, starting with the board itself. The Committee hoped the Amex would achieve "an organization and administration of the exchange that would

conform to the corporate type of organization and would minimize the possibility of rivalry between the president and the
chairman." In the Committee's view, the chairman and the
board should concern themselves only with policy making,
while the president would have "complete responsibility for administration." This would free the president from day-to-day
control by the board. Hopefully, a more autonomous president
would not have to rely upon the support of powerful brokers
to run the Amex. Nor would he come under their influence, as
had McCormick. In this way, the Levy Committee hoped to
"professionalize" the Amex administration far beyond anything
that had gone before. Under the old constitutions, presidents
could not hope to prevail against the will of powerful brokers;
with this change, they could.

The Committee recommended that no board member be
allowed to serve more than two consecutive three-year terms, in
order to avoid the cliquishness that marked previous boards
(what the report called rule by "self-perpetuating groups").
The composition of the board would be changed, decreasing
the power of specialists and increasing that of commission brokers, outsiders (public members), and non–New Yorkers.

The most drastic recommendation contained in the report
was one calling for an end to associate memberships. The Committee promised a future statement on this question, and a solution that would be fair both to regular and associate
members.

Finally, the report recommended that the Amex make
plans to submit constitutional amendments that would embody
these recommendations to the membership. Most important, it
should begin an immediate search for a new president.

Reilly accepted the Levy Committee report and was willing to carry out its recommendations. He established two committees to assist in the work. The first, to find a new president,
consisted of Vanderpoel Adriance, Charles Moran, Howard
Dean, and Harold Scott. The second, charged with expediting
the reorganization program, consisted of Posner, Henry Parish,
Litt, and James Dyer. Jackson was livid when he learned that
Dyer would be on the committee. A powerful specialist, and
one certain to be criticized in the SEC report, Dyer was hardly

the man for such a post. Jackson protested to Reilly, and spoke of possible SEC intervention in the matter. The Chairman backed down in the face of this warning, a sign of his waning power and influence.

Reilly would not resign—at least, not voluntarily. Tired and battered though he was, Reilly wanted vindication, and he believed he could have it at the polls that February. The contest appeared to be between Reilly and Jackson, and the Chairman thought he had sufficient votes to defeat an insurgent slate. But the Levy Committee did not want such a showdown, which would further rend the Amex fabric. Without indicating as much, it suggested that Reilly had outlived his usefulness to the Exchange. As a result, Reilly announced in late December his intention to withdraw from the race. He would serve out his term as Chairman and then, in March, retire from Amex affairs.

Some staff members of the SEC thought Jackson the best man for the presidency or the chairmanship, and members of the Levy Committee agreed. Jackson, who had always insisted he had no ambitions in either direction, rejected the call. He realized that he too had been a devisive figure: the man who had helped topple McCormick and Reilly, who had been the center of contention for the past half-year, could hardly serve as a binder of wounds. Jackson did recommend a candidate, however, a man he felt he could support: Edwin Posner.

Interestingly enough, Jackson and Posner had never liked one another. The rather imperious Posner, with a quick temper and a sharp tongue, was quite different from the gregarious, easy-going Jackson. Years earlier they had fought over personal matters, and were barely on speaking terms.* The two

* Despite this, the two men had respect for one another. Mr. Posner told the author that he believed Jackson to be a man of little ability and much ego, but added, "Of course, he was the first to take action against McCormick, and it couldn't have been done without him." On being asked whom he considered the most important person in the history of the Exchange, Jackson immediately responded, "Posner, without a doubt," and then added some pungent criticisms of the man. Both brokers admired Thomas McGovern, who returned to the Amex as counsel in December, replacing Mooney—who had replaced him in 1951. Perhaps the common bond with McGovern helped smooth their working relationship.

men had shared a distrust for McCormick, Posner refusing to serve on the board while he was in office and Jackson leading the campaign against him. In mid-1961, Jackson had asked Posner for his support, but the older man—Posner was seventy-one years old at the time—refused to enter the battle. As a result, he had been able to retain the trust and confidence of the old board, while at the same time the Young Turks recalled that he had led reform movements in the past, and had done so with skill and fairness.

Jackson knew Posner to be an honest and able man, but he also realized that Posner was closer to Reilly in some ways than he was to the Young Turks. Reilly preferred slow reform achieved through existing men and institutions. Posner, who might be called the puritan of the old Curb, could not abide the slightest hint of corruption, and would do all he could to root out those involved in any untoward activities. But Posner also rejected the idea of outside control in any form, and had a life-long dislike for the SEC, its policies, and its personnel. Posner would clean the Amex, but would be slow to accept institutional reforms, in particular those that might compromise Amex autonomy. Jackson, on the other hand, thought a strong SEC necessary for the district, and especially for the Amex. He not only welcomed the investigation, but cooperated with it fully, and wanted to assure a more permanent supervision of the Exchange. He also wanted a new constitution, one that would make for a more "open" Amex than previously had been the case. Posner was chagrined that the Levy Committee had been called into being. It was not so much that he opposed it; it was more the idea that outsiders on the Committee were investigating the Amex and making recommendations for change. He would cooperate with it, though bitter that such a body had been necessary. On the other hand, Jackson supported the Committee from the first. He endorsed its reports; Posner was not certain the outsiders were correct in their judgments of the Amex. Yet Jackson also believed Posner the best man for the job, and he convinced his allies at the SEC to support him.

Posner became President *pro tem* in January, serving with Reilly. In the elections in February, both factions cast their votes for him as the next chairman. Posner would begin the work of reform, but his major task would be to help select the new president, one capable of cleaning up the mess left by the scandals already known and the others to come.

On January 3, 1962—before Posner had had time to ease himself into his new office—the SEC released its report on the Amex. This report, the most important document in the modern history of the Exchange, covered a wide range of problems. It criticized the board, the management, the methods of stock listing and retention, trading methods, the specialist system— in fact, almost every aspect of the Amex. There was an attack on McCormick and Mooney, which, though gratuitous, served at that point to kill the last vestiges of support these men retained. The specialist system itself was criticized, with hints that perhaps a better way of dealing in stocks could be found. A key section of the report dealt with the power of Gilligan, Will. The SEC detailed the extent of Gilligan's power and his use of it, and the manner by which others were affected by his every action. It traced the connections between Gilligan and McCormick in such a way as to leave little doubt that both men had been acting contrary to rules. The report concluded with an indictment of the Amex for failing at self-regulation, and the promise of a more vigorous SEC role at Trinity Place in the future.

> It is not too difficult to identify the basic causes for the manifest failure of self-regulation in the past: the failure of an important segment of the financial community to exercise its share of responsibility for self-regulation of the Exchange; the resulting concentration of power in the hands of a small self-perpetuating group dominated by specialists; the disproportionate concern with quantity rather than quality, i.e., the emphasis on enlarging the market through new listings rather than on the functioning of the market; the delegation of responsibility for supervising floor conduct to a committee composed largely of specialists; the lack of adequate staff organization and the failure to grant adequate authority to staff members—all have played a part. . . .
>
> It is to be hoped that such correction can and will be ac-

complished promptly within the present statutory framework of self-regulation. But the Commission must be prepared to exercise its supervisory powers if the necessary reform is not forthcoming. The Commission's performance of its supervisory role must undoubtedly be strengthened in the future—even assuming maximum achievement in the Exchange's own program of reform—if there is to be durable assurance of proper performance by the Exchange as a major financial institution in the American economy.

This last paragraph was virtually the only indication that the SEC recognized that it too had a role, though indirect, in the Amex's problems. Throughout the 1940s and 1950s the agency had been moribund; this would have to change. It hadn't answered Reilly's question regarding its disposal of the 1957 report on the Res, and the report on the Amex did not mention or discuss how such widespread corruption could have taken place at an institution that was supposed to be regulated and policed by the very agency that, in 1962, condemned it.*

Reilly pledged "additional positive steps" in response to the report. He acknowledged that the "general tenor" of the report, "coupled with the recommendations contained in the recent report of the Levy Committee, indicate the necessity for an American Stock Exchange policy wherein actions will speak louder than words." No one was so unkind at the time to point

---

* The report may be criticized for misunderstanding several aspects of the Amex and its governance. For example, it identifies a "dominant group" at the Exchange as consisting of Reilly, Mann, Dyer, and Bocklet, since these men controlled the chairmanship, vice-chairmanship, chairmanship of the committee on floor transactions, and chairmanship of the finance committee, from 1952 to 1962. The impression given was that they worked in harmony with one another. Such was not the case. And at the Amex, like many institutions, the vice-chairman automatically succeeded to the chairmanship after the incumbent stepped down. Too, the report should have noted that one reason these men had such long records in administration was that the vast majority of members constantly refused to serve on committees, preferring instead to remain on the floor, where the money was to be made. The problem of attracting able people to committee work—often thankless and boring—remains a problem there, as it does elsewhere in American business.

out that, had Reilly upheld a policy of action instead of words, the report's impact might have been less than it was. As Frederick Barton, managing partner of Eastman Dillon Union Securities, put it, "This type of thing would not have happened to the ASE if everyone had been watching with a cold eye." Amyss Ames, managing partner of Kidder, Peabody & Co., predicted that in the future the commission houses would play an important role in the goverance of the Amex, and not leave the field to the specialists. "It's the only thing that makes sense."

Many brokers, remembering how they felt in 1962, now say that at the time they believed the Amex might not survive. In fact, however, the Exchange was never in danger of failure. But there seemed a strong possibility that control might pass from the hands of the specialists to those of the large commission houses, working in harmony with the SEC. The specialist system itself might be examined and, if found wanting, changed. To an Amex specialist of 1962, such might be tantamount to destruction.

Reilly and others on the board read the report carefully, and within a few days regretted their initial acquiescent attitude. In particular the members resented charges of lax administration. "I most strenuously reject this part of the report and emphatically deny that I was ever part of a group which was in joint control of the exchange for the past ten years," said Reilly in response to the charge that he was part of the "dominant group" at the Amex. By then, however, Reilly was out of power, if not out of office. The Posner interregnum had begun.

As had been expected, Posner acted abruptly and positively. First of all, on January 11 he insisted that Gilligan remove whatever funds he still had in the firm of Gilligan, Will; in the future, he said, Gilligan should have no contact of any kind with the Amex. Then he asked for additional funds, $75,000 in all, to be earmarked for legal work. He doubted that all this money would be spent, but he wanted to have it available should McGovern need it. He then said that he had met with Keith Funston, who promised him the help of the Big Board in his work. Posner said he might require the assistance of some lawyers, and Funston made them available for technical help. All of these actions required board approval. It was given without dissent.

Posner also met with SEC Chairman William Cary, and assured him that he planned to carry out all the recommendations contained in the SEC report. He also agreed substantially with the Levy Committee's report, with the exception of the suggestion regarding the end of associate memberships. The Levy Committee's recommendations also would be accepted. And Posner would go even further: the Levy Rport suggested the acceptance of amendments to the constitution, but Posner thought the Amex needed a completely new constitution, embodying most of the recommendations. In this, as in most of his actions during the months that followed, Posner took care to go beyond the maximum recommendations of the investigating bodies. But he always insisted that the Amex be permitted to reform itself; he wanted no outside controls. And he guarded the specialist system, which he considered the heart of the Exchange.

Cary concluded the meeting by asking Posner what would happen to the men mentioned in the report: Reilly, Bocklet, Dyer, and Mann. To this Posner replied, "I promise you, Mr. Cary, that there will be a very strict investigation of the whole operation, and there is going to be very definite action taken."

On January 18, James Dyer resigned his post of governor, effective February 12. This was not good enough for Posner: he demanded Dyer's immediate resignation, along with those of the others. Dyer complied, and changed the date of his resignation to January 22. Reilly fought the action, which was reported in the press. He had done nothing wrong, he said, and would not step down until after the election. This last attempt to salvage nothing more than his dignity was rebuffed. Along with Mann and Bocklet, he too resigned on January 22. His humiliation was only slightly less than that of McCormick, although Reilly had never been charged with wrongdoing himself.

Posner moved swiftly against Gilligan, Will, whose activities had been carefully documented in the SEC report, and which by that time had come to symbolize for many all that was wrong at the Amex. Will was still at the firm, as was James Patrick Gilligan, James Gilligan's son. On January 25, the committee on floor transactions held a special meeting, at which time the firm was suspended and its registration lifted "in the best interests of the Exchange, and in the best interests of the public." No specific charges were made against the firm, and neither Gilligan nor Will was charged with acts contrary to the constitution or the rules. Yet their registrations as specialists were suspended.

At first they accepted the suspension. Then, after consulting with his attorney, the younger Gilligan challenged the action as being contrary to the constitution. The committee replied that Gilligan and his firm had clearly violated provisions of the Securities Act of 1933 as well as SEC rules. Still, no specific violations were cited. James Patrick Gilligan had assumed the leadership of Gilligan, Will less than a year before (in April 1961). It would appear that the committee would have to detail his actions since that date in order to uphold the suspension.

The board scheduled a review of the case for February 6. Yet redistribution of Gilligan, Will stocks to other specialist units began in late January. It was as though the deceased's effects were given to his heirs while he was still alive in the hospital. James Patrick Gilligan may have been guilty of wrongdoing, and if only a part of the SEC charges was true, the firm was also guilty. The committee's action in redistributing the Gilligan, Will stocks indicated that neither could expect a completely impartial hearing.

The board review was thorough. The charges against the firm were presented, and detailed evidence introduced to substantiate them. Little was said about Gilligan himself, or his own actions. The board voted to uphold the committee's actions in toto, however. It marked the first time such action against an individual had been taken without substantial evidence having been introduced to support the case.*

* Gilligan, Will is still an important firm at the Amex, and James Patrick Gilligan is a prominent broker.

Posner was intent on removing from the Amex all individuals charged by the SEC of violations, and removing any doubts that the Exchange would not punish those who broke rules. He also wanted to discipline members connected with the Re case. One of these was Anthony Cordano, the broker who had serviced some of the dummy accounts Re had used in his dealings. Cordano, who was still at Josephthal & Co., had testified at the Re case, saying he had done nothing wrong, having followed the rules to the letter.

On March 14, Cordano appeared before the board to answer charges of violating rules and making false statements before Amex committees. Cordano insisted that such had not been the case, but the board introduced evidence of wrongdoing by him and two other brokers, Andrew Baird and Herman Froede. All were found guilty of "acts detrimental to the interests and welfare of the American Stock Exchange." Cordano was expelled from the Amex, while Froude and Baird were each fined $5,000 and given severe reprimands. In addition, Josephthal & Co. received a reprimand for allowing such activities to take place without proper investigation.

Posner's crusade helped remove men like Cordano from the Amex, and in this way both the Re and Gilligan eras at the Exchange were concluded. He also indicated that in the future careful surveillance would be the watchword on the floor. A large number of cases were heard by the committee on floor transactions and the committee on outside supervision in February and March; in most of these, those who had violated even minor rules were fined or suspended. Posner left no doubt in the minds of the SEC, the Levy Committee, or the public as to the new-found honesty of the Exchange.

The Levy Committee handed down its final report on February 16. It contained a series of recommendations, many of which either repeated earlier ones or were contained in the SEC report. Three, however, were more important than the others.

The first called for the replacement of the committee system by a paid staff. This would mean that effective control of the Amex would pass from the members to the president's office. Ownership of an Exchange seat would entitle its holder to trading privileges on the floor and commission advantages for his firm, but little else. He would have a hand in selecting the board, which in turn would choose the president. Once that was accomplished, the president and his staff would determine day-to-day operations.

The second recommendation repeated the earlier call for an end to associate memberships. In the future, all Amex brokers should have equal status, and this could be accomplished in part through the elimination of a system the reasons for which no longer existed.

Finally, the Committee called for far greater supervision of specialists than previously had been the case, and an increase in the capital required by specialist units. Specialists would no longer have a considerable responsibility for obtaining listings. And the qualifications for listing would be raised.

Most Amex brokers accepted the findings, resigning themselves to any program that would assure the continuation of the Exchange as a separate entity without direct governmental supervision. Some, however, objected to several of the Committee's recommendations. How would the holders of associate memberships be dealt with? Would the associate memberships be converted into regular memberships? If this happened, the equity value of a regular membership would be diluted. Would the associate memberships simply be eliminated, with the former holders required to purchase regular seats? In such a case, how would the prices be determined? At that time an Amex seat was selling for around $65,000, but the equity value was much lower. Which figure would be used? And, given the problems at the Exchange, would all associate members want to purchase seats? If they did not—if some firms simply gave up on the Amex—it would harm the Exchange, perhaps seriously.

Some members also railed against elimination of the committee system. They owned the Exchange, and should have the right to control it. To take away this right without their consent would appear to be a violation of the due process clause of the Fourteenth Amendment to the U.S. Constitution. Finally, the dissidents thought Amex listing requirements were high enough. To raise them further would be to compete with the Big Board and discourage small firms from seeking listing in the future. This would lead to a smaller list, which might result in turn in temptations to break rules. A lack of stocks had led the Amex to seek McCormick for the presidency in the first place. If the Levy Committee placed the Exchange in the same financial situation it had been in during the late 1940s, could not a new McCormick appear at some future date?

Posner ignored these criticisms, concentrating instead on his twofold task of mopping up the last vestiges of the McCormick administration and seeking a new president. The bulk of the work of reform was completed by February, at which time Posner dedicated himself to the search for his replacement as president.

There was no shortage of candidates. James Day, president of the Midwest Stock Exchange, who had a reputation for excellent administrative qualities and reform policies, was high on the list. Edward Grey, executive vice-president of the New York Stock Exchange, was another. Charles Ireland the former president of Allegheny Corporation and a man with wide financial and industrial contacts, was also mentioned. Several political figures were talked about, the most prominent of whom was Robert Meyner, the former Governor of New Jersey.

Posner rejected all of them. Having led in the search for his successor in 1947, he had experience in the task, and knew pretty much what he wanted in the next president. In 1947 he had helped select Francis Adams Truslow—a decent, intelligent man, who had a broad knowledge of the Amex but not very much interest in the job. A person like Truslow would not do in 1962. Nor could the Amex accept a modern version of Grubb, Moffatt, or Rea. The Exchange needed a person of force, vigor, intelligence—and political sophistication. He would have to be sufficiently like Posner to continue the work of reform. But he had to be independent of the old regime—all aspects of it, Posner not excepted. Such a person would have to harmonize the differences between the Young Turks and the former McCormick and Reilly supporters, most of whom were still on the floor. He would have to institute enough of the Levy Committee reforms to please Wall Street and SEC recommendations to satisfy the Commission, but not in such a way as to alienate the membership, many of whom disliked some or all of the proposed changes. His mandate would come from the Levy Committee and the SEC, as well as the Posner group. Most brokers retained their dislike for the SEC, felt the Levy Committee was composed largely of outsiders who didn't understand their problems, and accepted Posner as a necessary man, but not one to be followed after the problem period had passed. The new president would have to transfer his mandate from these organizations and men to the Amex membership, and in some way win the confidence of the brokers, even their enthusiastic support. By itself compliance would not suffice, for the brokers had to be convinced that change and reform were in their interest. The job required an educator as well as a businessman, a politician as well as a broker. The last such man to head the organization was Edward R. McCormick, who had led it indoors in 1921. The new president's tasks would be no less difficult. As one broker put it, "McCormick led us indoors; the new man had to lead us out of the woods."

SIXTEEN

The Fresh Start

Most committees rely heavily upon their staffs for the gathering of information and presentation of reports, and the Levy Committee was no exception. Ordinarily staff people remain in the background, and are often forgotten or overlooked; few have much to say in the way of policy. One man at the Levy Committee did not fit this description. Its special counsel, Edwin D. Etherington, was present at every meeting, drafted two of the three reports, incorporated many of his own ideas into them, and favorably impressed—perhaps a better word would be "awed"—those Amex members with whom he came into contact.

Individuals outside Wall Street knew little of Etherington in early 1962, at a time when dozens of names were bandied about as the next Amex president. But the financial community had for years recognized in him a man of unusual abilities. In 1958, while a vice-president at the Stock Exchange, he had been talked of as a logical successor to Keith Funston. At the time, Etherington was thirty-four years old.

Nineteen sixty-two was an unusual year, not only for the Amex, but for the country. The nation seemed entranced by President John F. Kennedy, a graceful, handsome young activist whose key word seemed to be "vigor." A premium was placed on people possessing his qualities. At any other time, a man like Etherington might have been groomed carefully for a top spot in industry or finance; hopefully, when the time came, he would be ready for it. But the early 1960s were tailor-made for rapid advancement for Kennedy-types, and Etherington, more than any other man in the financial district, had Kennedy's qualities.

Etherington had been born into a well-off New Jersey family. He had gone to Lawrenceville, and upon graduation had entered the Army, serving in the infantry for two years during World War II. On receiving his discharge, Etherington enrolled at Wesleyan. He graduated from there with honors and a Phi Beta Kappa key in 1948. Etherington stayed on for a year, working as assistant to the dean and teaching English. Then he entered Yale Law School, and graduated, again with honors, in 1952. During the next year he was clerk to a United States Court of Appeals judge, then went to Wilmer & Broun, a Washington law firm. Etherington came to New York in 1954 as a lawyer at Milbank, Twead, Hope & Hadley, and while there concentrated on Stock Exchange work. He joined the Big Board as assistant secretary in 1956, was promoted to secretary the same year, and became vice-president in charge of civil and governmental affairs in 1958. Much of Etherington's work consisted of SEC, congressional, and Federal Reserve negotiations and presentations. Throughout this period he received many offers of partnerships in major brokerage firms. In 1961 Etherington took one of these and joined Pershing & Co. He was there when called upon to serve by the Levy Committee.

Posner knew of Etherington's existence, but little else of the man. Then he came in contact with him during the Amex probes, and was impressed with his abilities. Still, Posner did not consider Etherington for the presidency until Levy raised the question while returning from Washington with Posner. Levy was convinced Etherington was the right man for the job, but added that he had talked the matter over with Etherington, who stated that he would not be in a position to consider it; he felt he could not leave Pershing & Co. after barely a year as a managing partner.

Soon after, rumors that Etherington was being considered appeared in the *Wall Street Journal*. Posner thought Levy had spoken to reporters of the matter, but such was not the case. Instead, others in the district had concluded that Etherington was exactly what the Amex needed—if he would take the job.

Now Posner and Etherington met for discussions. It seemed a strange match—the elderly Amex veteran and the young Stock Exchange star. Yet they found they had much in common; Etherington was one of the few men Posner ever had any strong affection for, and the two gradually gravitated to a father-son relationship that deepened over the years. Although Etherington was sincere in his disinterest in the Amex presidency, the more they met and the more Posner considered the matter, the more he was convinced that Etherington was the only person who had the right combination of qualities for the position. A generation earlier he had selected Truslow for the presidency, and Etherington—with his aristocratic bearing, his aura of glamour, and his youth—seemed quite like Truslow. But he had a toughness Truslow had lacked, and an interest in financial matters that had eluded the former president. Posner knew, however, that if Etherington, like Truslow, had reservations and yet took the presidency, it could prove disastrous to the Amex. In the end—late March—Etherington agreed to take the position. He assured Posner he did so with enthusiasm. Posner did not extract any pledges regarding programs and policies from his candidate. In any case, to try to do so would have been unwise, for he recognized in Etherington a man with a will as strong as his own. Posner was convinced that Etherington agreed with him on basic philosophy, and let it go at that.

The Chairman then spoke with members of the board of his interest in Etherington, and all agreed he would be a fine choice for the presidency. So did David Jackson, and former Reilly supporters. In fact, no important voice was raised against him. By then Posner was completely sold on the young man. On March 27, he told the board he would place Etherington's name in nomination for the presidency; it was "the happiest recommendation" he had made since joining the old Curb forty-one year earlier.

Etherington was selected unanimously. He was offered a five-year contract starting September 4, 1962, at $80,000 a year plus $20,000 in deferred compensation and other benefits worth about $20,000 a year. Posner explained that the reason Etherington would not join the Amex immediately, or at least sooner than September 4, was because he insisted on a period of time to acquaint himself with the Amex, enlist a staff, and be ready to move aggressively from the moment he took office. Then Posner escorted Etherington into the room, and the President-elect delivered a short, noncommittal acceptance speech.

During the next five months Etherington spent all of his time on Amex affairs, often working in tandem with Posner. Together with McGovern, they drafted a new constitution. At times Posner and Etherington differed over reforms and other changes, in the process learning more of each other's thoughts and how to work in tandem after September 4. At the same time, the Chairman continued his reform activities at the board and with the membership.

Posner continued to clash with Jackson, who watched all that was happening carefully. Jackson was particularly interested in the way Posner dealt with the specialists. On May 25, the Exchange adopted new rules regarding specialist finances. Under the previous rule, a specialist had to maintain a balance of $10,000 for each security he handled. Under the new rule, the cash balance was raised to $50,000. This meant the reassignment of several issues, with some brokers losing stocks and other gaining them.

One broker, James Rafferty, was badly overextended on his issues. A specialist in electronics stocks, Rafferty had accumulated many of them, but hadn't sufficient funds to service them all. Rafferty lost nine of his stocks under the new program, and some went to the biggest specialist units on the floor. Jackson thought the reassignment "capricious," and posed a series of questions to Posner. How long had the administration known of Rafferty's financial difficulties? Had Posner explored possibilities of helping Rafferty keep his stocks? What procedures were used in assigning the stocks to their new specialists? Did the committee on floor transactions have a policy to deal with such matters in the future? If so, what was it? Jackson was concerned for Rafferty's sake, but he was equally bothered by what he saw as a concentration of power in the hands of a few large specialists—just the situation the SEC had condemned.

Posner knew that Jackson was in regular communication with SEC officials, in particular with Chairman Cary and people at the Division of Trading and Exchanges. He suspected he was cooperating with the Commission in an attempt to bring it into closer relationship with the Amex, a situation Posner disapproved of. Posner chafed at this, but there was little he could do under the circumstances, for Jackson was an equally firm man, with a constituency of his own—including the press— that would have to be placated. At the same time, Posner wanted to make certain no rift developed between Etherington and Jackson, especially prior to the new President's assuming office.*

The reallocation question brought their differences to a head. Posner sought fairness in this: he wanted to make certain each specialist unit had its share, and could handle the stocks which were assigned to them. Jackson thought this was inadequate, and that the large units had to be broken up, as suggested by the SEC report.** He noted that the Dyer and Mann

---

* As before, the key difference between Posner and Jackson rested in their attitudes toward reform. Posner would punish those who violated rules to the point of expulsion, but he wanted no important change in the rules themselves. Jackson supported Posner's prodding of the committee on business conduct, but wanted to rewrite the rules too, so as to safeguard against future misdeeds. Posner's attitude seemed to be that if good and honest men were in control, the Amex would reflect their views. Jackson had less trust in human nature or the possibilities of changing long-held attitudes of brokers. An intelligent and able administration was needed, to be sure, but institutional changes were also necessary, and Jackson wanted to make certain they were carried out.

** The differences between the Posner and Jackson approach was reflected in politics as well, and went back to the early 1930s. Posner was a conservative Republican who admired Herbert Hoover, while Jackson

books were still quite large, and that they appeared to be getting larger, as they received additional securities in the post-McCormick period. The Rafferty situation merely intensified his anger at what he thought was happening. Then Cary contacted Posner, and spoke to him of what he thought was a major problem at the Amex.

Now Posner was angry. He confronted Jackson, demanding to know whether it was true he was in regular communication with Cary. Jackson said that was the case. Then Posner asked whether he thought there had been favoritism in the allocation of stocks, especially to Dyer and Mann. Jackson replied, "Eddie, I am against everything you do but I would never accuse you of favoritism."

The Chairman realized he could not move Jackson on the issue, and he also saw the logic in his position. He spoke to Dyer and Mann, and each voluntarily relinquished some of his stocks. Then he went to Washington to speak with Cary and Philip Loomis, Jr., the director of the Division of Trading and Exchanges. He emphatically denied favoritism of any kind. Posner told Loomis of the changes in reallocation. And he resented any suspicion that the slightest trace of chicanery existed in the Amex administration.

The SEC's leadership knew Posner well, and assured him that no such doubts existed. Cary and Loomis also understood Posner would do nothing to jeopardize Etherington's administration. Posner was satisfied with their statements, and returned to New York. He had made his point. At the same time, the securities had been reallocated as Jackson had wished. A compromise of sorts had been reached, as well as a clearing of the air. Together, though working separately, Posner and Jackson had succeeded in making several key reallocations, which represented a major shift of power on the floor. The two men understood this, and in the future would cooperate more than before.

---

had voted for Roosevelt. In the 1950s, Posner was a Taft Republican, while Jackson supported Stevenson. In 1962, Posner had great admiration for Republican Lieutenant Governor Malcolm Wilson, a conservative, while Jackson was a strong Kennedy supporter.

Posner was pulling the Amex to reform, while Jackson was pushing it, and in a somewhat different direction. Together these two veterans, who disliked one another, were remaking the Amex into a new kind of market and preparing the way for Etherington. The President-elect was able to keep Posner's confidence and win Jackson's in this period, another indication of his political abilities.

Etherington's position during the interregnum was difficult. In some areas Posner had granted him authority, but he lacked the power to make changes.* In others he had power, but lacked authority. All knew he would have a great deal to say in the framing of the new constitution, and that Etherington, a key figure on the Levy Committee, could be counted upon to incorporate many of its recommendations in the document. Should this happen, the reformers would be satisfied, but a majority of brokers would protest, and Etherington would take office with a badly divided constituency. If he accepted what appeared to be the will of the majority and made few changes, he would be viewed by the SEC with suspicion.

The Amex did adopt more stringent listing and delisting rules in the interregnum, as well as higher capital and performance requirements by specialists. Etherington pledged better statistical breakdowns of operations would be available in the future, and indicated in other ways that surveillance procedures would be strengthened. In this, he satisfied all, but most particularly Posner, who clung to the idea of self-regulation. Here too the constitution departed from the Levy Committee recommendations. It had been suggested that the market value of outstanding stock for Amex issues be set at $2.5 million. (Later the Committee lowered the figure to $2 million.) Under the new rules, Amex securities had to have outstanding stock in the hands of the public worth at least $1 million. Applicants had to have had net earnings of at least $150,000 after all charges, including federal taxes, in the fiscal year immediately

---

* Etherington took the tenth floor, cleared it of offices (including Gilligan's) and refurbished it for himself. He relegated the thirteenth floor—McCormick's old offices—to a meeting place. This was symbolic of his break with the past.

preceding the filing of the listing application, and net earnings averaging at least $100,000 for the past three fiscal years.* This represented reform, since prior to 1962 the Amex had had no requirements at all in these regards. In addition, the introduction of *delisting* rules would provide Etherington with the means by which he could remove many questionable issues from the Amex in his attempt to upgrade the market.

The higher listing standards were accepted by most members, even though they could mean a loss of listings. "It's the logical aftermath of the investigation," said one associate member, while a specialist called the change "a foregone conclusion."

The new constitution was ready for submission on June 12, and was voted upon during the next two weeks. In most respects it represented a victory for the Posner faction, but the Jackson group did have its share of gains. The committee system as previously constituted was eliminated, and most of the power was shifted to the president and his staff. As the SEC had recommended, professional administration would come to the Amex.

The board itself would be changed drastically. Five of the thirty-two-man board would be people from outside the New York metropolitan area. Twelve would be brokers, ten of whom spent most of their time on the floor; six of the twelve would represent the commission houses. Thus, the power of the specialists would be limited. Ten governors would be individuals engaged in office functions, while three would represent the public and be drawn from individuals outside the securities industry. The other two seats would be taken by the chairman of the board and the president of the Exchange.

One provision authorized an emergency committee, which would have powers in case of an enemy attack; this was new, and reflected the public mood at a time when the federal government was urging a bomb-shelter program. An advisory com-

* The listing requirements were raised in 1963, 1967, and again in 1972, in further attempts to upgrade the list.

mittee was also created. It would consist of seven governors who would serve on a rotating basis and advise the president but not have independent authority.

The constitution, adopted by a wide margin, was scheduled to go into effect on September 4, to coincide with Etherington's assumption of the presidency. Some reformers felt it didn't go far enough, while a group of old-timers were apprehensive about the new powers granted the president. By then, however, Etherington had met many members, and impressed them in such a way as to relieve them of their doubts.

Nevertheless, the division between the Posner and Jackson forces did result in a contest for the board. The nominating committee, composed of Posner people, put up a slate of candidates, including Posner himself, who ran for the chairmanship. An independent slate of five candidates was also filed, and a sixth joined them soon after. Then two additional candidates joined the contest, which promised to be the most hotly fought election in years.

As had been the case in previously contested Amex elections, personalities had a good deal to do with the rival slates, with some of the insurgents feeling they had been passed over in favor of "establishment" people. This time, however, the Posner-Jackson duel complicated matters. Most of the insurgents were men who were dissatisfied with the pace of reform, and wanted a more sweeping change at Trinity Place. Jackson himself did not seek office, and he insisted that the rival slate not criticize the work of Posner or the accession of Etherington. So far as he was concerned, there was nothing acrimonious about the fact that the election would be contested. "It simply means some members feel they want to participate more than they have in the past. They believe their unquestioning attitude in the past led to many of the troubles the Exchange found itself in. I think this is salutory and ought to happen more often. It's unreasonable to expect unanimity among 499 exchange members." Posner thought otherwise; in his view, Jackson had taken another opportunity to embarrass him in his efforts to assure smooth sailing for Etherington.*

* The candidates insisted they were not opposed to the new administration. One of them, Joseph Petta, said, "No concerted effort is being made

The Posner slate won an impressive victory; only two of the insurgents were elected. Posner hailed the results as an indication of "our members' confidence in the present board of governers." He had reason to rejoice. The new constitution had been written by moderate reformers and would be administered by the same kind of people. Jackson could also derive a measure of satisfaction from the results, since he had established the principle of contested elections. He viewed the campaign "as a magnificent victory for the free exchange of opinion as evidenced by the results."

The President-elect also showed moderation in constructing his new staff. He made it clear from the start that he would lead no purge of McCormick men, although no person with a taint of scandal could expect to remain. On April 15 he praised the administration as "made up of people who are capable and experienced," and added, "we will count on them." But Etherington ended by saying, "Our next job will be to find the people they need to help them in the new organizational setup."

What did this mean? Was Etherington saying he intended to keep *all* the old administrators, even though some were considered McCormick men? The Amex administrative staff was dispirited during this period, with many not certain where they would be after September 4. Some had been mentioned in the SEC report, and although they had not been criticized in any way for misconduct, and had in fact performed their duties efficiently and honestly in the face of great difficulties in the 1950s, they could not gauge Etherington's sentiments toward them. In the end all were retained, some to be promoted to higher office. They included director of the department of admissions and outside the supervision, H. Vernon Lee, Jr., Vice-President Martin Keena, who was in charge of the division of securities, and Bernard Maas, director of the department of securities.

---

and we're not plotting in dark corners. We just want this to be a free and democratic election." Another candidate added, "We're not opposed to the reforms and we're all behind Edwin Posner and Ted Etherington. We're running because of the feeling of some members that a couple of the regular candidates don't have as much experience or ability as we have."

Etherington did bring in over forty new staff members in 1962–63, most of whom filled newly created positions. The most important of them was Paul Kolton, who since 1955 had been at the Big Board, where he served as director of press relations and, in 1960, was named vice-president. Prior to that time Kolton had spent nine years in advertising and public relations. Now he would become executive vice-president of the Amex and work in tandem with Etherington, as he had at the Stock Exchange in the late 1950s. Kolton was a young man at the time—thirty-eight—and was considered an expert in public relations. His main task at the Amex at first would be to restore the Exchange's reputation for honesty and fair dealings. Soon after, he received additional duties, and worked with Etherington on the floor and in the back offices. This left the President free for outside activities, such as working with the SEC, repairing relations with the Stock Exchange, and planning for long-term changes at the market.* Kolton was named to his post in May and, like Etherington, spent much of his time learning the ropes at the Amex prior to taking office in September.

Other important Etherington additions were made in this period. One was Graham Bell, who became vice president in charge of floor operations, and William Moran, formerly of the SEC, who handled compliance. These four—Etherington, Kolton, Bell, and Moran—established the foundation for reform by the time the new administration took office in November. The old staff was still wary of the incoming President, but at least was confident in their positions, while the new men and women took care not to antagonize the older ones. But the key

* Unlike McCormick, however, Etherington did not plan to devote himself to seeking new listings. Such activities were a major source of McCormick's difficulties, and Etherington would not place himself in a position where he might be compared with his predecessor. On the other hand, he did not underestimate the problem of getting and retaining stocks, especially when standards had been raised and after the scandals. But he said, "With proper staff work it need not take an inordinate amount of my time." Instead, Vice-President Henry Riter instituted a nationwide program to contact companies in a more conventional fashion than had been done previously.

to Etherington's success or failure was not too different from what it had been for McCormick and other presidents: the attitude of the members. These men understood that a man like Etherington was vital for their well-being, to please the SEC and other outside agencies. In order to survive and flourish, the Amex needed a person who could assure the good will of the government, the industry, and the public. Etherington seemed admirably equipped for the task, as did Kolton. But the brokers also wanted business, which translated into profits. Would the scandals hurt their livelihoods? There had been a slight dip in volume in early 1961; although it was unconnected with the scandals, some brokers preferred to link them. Volume held for the rest of the year, however, and this satisfied most that customers would not boycott the Amex under the assumption that its stocks were somehow tainted.* Indeed, trading volume jumps at the Amex were not very different from those at the Big Board. Volume increased through most years of the decade, often sharply, as did profits.

The price of an Amex seat, as always a good indication of the morale of the membership, fell somewhat on the news of scandal, but picked up when volume figures did not decline. And in 1967 it eclipsed the 1929 high for the first time.

The apparent stabilization of seat prices in 1963–65 was not the result of indecision or a stagnant market, but of the operation of Etherington's solution to one of his most vexing problems: that of associate memberships.

The Levy Committee had recommended that associate memberships be ended within eighteen months. Etherington disagreed, and had done so even prior to the release of the re-

---

* Amex brokers of that period and today are convinced the investors' eye is on their activities all the time, and they fear the loss of public confidence. Yet there was no correlation between scandal and volume in 1959–62, or at any time before the McCormick era. Nor do most investors and speculators care very much where the stocks they purchase are listed, although they do make a distinction between listed and unlisted, or over-the-counter stocks, probably more because of the ease of finding quotations in the newspapers than anything else. Like many people, brokers assume their world is the center of their customers' universe, but such is not the case.

Trading Volume at the American Stock Exchange, 1960–69

Year	Shares Traded	Turnover Ratio	Daily Average
1960	286,039,982	18.0	1,112,996
1961	488,831,037	27.2	1,947,534
1962	308,609,304	17.1	1,224,640
1963	316,735,062	18.2	1,261,893
1964	374,183,842	21.2	1,478,988
1965	534,221,999	30.9	2,119,929
1966	690,762,585	37.8	2,741,121
1967	1,145,090,300	61.4	4,544,009
1968	1,435,765,734	65.5	6,352,945
1969	1,240,742,012	47.2	4,962,968

Source: *Amex Databook*, p. 30

port. He noted that approximately one quarter of all Amex revenues was brought in by the associates. To force them out, or to oblige them to purchase regular seats through the elimination of the associate status, would create grave dislocations. Some would leave, while others would compete with one another to purchase seats, driving their prices artificially higher and perhaps creating a speculative market in them that would be unhealthy for the Exchange.

Shortly after being named president-elect, Etherington met with reporters and was asked his views on the subject. "I

Price of an American Stock Exchange Seat, 1960–69

Year	First	High	Low	Last	No. of Transfers
1960	$ 60,000	$ 60,000	$ 51,000	$ 52,000	30
1961	52,000	80,000	52,000	65,000	51
1962	65,000	65,000	40,000	52,500	35
1963	54,000	66,000	52,500	66,000	43
1964	52,000	63,000	52,000	60,000	41
1965	59,000	80,000	55,000	80,000	57
1966	88,000	120,000	70,000	90,000	77
1967	100,000	230,000	100,000	230,000	104
1968	230,000	315,000	220,000	315,000	103
1969	320,000	350,000	150,000	170,000	135

Source: *Amex Databook*, p. 12

haven't yet seen a plan that is fair and equitable for the associate members or the regular members in this connection," he said. "However, I believe one can and will be formulated." *

Etherington's solution, one he had been working on since autumn, 1962, was to create 151 new seats, bringing the total to 650. These would be offered at favorable prices to the 415 associate members. A good part of the money raised through the sale would be used by the cash-short Amex to pay for the automation program then on the verge of being put into operation. The associate memberships would not be eliminated. Instead, the associates would be subject to a higher fee schedule and get less of a break on commissions than previously had been the case. In this way, Etherington hoped to lower the value of associate memberships and enhance that of the regular variety, and so encourage the associate members to seek regular status. The President had a "target list" of many large and influential brokerages that at the time held associate memberships, and had done so for many years. Etherington wanted them to purchase seats, not only to upgrade the membership, but also to give the major houses a larger stake in the Amex than before. When they had a vote in Amex policies, he felt, they would have an interest in a better market at Trinity Place. In time many firms did purchase regular memberships, and came to play an important role at the Amex.

Although the Etherington plan was not quite what the SEC had wanted, the Commission endorsed it as a "forward step" that would strengthen the Amex. It also won the approval of the commission houses and the Big Board. But it ran into difficulty with the Amex specialists.

Many specialists approved the plan, but some were dubious. Would the increased membership mean additional specialists? If so, the new men might take business from the old.

---

* Etherington argued that through associate memberships small firms could deal on the Amex; to end the category might be to exclude them, and this could at some time in the future be considered a breach of the anti-trust acts. He also viewed the associates as a means of bringing new brokerages to the market, as well as others that had never belonged to an organized exchange.

Volume was high in 1962 and 1963, and profits good. Yet the opposition faction claimed there still wasn't sufficient business for them to make decent livings.

This precipitated Etherington's first important conflict with the membership. He dealt with it by calling meetings after trading hours, which different groups of brokers attended on different afternoons and evenings. For the first time he met with and talked with the membership, not as a group but as individuals as well. Some were won over to his side, but even those who were not had been given an opportunity to get a closer look at their new president, and he won their respect if not total support.

The plan went through, and by a wide margin, partly as a result of the support of the major commission houses, the board, and leading specialists. And the higher volume of the next few years helped allay fears of economic failure on the part of opposition specialists. The new seats were sold slowly, and the bid/ask prices did not decline. In 1963, 93 were sold, at prices ranging from $50,000 to $61,000; 7 more were sold in 1964, at prices from $50,000 to $57,000. The remaining 51 were taken by former associate members at prices from $55,000 to $61,000 in 1965.

Partly in response to fears that new members would dilute the business of each specialist unit, but more to strengthen the specialist system, Etherington embarked on a program to consolidate the units. The SEC report had hinted at the need for major reforms in the system—perhaps its elimination. Posner had rejected the idea firmly, but offered no alternative to the system as then in existence. Etherington recognized the need for reform, but at the same time he knew of no alternative to the basic system.* Speaking on September 19, 1962, two weeks

* Later Etherington would explore the possibility of bringing bank and insurance issues to the Amex. At the time he came to office these were traded over the counter. He thought a "second" Amex floor might be created for them, and if this were done, some way of incorporating leading over-the-counter brokerages might be worked out. But the banks and insurance companies were not enthusiastic about the idea, and the Big Board turned it down insofar as cooperation was concerned. The idea

after assuming the presidency, he made his position on the issue clear:

> The subject of automation may remind you of the suggestion heard now and then that the work of the specialist might be done by a suitably wired-up black box. I am all in favor of progress. But I am waiting to see a black box with a sense of timing, a lasting charge of courage, and not least, some money of its own to put at risk. Until that day, I will stick by the wise statement of the Levy Committee that the success of the Exchange as an auction market depends in large measure on the effectiveness of the specialist. I would add that anything done to undermine his position is a potential disservice to the public. In my view, there is far too little mention of the need to strengthen the specialist system, to encourage the specialist as he handles his difficult assignment, and to recruit other capable men to join his ranks.

Jackson had criticized Posner in 1962 for making the major specialists bigger and withholding new issues from the smaller ones on the ground they lacked the capitalization to service them. Etherington came to the same conclusion as Posner, but for different reasons. Where Posner tended to argue that the natural flow of events meant the strong would get stronger and the weak, weaker, and that the Exchange's role was to assure this process took place honestly, Etherington said that volume was rising, costs increasing, and the business of specialization becoming more complex. Small units short of both manpower and capital simply could not service stocks and commission brokers as well as large ones. In the public interest, the specialist system had to be revamped. This did not mean the end of the small specialist, however, but his combination with others of his size to form large units, which would handle the stock involved as though a single firm. For the strength of the Amex and protection of the public, Etherington insisted on

---

died, but it did indicate a way by which the specialist and market-maker systems might have been united. Etherington believed that competing markets in these stocks might have been encouraged, and if it worked, other changes might have resulted.

ever higher financial status for the units, and this meant fewer and stronger ones.

He began this work in 1963. By the end of the decade, the number of units had been reduced from 60 to 35, but few specialists had been forced from the floor. The average number of specialists per unit increased from 2.9 to 4.8, while a new rule eliminated one-man units (and later two-man units) and fixed the minimum number of specialists per unit at three.

In a series of steps taken during the 1960s the units were strengthened financially as well. By the end of the decade each unit was required to have sufficient funds to handle at least 2,-000 shares, or $100,000 in cash, whichever was larger, for each security in which it specialized, and all had substantially higher funds than required. Each unit was able to handle additional securities as a result of this action, and the number of issues per unit rose from an average of 19 in 1964 to 37 by 1971. To enable the Amex to handle high-priced, high-volume stocks, several extra-large units with large blocks of capital were created. By 1971 the Exchange had 11 five-man units, 4 six-man units, and 1 each of nine- and twelve-man units.

Etherington's reforms in the specialist system, continued by his successors, were the only ways by which the system could have been continued; the days of wholesale competition were finished by the 1960s.

There were two additional reasons to revamp the system. The first involved the need to keep good specialists and floor brokers at the Amex. As we have seen, during periods of high volume many houses tended to use the Amex as a training ground. The best brokers, those who did well at the "junior market," would be promoted to the Big Board after an apprenticeship. Etherington realized that he could not prevent this from happening, but he wanted to create conditions at the Amex that would discourage such transfers. During the 1950s, as had been the case in the 1920s, many men left the Amex for the Stock Exchange. This continued in the 1960s, but increasingly the major commission houses assigned some of their top men to the Amex. The same was true of the specialists, for as the Amex was capable of handling important issues and managed to retain some of them, highly experienced specialists were needed to service them. Etherington worked behind the scenes to get and keep such people, and the campaign succeeded.

The second benefit of the specialist reform program was in the area of new listings and the retention of old ones. McCormick's program of going into the country to seek new stocks, and the specialists' own ventures, were replaced by Etherington's more sophisticated campaign to promote the Amex as a major exchange in its own right, a place where "better markets" could be had, with floor operations and brokers that need not apologize for quality and financing. Institutional publicity, rather than the McCormick approach, was the byword in the 1960s. It seemed to succeed. The list increased in size during every year but one of the decade, in spite of a program to delist marginal securities instituted at the beginning of the Etherington administration. Even the bond list, which had experienced setbacks in the 1950s, revived in the 1960s.

Issues on the American Stock Exchange, 1960–69

| Year | Stocks | | | Bonds | | |
	Listed	Unlisted	Total	Listed	Unlisted	Total
1960	731	219	950	33	30	63
1961	806	206	1,012	45	28	73
1962	842	184	1,026	57	27	84
1963	852	163	1,015	61	23	84
1964	893	139	1,032	72	21	93
1965	927	119	1,046	82	19	101
1966	942	109	1,051	81	17	98
1967	979	101	1,080	125	13	138
1968	1,010	93	1,103	158	11	169
1969	1,110	68	1,178	165	11	176

Source: American Stock Exchange

The insistence on higher standards resulted in one of the greatest turnovers of securities in Amex history. As had always been the case during previous bull markets, the Amex lost increased numbers of securities to the Big Board. Etherington delisted an even greater number, those that failed to meet the more stringent 1962 requirements. The fact that the total number of issues increased as it did was the most striking confirmation possible of the President's success at image-building.

Stocks Delisted at the American Stock Exchange, 1959–69

Year	Merged or Liquidated	Redeemed or Expired	Listed on NYSE	Failed to Meet Amex Standards	Other
1959	13	6	12	11	3
1960	17	3	14	3	—
1961	17	3	15	11	1
1962	24	1	13	24	1
1963	12	9	15	38	9
1964	33	2	17	13	8
1965	26	4	13	18	10
1966	32	6	20	23	4
1967	45	9	16	22	1
1968	42	10	39	24	1
1969	39	11	32	26	4

Source: *Amex Databook*, p. 24

Although continuing to boast that the Amex was the largest organized market for foreign stocks in the nation, the Exchange no longer pressed hard for such listings. International tensions (especially the Castro Revolution in Cuba) played a role in this. By the early 1960s the Canadian boom was over, and the public's interest had turned elsewhere. As a result, the Amex's reputation as the home of small, badly-financed uranium and gold stocks faded. This marked the end of still another McCormick program.

Etherington, Kolton, and others at the Amex used the upgraded list as evidence that the Exchange had become a better place at which to have listing. They tried to convince corporation executives that it would suit their interests to retain Amex listing, since stocks could be handled there as well, if not better, than at the Big Board. Etherington stressed the Amex training program for specialists, one of the most thorough in the nation. By 1965 the "stabilization rate" at the Amex topped that at the Stock Exchange for the first time. This meant that

Foreign Stocks on the American Stock Exchange,
1959–69

	Canadian Issues		All Foreign Issues	
Year	No. of Issues	Percent of List	No. of Issues	Percent of List
1959	107	12.3	147	16.9
1960	107	11.4	148	15.7
1961	103	10.3	142	14.2
1962	91	8.9	127	12.5
1963	73	7.3	106	10.6
1964	66	6.5	102	10.0
1965	63	6.1	99	9.6
1966	62	6.0	99	9.5
1967	58	5.5	91	8.6
1968	53	4.8	83	7.5
1969	46	4.0	73	6.3

Source: *Amex Databook,* p. 26

Amex specialists were doing as well as, and at times better than, their Big Board counterparts in stabilizing swift bull and bear moves.

Etherington and Kolton dramatized the higher floor standards by going on the floor during busy periods to bolster morale. In 1964 Syntex, a major Amex stock handled by a specialist unit headed by John Mann, began to act erratically. Volume increased, the result of many controversies regarding its birth-control pill. Etherington ordered an investigation, but found no sign of manipulation by outsiders. As before, he and Kolton went to the floor to investigate the trading, and it seemed that the Mann unit was not performing as well as it might have in maintaining the market in the stock. A few days later, with Etherington in Washington on SEC affairs, Syntex flared again. This time Kolton went to the floor to assist. That evening he called Etherington to tell him the Syntex specialists were "tired and harried," and were no longer willing to take the risks necessary to control the issue. The following morning Etherington met with Ralph Saul, who was still at the Division of Trading and Exchanges, and discussed the Syntex situation. He pointed out the need for a new unit, one better equipped to handle the stock. Saul agreed, and Etherington proceeded to put his plan into operation.

Etherington called Jackson to his office and asked him to head a new specialist unit in Syntex. Jackson agreed to do so, providing sufficient capital could be raised. Etherington called on other brokers to contribute to a pool of $1 million, which would be used to assure a "good market" in the stock. With this done, Etherington spoke to Mann and told him that he would have to relinquish the issue. Then the Jackson unit took over, and stabilized the stock.*

The incident garnered excellent publicity for the Amex, demonstrated the Exchange's willingness to keep the SEC informed as to developments, and helped keep Syntex at the Amex, for it remained there long after it qualified for Big Board listing.**

On other occasions Etherington acted promptly to suspend questionable issues, giving full publicity to the facts and reporting details to the SEC. His activities, together with institutional reforms, helped stave off several potential problems.

The following year, rumors appeared regarding heavy gambling losses incurred by R. W. Rosenblatt, a partner in the specialist firm of May, Borg. Etherington ordered an investigation, and learned that Rosenblatt had lost over half a million

* The Jackson unit was disbanded after the crisis was over, although Jackson probably could have held on to Syntex had he made the effort. Always aware that any of his actions would lead to rumors, Jackson made certain no one could accuse him of having acted in the matter for his own benefit.

** Shortly thereafter the Big Board decided to approach Syntex as an applicant for listing on the senior exchange. Etherington contacted the officers at Syntex, and convinced them that it was in their own interest to keep the stock at the Amex. As a result, Syntex remained at Trinity Place. This decision was little publicized at the time; newspapers do not print stories of events that don't happen. But it was the first time an Amex stock that qualified in every way for Big Board listing decided to remain at the Amex. The example was followed by others, and now there are many Amex stocks—Syntex among them—in this category. This little-noticed change was one of the most significant events of the Etherington administration, and the clearest sign of the new Amex status achieved during the 1960s.

dollars betting on football games; part of this had come from May, Borg accounts. He notified Saul, made certain the losses were made up from May, Borg's fidelity bond and contributions from the firm's other partners, and forced Rosenblatt from the Amex.

Previously such matters had been kept in the family. This time the Amex gave full publicity to the events, and made no secret of them in communications with the SEC or discussions with the press.

The Amex's relations with the SEC were good in this period, but Etherington was determined to keep the Exchange free from controls; he was a strong believer in self-regulation, in the Posner tradition. On taking office in 1962 he said:

> . . . I want to make explicit our attitude toward the SEC. The SEC's duty to administer the securities laws makes it the natural ally and not the natural enemy of the securities industry. The only time to worry about industry-government relations is when someone in either sector slips into thinking that hand-to-hand combat is preferable to a conference table conclusion. As long as I am President of the American Stock Exchange that will not happen at this end of the relationship.

The final SEC report on its investigations of the securities industry was released in 1963. At that time Etherington warned the brokers that it would be harsh and critical, but would take account of reforms already accomplished at the exchange.

> Our techniques for self-regulation may well be questioned, but our right to do the job is not at issue. Self-regulation by people and businesses is hardly a fad which may or may not remain fashionable. Civilized people have always regulated their own affairs. Something different would be something chaotic. The concept of government of, for, and by the people rests on the assumption that certain limited powers will be *given* to the government; it does not rest on the assumption that all authority will be *taken* by government, removing the duty of self-control.

The report was more an attack on Big Board practices than those at the Amex, a tribute in part to the Posner-Etherington reforms. It did urge the abolition of floor trading on the major exchanges, assailed the way in which odd lots were handled at the Big Board, and called for increased automation of securities transactions. As before, it was highly critical of the specialist system. But the Amex reforms, both those already accomplished and others in the planning stages, answered many of the criticisms.

Etherington was interested in automation, in this respect building on the work started by Reilly. In 1965 the board unveiled a long-term program of automation designed to prepare the Amex for 14-million-share days, expected within the next decade. The first step would be the mounting of electronic keyboards at every trading post for use in transmitting information from the floor to the stock tickers. This program was completed in 1966. Computers would also be used to take over operation of the ticker systems. A "talking computer," called Am-Quote, would receive price and volume information from the tickers. A broker wanting the latest information on a particular stock could dial a number on his telephone, and the computer would relay the information by means of special prerecorded tapes. The overall supervision of the program was placed in the hands of an eight-man committee charged with the task. The committee was not only to put the 1965 plan into operation, but prepare for further changes in the future. As always, Etherington viewed automation as a refinement of the specialist system; he assured the members he had no plans to change that key aspect of the auction market.

Within three years of having taken over at the Amex, Etherington had brought about more changes than any previous president. Of course, a good deal of the reform had been accomplished during the Posner interregnum, but this had been done with Etherington's knowledge and approval. Etherington had helped the Amex in not only recapturing its pre-1960 reputation, but enhancing it. Prior to his election, the Amex had been a very junior market, a somewhat dubious place at which to trade. Larger profits could be made there, but the risks were even greater. Etherington helped change this. Amex stocks were far better policed than they had been during any previous administration, and the public's trust in them, though not as important as was always believed, was in any case higher. Amex specialists, too, were of a higher order, and had little to apologize for in the way of training and performance. In this respect Etherington helped give the Exchange legitimacy, something it had always felt it lacked. Amex specialists in the past often were poor but honest, or wealthy but corrupt, although there were many exceptions to this rule. Now successful specialists were no longer considered somehow devious; it was possible to rise to the top through following the rules, not skirting them. Specialists were free to concentrate on business, and did not fly from place to place seeking listings. Firms that would have been wooed in the 1950s came to the Amex of their own volition to seek listing.

Was Etherington a reformer or a conservative? A case could be made for either position. The President cooperated with the SEC, and was on better terms with agency leaders than any previous president, and this pleased Amex reformers. His insistence on self-regulation, his defense of the specialist system, and his reluctance in going beyond the basic reforms introduced during the Posner interregnum endeared him to many conservatives. If the key to successful administration is to appear all things to all men, while at the same time making needed changes and preserving the values of the past, Etherington was a most successful administrator. The fact that he was able to remain on good terms with both Posner and Jackson was a sign of this success. Posner thought Etherington often moved too quickly, and he was doubtful about certain changes, but he cooperated in the reform movement. Jackson believed Etherington was too much of a showman and not a true reformer, but he too worked in harmony with the President. When Posner left the chairmanship to return to the floor in 1965, Jackson took his place. The transition was smooth. This too was a tribute to Etherington's political abilities.

New problems appeared in 1965, and these were discussed and debated. One involved the growth of the "third market," in which some Amex issues were traded. In the past the Amex often had attempted to raid the over-the-counter market. Now the reverse was taking place, with over-the-counter brokerages making markets in Amex securities. Several mutual funds and institutions were exploring the possibility of purchasing seats at the Amex, a situation forbidden under the constitution. There was talk of the merger of some Big Board and Amex facilities, such as the clearing houses, certificate systems, computer facilities, and the like. But the most intriguing involved the future of the President.

It would be incorrect to say that Etherington was at the height of his popularity in early 1966, for it rose every year, and was on the upswing at that time. Funston, who had come to the Big Board at the same time McCormick had taken over at Trinity Place, was completing fifteen years on the job, and felt himself due for retirement. Funston had been a masterful publicity man for the Big Board, but he was somewhat out of place in the new environment of the district, and was wise enough to know it. No one in the district doubted that Etherington could have the job if he wanted it. Or he could remain at the Amex for as long as he desired. Etherington gave signs of wanting a change. He had remained at the Amex for a longer period than he had at any previous position. His five-year contract would run out in 1966, and rumors had it he would step down at that time.*

If this were so, two questions were asked. The first: where would he go? The second: whom would the board select as Etherington's replacement?

Most Amex brokers expected Etherington to leave in 1966. A majority of them were convinced he would become Funston's successor, but others, equally certain, said he would go into politics. By 1966 the disillusionment with President Lyndon Johnson had begun, and the critiques of the Kennedy administration were yet to come. There seemed a national longing on the part of many for a return to the Kennedy years —to "Camelot." Throughout the nation young, attractive poli-

---

* Rumors as to changes in jobs and official reactions to programs are often accurate when spread throughout Wall Street. More often than not, such "leaks" are planned, and can be trusted. On the other hand, stock tips and the like are worthless, even when coming from "insiders" in the district and guaranteed as to accuracy and freshness.

ticians were making their mark; and most of them were liberals. Etherington fit the bill perfectly. He had all the qualities of a fine politician, the charismatic features so attractive to many voters, the kind of experience and background to appeal to conservative businessmen with reformist ideas, and the driving ambition to succeed needed to put them all together. Noting this, many brokers thought Etherington would announce his candidacy for elective office sometime early in 1966.

On July 13, Etherington confirmed one of the rumors: he would leave the Amex, but not for the Big Board or politics. Instead, he would assume the presidency of Wesleyan University, from which he had graduated and where he had taught from 1948 to 1949. "It is not easy for me to leave the exchange and the securities industry," he told reporters, "but it would not have been possible for me to say no to this opportunity. Eighteen years ago, at the outset of my post-college career, my sights were set lower but in this same direction. My values have not changed."

The news came as a shock to the financial community. Such a move had not been expected. Then the brokers rationalized the statement and announcement. It seemed to confirm that Etherington indeed had political ambitions, but of a higher order than they had thought. Wesleyan would be a better launching pad for a try at the governorship of Connecticut —or even the presidency—than would the Amex. The fact that such talk took place, and seriously, was another measure of the esteem in which they held Etherington at that time.

This made the second question all the more pressing. Who would succeed to the Amex presidency? Paul Kolton appeared the front-runner, but there were many others in the race, including former New York Mayor Robert Wagner and a host of other politicians. David Jackson, in accepting Etherington's resignation "with deep regret," reflected on the need for an able successor. He might also have considered that, although it would be a difficult problem, the pressures on the next president would be far less than those that Etherington had faced in 1962.

SEVENTEEN

The Amex as Establishment

On July 14 Jackson named a five-man panel charged with selecting Etherington's successor. The outgoing President declined to serve on it, but would offer suggestions and recommendations. Jackson thought the panel should conclude its work quickly, even though Etherington would not leave his post until November. The Chairman thought the rumors as to who would fill the post could not do the Amex much good, and would raise the hopes of many, while only one man could assume the post. There was an even more pressing reason to conclude the job quickly. It was known that Funston might soon announce his own retirement, at which time the Big Board would establish a search panel of its own. Candidates who might otherwise have wanted the Amex job then might hold back in hope of winning the prize at the Stock Exchange.

Within a week Trinity Place gossip had it that one of three men would be the next president. Kolton was given a chance at winning the post, and was the only insider being considered. The other two were men with SEC experience at the highest level. Former Chairman William Cary, who had left the agency to accept the Dwight Professorship of Law at Columbia University in 1964, was mentioned prominently. The other was Ralph Saul, who had kept in close contact with Etherington while heading the Division of Trading and Markets.*

Jackson insisted that the field was not closed, but by early August it seemed the panel was choosing among the three. By then Kolton had become a long shot. He was popular with the members and administration, and had served a successful apprenticeship under Etherington. But many brokers seemed to feel the Amex needed a man with an SEC background. As one broker put it, "I think the man who succeeds Ted Etherington will be someone with Washington connections."

On August 15 the panel announced the selection of Ralph Saul, who accepted on that date. Saul was forty-four years old, had been born in Brooklyn, gone to Long Island schools, and then to the University of Chicago. After serving in the Navy during World War II he returned to Chicago to complete his undergraduate education. At the time he considered making diplomacy his career, and served in the Prague embassy during the early days of the Cold War. But he left the diplomatic service to enter Yale Law School, and graduated in 1951.** After a year with the New York law firm of Lyeth & Voorhees, Saul reentered government service, this time as confidential law assistant for New York Governor Thomas E. Dewey. He remained with Dewey until 1954, when he took a position with the legal department at Radio Corporation of America. Saul joined the SEC in 1958, and almost immediately was plunged into the study of the securities markets. He was responsible for the staff study of the Amex that had been harshly critical of the Exchange's practices. In 1962 it was Saul, not Cary, whom the Amex leaders felt was the radical of the Commission, the man who wanted to drastically revamp the market.

Saul was capable of blunt, often hard language. He was a man of strong convictions, not easily swayed, though his appearance and manner gave a very different impression. Tall

* Others were talked about in this period, and a few had been mentioned. One of them was John Roosevelt, son of Franklin D. Roosevelt, who at the time was Vice President and Director at Bache & Co.

** Saul had graduated from Yale Law a year before Etherington. The two men had met there, but were not close friends at the time.

and gangly, Saul often seemed quite shy and soft-spoken, someone who might be thought a head librarian at a major university rather than the relentless SEC prober. He was quite different from the handsome, polished Etherington, and would offer a different kind of public image than his predecessor. Yet the two had worked well together while Saul was at the SEC, and had developed a mutual respect. Saul could not have become president without Etherington's confidence, and he had it.

Saul had left the SEC in 1965 to become Vice-President for Corporate Development at Investors Diversified Services, a major financial corporation, which managed mutual funds with assets of over $5.3 billion. His experience there gave him a new view of finance—from the inside. This was comforting to some brokers, who remembered with some dislike the Saul of 1962. He was a man who knew more of inside Amex operations than any other outsider. During the next six years he had remained in close communication with the Exchange's leaders. Unlike Etherington, who, despite his work on the Levy Committee, was still a novice so far as the Amex was concerned, Saul would enter office well prepared with current information; he would not need the long weeks of study Etherington had undergone in the summer of 1962. He would also have an easier task than his predecessor; Saul would inherit from Etherington few of the vestigal remains of the McCormick years.

On taking office in November, Saul indicated his belief that most of the problems the Amex had faced in 1962 had been resolved. He told reporters:

It's a new American Stock Exchange. Mr. Etherington and the board have installed a first-rate organization. There's been a whole change in attitude and tone among membership and management. They're aware of their public responsibility, and they're fulfilling it. Now, we must continue to grow, be prepared to innovate and give better quality and services to the public.

Saul further strengthened the administrative staff. Kolton remained as executive vice-president, and a new level of senior vice-presidents was established to further centralize administrative functions.

Much of Saul's initial work consisted of completing projects begun by Etherington, and maintaining the improved surveillance of that period. Floor operations were watched closely, and Amex control of back offices also improved. On several occasions, when the administration heard rumors of possible manipulation by brokers, Saul organized investigating teams to track down the rumors. Such activities had taken place under Etherington; they were refined in the Saul period as the new President brought SEC techniques to the Amex.

Saul also broadened the scope of his authority, just as Etherington had before him. Previously the administrations had been charged with overseeing the Exchange; speculation on the part of the public was beyond their ability to control. Saul took a different point of view, holding that when speculators attempted to manipulate Amex stocks, even though members were not involved, the Exchange's duty was to investigate and report. In March of 1966, several non-Amex brokers and speculators met to plan the manipulation of several Amex stocks. Soon after Saul took office he learned of these developments, and a quick study of volume figures indicated irregularities. An initial reconnaissance satisfied him that nothing untoward had taken place on the floor. Going beyond that, Saul continued the probe, investigating all rumors. By mid-April he had uncovered the ring, and the Amex issued a report on its findings.

> The pattern of activity which is emerging . . . indicated that certain customers, acting in concert, were taking sizable positions in a small number of securities. Other members of the public were then urged to purchase the stocks on the strength of merger possibilities, favorable earnings forecasts or technical considerations. As public interest was aroused and prices rose, the original group was in a position to sell out at substantial profits. The Exchange's investigation also indicates that unregulated lenders have financed, to a significant degree, the capital needed by persons engaged in these activities.

In this way the Amex uncovered a pool, not very unlike those of the 1920s. And although the Exchange was in no way a party to the deals, it launched a much-needed investigation. This was a step beyond self-regulation: the Amex was doing the job the SEC should have done.*

Nor did the Exchange stop there. Saul warned commission houses involved in the ring of continued investigations into such rumors, and asked them to tighten up their control of registered representatives, just as the Amex was improving the quality of specialists and floor brokers. Most complied. One issued this memo to its brokers after receiving the Saul statement:

> We will not tolerate some customers' man calling his customers and selling them on the idea of buying a low-priced radical speculation solely because some other customers' man, who has a wealthy and knowledgeable client, decides to take a position in the stock. Nor will we tolerate recommendations that in the end reflect on the character and integrity of the firm.

In the past only Big Board warnings had been heeded by the commission houses. Only five years earlier these brokers had mounted a strong attack against the Amex, and seemed capable of controlling its specialists. The threat was not gone. By 1967 the large commission houses heeded Amex warnings, and the Exchange for the first time was in a clearly dominant position vis-à-vis the commission houses.

The SEC took note of the progress made at the Amex during Saul's first year in office. The Commission's surveillance of the Amex had lessened during the Etherington presidency; now it was nominal. "Overall, I think they're doing a fine job," said Mahlon Frankhauser, New York regional administrator. "I think they have been making good progress and the difference between this administration and those prior to 1961 is like night and day." An SEC lawyer, commenting on Saul's investigating teams, said he thought them the most capable in the district—more so than their Big Board counterparts.

By that time, too, the public's attitude toward the Amex had also changed. There were signs of heightened respect at

---

* Compare this probe with that of Birrell in 1957, when the Amex claimed it could not control customers and registered representatives.

the Stock Exchange. Ever since 1792, when a small group of major businessmen had gone indoors to form what amounted to a private organization where securities would be auctioned —the forerunner of the Stock Exchange—those who remained outdoors had been viewed as second-class citizens or worse. The organization of the Curb Market Association did not change this, and even the move indoors in 1921 had not altered the relationship between the Big Board and Curb brokers. The public tended to view curbstone and later Curb Exchange stocks as something akin to "fallen women": racy but rather risky, and sometimes dangerous. Events of the Re and Gilligan period served only to intensify these feelings. After four years of the Etherington administration, the Amex had become respectable, and during Saul's presidency the Exchange's status increased.

This is not to say that the Amex was considered equal to the Big Board, or that it had the same sort of prestige. Amex brokers who moved to Wall Street from Trinity Place in the late 1960s still considered it a promotion. But those who remained, including many who chose to do so, no longer felt they had anything to apologize for, and a transfer from the Big Board to the Amex was no longer considered Siberia.

Even during the McCormick era the Amex was considered a place for securities unwanted by the Big Board—for men who either couldn't make the switch or were content to remain in the "minor leagues." This attitude was fading during the Saul administration. The sentiment grew that in some way the Amex was a junior partner in the exchange complex. More could not be expected. But that much progress had not been thought possible as late as 1962.

This change took place for three reasons beside the reforms and other evolutions already discussed. These were the wild, often unmanageable markets of the late 1960s and the problems they created, along with the need for cooperation between the exchanges; the increased necessity for rationalization and consolidation of facilities, in part resulting from higher volume; and attacks and challenges from the outside.

As late as 1963 some specialists were concerned that they would have too little business to maintain their financial posi-

tions. Four years later they enjoyed prosperity greater than that
of the late 1920s, but were ragged with overwork. Speculation
was rife in the late 1960s, and the Amex experienced more
than its share. Trading volume in 1968—when the exchanges
were closed on Wednesdays for more than half a year—
amounted to almost four times what it had been in 1963. In
1961, the Amex had its first 5-million-share day; the first 6-mil-
lion-share day came in 1966; the 8-million level was passed in
1967, the 10-million the following year. On the last day of
1969, a record 11,355,410 shares were traded. There was not a
single day in 1966 in which fewer than one million shares were
traded, and there hasn't been one since. Unlike volume surges
of earlier years, this increased activity could not be attributed
to a penchant for low-priced securities alone. The average price
of Amex listed shares rose steadily throughout the period.

Trading Volume at the
American Stock Exchange,
1963–70

Year	Shares Traded	Turnover Ratio
1963	316,735,062	18.2
1964	374,183,842	21.2
1965	534,221,999	30.9
1966	690,762,585	37.8
1967	1,145,090,300	61.4
1968	1,435,765,734	65.5
1969	1,240,742,012	47.2
1970	843,116,260	29.5

Source: *Amex Databook*, p. 30

This substantially higher volume came at a time when
many commission houses had only begun to automate their facilities. The back offices, never well organized in the past, were
in a shambles. A number of commission houses, which had
taken advantage of lax and poorly written regulations to keep
bank balances of the most meager reserves, found that their
cash flows were inadequate to maintain them. Lost and stolen
securities became a scandal, and several of these houses failed.
This soon developed into one of the biggest cascades of

failure in Wall Street history, though it was not recognized as such by the general public, since the brokerage tangles were quite different from anything that had happened before. Previous wrongdoings had been associated with manipulations by insiders or plungers, at times thefts by Exchange personnel or brokers, and even thievery at the commission houses. In each case one or several people or firms had been the focus of attention and scandal, and this had personalized them for the public. But in the late 1960s the entire commission-house nexus was ridden with institutional rather than individual problems. The commission houses for the most part were operating within the letter of the law—but the law itself was outmoded, and written in such a way as to encourage questionable financial and accounting practices. This was perhaps the most surprising revelation of all.*

The SEC was concerned about the back offices and financial problems at the commission houses, and in January 1968 wrote to the Stock Exchange, the Amex, and the National Association of Securities Dealers, expressing its fears regarding "accounting, record keeping, and back office problems and their effects on the prompt transfer and delivery of securities." The "fail rate"—the ratio of transactions completed within specified time limits to those not completed—was rising steadily at the commission houses. Now the exchanges and the NASD were asked to do what they could to help.

The key men were Stock Exchange President Robert Haack and Saul. Haack was the industry's spokesman, a task that fell naturally to one in his position. But throughout the crisis period, Saul emerged as a major factor within the district, a new and unaccustomed role for an Amex president.

The commission house crisis lasted until 1971, and even then debris remained in the district. The exchanges had been only marginally helpful in alleviating pressures. Declining volume, government action, and salvaging operations by leading commission houses were more important than anything Haack

* The best study of the brokerage crisis is Hurd Baruch, *Wall Street: Security Risk* (Acropolis, 1971). At the time of its writing, Baruch was special counsel to the SEC's Division of Trading and Markets.

and Saul could do or actually did. The two men, however, co-operated by voluntarily cutting back on trading hours in 1967–68 in the hope that volume would decline and the brokerages would use the extra time to catch up on paper work. When this did not happen, the exchanges closed down on Wednesdays during the second half of 1968. Saul applied pressures to the commission houses on trading in low-priced securities, urging them to place limits on such transactions. The Amex also raised fees, leading several small companies, most of them with unlisted status, to leave the Exchange. Saul insisted that presidents of corporations whose stocks traded on unusually heavy volume report the possible reasons for the activity. Amex clearing facilities were extended to certain over-the-counter issues that until 1968 had not used the Amex facility.* And in 1968 he issued a ban on all credit purchases on 103 securities, which effectively ended floor dealings on the part of private members in these stocks.

Fortunately, a modernization program on the floor, by

Over-the-Counter Clearances at the ASE Clearing House

Year	Trades	Shares	Value
1963–1964	580,000	83,184,469	$ 1,681,503,120
1965	537,609	79,590,961	1,677,838,047
1966	549,644	83,790,377	1,780,697,535
1967	946,904	155,502,736	3,330,294,835
1968	1,674,564	317,932,157	6,677,531,573
1969	4,914,873	551,438,327	10,716,289,861

Source: *Amex Databook*, p. 46

which fewer but larger posts were created and traffic flow improved, was ready in time for the heavy trading of 1968–69, but even then Amex facilities were taxed as never before.

The crisis affected the entire securities industry, and could not help but bring the exchanges closer together. Haack and

---

* The ASE Clearing Corporation had begun clearing certain over-the-counter transactions on August 1, 1963, in cooperation with the National Over-The-Counter Clearing Corporation. But the list was extended in 1968. The rise in volume was impressive.

Saul often operated as a team; the Amex President's views and plans were second only to those of Haack in dealing with the situation.* As much as anything else that happened in the late 1960s, the fiasco created a community of interest where only the bones of one had previously existed, and, significantly, a sense on the part of both exchanges that future cooperation, as equals, should and would be continued.**

The increasingly apparent need for rationalization of facilities also resulted in higher Amex status. The complex markets of the 1960s, the growth of interest in securities, and the development of new technologies provided the impetus, while the brokerage failures gave it more urgency than might otherwise have been the case.

Saul and Etherington before him had recognized the need for technological change. In 1969, North American Rockwell Information Systems prepared a special study for the Amex on the subject. It explored the use of computers to speed processing and minimize errors throughout the trading cycle—at order entry, trading, settlement, and transfer. The major recommendation was to develop a nationwide system for netting (clearing) and settling trades between brokers. This included a system of depositories for stock certificates so that securities movements between brokers could be accomplished by bookkeeping entries rather than by actually moving certificates around. In this way it would be possible to eliminate much of the cause of the paperwork crisis.

---

* It is interesting to compare the situation in 1969 to that forty years earlier, during the great crash. In 1929 the Stock Exchange spoke for the district, usually through its Vice-President, Richard Whitney. Curb President Muller said nothing of the crash, and offered no opinions on its meaning for the nation and the district. Muller remained quiet for several reasons, and one of these was that no reporter thought it necessary to ask the Curb President his views. The opinion of a man in that office carried little weight in 1929.

** In 1970 the Amex did work with other industry groups and the SEC to help frame legislation that created the Securities Investor Protection Corporation (SIPC). The organization insures investors against losses directly resulting from broker-dealer insolvencies up to $50,000. The Amex contributed $3 million from its special trust fund to SIPC.

In the late 1960s the exchanges explored methods by which their operations might be coordinated, and in some cases joined. In June 1970, Kolton and Big Board Executive Vice-President R. John Cunningham set up staffs to prepare reports on the subject. Shared computer time seemed a natural area for cooperation. Another would be the introduction of Amex securities into the Stock Exchange's Block Automation System, a computerized network aimed at facilitating large block transactions. A unified clearing house was also considered, and Kolton and Cunningham saw little reason why the exchanges could not cooperate in the establishment of a central depository for all exchange securities.

In 1970, Saul was instrumental in bringing New York clearing-house banks and securities industry groups together to form the Banking and Securities Industry Committee (BASIC). Herman Bevis, Executive Director of BASIC, cooperated with the exchanges in preparing a new program for dealing with certificates. During the first half of 1971, over $500 million of these were lost or stolen. Some were regained, but many were permanently lost. Rumors spread that the underworld was behind many of the losses.

The Bevis proposal called for the creation of a Central Securities Depository System, which would incorporate the Big Board's Central Certificate Service. The new facility would provide services for both exchanges, as well as the regional markets and the over-the-counter market. Bevis believed it could reduce the movement of securities by as much as 50 percent or more. This would go far toward the goal of "immobilizing certificates," ending abuses and losses, and automating the district.* Haack and Saul agreed, and as a first step, all eligible Amex securities entered into the Stock Exchange's CCS in 1971.

In 1971 the exchanges and commission houses adopted better standardization procedures on clearances. By then automation and standardization had become key words in the district. "Those that standardize on automation will survive," said

---

* Saul favored the elimination of certificates. He saw them as vestigal remnants of the past that made little sense in the 1970s. He accepted the Bevis proposal as a first step in this direction.

one executive. "Those that don't will end up as another blurb in the *Wall Street Journal.*" What would be the end product of such efforts? To some it seemed a complete merger of the exchanges made sense. This was the view of Amex Chairman Frank Graham. James Davant, Managing Partner of Paine, Webber, Jackson & Curtis, added his belief that a merger would save millions of dollars. In late 1970 Wall Street buzzed with rumors of a secret Big Board report on the merger, and some said it would come within the year. The report, entitled "The Potential for Joint Management of the New York and American Stock Exchanges," did indeed call for additional forms of cooperation, but noted that a merger, resulting in a saving of only five million dollars, seemed out of the question for the time being. The report did note that some 80 percent of the Big Board members had Amex seats as well, and there seemed no reason why Amex and Big Board specialists could not coordinate their efforts.

A half-century before, the Stock Exchange offered to "take over" the Curb by giving the curbstone brokers a room in the Exchange building. In 1971 the talk of the district was of merger, not takeover. The merger did not take place, but the plan, as discussed, was another sign of increased Amex prestige.

Saul and Haack did agree that the structure of the district was outmoded, and that change—perhaps drastic change—was needed. In November, 1970, Saul said,

> Organizations conceived in other times and under other circumstances may no longer be adequate in many respects to meet the needs of an industry that has expanded and diversified into something different from what it was thirty years ago.

Haack agreed. But what did the two men have in mind? Neither would go into details on the subject, but Haack did speak of the need for revisions in rates, procedures, and programs. Unless this were done, he implied, the exchange system might wither.

Although neither president would spell out his plan, Wall Street knew what they were talking about, and the nature of the challenges to which they referred. These were unrelated but in some ways similar pressures from two different directions and groups: the institutional investors and the over-the-counter dealers.

The first, from the mutual funds, pension funds, and the like, arose when these organizations attempted to purchase seats on both exchanges, as they had on some regional exchanges. The two New York markets rejected their bids under the terms of their constitutions. Had they been accepted, the large institutions would have been able to buy and sell securities without going through the commission houses, thereby saving themselves sizable fees. This might have destroyed the commission houses, which increasingly relied upon block orders at a time when the percentage of small investor purchases in terms of net volume continued to decrease. The institutions did use their positions on the regionals to buy and sell securities, and this resulted in a loss of business by the Big Board and gains by the regionals. The Amex was not hurt directly by this situation, but, as part of the New York exchange complex, it was concerned.

A more significant challenge came from the over-the-counter dealers in the form of the "third market" that dealt in Big Board stocks.* Such securities had long been traded off the exchange floor; in 1941 some $84 million worth of stock was bought and sold in this fashion. By 1961 the figure was $2 billion, and it rose to $2.5 billion in 1965. Then volume shot even higher, as institutions began to patronize the third market in increasing numbers. In 1971 the third market, using National Association of Securities Dealers Quotation System (NASDQS) mounted a major challenge to the Big Board. By then a "fourth market," under which institutions dealt directly with one another, had also been organized.**

None of this affected the Amex directly—in 1971, only

---

* The third-market operation is beyond the purview of this book. For a good analysis of it, see *St. John's Law Review* (Vol. 45, No. 4, May 1971). Especially see "NYSE Rules and the Antitrust Laws—Rule 394—Necessary Restriction or Illegal Refusal to Deal?" on pp. 812–64.
** The most important of the fourth market firms is Institutional Networks, formed in 1967 and more commonly called "Instanet."

one Amex stock was covered regularly by third-market firms. But this market, which used computers, scanners, and telephones rather than the exchange floors, sometimes with tighter bid-asked questions than specialists, bypassing the "middle man," represented the greatest threat to the specialist system Wall Street had ever known. Stock specialists were the heart of the exchanges, the Amex included. Part of the reason for Etherington's reform success was his dedication to the system, and his defense of it against all who threatened. In 1971 the system at the Big Board was being challenged by the over-the-counter dealers. And although the Amex was not directly involved, its brokers had a direct interest in its resolution. For if the specialist system at the Big Board was destroyed, that at the Amex could not survive. The result? The greatest institutional market change in over a century. Naturally, the threat brought the two major exchanges closer together than ever before.*

The complex of Wall Street problems led the Big Board to commission former Federal Reserve Board Chairman and Stock Exchange President William McChesney Martin to make a study of the markets and their needs. This report began early in 1971, and was released on August 6.** It was a highly controversial report, one that was to be debated for months. In effect, Martin recommended the centralization of the exchange-market system. He opposed institutional memberships on stock exchanges, but would preserve and defend the specialist system.

> There has been a great deal of criticism of the role and function of specialists. However, no better system of maintaining a continuous and responsible market has been suggested. The capital resources of specialists, however, should be increased to meet the requirements of today's trading, and methods should

* The introduction of negotiated commissions at both exchanges in 1971 did not cause an appreciable impact on the third market, which continued to grow.
** The report was issued two months after the Amex celebrated its fiftieth anniversary, and so falls beyond the limit of this work. But its impact was so great that a brief discussion was felt necessary.

be developed to encourage and enable specialists to improve performance of their functions in instances where securities are offered in unusually large volume.

Martin commended the exchanges for their work in automation, and asked for its continuation. In particular the report spoke of the "consolidation of certain computer facilities of the New York Stock Exchange and the American Stock Exchange," which "will provide maximum economy in their use."

Haack supported the report in its essentials, as did Saul. As might have been expected, the over-the-counter houses viewed it as another attempt to impose monopoly conditions on the securities industry. They had good reason: in one of its most important recommendations the report suggested "that the Exchange ask the Congress to enact legislation granting all registered national securities exchanges certain immunities under the anti-trust laws."

In June 1971, Saul left the Amex, prior to release of the Martin report and soon after the celebration of the Amex's fiftieth anniversary. He accepted a position as Vice-President of First Boston Corporation, a major Wall Street house. There was no prolonged debate as to who would succeed to the presidency: Paul Kolton was the one serious contender for the post. No previous president had been so well-prepared for the assignment, and the change in administrations was accomplished smoothly.

Kolton assumed the presidency at a time when the Amex was secure financially and established as a major exchange. Common problems and needs had resulted in strong ties and common bonds with the Big Board. These would be strengthened if the main lines of the Martin report were accepted. Both Saul and Kolton might have been thinking of this new status as they walked through Trinity churchyard to Broad Street in June 1971 to participate in the celebration. A half-century before, the curbstone brokers had crossed this same churchyard—in triumph but in the opposite direction—to go indoors. At that time, some wanted status, and others, financial success. Neither group was convinced it could have both.

Throughout much of the history of the Curb, as well as the Amex, these two desires had come in conflict. The conflict ended in the 1960s, and was sealed by 1971. When Amex officials and brokers went back to Broad Street in June 1971, they had arrived, in more ways than one. The Amex had both status and prosperity. The question for the future seemed to be, how would the Exchange use them?

Conclusion

The history of the Curb/Amex has been one of struggle
and conflict. The men who led the Exchange—and those who
were led by the membership—usually reflected the aspirations
of the main body of brokers. The combination of a strong
leader and indecision and fear on the part of the membership
enabled the curbstone brokers to move indoors in 1921. At the
time a small group, resentful of their second-class status and
unable to move to the Big Board, hoped that through the move
and the creation of a stronger, more honest market, they could
become respectable. Marginal men and inferior securities
would be excluded. The Curb would rise and, in time, win acceptance by the district's leaders.

A price would have to be paid, and it would be in volume
and listings. President Edward R. McCormick realized this, as
did the brokers who opposed the move. Ever since its first beginnings, the outdoor market had been a place for securities
that did not qualify for the Big Board but were slightly better
than those traded over the counter. The Curb could raise standards, but if it did, men and securities would be forced elsewhere. To lower standards meant more business, but also investigations and lack of respect.

McCormick was willing to pay the price. Under his
leadership both shady securities and thieving brokers were re-

moved from the outdoor market. Such was his political acumen and abilities at persuasion that he carried it off. Without him, the move would not have taken place when and in the manner it did.

The specialists were the key individuals *of* the Curb. These brokers, who made markets in securities, would accept the move so long as it increased their well-being or wealth—or both, if that could be arranged. They would also go along with reforms in order to remain in business, for at times many of them were not certain the Curb would survive. McCormick was able to convince leading specialists that the move would give them new respectability, not harm business, and was the only way by which the market could survive.

The commission brokers, the second largest category of brokers, were *at* the market in 1920. These men represented the powerful Wall Street brokerages. Many were dubious as to the value of the move indoors. But they had less sway with McCormick than did the specialists. In addition, many commission brokers had associate memberships, and not full memberships, which meant they had no vote in organizing the administrations. The move indoors was made by specialists, not commission brokers; from the first, this group dominated the indoor market, even to the extent that it became such a market.

The Curb Market's fortunes were not very different from that of the Big Board in the 1920s. At a time when money and its accumulation seemed to indicate and enhance status, Curb brokers scrambled for the dollar, and got it by fair means when possible, by skirting the law when it was not. By today's standards the market of that period was corrupt. But the Curb was no different than other securities exchanges of its time, no more corrupt by its own values. It was generally understood that brokers were out to get what they could for themselves. A desirable broker was not necessarily an honest one, but rather a person who used inside information and even manipulation to make money for his clients. Few customers complained of pools, rebates, and similar deals—unless they were not included in them. And throughout this period, government did nothing.

If the Curb brokers of the 1920s hoped to rise through wealth, depression brokers would willingly have sacrificed both simply for survival. Listings and higher volume were what counted, and they had to be obtained by whatever means possible. Honesty didn't seem the way, for if the rather lax listing rules then in force were actually applied, many important securities would have been delisted. The same was true of the men. If petty deals, in which no outsider was hurt, were not overlooked, most of the members might have become permanent fixtures before the committee on business conduct.

This was the milieu of Jerome Cuppia. A man of unusual intelligence, charm, and ability, Cuppia had plans to reform the Curb so as to bring it closer to the Big Board. A natural leader of the commission houses, he also became a serious foe of the specialists. Cuppia was also a wheeler-dealer and a blundering one at that. The nature of his misdeeds was not unusual, but their scope was. He fell from power, and this resulted in a reform wave that also served to solidify the power of the specialists.

Business was bad in the 1940s, even worse than it had been during the depression. Under the leadership of rigorous reformers, the Curb was honest but, as many had feared in 1921, honesty also meant lower volume and fewer listings. Brokers realized that the SEC, so activist in the 1930s, had declined in power and influence. They also felt that more business could be obtained if only the right leadership was there to get it for them. Toward the end of the decade the puritans were challenged by the crowd of hungry brokers, and they hadn't the power to resist even had they so desired. Although neither group could have realized it at the time, Edward T. McCormick was the symbol of the puritans' defeat.

The reformers of the 1940s had not been responsible for the slump; business in the district would have been bad no matter who was in control. Similarly, Ted McCormick, the super-salesman, arrived at a time when business was picking up, and he received much credit where less was due.

As had been the case in the 1920s, prosperity also brought wrongdoing of several varieties. The Amex administration in the 1940s and 1950s did little to correct abuses, and in some instances actually participated in questionable activities. McCormick proved not to be the mover of men and events many believed him to be. Rather, he reflected forces already present at the exchange, and enlarged them. And because of this, he had to go.

The Cuppia Scandal had been followed by puritan administrations. The much larger Re scandal and allied disclosures might well have resulted in a new, bigger reform movement. Edwin Posner, a leader in the post-Cuppia period, became a dominant force once again, and he gave every indication of cutting off the necks of questionable brokers and delisting suspected stocks.

To a degree this did happen, but it was not a replay of the 1940s. Instead, the Amex's new President, Edwin Etherington, proved to be in the mold of Edward R. McCormick, the first indoor President. Unlike Ted McCormick, he did not merely reflect forces, and, like Edward R., he was a man whose administration made a major difference for the men and institutions of the market.

Etherington led the reform movement, won the cooperation of not only Posner but of his opponents, cleaned the market of its rabble of securities and questionable men, but at the same time preserved its institutional structure. Those reformers who wanted a radically restructured market were disappointed, as were others who wanted to keep low-priced securities and men of low ethics. Both supported Etherington, whose administration was one of continuous success. It has been said that Etherington saved the Amex, meaning that without him the market might have been destroyed. This is a gross overstatement, for the Amex was too important an institution to be demolished, by the SEC or any other outside force. What Etherington did do was to save the Amex's institutional structure, and in particular the specialist system.

Etherington's successes redounded both to his reputation and to the benefit of his successors. At the same time his failure to challenge the institutions at Trinity Place made the jobs of Saul and Kolton more difficult than they might otherwise have been. The grip of institutional investors was tightening in the 1960s, and change was in the air. Saul had to face these problems in the late 1960s, and in so doing gave the Amex added prestige while brokers were making larger profits than ever before.

Kolton faces the challenges today. In many ways the new challenges are greater than those of any president since Edward R. McCormick, for it appears certain—given reform talk both on Wall Street and in Washington, a revived SEC, pressures from the third and fourth markets, and the role of institutional investors—that the markets will change dramatically during the next decade.

The Amex seems prepared for such changes—more so than the Big Board, which never underwent the Etherington-Saul-Kolton transformation. Saul's recommendations for change were not much more drastic than those put forth by Big Board President Robert Haack. Yet Haack was severely criticized by Stock Exchange brokers for his "radicalism," while Saul was praised for his statements. Soon after, Haack announced his planned resignation from the Big Board presidency—and hours later Saul was named to the Board of Governors.

There has been talk of the need for a "czar" for all the markets that comprise the securities industry. Often Saul is mentioned as a natural selection for such a position, while Kolton is considered an outside possibility, due in part to his recent arrival at the Amex presidency. Meanwhile Etherington, "the strong man from the outside," remains a dark horse for such a post, if and when it is created. Significantly, the last three Amex presidents are talked of for such a position, while no recent Big Board president or chairman seems in the running.

The American Exchange brokers are confident. Although the specialist system again appears threatened, the Amex is better prepared psychologically for change than are the members at the Big Board. And Amex brokers have respect—greater than any dreamed of by Edward R. McCormick in 1921, as he traded outdoors and looked across Broadway at the new indoor market rising on Trinity Place.

Bibliographical Essay

Historical literature on the American securities markets in the twentieth century is meager. Special aspects of the markets have been dealt with in government reports, articles in popular magazines, a few scholarly articles in professional journals, and a handful of trade books. Economists have explored the industry, as have lawyers. Historians have largely avoided it. To be sure, there are many works on the markets of the 1920s and the crash of 1929, as well as biographies of major financial figures. Most of these are by scholars looking from the outside in; few historians have shown much interest in exploring the anatomy of Wall Street. Their work shows little more than theoretical knowledge of how the market operated, or of the motivation of the people in the financial district and the evolution of its institutions. I am at a loss to explain why.* Hopefully, this situation will change, for the many histories of Wall Street institutions remain unwritten.

---

* Even more disappointing is the failure of sociologists and anthropologists to study the district. There have been few sociological studies of financial businessmen. The anthropologist might consider studying Wall Street as one might view an alien society, with interesting folkways and mores, values, etc. We know more of some small tribes in the Congo than we do of the financial community.

For this reason I have not been able to use many secondary sources for this history of the American Stock Exchange. The sources used were varied, and can best be discussed through the medium of a bibliographical essay rather than a more conventional list of works consulted.

Certain newspapers have been useful in illuminating the half-century covered in this work. These are the conventional ones, such as the *New York Times,* the *New York Herald Tribune,* the *New York Journal American,* the *Wall Street Journal,* the *New York World Telegram,* and their antecedents. The *Tribune* had the best coverage of Curb and Amex affairs. The *Times* carried little on the subject until the 1950s. Surprisingly enough, the *Wall Street Journal's* coverage was poor until after World War II. For the 1960s, however, the *Journal* was one of the better sources.

Few financial columnists showed much interest in the Curb. Alexander Noyes of the *Times* did not write of it, and the other columnists followed that dean of financial journalists in the 1920s. Only one—Leslie Gould—devoted more than a half dozen or so articles to the Curb each year during the 1930s and 1940s. Gould's work, which will be discussed in greater detail below, can be followed through articles and series in the *Journal American.*

Among the magazines consulted were *Fortune, Time, Newsweek, U.S. News and World Report, Forbes, Barron's,* and the *Institutional Investor. Business Week* was the only major business magazine to run more than brief items on the Curb, and was the best of the group until the 1960s. The *Institutional Investor's* articles in recent years have been most worthwhile. The *American Investor,* a monthly publication of the Amex, first appeared in 1956 and, as might be expected, was a useful source. Law journals, especially those of Harvard, Yale, and St. John's, have also published interesting and well-researched articles on Wall Street, including Curb/Amex material.

Leslie Gould left his papers and files to Hofstra University, and I have gone through these with great care. At one time Gould thought he might become the president of the

Amex; perhaps this was the reason for his interest. In any case, there are three categories of material in the Gould Papers of interest. The first is an extensive file of clippings going back to the late 1920s. Useful as these may be, they can be found elsewhere. Gould also collected news releases, and his file is the best available for the 1920s and 1930s. But the most important part of the collection is his file of signed and unsigned correspondence with Curb/Amex figures, together with material these men sent to him. Almost from the first, Gould had confidential contacts at the Curb/Amex, which continued through forty years. I do not know who all of these people were, although one was Jerome Cuppia. I have mined this material extensively, and without it this work would have lacked an important dimension.

When possible I checked Gould's material with the people involved. In a large majority of cases they verified my information. One broker told me he read Gould's column in the 1930s and 1940s to find out what was going on "upstairs." Another said that Gould had more inside information regarding the Re scandal than any man outside the board. Some brokers called him a muckraker, and he was that. A prominent Amex leader thought Gould was what he called "the Walter Winchell of Wall Street," and he spoke these words in an uncomplimentary fashion. Whatever else, Gould was a man to be feared and respected. His files indicate why this was so.

Less valuable was the historical section of the Martin Keena Library at the Amex. This library has an excellent collection of material of interest to brokers, such as SEC rulings, registrations, and the like. But there is less of a historical nature, with the exception of press releases and similar material.

Interviews were one of the most important sources of information. Neil Sheridan, who had been at the Clearing Corporation almost from its inception, provided insights as to the operation of the facility. Bernard Maas, Vice-President of the Securities Division, helped me understand how securities were listed in the 1920s and 1930s, and cleared up several thorny points. Charles Jacobs made available material on committee work of leading Amex figures. Vice-President of the Member-ship Services Division H. Vernon Lee made available to me the resources of his section. Vice-President of the Press Relations Division John Sheehan enlightened me on some neglected as-pects of public relations at the Amex and on operations during the late 1940s, 1950s, and 1960s. Vice-President of Information Services Robert Coplin put me in contact with many Amex fig-ures, opening doors whenever necessary. Edwin J. Wheeler, a former board member and now a specialist at the Big Board, spent hours discussing Curb/Amex policies and politics. Mr. Wheeler, whose father, Edwin P. Wheeler, was also an Amex governor, has a great interest in the institution's history, and has been encouraging throughout my work. Members of the Cuppia family provided me with information regarding that big Curb Exchange leader. One of my most important inter-views was to have been with Thomas McGovern, the Amex general counsel, whose knowledge of the Exchange's affairs was unparalleled. I was to have met with Mr. McGovern on a Friday; he died on Thursday.

I have read the court records of all the trials and investiga-tions described in this work. SEC records were useful, and this material will be described later in this essay. The same was true of congressional hearings.

Books, reports, and investigations were used in the study of the Curb in the 1920s. There are many such works, almost all dealing with the wild speculation of the period. After the 1929 crash dozens of exposés appeared. Some were useful, al-though a majority were exaggerated and more imaginative than factual. A. Newton Plummer, *The Great American Swindle, Inc.* (Plummer, 1932), documented several pools and methods by which newspapermen were implicated in them. Watson Washburn and Edmund DeLong, *High and Low Financiers* (Scribner's, 1932), deals more with the New York Stock Ex-change than with the Curb, and is less useful. David Salmon, *Confessions of a Former Customers' Man* (Vanguard, 1932), is an interesting study of how commission brokers and specialists op-erated, although, like most such works, it tends toward morali-zation. Other exposés, such as Earl Sparling, *Mystery Men of*

Wall Street (Vanguard, 1930) and Rudolph Weissman, *The New Wall Street* (Harper & Bros., 1939), contain little information on the Curb. The same is true of classics such as Ferdinand Pecora, *Wall Street Under Oath* (Simon & Schuster, 1939). Like others of his period in government service, Pecora ignored Trinity Place. This is true of such contemporary historians and economists as John K. Galbraith, Arthur Schlesinger, Jr., and Donald Rogers. When exploring the great bull market of the 1920s and the 1929 crash, most scholars have concentrated on the Big Board and ignored the Curb. Similarly, there is no recent work—not even an article—on the Consolidated Stock Exchange. Material on this market had to be gleaned from newspapers, court records, and memories of old-timers.

The coming of the Securities and Exchange Commission changed this situation somewhat. The best sources for the Curb's history in published form can be found in SEC hearings and investigations. The more important of these are:

U.S. Securities and Exchange Commission. *Annual Report* (USGPO, 1935–present).

———, *In the Matter of Richard Whitney et al.,* 3 vols. (USGPO, 1938).

———, *Report on the Feasibility and Advisability of the Complete Segregation of the Functions of Brokers and Dealers* (USGPO, 1936).

———, *Report on the Government of Securities Exchanges,* 74th Cong., 1st GD50 Session. House Document No. 85 (USGPO, 1935).

———, *Securities Act Releases* (USGPO, 1934–present).

———, *Trading in Unlisted Securities* (USGPO, 1936).

Michael Parris, *Securities Regulation and the New Deal* (Yale University Press, 1970), is an excellent introduction to the history of the Commission and contains material on the Curb Exchange. It is written from the outside looking in, and tends to reflect SEC rather than Wall Street attitudes. Still, it is a groundbreaking work, and one of the best histories of a government agency we have. Ralph de Bedts, *The New Deal's SEC: The Formative Years* (Columbia University Press, 1964), contains less material on the Curb.

The New Deal Congresses probed Wall Street thoroughly, and at times also looked into Trinity Place. Curb leaders journeyed to Washington to offer testimony every year of the New Deal, appearing before various congressional committees and the SEC. Testimony and other important information may be found in:

U.S. House of Representatives, Committee on Interstate and Foreign Commerce, 73rd Cong., 2d sess., *Federal Securities Act.* House Report No. 85 and No. 152 (USGPO, 1933).

———, Committee on Interstate and Foreign Commerce, 73rd Con., 2d sess., *Stock Exchange Regulation.* House Report No. 1383 and No. 1838 (USGPO, 1934).

———, Committee on Interstate and Foreign Commerce, 74th Cong., 2d sess., *Unlisted Securities.* House Report No. 2601 (USGPO, 1936).

———, Committee on Interstate and Foreign Commerce, 75th Cong., 3rd sess., *Regulation of the Over-the-Counter Markets.* House Report No. 2307 (USGPO, 1938).

U.S. Senate, Committee on Banking and Currency, 73rd Cong., 2d sess., *Regulation of the Stock Exchange* (USGPO, 1934).

———, Committee on Banking and Currency, 73rd Cong., 2d sess., *Stock Exchange Regulation.* Senate Report No. 792 (USGPO, 1934).

———, Committee on Banking and Currency, 74th Cong., 2d sess., *Trading in Unlisted Securities Upon Exchanges.* Senate Report No. 1739 (USGPO, 1936).

Material on the Cuppia-Plate controversy was more difficult to find. In the first place, few brokers remember the men very well or knew much about what had happened, and not many of these would talk about it. The Curb hearings on the case were secret, but when the SEC took an interest in the case, the records were deposited with the Commission. The SEC investigation was well-reported in the press and open to reporters, but the Commission did not publish a record of the hearings. Transcripts may be found at SEC headquarters in Washington; they are not in the New York office.

Like the rest of the financial district, the Curb was in decline in the World War II period and the late 1940s. The

SEC was moribund too, as the nation and Congress were interested in other matters. Material on this period was hard to come by, and for the most part I had to rely upon sources already discussed. My interviews with Edwin Posner and James DuHamil were useful in finding out how brokers and clerks survived this period. Other brokers recalled their feelings at the time, but none of them kept records.

Interest in the district picked up in the early 1950s, and magazine articles on the Curb began to appear with more regularity. Many of these revolved around President McCormick, who had captured the imagination of financial writers. A sketchy picture of the Amex at mid-decade can be found in Martin Mayer, *Wall Street: Men and Money* (Harper & Bros., 1955), which, like most such pieces, concentrates on McCormick. The President and other administrators appeared regularly before Congressional committees too. Important testimony may be found in:

U.S. House of Representatives, Committee on Interstate and Foreign Commerce, 82nd Cong., 2d sess., *Study of the Securities and Exchange Commission* (USGPO, 1952).

————, Committee on Interstate and Foreign Commerce, 84th Cong., 2d sess., *Amendments to Securities Act of 1933* (USGPO, 1956).

U.S. Senate, Committee on Banking and Currency, 84th Cong., 1st sess., *Stock Market Study* (USGPO, 1956).

————, Committee on Banking and Currency, 86th Cong., 1st sess., *SEC Legislation* (USGPO, 1959).

When the Re scandal broke, several popular books on the subject, hastily written, appeared. Later on two books were published of a more scholarly nature, which presented the background to the scandals and also explored the Amex under McCormick. These are Frank Cormier, *Wall Street's Shady Side* (Public Affairs Press, 1962), and Hillel Black, *The Watchdogs of Wall Street* (Morrow, 1962). Of the two, Black's book is wider in scope, but Cormier's explores the problems of the Amex in greater detail, and is more useful.

The financial magazines and press had a field day during the SEC probe, and many articles on the Amex appeared in most journals. The best coverage of the period may be found in the *Wall Street Journal* and *Business Week*. A key document for this period is the massive SEC report on the financial district: Securities and Exchange Commission, 88th Cong., 1st sess., *Report of the Special Study of the Securities Markets,* House Document No. 95, 6 pts. (USGPO, 1963). The appendix to part 4, entitled "Staff Report on Organization, Management, and Regulation of Conduct of Members of the American Stock Exchange," was prepared by the Division of Trading and Exchanges, and is the most important document in recent Amex history.

Material on the post-1962 period came from Amex files, interviews with Presidents Etherington, Saul, and Kolton, and with Chairmen Posner and Jackson, as well as other executives at the Amex. The market problems of the late 1960s are covered ably in Hurd Baruch, *Wall Street: Security Risk* (Acropolis, 1971). I also had interviews and discussions with Donald Weeden and Fred Siesel of Weeden & Co., a leading third-market firm, regarding the conflicts between the exchanges and the over-the-counter markets. Such documents as the Martin Report and the Amex's reports on automation may be found in the American Stock Exchange library.

Statistical Summary from the
Amex Databook: 1971

Presidents of the American Stock Exchange

	Effective Date	
John L. McCormack	March	1911
Edward R. McCormick	June	1914
John W. Curtis	February	1923
David U. Page	February	1925
William S. Muller	February	1928
Howard C. Sykes	February	1932
E. Burd Grubb	February	1934
Fred C. Moffatt	February	1935
George P. Rea	April	1939
Fred C. Moffatt (pro tem)	July	1942
Edwin Posner (pro tem)	February	1945
Edward C. Werle (pro tem)	February	1947
Francis Adams Truslow	March	1947
Edward T. McCormick	April	1951
Joseph F. Reilly (pro tem)	December	1961
Edwin Posner (pro tem)	January	1962
Edwin D. Etherington	September	1962
Ralph S. Saul	November	1966
Paul Kolton	June	1971

Chairmen of the Amex Board of Governors

	Effective Date	
Clarence A. Bettman	February	1939
Fred C. Moffatt	February	1941
Edwin Posner	February	1945
Edward C. Werle	February	1947
Mortimer Landsberg	February	1950
John J. Mann	February	1951
James R. Dyer	February	1956
Joseph F. Reilly	February	1960
Edwin Posner	February	1962
David S. Jackson	February	1965
Macrae Sykes	February	1968
Frank C. Graham, Jr.	February	1969

Prior to 1939, there was no Board Chairman. The President was elected from among the Board of Governors. The Exchange's first paid president was George P. Rea.

Regular Membership Sales

Year	High	Low	Last	No. of Transfers Public	No. of Transfers Private	No. of Transfers Total
1921(a)	$ 6,800	$ 3,750	$ 5,500	39	3	42
1922	10,000	4,200	7,000	66	8	74
1923	9,500	3,600	4,500	48	7	55
1924	9,000	4,000	9,000	55	8	63
1925	37,500	8,500	32,000	53	9	62
1926	35,000	17,500	32,000	31	6	37
1927	67,000	22,000	67,000	41	7	48
1928	170,000	56,000	170,000	43	14	57
1929	254,000	150,000	160,000	49	19	68
1930	225,000	70,000	95,000	34	22	56
1931	137,500	38,000	38,000	27	14	41
1932	55,000	16,500	30,000	32	12	44
1933	50,000	25,000	25,000	26	9	35
1934	40,000	17,000	20,000	17	9	26
1935	33,000	12,000	30,000	17	9	26
1936	48,000	26,000	34,000	23	19	42
1937	35,000	17,500	17,500	15	17	32
1938	17,500	8,000	12,000	18	9	27
1939	12,000	7,000	8,500	14	11	25
1940	7,250	6,900	6,900	6	8	14
1941(b)	2,600	1,000	1,000	24	3	27
1942(c)	1,700	650	1,700	22	3	25
1943	8,500	1,600	6,300	18	2	20
1944	16,000	7,500	14,000	14	6	20
1945	32,000	12,000	32,000	19	16	35
1946	37,500	19,000	19,000	13	12	25
1947	25,000	13,500	16,000	16	19	35
1948	23,000	12,500	15,500	8	11	19
1949	10,000	5,500	8,000	12	4	16
1950	11,000	6,500	9,500	17	13	30
1951	15,500	9,500	11,500	17	9	26
1952	14,000	12,000	14,000	15	8	23
1953	15,000	10,100	10,100	9	3	12
1954	19,000	10,000	18,000	14	8	22
1955	22,000	17,500	20,500	15	11	26
1956	31,500	21,500	28,000	18	8	26
1957	26,000	21,500	22,000	14	9	23
1958	42,000	18,000	42,000	20	10	30
1959	65,000	44,000	60,000	17	14	31
1960	60,000	51,000	52,000	14	16	30
1961	80,000	52,000	65,000	20	31	51
1962	65,000	40,000	52,500	18	17	35
1963(d)	66,000	52,500	66,000	27	16	43
1964(e)	63,000	52,000	60,000	15	26	41
1965(f)	80,000	55,000	80,000	29	28	57
1966	120,000	70,000	90,000	23	54	77
1967	230,000	100,000	230,000	32	72	104
1968	315,000	220,000	315,000	35	68	103
1969	350,000	150,000	170,000	31	104	135
1970	185,000	70,000	125,000	42	87	129

(a) The figures given for 1921 are from June 27, when indoor trading began in the New York Curb Market.
(b) Not included are 21 memberships purchased by the New York Curb Exchange at $1,000 each and subsequently retired.
(c) Not included are 30 memberships purchased by the New York Curb Exchange at $1,000 each and subsequently retired.
(d) Not included are 93 memberships sold by the American Stock Exchange to associate members for prices ranging from $50,000 to $61,000.
(e) Not included are 7 memberships sold by the American Stock Exchange to associate members for prices ranging from $50,000 to $57,000.
(f) Not included are 51 memberships sold by the American Stock Exchange to associate members for prices ranging from $55,000 to $61,000.

Stocks Traded

Common Stock (a)					Preferred Stock (b)				
Dec. 31	No. of Issues	No. of Shares Outstanding	Market Value	Average Share Price	Dec. 31	No. of Issues	No. of Shares Outstanding	Market Value	Average Share Price
1938	786	637,500,921	$ 8,420,891,785	$13.21	1938	320	55,744,110	$2,380,391,185	$42.70
1939	764	623,274,872	7,638,633,567	12.26	1939	313	54,647,856	2,489,286,766	45.55
1940	749	622,861,597	6,258,846,708	10.04	1940	310	53,775,327	2,353,191,153	43.76
1941	724	616,466,577	5,218,690,704	8.47	1941	294	51,542,224	2,135,621,132	41.43
1942	697	576,434,487	5,853,026,343	10.15	1942	278	50,957,901	1,992,925,827	39.11
1943	676	594,553,884	7,530,044,985	12.67	1943	259	47,295,011	2,362,349,391	49.95
1944	652	580,089,716	8,803,575,493	15.18	1944	231	43,679,607	2,372,467,496	54.32
1945	646	592,029,974	11,957,095,471	20.20	1945	213	39,684,887	2,402,938,098	60.55
1946	668	634,193,250	11,187,334,409	17.64	1946	171	36,672,788	1,967,928,989	54.66
1947	659	619,803,495	10,601,871,345	17.11	1947	156	33,394,576	1,542,998,851	46.21
1948	651	624,105,323	10,419,236,793	16.69	1948	150	34,148,000	1,465,070,983	42.90
1949	627	584,671,380	10,492,115,479	17.95	1949	151	37,260,855	1,658,857,847	44.52
1950	621	574,572,841	12,311,848,317	21.43	1950	136	36,220,558	1,562,445,440	43.14
1951	637	654,484,580	15,083,608,093	23.05	1951	126	34,753,508	1,408,527,890	40.53
1952	654	750,003,156	15,386,134,587	20.51	1952	124	36,704,792	1,525,155,031	41.55
1953	672	811,151,134	13,873,959,003	17.10	1953	122	33,593,516	1,424,382,853	42.40
1954	684	877,579,086	20,672,352,496	23.56	1954	124	33,627,966	1,460,500,684	43.43
1955	700	1,030,630,924	25,566,019,818	24.81	1955	118	42,835,265	1,580,140,715	37.89
1956	728	1,182,685,159	29,532,256,332	24.97	1956	121	45,268,885	1,487,842,460	32.87
1957	737	1,329,017,309	24,126,405,973	18.15	1957	118	46,020,893	1,418,831,711	30.83
1958	740	1,376,445,390	30,361,136,441	22.06	1958	115	43,754,332	1,368,349,169	31.27
1959	757	1,430,821,914	25,116,886,744	17.55	1959	114	44,177,353	1,312,707,247	29.71
1960	828	1,539,268,585	22,822,499,838	14.83	1960	114	45,620,587	1,348,432,687	29.56
1961	891	1,752,945,670	31,619,755,022	18.04	1961	110	46,498,424	1,391,115,208	29.92
1962	910	1,757,849,123	23,005,116,387	13.09	1962	108	45,372,023	1,360,027,153	29.98
1963	908	1,706,435,036	24,903,501,616	14.59	1963	95	35,796,812	1,226,107,209	34.25
1964	930	1,725,761,814	26,916,066,899	15.60	1964	92	35,800,408	1,303,928,189	36.42
1965	939	1,690,626,462	29,752,326,279	17.60	1965	89	35,574,784	1,234,382,303	34.70
1966	947	1,789,569,000	26,702,661,816	14.92	1966	91	38,550,000	1,155,842,275	29.98
1967	968	1,823,765,475	41,562,497,508	22.79	1967	93	40,296,846	1,402,526,997	34.80
1968	994	2,142,702,703	59,212,671,744	27.63	1968	90	49,288,482	2,000,758,250	40.59
1969	1,079	2,582,977,509	46,727,504,165	18.09	1969	73	47,829,878	988,146,230	20.66
1970	1,151	2,806,692,369	38,441,892,174	13.70	1970	71	50,585,000	1,093,787,200	21.62

(a) Excluding suspended issues; including warrants   (b) Excluding suspended issues

Stock Issues Delisted

Year	Merged or Liquidated		Redeemed or Expired		Listed on NYSE		Failure to Meet Amex Standards		Other		Total	
	No.	Shares	No.	Shares	No.	Shares	No.	Shares	No.	Shares	No.	Shares
1955	25	12,368,771	14	1,583,742	10	19,742,742	7	1,481,217	—	—	56	35,176,472
1956	18	12,247,619	8	282,577	6	5,472,007	2	6,232,059	5	3,753,137	39	27,997,399
1957	15	6,522,503	3	45,278	18	22,836,332	13	22,966,723	—	—	49	52,370,826
1958	13	20,199,418	1	1,319	5	27,631,112	14	15,302,831	5	2,515,117	38	65,649,797
1959	13	95,393,496	6	2,787,487	12	24,576,526	11	3,307,615	3	1,358,500	45	127,423,624
1960	17	38,172,106	3	386,841	14	27,972,811	3	13,291,257	—	—	37	79,823,015
1961	17	20,857,431	3	47,726	15	40,428,913	11	17,723,747	1	79,600	47	79,137,417
1962	24	38,041,732	1	705,014	13	59,925,603	24	33,725,170	1	291,843	63	132,689,362
1963	12	12,046,793	9	827,582	15	47,777,648	38	71,408,138	9	15,822,062	83	147,880,223
1964	33	42,797,457	2	71,171	17	31,824,258	13	11,490,986	8	3,906,038	73	90,089,910
1965	26	28,230,870	4	348,930	13	87,708,292	18	25,987,093	10	7,857,361	71	150,132,546
1966	32	45,544,428	6	494,797	20	66,738,681	23	52,596,924	4	2,871,841	85	168,246,671
1967	45	72,719,558	9	4,651,154	16	29,244,557	22	27,492,698	1	2,086,950	93	136,134,917
1968	42	64,039,023	10	4,074,217	39	98,852,370	24	61,018,913	1	525,960	116	228,510,483
1969	39	78,226,984	11	4,664,319	32	123,461,606	26	74,634,862	4	4,066,683	112	285,054,454
1970	19	52,749,726	—	—	30	103,502,265	29	50,852,984	—	—	78	207,084,975

Issues Gained and Removed

Stocks (a)

Year	Issues Approved	Issues Admitted	Issues Removed	All Issues (Dec. 31)	Net Gain (Loss)
1941	8	8	55	1,023	(47)
1942	6	6	45	984	(39)
1943	10	11	49	946	(38)
1944	13	10	53	903	(43)
1945	31	38	61	880	(23)
1946	54	52	76	856	(24)
1947	28	31	51	836	(20)
1948	21	21	38	819	(17)
1949	15	16	39	796	(23)
1950	21	21	50	767	(29)
1951	45	38	28	777	10
1952	45	46	30	793	16
1953	43	39	24	808	15
1954	43	40	24	824	16
1955	68	64	56	832	8
1956	70	70	39	863	31
1957	45	48	49	862	(1)
1958	42	37	38	861	(1)
1959	63	64	45	880	19
1960	110	107	37	950	70
1961	112	109	47	1,012	62
1962	73	77	63	1,026	14
1963	73	72	83	1,015	(11)
1964	87	90	73	1,032	17
1965	87	85	71	1,046	14
1966	92	90	85	1,051	5
1967	121	122	93	1,080	29
1968	145	139	116	1,103	23
1969	187	187	112	1,178	75
1970	147	149	78	1,249	71

Bonds (a)

Year	Issues Approved	Issues Admitted	Issues Removed	All Issues (Dec. 31)	Net Gain (Loss)
1941	16	18	31	269	(13)
1942	—	—	32	237	(32)
1943	4	4	17	224	(13)
1944	—	—	34	190	(34)
1945	1	3	29	164	(26)
1946	1	1	32	133	(31)
1947	4	4	23	114	(19)
1948	2	3	7	110	(4)
1949	3	3	9	104	(6)
1950	1	1	16	89	(15)
1951	4	4	10	83	(6)
1952	2	2	2	83	—
1953	2	2	1	84	—
1954	5	4	6	82	(2)
1955	1	2	12	72	(10)
1956	2	2	1	73	—
1957	4	4	13	64	(9)
1958	1	1	6	59	(5)
1959	6	6	3	62	3
1960	5	5	4	63	—
1961	16	14	4	73	10
1962	12	14	3	84	11
1963	7	7	7	84	—
1964	14	13	4	93	9
1965	13	13	5	101	8
1966	13	13	16	98	(3)
1967	61	56	16	138	40
1968	47	49	18	169	31
1969	28	29	22	176	7
1970	18	17	18	175	(1)

(a) Including suspended issues

Listed and Unlisted Issues

Stocks (a)

Dec. 31	Issues Listed	Percent of Total	Issues Unlisted	Percent of Total	All Issues
1938	501	45.3	605	54.7	1,106
1939	499	46.3	578	53.7	1,077
1940	493	46.6	566	53.4	1,059
1941	472	46.4	546	53.6	1,018
1942	459	47.1	516	52.9	975
1943	439	47.0	496	53.0	935
1944	422	47.8	461	52.2	883
1945	421	49.0	438	51.0	859
1946	437	52.1	402	47.9	839
1947	441	54.1	374	45.9	815
1948	434	54.2	367	45.8	801
1949	431	55.4	347	44.6	778
1950	424	56.0	333	44.0	757
1951	443	58.1	320	41.9	763
1952	470	60.4	308	39.6	778
1953	498	62.7	296	37.3	794
1954	520	64.4	288	35.6	808
1955	544	66.5	274	33.5	818
1956	588	69.3	261	30.7	849
1957	609	71.2	246	28.8	855
1958	618	72.3	237	27.7	855
1959	647	74.3	224	25.7	871
1960	726	77.1	216	22.9	942
1961	797	79.6	204	20.4	1,001
1962	834	81.9	184	18.1	1,018
1963	841	83.8	162	16.2	1,003
1964	883	86.4	139	13.6	1,022
1965	910	88.5	118	11.5	1,028
1966	929	89.5	109	10.5	1,038
1967	960	90.5	101	9.5	1,061
1968	995	91.8	89	8.2	1,084
1969	1,088	94.4	64	5.6	1,152
1970	1,160	94.9	62	5.1	1,222

Bonds (a)

Dec. 31	Issues Listed	Percent of Total	Issues Unlisted	Percent of Total	All Issues
1938	71	18.5	313	81.5	384
1939	63	18.9	270	81.1	333
1940	33	11.8	247	88.2	280
1941	33	13.5	212	86.5	245
1942	29	13.6	185	86.4	214
1943	28	13.9	173	86.1	201
1944	23	14.1	140	85.9	163
1945	22	15.9	116	84.1	138
1946	18	16.8	89	83.2	107
1947	19	20.4	74	79.6	93
1948	19	21.3	70	78.7	89
1949	18	21.7	65	78.3	83
1950	11	15.9	58	84.1	69
1951	14	22.2	49	77.8	63
1952	16	25.4	47	74.6	63
1953	17	26.6	47	73.4	64
1954	19	24.1	60(b)	75.9	79
1955	19	27.5	50	72.5	69
1956	21	30.9	47	69.1	68
1957	23	39.0	36	61.0	59
1958	24	40.7	35	59.3	59
1959	29	46.8	33	53.2	62
1960	33	52.4	30	47.6	63
1961	45	61.6	28	38.4	73
1962	57	67.9	27	32.1	84
1963	60	72.3	23	27.7	83
1964	70	76.9	21	23.1	91
1965	79	80.6	19	19.4	98
1966	81	82.7	17	17.3	98
1967	124	90.5	13	9.5	137
1968	156	93.4	11	6.6	167
1969	164	93.7	11	6.3	175
1970	164	97.0	5	3.0	169

(a) Excluding suspended issues (b) Increase due to reinstatement of 17 bond issues previously suspended

Annual Volume

Year	Shares	Year	Shares	Year	Shares	Year	Shares
1921	15,522,415	1926	115,531,800	1931	110,413,687	1936	134,845,196
1922	21,741,230	1927	125,116,566	1932	57,108,543	1937	104,178,804
1923	50,968,680	1928	236,043,682	1933	100,916,602		
1924	72,243,900	1929	476,140,375	1934	60,050,695		
1925	88,406,350	1930	222,268,045	1935	75,747,764		

Year	Shares	Dollar Volume	Shares Outstanding	Turnover Ratio	Daily Average(a)	High Day Date	High Day Shares	Low Day (c) Date	Low Day (c) Shares
1938	49,640,238	$ 687,200,992	693,245,031	7.2	199,358	Oct 17	669,075	June 17	62,245
1939	45,729,888	749,892,033	677,922,728	6.7	183,654	Sept 5	950,025	July 3	40,185
1940	42,928,377	646,146,547	676,636,924	6.3	171,029	May 21	659,550	Aug 26	26,470
1941	34,656,354	465,340,082	668,008,801	5.2	139,182	Dec 29	636,395	May 19	45,800
1942	22,301,852	284,804,875	627,392,388	3.6	89,566	Dec 29	378,395	July 20	28,895
1943	71,374,283	803,639,346	641,848,895	11.1	286,644	May 10	1,258,770	Jan 6	91,045
1944	71,061,713	911,447,710	623,769,323	11.4	285,389	July 5	637,840	May 15	113,890
1945	143,309,292	1,759,899,715	631,714,861	22.7	582,558	Nov 13	2,354,345	Apr 4	165,695
1946	137,313,214	2,021,047,018	670,866,038	20.5	549,253	Jan 29	1,748,295	Aug 19	201,560
1947	72,376,027	1,016,933,852	653,198,071	11.1	289,504	Feb 7	872,370	Aug 27	114,965
1948	75,016,108	1,041,778,268	658,251,323	11.4	297,683	May 14	920,760	Sept 16	132,775
1949	66,201,828	906,909,867	621,932,235	10.6	264,807	Dec 2	524,435	June 17	123,159
1950	107,792,340	1,494,095,914	610,793,399	17.6	434,647	Dec 18	917,195	July 3	230,205
1951	111,629,218	1,610,671,702	689,238,088	16.2	448,310	Oct 8	953,040	July 11	173,775
1952	106,237,657	1,285,366,862	786,707,948	13.5	426,657	Apr 3	1,388,910	Sept 11	203,495
1953	102,378,937	1,134,889,391	844,744,650	12.1	407,884	Sept 15	982,800	June 19	213,275
1954	162,948,716	1,910,478,693	911,207,052	17.9	646,622	Dec 20	1,697,805	Jan 11	340,545
1955	228,956,315	2,657,015,518	1,073,466,189	21.3	912,177	Sept 26	1,853,315	Nov 1	459,040
1956	228,231,047	2,731,359,623	1,227,954,044	18.6	912,924	Mar 26	1,878,885	Oct 9	499,595
1957	214,011,566	2,361,939,394	1,375,038,202	15.6	845,896	Dec 31	2,022,670	Nov 11	429,055
1958	240,358,524	2,864,485,901	1,420,200,252	16.9	953,804	Dec 4	1,954,500	Feb 8	388,810
1959	374,058,546	4,954,568,030	1,474,999,267	25.4	1,478,492	Mar 20	3,523,410	Oct 12	640,305
1960	286,039,982	4,235,685,712	1,584,889,172	18.0	1,112,996	Dec 30	2,440,760	Aug 1	739,590
1961	488,831,037	6,863,109,560	1,799,444,094	27.2	1,947,534	May 12	5,430,965	July 3	779,695
1962	308,609,304	5,736,618,490	1,803,221,146	17.1	1,224,640	May 29	5,332,770	Oct 8	460,520
1963	316,735,062	4,844,911,758	1,742,231,848	18.2	1,261,893	Dec 31	2,796,420	Jan 2	636,660
1964	374,183,842	6,127,236,386	1,761,562,222	21.2	1,478,988	Apr 3	2,882,625	Sept 16	900,830
1965	534,221,999	8,874,874,754	1,726,201,246	30.9	2,119,929	Dec 8	4,963,495	July 22	792,710
1966	690,762,585	14,647,166,165	1,828,119,000	37.8	2,741,121	Apr 14	6,566,600	Oct 14	1,043,075
1967	1,145,090,300	23,491,311,698	1,864,062,321	61.4	4,544,009	Oct 26	8,291,884	Jan 3	1,740,050
1968(b)	1,435,765,734	34,775,384,635	2,191,991,185	65.5	6,352,945	June 13	10,809,215	Mar 25	2,111,765
1969(d)	1,240,742,012	30,074,031,388	2,630,807,387	47.2	4,962,968	Dec 31	11,355,410	Aug 12	2,540,080
1970(e)	843,116,260	14,266,040,599	2,857,275,369	29.5	3,319,355	Sept 24	7,876,654	Aug 17	1,445,005

(a) Based on five trading days a week. When half-day Saturday trading was discontinued in 1952, weekday closings were extended from 3 to 3:30 P.M., providing approximately the same number of trading hours per week.
(b) Based on 226 trading days, compared with 252 in 1967, with activity limited to a four-day week as of June 12, 1968; the policy remained in effect until the year end.
(c) Excluding Saturday trading.
(d) Based on 250 trading days, compared with 226 trading days in 1968. On July 7, 1969, market hours changed from 2:00 to 3:00 P.M. closing.
(e) As of May 4, 1970, market hours were extended to 3:30 P.M.

369

Index

371

Printed in the United States
88662LV00005B/63/A